MEETINGS, EXPOSITIONS, EVENTS, AND CONVENTIONS

An Introduction to the Industry

GEORGE G. FENICH, Ph.D.

PEARSON

Prentice
Hall

Upper Saddle River, New Jersey

A CIP catalog record for this book can be obtained from the Library of Congress.

Executive Editor: Vernon R. Anthony
Editorial Assistant: Beth Dyke
**Director of Manufacturing
and Production:** Bruce Johnson
Managing Editor: Mary Carnis
Creative Director: Cheryl Asherman
Production Liaison: Janice Stangel
Production Management: Susan Free,
The GTS Companies, York, PA Campus

Manufacturing Buyer: Cathleen Petersen
Manufacturing Manager: Ilene Sanford
Design Coordinator: Mary Siener
Cover Design: Allen Gold
Cover Illustration: Vancouver Convention and
Exhibition Center
Printer/Binder: R. R. Donnelley–Harrisonburg

Pearson Education LTD.
Pearson Education Singapore, Pte. Ltd
Pearson Education, Canada, Ltd
Pearson Education–Japan

Pearson Education Australia PTY, Limited
Pearson Education North Asia Ltd
Pearson Educación de Mexico, S.A. de C.V.
Pearson Education Malaysia, Pte. Ltd

10 9 8 7 6 5 4 3 2
ISBN 0-13-112587-7

In memory of George Fenich, Sr.

◆ TABLE OF CONTENTS

PREFACE

The **M**eetings, **E**xpositions, **E**vents, and **C**onventions (MEEC, pronounced like *geese*) industry continues to grow and garner increasing attention from the hospitality industry, communities, and college faculty. This book is meant to provide a broad overview of this industry and is thus an introduction. It is not meant to provide a hands-on or step-by-step method for handling gatherings in this industry.

This book is being produced at this time for a number of reasons. One is the continued growth of this industry. In spite of the economic downturn of late, and the events following the 9/11 disaster, the MEEC segment of the hospitality industry remains resilient. Communities continue to build or expand MEEC venues unabated. The private sector has become a player in convention center construction and operation. People still find a need for face-to-face meetings. The MEEC industry appears to be on a growth curve and of interest to many people, not unlike the casino industry was in the early 1990s.

Also, college faculty have indicated a need, and pent-up demand, for a book such as this. The author/editor has been teaching an introductory MEEC course for many years and has found himself having to continually supplement the existing books to make them (1) current and (2) more complete in addressing the various segments of the MEEC industry. Therefore, he began to contemplate the development of a book on the subject. Then, at a meeting of the Convention Special Interest Group at the Council on Hotel, Restaurant and Institutional Education (CHRIE) Convention in 2001, the need for a new text was discussed. The members of this group all noted the need, and the author/editor volunteered to spearhead an effort to put together a new book using faculty and industry experts to write chapters. This book is a culmination of that effort. The result is a text where some of the best and most notable people in the MEEC industry have made a contribution. As you will see, there is a fairly even balance of educators and practitioners among the chapter contributors.

The approach to deciding on topics was unusual. Rather than have a list of topics or chapters based on people's willingness to contribute, a more scientific method was used. The author/editor reviewed all existing books, both theoretical and practical, to ascertain which topics to cover. Topics that appeared in more than one text were compiled into a list. Then, a number of meetings were held with educators, and the relative importance of topics was discussed. This led to the development of a comprehensive list of topics. The list was sent to educators and practitioners, who were asked to rank the importance of each topic as either critically important, important, or not important. Results were used to pare down the list, and this iterative voting procedure (Delphi technique) was used to reach the decision as to the topics to include in the book.

Meetings, Expositions, Events, and Conventions should be of interest to practitioners, educators, students, and the general public. It is the most up-to-date book on the MEEC industry and will provide users with an overview of the industry. It is also comprehensive and covers a wider range of MEEC topics than any other book available. It can easily serve as the basis for an introductory college course on the subject or for orientation sessions for new employees in the industry. It should meet the needs of anyone interested in knowing more about the MEEC industry.

George G. Fenich, Ph.D.

◆ ACKNOWLEDGMENTS

I would like to thank Kathryn Hashimoto for her unabated support, patience, and encouragement; the University of New Orleans, Lester E. Kabacoff School of Hotel, Restaurant and Tourism Administration, College of Business Administration, for allowing me to undertake this book as the primary activity during my sabbatical leave in the fall of 2002; Michael Davidson, Ph.D., director, for his support and encouragement; and the students for their interest in the Meetings, Expositions, Events, and Conventions (MEEC) field. Also, thank you to the educators teaching in the MEEC field for helping to develop the concept for this book: Patti Shock, UNLV; Howard Reichbart, NVCC; Curtis Love, UNLV; Court Carrier, Mt. Hood CC; Tyra Hilliard, George Washington University; M. T. Hickman, Richland College; and the Meetings/Conventions SIG of CHRIE. In addition, I would like to extend my appreciation to the reviewers of the text: Sandra K. Strick, University of South Carolina; Sotiris H. Avgoustis, Indiana University, Purdue University–Indianapolis; and Linda Brothers, Indiana University, Purdue University–Indianapolis. And finally, my thanks to the chapter contributors: Joan L. Eisenstodt, Curtis Love, Howard Reichbart, Bob Cherny, Ben McDonald, Cynthia Vannucci, Patti Shock, Terrence J. Epton, Susan L. Schwartz, Elaine Rosquist, James M. Goldberg, Denis P. Rudd, Kathleen Taylor Brown, M. T. Hickman, and William Host.

1

INTRODUCTION TO THE MEETINGS, EXPOSITIONS, EVENTS, AND CONVENTIONS INDUSTRY

Vancouver Convention Center.
Photo by George G. Fenich, Ph.D., Professor, School of HRTA, University of New Orleans

◆ Chapter Objectives

This chapter provides the reader with an understanding of the following:

- The history of the Meetings, Expositions, Events, and Conventions (MEEC) industry
- Where MEEC fits in relation to the hospitality industry

- The magnitude and impact of MEEC
- Careers in MEEC
- Different types of gatherings

◆ Chapter Outline

THE BIG DAY

Picture this: The sun rises above the horizon, releasing rays of blue and pink light that whisk across the ocean and spill onto the beautifully manicured greens of the resort hotel's championship golf course. Against the backdrop of the crashing surf and pleas of hungry gulls, you can also hear the sounds of morning stirring at the resort hotel. Car doors slamming, muffled voices sharing greetings and farewells, china and silver clashing, and the squeaking wheels of fully laden carts, each heading off to its appointed area under the guiding hand of one of many hotel staff who have arrived before most guests are awake.

Today is a big day. The Association of Amalgamated Professionals (AAP) will open its 35th Annual Congress with an evening reception, and before the day is done, 1,900 guests and hundreds of vendors will have descended on this resort hotel.

Todd Cliver, Convention Services Manager (**CSM**) for the resort hotel, convenes a last-minute meeting for the hotel's team that is handling

A fully laden pastry cart ready to head to its appointed destination.
Source: Courtesy of Wayne Sorce

the Annual Congress. Todd has worked tirelessly for nearly nine months, coordinating all the plans, wants, and needs of his client, the association's senior meeting manager, Barbara Tain. Today represents the culmination of hundreds of faxes, e-mails, phone calls, and personal meetings between Todd and Barbara. Todd interacted with every department in the resort hotel. Barbara worked closely with AAP staff and volunteers, and also worked with other vendors as well as supervised AAP support staff for the AAP's 35th Annual Congress.

Donna Miller, Director of **Sales and Marketing**, whose department was responsible for contracting this—the largest meeting the resort hotel will have ever managed—reports on her client's last-minute changes and concerns, all meticulously logged since her client, Barbara Tain, arrived two days ago. David Stern, Front Desk Manager, recaps the latest report on expected room occupancy and on the timing and numbers of anticipated arrivals. Throughout the day, he will continue to check with his staff to ensure that there will be adequate (and contracted!) numbers of front desk clerks to support the check-in flow, bell staff to

(continued)

manage the deluge of luggage and golf clubs, and doorstaff, valet parkers, concierge and guest services staff, and housekeeping support.

David Fenner, Director of Catering, provides his final status report, commenting on the readiness of the kitchen and serving staff to serve, over the next three days, the equivalent of almost 12,000 meals and untold gallons of juice, milk, coffee, tea, soda, and alcoholic beverages. In addition, the resort hotel's **outlets** (restaurants and lounges) expect a much higher than average volume and have planned accordingly for supplies and personnel.

Other resort hotel staff members report in to the director of sales and the CSM. These include those involved with recreation (golf, tennis, health club, and pool), maintenance, security, and accounting. Even the animal handlers who work with the parrots, an attraction as guests enter the resort, want to ensure there are only healthy, well-behaved birds to greet the guests!

This one **convention** has already impacted and will impact every area of the resort hotel's operations. Armed with all this information, Todd leaves for his final preconference meeting (pre-con) with Barbara Tain, his client.

Meanwhile, on the other side of the country, Jane Lever steps onto Concourse B of the Philadelphia International Airport, her airline boarding pass, e-ticket receipt with its special "meeting discount" price, and photo ID firmly in her grasp. She has checked her luggage, making sure to leave it unlocked for a possible security search. She scans the bank of monitors for her flight information. Before her day ends, she will have touched down at two other airports, eaten one airline snack, grabbed a candy bar on her way through a change of planes at another airport, made numerous cell phone calls, bought a newspaper and a few magazines, and paid for a taxi to the resort hotel. Around the country, 1,899 other professionals just like Jane will do the same thing and travel to the same place, for the same purpose—a **meeting**.

In the resort hotel's **destination** (city), Kathy Sykes, the owner and president of Skylark Destination Management Company (**DMC**), is already at her office reviewing final arrangements for ground transportation, event theme preparations, and entertainment for the AAP meeting. Kathy has already received two complaints from the manager of the headliner rock star booked for tonight's reception: He wants only chilled glasses for his orange juice—which he expects to be freshly squeezed in his suite—and can only get dressed if he is provided with navy blue towels for his after-shower rubdown. Kathy, of course, ensures compliance with these requests; she wants to avoid any problems before tonight's event.

With a thunderstorm threatening for tomorrow afternoon, her mind is already racing through alternatives for the golf tournament. She knows the golfers can play in the rain, but a thunderstorm would endanger their safety.

Jack Ardulosky, a senior technical engineer for an audiovisual company, pulls into the hotel's delivery area, completing his mental checklist for final site review, satellite link integrity, picture clarity, and sound quality. With three global broadcasts and webcasts, there will be little room for error.

He sees the florist unloading the last of the fresh floral arrangements and makes a note to himself that leaves and petals can cause just as much of a viewing obstruction as meeting room columns. He scans the area around him for a parking spot: not too much available with all the trucks and vans unloading the trade show booths. Jack notices the rising temperature and expects a long, hot day. He will feel better as long as he can find parking in the shade, even if he has to walk a greater distance.

Barbara Tain, the senior meeting manager for the association, wipes the beginning of fatigue from her eyes—she has already been on site for two days, and her constant checking of details has not allowed her to sleep as well as she would have liked—and continues her walk-through of the registration area, information center, and cyber cafe—en route to a meeting with Todd Cliver and David Fenner. Having eaten just a few bites of her breakfast during a meeting with association executives and key committee members, she will still be late to her meeting with Cliver and Fenner because of last-minute details and concerns expressed in the meeting with association staff and volunteers.

Only half glancing at the space around her, she again reviews her lengthy checklists: banquet event orders (**BEOs**), transportation schedules, badges, staffing, centerpiece design and delivery, phone lines, computers and printers, exhibitor booth setup, VIP procedures, concerns about tomorrow's weather, special check-in process, audiovisual equipment, opening production needs, PowerPoint files, handouts, arrangements for participants with disabilities and special needs for those who have specified food allergies, amenities for VIPs . . . her mind is crowded with details.

(continued)

> With all this and more going through her mind, the most dominant thought is, "What could go wrong over the next three days—weather? delayed arrivals? delayed departures? illness, or worse, death, of a participant? How prepared am I and the resort hotel to respond quickly and effectively?" The fact is, although it is almost never apparent to a meeting participant, some things may not proceed as planned. The meeting planner and CSM are never more important than at that moment when a crisis must be averted.
>
> It is opening day at last, and everything is in motion.

INTRODUCTION

WHAT A DIFFERENCE A DAY MAKES

Planning for AAP's 35th Annual Congress began long before the previous year's program ended. The scenario in the opening of this chapter is only a brief glimpse of the multitude of complexities that support the planning and management, and of the jobs that employ those who work in and around the **MEEC** industry, all of which contribute to a meeting's success.

By the time the AAP program is over, roughly 1,900 people (participants and exhibitors) will have flown approximately nine different major airlines and regional carriers on 200 different flights, covered 4 million air miles, consumed 1,000 airline snacks, thousands of bags of candy or snacks grabbed on runs through airports; sat through 60,000 people hours of presentations and education, played 4,000 person hours of golf, and eaten approximately 12,000 catered meals. They will have made about 80,000 telephone calls, purchased and read 5,700 newspapers, transmitted and received more than 500 faxes, and injected about $5,000,000 into the local economy. Their presence will generate about $500,000 in taxes toward state and local coffers. Countless local business owners will make sales in everything from clothing to artwork to souvenirs. Dry cleaners, cab drivers, area restaurateurs, sports facilities, attractions, and hotels will all see jumps in their average weekly revenue. There may also be a significant boost to the local underground, cash-only economy, with contributions made by the seamier side of this phenomenon such as gambling, drugs, and prostitution. In total, the convention-related activities for this single event will touch more than 250 local jobs.

Performing poorly at any of the hundreds of potential failure points can cause dramatic immediate financial loss to the geographic area. In addition, the financial impact could result in positive or negative impact for years to come: A good experience by each delegate will result in praise to many others; a negative experience will result in even more people hearing the results of the stay in that destination. Each of these people can bring or deny more business to the destination and the resort.

WHAT IS A MEETING?

What are these things called "meetings," "exhibitions," "symposia," "congresses," "events," and "conventions"? Why are they so important to the economy? Will these face-to-face gatherings be eliminated in the years ahead? Why have them at all? Are they all the same, or are they different, and if so, what are those differences, and why are they present? All of these questions are addressed in this chapter. Welcome to the fast-paced, tense, and fulfilling world of meetings, expositions, events, and conventions.

The Convention Industry Council's **APEX** (Accepted Practices Exchange) initiative proposes the generic definition of *meeting*: A gathering for business, educational, or social purposes. Associations often use the term to refer to a combination of educational sessions and exhibits. This can include seminars, forums, symposiums, conferences, workshops, clinics, and so on.

In various online tools, synonyms for "meeting" include the following:

Entry:	meeting
Function:	noun
Definition:	gathering
Synonyms:	affair, assemblage, assembly, assignation, audience, bunch, buzz session, call, cattle call, clambake, company, competition, conclave, concourse, concursion, confab, **conference**, conflict, confrontation, congregation, congress, contest, convention, convocation, date, encounter, engagement, gang, get-together, gig, huddle, introduction, meet, nooner, parley, powwow, quickie, rally, rap session, rendezvous, reunion, session, showdown, sit-in, talk, tryst, turnout
Concept:	business action

Source: *Roget's Interactive Thesaurus, First Edition (v 1.0.0)*

Other words from the same source were "assembly," "congregation," and "caucus."

Meetings are a form of, and build, community. From the same sources, words that are also used for "meeting" are synonymous with "community."

Entry:	community
Function:	noun
Definition:	society
Synonyms:	association, body politic, brotherhood, center, colony, commonality, commonwealth, company, district, general public, hamlet, jungle, locality, nation, neighborhood, people, populace, public, residents, society, state, territory, turf
Concept:	social entity

Source: *Roget's Interactive Thesaurus, First Edition (v 1.0.0)*

A dictionary definition was (1) "The act or process or an instance of coming together; an encounter"; and (2) "An assembly or gathering of people, as for a business, social, or religious purpose" (*American Heritage Dictionary of the English Language*, 4th ed.).

INDUSTRY TERMINOLOGY AND PRACTICE

Our industry has struggled for years, before and since the founding of the Convention Industry Council, with terminology and practices that are specific to the work we do. **CIC**'s APEX (http://glossary.conventionindustry.org) is attempting to put into place words that will help all those in the United States, and eventually in all of North America, "speak the same language" as it pertains to types of meetings as well as to other aspects of our industry. This is no easy task.

We have always, generically, referred to gatherings of two or more people as "meetings." This term clearly could encompass meetings that are also called "conventions," "congresses," "symposia," and so on, some of which could have tens of thousands of people in attendance. If one adds displays of materials or products to a meeting, the meeting then has a trade show or **exposition** or **exhibition** component.

The following list of terms is important for anyone involved in MEEC to know. The terms were developed by the terminology panel of APEX and are a small sample of the thousands of words that apply to this industry. Although these terms have, as of this writing, not been formally accepted by CIC or all APEX stakeholders, there is growing acknowledgment that they will be used. The complete glossary of terms used in the MEEC industry can be found online at http://glossary.conventionindustry.org.

- *Meeting:* An event where the primary activity of the attendees is to attend educational sessions, participate in meetings and discussions, socialize, or attend other organized events. There is no exhibit component to this event.
- *Exhibition:* (1) An event at which the primary activity of the attendees is to visit exhibits on the show floor. These events focus primarily on business-to-business (B2B) relationships. (2) Display of products or promotional material for the purposes of public relations, sales and/or marketing. Same as Exposition or Trade Show.
- *Trade Show:* Exhibit of products and services targeted to a specific clientele and not open to the public.
- *Exposition:* A display of products and/or services. Same as Exhibition.
- *Convention:* A display of products and/or services. Same as Exhibition.
- *Seminar:* (1) Lecture and dialogue allowing participants to share experiences in a particular field under the guidance of an expert discussion leader. (2) A meeting or series of meetings of ten to fifty specialists who have different specific skills but have a specific common interest and come together for training or learning purposes. The work schedule of a seminar has the specific object of enriching the skills of the participants.
- *Workshop:* (1) Meeting of several persons for intensive discussion. The workshop concept has been developed to compensate for diverging views in a particular discipline or on a particular subject. (2) Informal and public session of free discussion organized to take place between formal plenary sessions or commissions of a congress or of a conference, either on a subject chosen by the participants themselves or else on a special problem suggested by the organizers. (3) Training session in which participants, often through exercises, develop skills and knowledge in a given field.
- *Conference:* (1) Participatory meeting designed for discussion, fact finding, problem solving, and consultation. (2) An event used by any

organization to meet and exchange views, convey a message, open a debate, or give publicity to some area of opinion on a specific issue. No tradition, continuity, or periodicity is required to convene a conference. Although not generally limited in time, conferences are usually of short duration with specific objectives. Conferences are generally on a smaller scale than congresses. See also Congress, Convention.

- *Clinic:* Workshop-type educational experience where attendees learn by doing.
- *Break-Out Sessions:* Small group sessions, panels, workshops, or presentations offered concurrently within the event, formed to focus on specific subjects. The meeting is separate from the general session, but within the meeting format, formed to focus on specific subjects. These sessions can be arranged by basic, intermediate, or advanced information, or divided by interest areas or industry segment.
- *Assembly:* (1) The process of erecting display component parts into a complete exhibit. (2) A general or formal meeting of an organization attended by representatives of its membership for the purpose of deciding legislative direction, policy matters, the election of internal committees, and approval of balance sheets, budgets, and so on. Consequently, an assembly usually observes certain rules of procedure for its meetings, mostly prescribed in its articles and bylaws.
- *Congress:* (1) The regular coming together of large groups of individuals, generally to discuss a particular subject. A congress will often last several days and have several simultaneous sessions. The length of time between congresses is usually established in advance of the implementation stage and can be either semiannual or annual. Most international or world congresses are of the former type, whereas national congresses are more frequently held annually. (2) Meeting of an association of delegates or representatives from constituent organizations. (3) European term for convention. See also Conference, Convention.
- *Forum:* (1) Open discussion with an audience, panel, and moderator. (2) A meeting or part of a meeting set aside for an open discussion by recognized participants on subjects of public interest. Also for

legal purposes, as part of the proceedings of a tribunal, court, or similar body.

- *Symposium:* A meeting of a number of experts in a particular field, at which papers are presented and discussed by specialists on particular subjects with a view to making recommendations concerning the problems under discussion.
- *Institute:* In-depth instructional meeting providing intensive education on a particular subject.
- *Lecture:* Informative and instructional speech.
- *Panel:* Discussion with a moderator and two or more participants.
- *Incentive Travel:* A travel reward given by companies to employees to stimulate productivity. Also known as an incentive trip.

ORGANIZATIONAL STRUCTURE OF MEEC

MEEC is a part of, and encompasses, many elements of the hospitality and tourism industry. In order to understand how MEEC is related, one must understand the organization and structure of the tourism and hospitality industry.

There are six major divisions, or segments, of the tourism and hospitality industry: lodging, food and beverage, transportation, attractions, entertainment, and shopping.

Lodging: The lodging segment consists of all types of places where travelers may spend the night. These can include hotels, motels, bed-and-breakfasts, cruise ships, trailer parks or campsites, condominiums, and college dormitories. The important characteristics of this segment are that they are available to the public and charge a fee.

Food and Beverage: Obviously, this segment actually contains two sub-segments: food service operations and beverage operations. Food service operations can include the following: table service facilities that can be further broken down by price—high, medium, and low; by type of service—luxury, quick service, and so on; or by cuisine—American, Asian, Italian, Chinese, and the like. Food service also embraces other types of operations including catering, chains, and institutional feeding. Beverage operations can also be broken down by price or type of service, and even whether they serve alcoholic beverages or not.

Transportation: This segment includes any means, or modality, people use to get from one place to another, including walking. The better-known elements include air transportation, water transportation, and ground transportation.

> *Air transportation:* This subsegment includes regularly scheduled carriers such as Delta or Southwest and charter air service that can involve jets, propeller aircraft, and helicopters.
>
> *Water transportation:* This subsegment includes cruise ships and paddle wheelers, charter operations, ferries, and water taxis.
>
> *Ground transportation:* This subsegment includes automobiles, taxis, limousines, jitneys, buses, trains, cog railways, cable cars, and monorails.

Attractions: This segment includes anything that attracts people to a destination and can be further divided into natural and man-made attractions.

> *Natural attractions:* This subsegment includes mountains, seashores, lakes, forests, swamps, climate, and rivers.
>
> *Man-made attractions:* This subsegment consists of things made or constructed by human beings, including buildings such as convention centers, hotels, and monuments; museums, theme parks, and some restaurants.

Entertainment: This subsegment includes anything that provides entertainment value for a guest such as movie theaters, playhouses, orchestras, bands, theme parks, and festivals.

Shopping: This is an important segment of the hospitality and tourism industry, and an area in which people spend considerable sums of money. Many attractions have developed products that carry their theme or logo and result in significant revenue streams for the operator. Probably the best known is Disney, whose products are sold not only at its attractions but also in stand-alone retail centers.

As can be seen, the hospitality and tourism industry is multifaceted. Further, the framework offered in the preceding list is meant to help provide an understanding of the industry and is not intended to be a well-delineated typology. There are many overlaps between the categories: A hotel may be an attraction in itself, such as the Luxor or Treasure Island in

Shopping, such as in a Disney store, is an important segment of the hospitality and tourism industry.

Source: Courtesy of Getty Images, Inc.—Liaison

Las Vegas; the same is true of some stores, such as FAO Schwartz in New York City or the Mall of America in Minneapolis. Hotels often have food and beverage outlets, retail stores, and even entertainment. Further, some of the businesses mentioned above cater to both the tourist and local resident, making it difficult, if not impossible, to determine how much business is derived from each constituency.

It would seem, then, that the MEEC industry is involved with all segments of the hospitality and tourism industry. Understanding the interactions and complexities of the hospitality and tourism industry, along with MEEC, helps explain why it is difficult to determine the size and scope of these industries. Until the late 1990s, the U.S. government, using its Standard Industry Classification (SIC) codes, did not even track many elements of these industries. For example, the government did not even list "meeting planner" as a recognized profession until the late 1980s.

BACKGROUND OF INDUSTRY

Gatherings, meetings, events, and conventions (of sorts) have been a part of people's lives since the earliest recorded history. Archeologists have found primitive ruins of ancient cultures that were used as meeting areas where citizens would gather to discuss common interests such as government, war, hunting, or tribal celebrations. Once humans developed permanent settlements, each town or village had a public meeting area, often called a town square, where residents could meet, talk, and party! Under the leadership of Alexander the Great, over half a million people traveled to what was then Ephesus (now Turkey) to see exhibitions that included acrobats, magicians, animal trainers, and jugglers. Andrew Young, the former U.S. ambassador to the United Nations, said at an MPI (Meeting Professionals International) meeting in Atlanta in the middle 1990s that he was sure there would have been a meeting planner for the Last Supper and certainly for the first Olympics. In Rome, the Forum was a type of organized meeting to discuss politics and decide the fate of the country. Ancient Rome had the Coliseum, which was the site of major sporting events such as gladiatorial contests—someone had to organize them. Through the use of excellent roadways, the Romans were able to establish trade markets to entice people to visit their cities. In Old England, there are stories of King Arthur's Round Table, another example of a meeting to discuss the trials and tribulations of the day. Religious gatherings of various faiths, pilgrimages to Mecca, and others are examples of ancient religious meetings and festivals. The Olympics are an ancient sporting event that was organized just like similar events today. World's fairs and expositions are still another piece of the MEEC industry.

The MEEC industry has also been a part of American culture and development. The white steeples surrounded by snow-covered ground from Currier and Ives prints actually depicted the town square of New England cities. In one of the oldest communities in North America, Santa Fe, the square not only houses the seat of government but also has been used traditionally as a festival marketplace. Even today, Native Americans can be seen around the perimeter of the square displaying their handicrafts for sale. The First Continental Congress in Philadelphia is an example of a "formal meeting," in this case to decide on governance of the thirteen colonies. Political conventions have a long history in the United States and are part of the MEEC industry. Americans have made festivals and celebrations of every sort, such as Mardi Gras in New Orleans, part of their lives since the early days of this country.

Today, structures supporting the MEEC industry are integral parts of major cities. It is a well-known fact that in order to be considered a "world class city" a community must possess a convention center and a stadium or arena for sports and events. The largest cities all have them, including New York, Los Angeles, Chicago, Washington, San Francisco, and even New Orleans. The hope is that these public facilities will attract out-of-town attendees for conventions and events who will spend money in the community.

In spite of its long history, meeting planning as a recognized profession did not develop until 1972, when MPI was founded. Only 120 planners and suppliers attended their first convention. The first board of directors was headed by "Buzz" Bartlow and led to the development of the first academic meeting planning program. This program, approved by the state of Colorado in September of 1976, was implemented by Metropolitan State College in Denver. This initiative was followed closely by the meeting planning program at Northeastern Oklahoma University in Tahlequah. In 1979, Patti Shock started the convention service management (hotel perspective) and meeting planning classes at Georgia State University (GSU). In 1983, trade show classes were added with the financial support of the National Association of Exposition Managers (NAEM) (now the

Mardi Gras Festival in New Orleans.
Source: Getty Images Inc.—Image Bank.

International Association of Exposition Managers, or IAEM) and IAFE (International Association of Fairs and Expositions). GSU was the first to implement trade show classes and therefore the first to cover the whole convention industry.

There were two factors that contributed to the rapid development of both industry workshops and academic programs during the 1980s. The first was the development and implementation of the Certified Meeting Professional (CMP) examination and designation by the Convention Liaison Council (CLC). This certification gives both status and credence to the person who achieves it. A second factor was the development of a "model" meeting curriculum by the Professional Convention Management Association (PCMA). Once PCMA had its model curriculum, it actively pursued the inauguration of its program in several colleges and universities.

Since its founding in New York in 1949 by four organizations—the American Society of Association Executives (ASAE); American Hotel and Motel Association (AH&MA, now the American Hotel Lodging Association); Hospitality [then Hotel] Sales and Marketing Association International (HSMAI); and International Association of Convention and Visitor Bureaus (**IACVB**)—the Convention Industry Council (then, the Convention Liaison Council) has traditionally followed the lead of its constituent organizations, which now number thirty-one (from the CIC Web site: http://www.conventionindustry.org).

In 1895, "[t]he roots of present-day convention & visitor bureaus (CVBs) [were] planted when journalist Milton Carmichael suggest[ed] in *The Detroit Journal* that local businessmen band together to promote the city as a convention destination, as well as represent the city and its many hotels to bid for business. Two weeks later, what [became] the Detroit Convention and Businessmen's League form[ed] to do just that. Carmichael head[ed] the group, which . . . later evolve[d] into the Detroit Metro CVB." (From *EXPO Magazine* at http://www.expoweb.com/expomag/BackIssues/2001/Apr/feature2.htm).

The role of CVBs has changed over time. As in Detroit, most began by trying to attract only conventions and business meetings to their community. Later, they realized leisure visitors were an important source of business and added the "V" for visitors to their name. Today, virtually every city in the United States and Canada, and many cities throughout the world, has a CVB or convention and visitors association (CVA). CVB or CVA is a membership organization that helps promote tourism and meetings and related business for their cities.

ECONOMIC IMPACT

The MEEC industry is diverse. As a result, it is hard to estimate the size, magnitude, and impact of the MEEC industry. Further, only limited research has been done in the field. The CIC commissioned Deloitte & Touche, LLP, to study the economic impact of the meetings and hospitality industry. The study, from the mid-1990s, states that the industry encompassing meetings, conventions, expositions, and incentives contributed more than $82.8 billion to the U.S. economy, making it (then) the twenty-second largest contributor to the gross domestic product of the United States. (From PCMA at http://www.pcma.org/resources/industry/research/clc_study.asp).

One of the most comprehensive accounts of the impact of the MEEC industry is published biannually in the "Meetings Market Report" in *Meetings & Conventions Magazine.* It shows that in 2001 there were 844,100 corporate meetings, 177,700 association meetings, and 11,800 conventions for a total of 1,033,600 meetings held in the year. The number of people attending MEEC is also significant. In 2001, 51,500,000 attended corporate meetings, 15,900,000 attended association meetings, and 12,500,000 attended conventions for a total meeting attendance of 79,900,000 in the year. Total expenditures included $10.3 billion for corporate meetings, $13.9 billion for association meetings, $16.6 billion for conventions, and $40.8 billion aggregate expenditures for all meetings in 2001. Readers are reminded that these figures are for direct spending and do not include the "multiplier effect." When the latter is considered, the amounts above are doubled. Thus, the "total impact" of the MEEC industry sector studied by this magazine is $93.6 billion.

Another source of information on the impact of MEEC is provided by the Trade Show Exhibitors Association. They found that in 2001 trade shows and exhibits alone had total direct spending amounting to $20.5 billion, while spending by exhibitors totaled $3.6 billion. There were 4,983 events at an exhibition or convention center, 1,070 events at a conference center or seminar facility, 4,870 events at a hotel, and another 2,262 that were not classified. Of all the direct spending, 63.1% was done at conventions and expositions, 32.7% was done at meetings, and 4.2% was on incentive travel. The recipients of direct spending included hotels with 32.5%, air transportation with 22.3%, restaurants with 12.1%, ground transportation with 8.6%, retail trade with 6.7%, business services with 6.6%, and entertainment with 4.5%; the remainder was unspecified.

Current meeting economic impact statistics, although not collectively available, have shown that the impact of the September 11, 2001, terrorist attacks on the World Trade Center in New York City and on the Pentagon in Washington, DC, as well as that involved in the plane crash in Pennsylvania, resulting in the subsequent softening of the U.S. economy, was devastating to the meetings, conventions, expositions, and incentive industry.

A study conducted by Meeting Professionals International in October 2001 showed that 68% of those surveyed canceled up to five meetings each for October 2001; 43% canceled up to five meetings for November and December 2001; 25% canceled meetings for some time in 2002. Seventy percent of those respondents said they hoped to rebook their meetings. (Data is not available to know how many meetings were rebooked.) Many meetings were cancelled or terminated, hotels and other meeting venue and service providers cut staff, and hotels profits were devastated.

The following article is available from the Web page of the International Association of Convention and Visitors Bureaus and was released on October 17, 2002:

Mayors, Industry Leaders Propose Plan to Help Boost Travel

Travel and tourism is a key contributor to the economies of the nation's 100 largest metropolitan areas, according to new data released today by the U.S. Conference of Mayors, the Travel Business Roundtable, and the International Association of Convention and Visitor Bureaus. The research finds international travel to the [United States] significantly suppressed because of the weak economy and 9/11[01] and predicts it will remain threatened, barring a concerted effort by the public and private sectors. A summit of mayors, CEOs of convention and visitor bureaus, and travel industry experts meeting here today endorsed a detailed plan to stimulate travel and thereby boost metro economies.

"We are here today because we realize the importance of being proactive in the effort to stabilize this important industry," said Atlanta Mayor Shirley Franklin, who chairs the U.S. Conference of Mayors Travel and Tourism Task Force. "As tourism goes, so goes the economic well-being of our communities. We cannot and will not leave it to chance. This task force will be very aggressive in pursuing the implementation of our ten-point action plan to boost travel and tourism."

The report, developed by DRI-WEFA, an economic research firm, is accessible at http://www.usmayors.org. Key findings include—

- In 2000, travel and tourism was a $263.4 billion industry in the nation's top 100 metro areas, including $17.6 billion in New York, $14 billion in Chicago, $13.6 billion in Los Angeles–Long Beach, $11.2 billion in Atlanta, $3.5 billion in Pittsburgh, and more than $1 billion in Colorado Springs. Travel and tourism is the largest share of the gross metropolitan economy in Las Vegas (14.4%), Honolulu (13.9%), and Orlando (12.3%).
- In 2000, tourism supported 3.9 million jobs in the nation's 100 largest metro areas, including Chicago (207,436 jobs), New York (198,998), Los Angeles–Long Beach (177,264), Atlanta (172,954), Washington (152,891), Dallas (140,661), Detroit (76,775), and Salt Lake City (45,175).
- A significant travel slowdown, the result of the weak economy and 9/11, has hit metro economies disproportionately hard, cutting more than 536,000 tourism-related jobs in the top 100 metro areas through 2002. Tourism job losses have been particularly severe in Phoenix (−27.2%), Orlando (−24.5%), San Diego (−23.8%), Lancaster (−22.9%), and Houston (−22.7%).
- A reduction in international visitors will cost metro areas more than $22.6 billion in lost economic activity in 2001 and 2002, of which more than $12.5 billion is attributed to 9/11. Losses were largest in New York ($5.9 billion, of which $3.3 billion is attributed to 9/11), San Francisco ($2.1 billion, of which $1.2 billion is attributed to 9/11), Los Angeles ($1.75 billion, of which $970 million is attributed to 9/11), and Miami ($1.6 billion, of which $861 million is attributed to 9/11).
- International visits to the United States are not expected to recover soon without aggressive efforts by the public and private sectors. The report projects that the nation could achieve an additional $100 billion in international tourism spending from 2003 to 2007 if key strategic and policy decisions were made to foster the recovery and growth of key tourism export markets.

"The United States is losing tourism market share, and with it jobs and tax revenue, to our foreign competitors who are spending vast sums of money to promote their countries," said Jonathan Tisch, Chairman of the Travel Business Roundtable and Chairman & CEO of Loews Hotels. "We are the only developed nation in the world that does not make a strategic federal investment to promote our country as an international destination. In fact, the [United States] is now the third most visited country, behind France and Spain. The public and private sectors must work together to reverse this trend."

Today, the economic uncertainty in the United States and throughout the world, the reality of civil war, the possibility of international war, and the disarray and financial woes of the airline industry have made the traveling public skittish about leisure and business travel. Hotel occupancy rates in all cities have fallen—more dramatically in what the industry calls "first-tier" cities, which are those that host large conventions and trade shows. Cities continue to build convention centers and new hotel projects, planned before the economic downturn, and hope to be able to fill them with meetings that will in turn bolster the local economy.

WHY HAVE MEETINGS?

In the early to mid-1980s, there was talk, as there was immediately after September 11, 2001, that face-to-face meetings would be a thing of the past—that teleconferencing or other e-conferencing and learning would supplant face-to-face gatherings. The Foundation of Meeting Professionals International (MPI) conducted studies in the mid-1990s that focused on what makes meetings work for associations and corporations (http://www.mpiweb.org and directly to the studies at http://www.mpiweb.org/resources/mpif/pdfs/whitepaper.pdf). These studies show that people prefer meeting face-to-face, that one of the most important values of gatherings is the ability to meet with and learn from peers. "Virtual" meetings in all forms (audio and video conferences, online learning and exchanges) do not yet create the desired effect. Further, face-to-face meetings have the added benefit of including all forms of communication, including verbal and nonverbal. For example, when you meet people for the first time and the palms of their hands are sweaty, are you concerned whether they are telling the truth or are nervous for some reason? What does the strength and style of a handshake tell you about people? Facial expressions can support a message or send one that is completely different from the verbal message.

Shaking hands is a form of nonverbal communication.
Source: Dorling Kindersley Media Library

How do you feel if the people to whom you are speaking never look you "straight in the eye"? Nonverbal communication is very important.

When we meet, we build "communities of practice." Through these communities of practice, we are able to strengthen skills (at sales or association educational meetings, symposia), impact change (political conventions, governance meetings), observe accomplishments (incentive meetings, celebrations), renew acquaintances (reunions), and learn about new products in our field (exhibitions, trade shows).

EMPLOYMENT IN AND AROUND THE MEEC INDUSTRY

The meetings, expositions, events, and conventions industry is a subsegment of the hospitality industry, which itself is part of the larger services industry. It encompasses many areas of the hospitality industry. Thus, the readers are challenged to conceptualize their personal ideal job and then determine how and where in the MEEC industry they could be employed doing what they dream of.

Some of the careers in MEEC include the following:

- *Event Planner:* Puts together special events like the Super Bowl of football, the Final Four in basketball, festivals, and celebrations.
- *Meeting Planner:* Organizes meetings and other gatherings for companies, corporations, and associations. These gatherings can range from a small board of directors meeting, a stockholders meeting, and new product introductions to educational seminars and national conventions.
- *Wedding Planner:* Did you ever think that *someone* needs to organize all the weddings that occur each year?
- *Hotel Sales:* The majority of positions in hotel sales deal with groups, and MEEC covers most of those groups.
- *Restaurant Sales:* While most people think of restaurants attracting walk-in clientele, many rely heavily on the MEEC industry for business. Food and beverage (F&B) venues employ significant numbers of people on their group sales staff. In New Orleans, Arnaud's, Emeril's, and even the Crescent City Brewhouse have convention sales teams.
- *Entertainment Venue Sales:* Although these places attract individual patrons primarily, most also devote much time and effort to selling and producing events for groups. Further, groups have lots of money and can afford lavish productions.
- *Destination Management:* Destination Management Companies (DMCs) function as the "local experts" for companies and associations in organizing gatherings and events. People employed for DMCs usually work in either sales or production.
- *Hotels:* Hotels are one of the primary locations where MEEC events are held using ballrooms, meeting rooms, break-out rooms, etc., for their gatherings along with sleeping rooms and F&B for their attendees. The two departments in hotels that deal with the MEEC industry are sales and convention services.
- *Convention Centers:* These venues include dedicated facilities like McCormick Place in Chicago, the Jakob Javits Convention Center

in New York, and the Sands Expo in Las Vegas. Also included in this category are multipurpose venues like the Superdome in New Orleans or the Astrodome in Houston. Once again, careers are found in either sales or operations.

- *Exposition Services Contractors:* Do you like to build things? Have you thought about being an engineer or architect? Well, exposition services contractors (ESCs) may be the place for you. These businesses design and erect the booths, backdrops, staging, etc., for meetings and conventions. The decorations and backdrops for your school prom may have been done by an ESC. Again, career paths exist in sales and in production.
- *Convention and Visitor Bureaus:* CVBs serve to represent a wide range of MEEC companies and market the destination to business and leisure travelers. CVBs have many departments and careers, including convention sales, tourism sales, housing bureaus, convention services, marketing, research, and member services.

Gaming industry trade show held in Las Vegas.
Photo by George G. Fenich, Ph.D., Professor, School of HRTA, University of New Orleans

As you can see, MEEC is a vibrant, dynamic, and exciting part of the hospitality industry. It may also serve as an ideal work environment for someone who has tried or worked in many different areas and likes them all. Many careers in MEEC involve multiple aspects of the hospitality industry. For example, someone who works in convention or group sales in a hotel must interface with, and be knowledgeable about, hotel sleeping rooms, front desk, food and beverage, catering, and all the meeting facilities. Further, unlike at a front desk, hotel convention employees develop long-term friendships and relationships with their MEEC clientele. These hotel employees have been known to be invited to clients' homes, vacation retreats, birthdays, weddings, and so forth. In fact, one of the most important considerations for anyone involved in MEEC is the building of long-term relationships with clientele. In marketing jargon, this is called "relationship marketing."

Think for just a moment about all the lives and jobs that could impact one of the meeting participants and the meeting organizers involved in the scenario for the Association of Amalgamated Professionals. They include what follows:

The Meeting Sponsor

The Association of Amalgamated Professionals

Meeting planner

Executive director or chief executive officer (CEO)

Staff specialists in departments that include marketing, governance and government affairs, education, membership, information technology, and accreditation

Others who staff call centers, copy materials, process registrations, manage human resources, control purchasing, and more

Board of directors

Committees

Sponsors

The Facility

Owners

Executive staff including but not limited to general manager, revenue manager, resident or hotel manager, directors of sales, marketing, convention services, catering, housekeeping, engineering, maintenance, purchasing, human resources, food and beverage, front office operations, and security

The thousands of other full- and part-time, year-round and seasonal staff: grounds keepers, animal handlers, housekeepers, food servers (for banquets, room service, and the resort's outlets), maintenance, security, and engineering

The Destination

Convention and visitors bureau (president, directors of sales, marketing, convention services, membership, registration, and all support staff)

Restaurants

Attractions

Off-site venues

Theaters (movie and legitimate)

Copy and printing companies

Transportation (buses, airport shuttles, taxicabs, limousines)

Airport concessions

Doctors and medical personnel

Pharmacies

Florists

Department and other stores

Destination management companies

Audiovisual suppliers

General services contractors

Specialty services contractors

Dry cleaners and tailors

City, county, and state employees

And All the Others Who Provide Services for Meetings

Talent (entertainers, disc jockeys, bands, magicians)

Education (speakers, trainers, facilitators)

Sound and lighting

Transportation (air, rail, car, boat, and travel agencies)

Printing

Shipping

Promotional products

Off-property food and beverage

Translators for those who speak American Sign Language and other languages

Americans with Disabilities Act (ADA) equipment

Carpentry

National sales (hotels, conference centers)

"Third-party" or independent meeting planners

Is there anyone who does not have some influence on the MEEC industry? A case can be made that every person has an impact, in some way, on each and every meeting—even those meetings of two or three that take place in an office or restaurant. Take a few minutes and add to the jobs or functions above that might affect a meeting. Then think again. Even the president of the United States and all members of Congress impact our industry by determining trade regulations, security issues, and whether or not our country goes to war.

WHAT DOES A MEETING PLANNER DO?

When asked about a "typical day," there are few if any meeting professionals, whether they work in an organization or operate an external meeting planning company, who could say that any day is "typical." Our jobs are ideal for those who love to multitask, who have broad interests, who enjoy problem solving, and who care passionately about building community through meetings.

Doug Heath, Certified Association Executive (CAE) and Certified Meeting Planner (CMP), who was the second executive director of MPI, said many years ago, "Meeting planners have to be more than coffee-cup counters." When Mr. Heath said that, it was a time when most meeting planners were concerned only with logistics—ensuring room sets, coffee and refreshment breaks, meals, and audiovisual setup.

Today, our jobs are strategic. We are charged with supporting the work toward an organization's bottom line. To do that, and in the course of planning a meeting, a meeting planner may do any or all of the following, and more:

- Define meeting goals and objectives.
- Develop a request for proposal (RFP) based on a meeting's objectives, audience profile, budget, and program (see Appendix A of this book for examples).
- Send the RFP to national sales offices of hotel and conference center companies, to convention and visitors bureaus, and to external meeting planning companies.
- Prepare and manage a budget and expenditures that can range from a few hundred dollars to well over $2 million.
- Negotiate contracts with a facility, transportation providers, decorators, speakers, entertainers, and all the vendors and venues that will support a meeting.
- Market the meeting electronically and in print, and track results.
- Invite and manage needs (travel, lodging, registration, room setup, and audiovisual) for all speakers, trainers, and facilitators involved in delivery of information and knowledge for the meeting.
- Invite and manage contracts and needs for entertainers.
- Design food and beverage events, and negotiate contracts for these events. To do so, a planner must know the audience (age of participants, gender, abilities, allergies, geographic location, and more) and timing for the program.
- Prepare a crisis management plan in conjunction with other staff, facilities, vendors, and emergency personnel.
- Register participants, ensuring data is accurately entered.
- Manage the multitude of changes that happen from first conceptualizing a meeting to the execution.
- Monitor industry and business publications for strikes and other issues.
- Calm others' nerves and remain calm.

The following are some questions you might answer in order to determine if you have what it takes to be a successful meetings professional:

- Do you like to plan parties, work schedules, your day, and so forth?
- Do you have a date book or personal digital assistant (PDA) that you update regularly and that includes everything you need to do for weeks or months into the future?
- Do you like to organize your bedroom, car, workplace, and so on? Is your idea of fun organizing a closet for someone?
- Are you very organized, almost to the point of obsession?

If you answered "yes" to all of those questions, you have the aptitude to be a good meetings professional.

To be prepared for short- and long-term change, *meeting professionals*— a term that encompasses those who plan and execute meetings, those who work for and in facilities in which meetings are held, and the many vendors who supply services for meetings—must begin to anticipate changes that will occur as the nature of meetings changes. In the scenario at the beginning of the chapter, there is a designated vendor to work with satellite and other e-communication tools. In the future, meeting professionals will need a greater working knowledge and will be charged with selecting meeting destinations (cities) and sites that can facilitate distance learning and e-communications.

End of the First Day

It is the end of the first day of the AAP's 35th Annual Congress, which, internally, Barbara Tain, the AAP Meeting Planner, refers to as the "Annual" or "Annual Meeting," and so far all has gone well.

Barbara will have had formal, prescheduled meetings with Todd Cliver, the resort hotel's CSM. Via radio (sometimes referred to as a "walkie-talkie") and mobile phone, and through chance meetings, Barbara will also have talked with Todd and with many others who work for the resort hotel. These talks include a review of banquet checks with various departments, one of which will be include accounting. She will have talked with those on the AAP staff and in volunteer leadership and with outside vendors. She will, on her PDA, through television and radio and the newspaper, check weather many times. Barbara will have eaten on the run, tried to find a few minutes to check office voice mail and e-mail, and, through it all, kept a smile on her face.

At the end of the day, she will review her notes and check room sets for the next morning's sessions and crawl into bed for a few hours sleep before it all begins again.

When the final curtain closes on the AAP's 35th Annual Congress, Barbara Tain will be one of the last to leave the resort hotel. Before leaving for the airport to fly home, she will review all the master account charges, conduct a postconvention ("post-con") meeting with the property staff and her vendors, and make notes for next year's meeting.

For meeting professionals, meetings never truly end. No matter how we define a "meeting," each meeting is a matter of intense planning and execution, evaluation, follow-up, and starting over. Our role is critical in ensuring outcomes, and from those outcomes, we contribute to a sound economy.

◆ SUMMARY

In this chapter, you are introduced to the world of MEEC. As can be seen, MEEC is multifaceted and exciting, and offers diverse career opportunities. MEEC is also very large and incorporates many facets of the hospitality industry. It has tremendous economic impact. You are now prepared to continue with the remaining chapters in this book. They expand on and provide more detail about the concepts and practices of MEEC that this first chapter only touches on.

KEY WORDS AND TERMS

For definitions, refer to http://glossary.conventionindustry.org.

APEX

BEO

CIC

Conference

Convention

CSM

Destination

DMC

Exhibition

Exposition

IACVB

MEEC

Meeting

Outlet

Sales and Marketing

REVIEW AND DISCUSSION QUESTIONS

1. What are meetings?
2. Describe some events from the past that were "meetings."
3. Describe some current aspects of MEEC industry jobs.
4. Who attends meetings?
5. What can be accomplished by convening or attending a meeting?
6. What are five key jobs in a facility (hotel, resort, conference center) that contribute to the successful outcome of a meeting?
7. What is CIC?
8. What is APEX, and what does it hope to accomplish?
9. What is the impact on the U.S. economy of meetings?
10. What is the future of electronic meetings?

ABOUT THE CHAPTER CONTRIBUTOR

Joan L. Eisenstodt, a facilitator, trainer, and meeting manager with 30+ years' experience, is president of Washington, DC-based Eisenstodt Associates, LLC, a company she founded in 1981. Eisenstodt is moderator of the "MIMList," an international online community. In her community, she serves on the Board of Governors of George Washington University–Hillel and on the Advisory Board of Speaking From the Heart. She has been recognized by hospitality industry organizations as Planner of the Year (MPI), Teacher of the Year (PCMA), and a "Pacesetter" (HSMAI). Joan has been included in the *"One of the 25 Most Influential People in the Meetings Industry"* list since its inception. She has also been recognized as one of the "Power Players" ("10 Women Who are Changing the Industry") and appears in "The 'A' List: 10 Women Meeting Industry Leaders." Joan is the recipient of the Pyramid Award from the International Association of Conference Centers.

◆2

PLANNING, ORGANIZING, DIRECTING, AND CONTROL IN MEEC

Planning and organizing of national political conventions is a function of the MEEC industry.
Source: Pearson Education/PH College

◆ Chapter Objectives

This chapter provides the reader with an understanding of the following:

- The differences in association and corporate meeting planning
- The motivations that influence meeting objectives
- Writing clear and concise meeting objectives using the *SMART* technique
- The purpose of a needs analysis
- The process of site selection
- The information needed on an RPP

- Establishing budgetary goals
- The process of registration for a meeting or event
- The process of arranging housing for a meeting or event
- The elements of a meeting and event specification guide
- The importance of a pre- and post-convention meeting
- Effective evaluation instruments

◆ Chapter Outline

Planning
    Creating Meeting Objectives
Needs Analysis
Developing *SMART* Objectives
Site Selection
Request for Proposal
Budgetary Concerns
    Step 1: Establish Goals
    Step 2: Identify Expenses
    Step 3: Identify Revenue Sources
Cost Control
Organizing and Directing
    Registration

Housing
Meeting & Event Specification Guide
Pre- and Post-Con Meetings
    Preconvention Meeting
    Postconvention Review
Control in MEEC
    Designing the Evaluation
Summary
Key Words and Terms
Review and Discussion Questions
References
About the Chapter Contributor

PLANNING

CREATING MEETING OBJECTIVES

All meetings and events should begin with clear, concise, and measurable objectives. Webster's dictionary defines an *objective* as "something aimed at or strived for" along with "being the aim or goal" (*Webster's Unabridged Dictionary,* 2nd ed., S. V. "objective"). Meeting objectives are the basis for virtually all components of the planning process, whether it is for corporate meetings, association meetings, special events, trade shows, or virtual meetings held via the Internet. It is meaningful to illustrate one key difference between corporate meetings and association events. Attendance at corporate meetings and events is typically mandatory. If management dictates that all sales managers must travel to Dallas on October 3 for a sales meeting, there is little question of where the managers will be on October 3. However, association meetings and most trade shows do not have the luxury of a built-in audience. Attendance to association events is typically voluntary. Organizers must rely on marketing and program content to drive participation. Thus, meeting objectives may differ depending on the goals of the sponsor of the event. An important objective for an association may be to increase membership by 5%. An important objective for a corporation may be to increase the attendee's product knowledge of a new software program by 50%.

Good meeting objectives should focus on the attendees. What will make the attendees want to attend the meeting? What will be their **Return on Investment** (ROI)? What makes your event more desirable than your competitor's event? Some of the key meeting planning components that are directly affected by the meeting objectives are discussed in the following text.

Program Design and Room Set

What educational approach is appropriate for the group? If the objective is to disseminate new corporate policies and procedures, then a lecture format may be used. A classroom-style room set with tables and chairs would be needed to provide adequate working space. If the objective is to teach attendees how to use a new airline reservation software package, then a "hands-on" computer simulation may be needed, which would require a room with multiple computer stations and possibly an Internet connection. However, if the objective of the event is to hold an awards ceremony for top achievers in a company, then a large ballroom at a hotel that can accommodate 2,000 attendees set theater style (only chairs) may be best.

Logistics

The physical location for a meeting is also impacted by the objectives. For a meeting of the incoming board of directors for the American Medical Association to get acquainted and conduct strategic planning, a relaxing environment at a resort location would be appropriate. On the other hand,

Classroom-style layout for an event in a tent.
Used by permission of Paradise Sound & Light, Orlando, Florida

if a one-day sales meeting for regional directors of a corporation in the Southeast needs to occur, then selecting an easily accessible location, such as Atlanta, and holding the meeting close to the airport would allow many people to arrive and depart on the same day. This would eliminate the costs of an overnight stay and allow people to get back to work as soon as possible. If an intensive three-day seminar is to be held with morning-to-evening mandatory workshops, then an exciting casino property in Atlantic City is probably not a good choice of venue. There would be too many distractions. It may also elicit a negative attitude by the attendees. Who wants to be in an exciting location if no one can participate in the activities?

Affordability

Cost is another factor in site selection. If keeping meeting costs low is a primary objective, then the planner may elect to hold the event in a

second-tier city. Second-tier cities like Albuquerque, Columbus, and Birmingham are often more affordable than **first-tier** cities like New York, Orlando, San Francisco, Atlanta, Dallas, Chicago, or Las Vegas. Second-tier cities offer value and can be quite enjoyable. They are often more "hungry" for convention business and will be more likely to negotiate the best prices for accommodations and services. However, for some affluent associations or corporations, cost is not a major consideration.

Overall, the planner tries to match the meeting environment to the overall objectives for the event. The planner must consider both the objectives of the sponsoring organization (association or corporation) as well as the objectives of the prospective attendees. For example, a planner would not want to schedule a meeting for Mormons in New Orleans. So, how do we determine what these objectives are? The first step is to conduct a needs analysis.

NEEDS ANALYSIS

A **needs analysis** is a method of determining the expectations for a particular meeting. A needs analysis can be as simple as asking senior management what they want to accomplish at a meeting and then designing the event around those expectations. If the CEO wants to hold the meeting at the exclusive Ritz Carlton Buckhead in Atlanta, provide deluxe suites for all attendees, have all meals catered and expense is no object, then the meeting planner's job is much easier. However, in the real world, it takes more work to develop a needs analysis. The first step is to know your attendees. The question "Who are they?" should be asked. Collect demographic information of both past and prospective attendees. This is much easier for an annual event, such as an association meeting or corporate management meeting. The planner keeps a detailed **history** of who attended the meeting, their likes and dislikes, and all pertinent information that can be used to improve future meetings. Questions to consider include the following:

- What is the age and gender of past attendees?
- What is their level of expertise—beginner, intermediate, advanced?
- What is their position within the organization's hierarchy—new employee, junior management, or senior management?

- What hotel amenities are preferred—indoor pools, spas, tennis courts, exercise rooms?
- Are there specific dietary restrictions for the attendees?
- Who is paying the expenses? Most people are more cost-conscious if they are paying out of their own pocket rather than a company expense account.
- Will meeting attendees bring guests or children to the event?
- Are networking opportunities important?
- How far are attendees willing to travel to attend the meeting?
- Will international guests attend who require interpreters?
- Are special accommodations needed for people with disabilities?
- What are the educational outcomes expected at the meeting?

Some of this information can be answered by questions on the meeting registration form. Other information can be obtained through association membership or company records. Most planners do some type of evaluation after an event to provide feedback that can be used to improve the next meeting. This is covered later in the chapter.

DEVELOPING *SMART* OBJECTIVES

Once the planner has determined the needs of the attendees and sponsoring organization, objectives must be written in a clear and concise format so all parties involved in the planning process understand and are focused on common goals. A common method of writing effective meeting objectives is to use the **SMART** approach. Each letter of the SMART approach reminds the planner of critical components of a well-written objective.

*S*pecific: Only one major concept is covered per objective.

*M*easurable: Must be able to quantify or measure that you have, or have not, achieved the objective.

*A*chievable: Is it possible to accomplish the objective?

*R*elevant: Is the objective important to the overall goals of the organization?

*T*ime: The objective should include when the objective must be completed.

It is also good to begin meeting objectives with an action verb (e.g., *achieve*, *promote*, *understand*, *design*) and include cost factors if applicable. List by name the person or department responsible for achieving the objectives.

Examples of Meeting Objectives

- The Meetings Department of the International Association of Real Estate Agents will "generate attendance of 7,500 people at the 2008 annual meeting to be held in Orlando, FL."
- The Education Committee of the National Association for Catering Executives (NACE) will "create a NACE professional certification program by the 2008 annual meeting."
- The Brettco Pharmaceutical Corporation will "hold a two-day conference, October 2 and 3 in Chicago, IL, for the 12 regional sales managers to launch 5 new product introductions for 2008. Total meeting costs not to exceed $15,000."
- Jill Miller will "complete the graphic design for the convention program by May 3, 2008."

Tests for Evaluating Objectives

1. Is the objective written using SMART?
2. Can the ultimate outcome be measured?
3. Can the objective be clearly understood by those responsible for accomplishing it?
4. Is the objective realistic and attainable while still presenting a challenge?
5. Is the ultimate outcome of the objective justified by the time, effort, and expense utilized in achieving it?
6. Is the objective consistent with company and organizational goals?
7. Can accountability for outcomes be clearly established from the objective?

Adapted from Meetings and Conventions: A Planning Guide (MacLauren and Wykes 1997, 13).

Designing well-written meeting objectives can be a very positive activity for the meeting planner. Objectives serve as signals to keep the planning process focused and on track. At the end of the meeting, the planner can communicate to management what goals were achieved or exceeded, or what was not achieved and why. If objectives are met, it helps demonstrate the ROI that the meeting planner provides to the organization. If objectives are not met, then management can focus resources on finding out the causes of failure and correcting them for the next meeting.

SITE SELECTION

The site selection process can begin after meeting objectives are developed. The objectives will guide the planner in deciding the physical location for the event, type of facility to use, transportation options, and many other meeting components. Depending on the type of meeting, site selection may take place days, weeks, months, or years before the actual event. For major conventions, a city is usually selected three to five years in advance. Some large associations, such as the American Library Association, have determined meeting sites (cities) decades into the future. However, small corporate meetings usually have a much shorter lead time. Results of a study by *Successful Meetings* (2003) indicates that approximately 75% of management meetings, 64% of training and education meetings, and 80% of sales meetings are planned six months or less in advance.

Professional Meeting Management (Connell et al. 2002) lists eight steps to the **site selection** process (42):
1. Identify the meeting objectives.
2. Gather historical data.
3. Determine the physical requirements.
4. Consider attendee expectations.
5. Select general area and type of facility.
6. Prepare a RFP.
7. Review and evaluate choices.
8. Select site.

Contrary to popular belief, the association meeting planner is usually not the final decision maker when it comes to which city will be selected to host a convention. Typically, determining the actual site selection is a group decision made by the association staff with much input from the board of directors and volunteer committee members. The meeting planner will review numerous reference materials, talk with other planners, and may make recommendations but usually does not personally make the final decision. The corporate planner may have more influence over site section, especially for smaller meetings. But for larger corporate meetings, the CEO or chairman of the board may make the decision. Sometimes locations are chosen because of the availability of recreational activities like golf, not because the meeting facilities are outstanding. It differs with each organization.

Meeting planners are regularly bombarded with site selection information. There are several trade publications like *Successful Meetings*, *Meetings and Conventions*, *Convene*, *Corporate Meetings and Incentive Travel*, and *Expo*

The Links at Spanish Bay, part of the famous Pebble Beach Golf Resort, is often chosen as a site for small meetings and incentive trips.
Photo by George G. Fenich, Ph.D., Professor, School of HRTA, University of New Orleans

that meeting planners may subscribe to for low or no cost. These magazines are either independently owned or are affiliated with one of the major meetings-related professional associations, such as the PCMA and MPI. The magazines are funded through advertising sales from hotel chains, transportation companies, convention facilities, and many other service providers to the meetings industry. Other key advertisers are the actual locations competing for the convention dollar. Special advertising inserts or destination guides are common that promote regions ("Meetings on the Gulf Coast"), individual cities ("San Antonio Meeting Planners Guide"), states ("Conventions in California"), and countries ("The Korean Connection: Asia's Convention Destination"). These special advertising segments can showcase local culture, attractions, and facilities; provide testimonials of past events; and serve to entice the planner to consider their location. Other special supplements are designed to showcase other characteristics like "Second-Tier Cities," "Unique Venues," "Meetings on College Campuses," "Cruise Ship Conventions," "Affordable Meetings," or "Golf Destinations."

Conventions are big business and can have dramatic economic impacts on a city. For example, in Las Vegas in 2001, approximately 4.1 million convention delegates came to meetings, conventions, and trade shows. The combined economic impact of the convention industry is estimated to have been over $4.84 billion on the local economy (Convention and Visitors Authority, "Las Vegas" 2003). CVBs (see chapter 11, "Convention and Visitors Bureaus") spend thousands to tens of millions of dollars each year promoting their location for tourism and convention business. Las Vegas alone spent approximately $83 million on marketing expenses in 2002 (Las Vegas Convention and Visitors Authority, "Expenditures" 2003). CVBs also provide planners with assistance for housing, arranging tours, and connecting with service providers, such as security, audiovisual, computer rentals, temporary staffing, banking, and florists. CVBs from across the globe have their own professional association called the International Association of Convention and Visitor Bureaus (IACVB). Their Web site provides links to member CVBs worldwide and can be viewed at http://www.officialtravelinfo.com. Many of the Web sites include options like streaming audio and visual, interactive local maps, direct links to other service providers, cultural highlights, language translators, currency exchange rates, and safety and security issues. Some CVBs and convention facilities promote their services through videotapes, DVDs, or

CD-ROMs. These media are desirable, as they provide a visually stimulating and often interactive experience for the planner and others involved in the process.

Other factors to consider in site selection are the rotation of locations and the location of the majority of the attendees. In the United States, the planner may want to hold a major convention in the East (Boston) one year, the South (New Orleans) the next, the Midwest (Chicago) the third year, and the West (San Francisco) the fourth year. This allows attendees to enjoy a wide variety of meeting locations, and attendees who live on one side of the country are not always traveling many hours and through several time zones to attend the meeting. But if most of the attendees live on the East Coast, it may be preferable to hold the meeting in a city conveniently located. However, some association meetings, such as the National Association of Broadcasters or the Consumer Electronics Show, are so large that they are extremely limited to their choice of cities. In 2003, approximately 116,687 people attended the Consumer Electronics Show (CES), one of the largest trade shows in the United States. CES used 1.3 million net square feet of exhibit space (Jones 2003) and most of 127,000 sleeping rooms available in the city. Few cities can compete with Las Vegas as far as total amount of exhibit space and sleeping rooms that are concentrated in a relatively small area.

Cost is another consideration. In addition to the costs incurred by the meeting planner for meeting space and other essentials, the cost to the attendee should be considered. Some cities, mostly first-tier cities, are notoriously expensive for people to visit. For example, *Convene* magazine (Hanson 2002, 20) reports that New York is the most expensive at over $400 per day, Boston costs approximately $360 per day, and San Francisco can cost about $297. These figures represent costs associated with the average year-round cost for one night, single room, corporate rate, plus three meals per day, and taxes at a first-class hotel. On the other side of the spectrum, Salem, Oregon, Biloxi, Mississippi, and Lubbock, Texas, can all be enjoyed for about $130 per day for similar first-class lodging and food. It all depends on what is important to your attendees—cost or location. Another option is to hold a meeting in a first-tier city at a first-class property in the off-season or during slow periods, such as around major holidays. Most hotels discount prices when business is slow.

The mode of travel is another factor in site selection. How will the attendees get to the location? Air? Road? Rail? In the post-9/11 business climate, airline carriers have been struggling to survive. Many people are still cautious about flying, and checking in at airports has become such an ordeal that many people prefer to drive to meetings rather than fly. For example, a fifty-minute flight from Las Vegas to Los Angeles can take five hours or more with all the security precautions and delays. You can usually drive that distance in less time. Some cities, such as Baltimore, Maryland, are actively promoting their convention facilities to this drive-in market, especially from the Washington, DC, area.

The type of hotel or meeting facility is another a major consideration. There are a variety of choices, including metropolitan hotels, suburban hotels, airport hotels, resort hotels, and casino hotels. In addition, there are facilities especially designed to hold meetings called "conference centers." The **International Association of Conference Centers** (IACC) is an association in which the member facilities must meet a list of over thirty criteria to be considered an approved conference center. Visit http://www. iaccnorthamerica.org for more information. Other options are full-service convention centers, cruise ships, and university campuses. These facilities are discussed at length in chapter 4, "Meeting and Convention Venues."

Meeting space requirements are also critical in the site selection process. How many meeting or banquet rooms will be needed? How much space will staff offices, registration, and prefunction areas require? Floor plans with room dimensions are readily available in the facilities' sales brochures or on their Web sites. Good diagrams will also provide ceiling heights, seating capacities, entrances and exits, and location of columns and other obstructions. Most major hotel chain Web sites (http://www.hyatt.com, http://www.marriott.com, http://www.hilton.com) will provide direct links to their hotels and their specifications information.

REQUEST FOR PROPOSAL

Once the meeting objectives are clearly defined and the basic location and logistics are drafted, the meeting manager creates an RFP. The RFP is a written description of all the major needs for the meeting. The **CIC**, a federation of over thirty MEEC industry associations, has created a standardized

REQUEST FOR PROPOSAL

Meeting Name: _____

Contact Information:

Prefix: ☐ Mr. ☐ Ms. ☐ Other: _____ **Proposal due date**: _____

Last Name: _____

First Name: _____

Address: _____ City: _____

State/Province: _____ Postal Code: _____

Country: _____

Phone: _____ Fax: _____

Email: _____ Web: _____

Meeting Information:

Sponsor of meeting: ☐ association ☐ corporate ☐ other: _____

Type of meeting:

☐ Board	☐ Committee	☐ Incentive
☐ Education	☐ Convention	☐ Management
☐ Retreat	☐ Trade Show	☐ Other: _____

Decision made by:

☐ Primary Contact	☐ Board	☐ Committee
☐ Chief Staff Officer	☐ Management Company	☐ Other

Meeting Dates (mm/dd/yy) Start: _____ End: _____

Alternate Dates (mm/dd/yy) Start: _____ End: _____

Expected meeting attendance: _____

Largest Meeting Setup

☐ Theatre	☐ Herringbone	☐ Hollow square
☐ School room	☐ Rounds of 8	☐ Board
☐ U-Shape	☐ Rounds of 10	☐ Other: _____

On-site Food/Beverage Functions Required

☐ Breakfast	☐ Dinner	☐ Morning break
☐ Lunch	☐ Reception	☐ Afternoon break

LARGEST meal period

☐ Breakfast	☐ Dinner	Largest Function Attendance: _____
☐ Lunch	☐ Reception	

Preferred Arrival Dates (mm/dd/yy)

   Arrive: _____ Depart: _____

Alternate Arrival Dates (mm/dd/yy)

   Arrive: _____ Depart: _____

Preferred Location/Facilities

☐ Airport	☐ Conference Center	☐ Convention Hotel
☐ Golf Resort	☐ Ocean Resort	☐ Citywide
☐ Downtown	☐ Rounds of 10	☐ Mountain resort
☐ Gaming	☐ Suburban	☐ Other: _____

Rates:

☐ under $100	☐ $126 – 140	☐ $156 – 170	☐ over $200
☐ $101 – 125	☐ $141 – 155	☐ $170 – 200	

Special Requirements: Check items for which you would like additional information sent to you.

☐ Audio-Visual Services	☐ Shopping
☐ Beach	☐ Shuttle/ground transportation
☐ Child care	☐ Special Assistance/Disabilities
☐ Diabetic	☐ Spouse/guest/youth programs
☐ Fitness facilities	☐ Teleconferencing
☐ Golf	☐ Tennis
☐ Hired entertainment or speakers	☐ Theme parties/special events
☐ Kosher food	☐ Tours/sightseeing
☐ Off premise catering/banquet facilities	☐ Vegetarian
☐ Official airline	☐ Water sports
☐ Official car rental company	☐ Other: _____
☐ Official travel agency	

Group History:

Past Start Date(s)	Past End Date(s)	City	State/ Province	Hotel/Facility name	Total # People	Exhibit Facility Type	Total Room Pick Up

(continued)

Exhibit Information:

Type of Show: ☐ Consumer Show (public)   ☐ Trade Show (private)
Exhibit Booth Size _____ 8 × 10   _____ 10 × 10   _____ table top
Gross Exhibit Area (sq. feet) _____

Exhibit Move In:	☐ Sun	☐ Mon	☐ Tues	☐ Wed	☐ Thurs	☐ Fri	☐ Sat
Exhibit Move Out:	☐ Sun	☐ Mon	☐ Tues	☐ Wed	☐ Thurs	☐ Fri	☐ Sat
Show First Day:	☐ Sun	☐ Mon	☐ Tues	☐ Wed	☐ Thurs	☐ Fri	☐ Sat
Show Last Day:	☐ Sun	☐ Mon	☐ Tues	☐ Wed	☐ Thurs	☐ Fri	☐ Sat

Preferred Location *(list all that apply)*:
State: _____   City: _____
Region: _____   Country: _____

format that may be used. It is copyright free and may be downloaded at http://www.conventionindustry.org.

The RFP will contain basic information such as:

- Meeting name
- Meeting start and end dates
- Key contact information
- Expected attendance
- Number and type of sleeping rooms required
- Number and size of meeting and exhibition space required
- Food and beverage requirements
- Acceptable rates for rooms, meeting space, and food and beverage
- Expectations of "comps" or free services
- Cutoff date for the submission of RFPs

Once the RFP is completed, it is disseminated to hotel properties and convention facilities that may be interested in submitting a bid for that meeting. Typically, the meeting planner can submit the RFP via the Internet directly to preferred hotels and the CVBs of desirable cities for distribution to all properties, or can submit it to the IACVB's Web site at http://www.officialtravelinfo.com). Some hotel chains, such as Hyatt, guarantee a response to an RFP within twenty-four hours of receipt. The RFP also serves to allow hotels to examine the potential economic impact of the meeting and decide whether or not to create a bid for it. If the group has limited resources and can only afford an $89 room rate, then major luxury hotels may not be interested in the business. However, smaller properties or hotels in second-tier cities may be very interested in hosting the event. If a meeting facility decides to submit a proposal, then the sales department will review the meeting specifications and create a response.

Fam trips (familiarization) are another method of promoting a destination or particular facility to a meeting planner. Fam trips are a no- or low-cost trip for the planner to personally review sites for their suitability for a meeting. These trips may be arranged by the local **CVB** or by the hotel directly. During the fam trip, the hotel or convention facility tries to impress the planner by showcasing their property, amenities, services, and overall quality. Throughout the visit, the planner should visit all food and beverage outlets, visit recreational areas, see a variety of sleeping rooms, check all meeting space, monitor the efficiency of the front desk and other personnel, note the cleanliness and overall appearance of the facility, and if possible, meet with key hotel personnel. A seasoned meeting planner always has a long list of questions to ask. A lot depends on the selection of hotel. Make a mistake and the whole meeting could be in jeopardy.

The ultimate goal for the facility is to balance what the planner wants and can afford with what revenues need to be generated by the property. There are many factors to be considered. If low room rates are important to the planner, then perhaps a guarantee of providing all food and beverage during the meeting will balance out the reduced room rates. Conversely, if the group does not want to have the facility provide food and beverage, then additional charges for rooms or meeting space rental will be assessed.

Once the planner has reviewed the RFPs, then the negotiations between the planner and the sales department at a facility can begin. This process can be quite complex, and careful records of all communications, concessions, and financial expectations should be well documented.

BUDGETARY CONCERNS

Following the objectives, budgetary issues are usually the next major consideration in planning a meeting. How much will it cost to produce the event? Who will pay? How much will attendees be charged for registration, if anything? What types of food and beverage events are planned, and what will be served? Will meals be provided free or at an additional cost to the attendee? What additional revenue streams are available to produce and promote the meeting? If the event is being held for the first time, the planner will have to do a lot of estimating of expenses and potential revenues. An event that is repeated benefits by having some historical data to compare and project costs. The basis for a meeting budget can be developed by establishing goals, identifying expenses, and identifying revenue sources.

STEP 1: ESTABLISH GOALS

Financial goals are important and should incorporate SMART. They may be set by the meeting planner, association management, or by corporate mandate. Basically, what are the financial expectations of the event? Not every meeting or event is planned for profit. For example, an awards ceremony held by a company to honor top achievers represents a cost to the company. No profit is expected. Similarly, a corporate sales meeting may not have a profit motive. The ultimate goal of the meeting may be to determine how to increase business and thus "profit," but the meeting itself is not a profit generator, it is an expense for the company. Most association meetings, on the other hand, rely heavily on conventions to produce operating revenue for the association. For most associations, the annual meeting (and often accompanying trade show) is the second highest revenue producer after membership dues. The financial goal for an annual meeting may be based on increases or decreases in membership, general economic trends, political climate, competing events, location of the event, and many other influences. In the post-9/11 economy, many associations had to realign their revenue expectations because of decreases in attendee travel budgets and paid association memberships. For any event, there are three possible financial goals:

- Break even: revenue collected from all activities cover the expenses. No profit is expected.
- Make profit: revenues collected exceed expenses
- Deficit: expenses exceed revenues

STEP 2: IDENTIFY EXPENSES

The CIC manual (2000) suggests categorizing expenses by their different functions:

- **Indirect costs** are listed as overhead or administrative line items in a program budget. These are organizational expenses not directly related to the meeting, such as staff salaries, overhead, or equipment repair.

McLaurin and Wykes (1997) list a number of possible expense items. Can you determine which are direct, indirect, or variable costs?

- Administrative overhead
- Registration materials
- Speaker travel, expenses, honoraria
- Signs, posters, and banners
- Gratuities and gifts
- Printing and photocopying
- Room rental
- Decorations and flowers
- Car rental
- Shipping and freight charges
- Complimentary registrations
- Translators and interpreters
- Temporary staff
- Web site design and administration
- Child care

- Food and beverage functions
- Promotion
- Multimedia equipment
- Staff travel and expenses
- Taxes
- Office furniture and equipment
- Insurance
- Supplies
- Labor charges
- Session taping
- Shuttle service
- ADA compliance
- Telecommunications
- Security guards
- Postage and overnight delivery costs

- **Fixed costs** are those expenses incurred regardless of the number of attendees, such as meeting room rental or audiovisual equipment. You could even set a specific dollar amount for profit as a fixed cost.
- **Variable costs** are those expenses that can vary based on the number of attendees (e.g., food and beverage). (CIC, 29)

Expenses will vary according to the overall objectives of the meeting and will be impacted by location, season, type of facility, services selected, and other factors. For example, a gallon of Starbucks coffee in San Francisco at a luxury hotel may cost you $80 or more. A gallon of coffee at a moderate-priced hotel in Oklahoma City may only cost $25 or less.

STEP 3: IDENTIFY REVENUE SOURCES

There are many ways to fund meetings and events. Corporations include meeting costs in their operating budgets. The corporate planner must work within the constraints of what is budgeted. Associations usually have to be a bit more creative in finding capital to plan and implement an event.

Associations have to justify the cost of the meeting with the expected ROI of the attendee. It can be quite expensive to attend some association meetings. Consider a hypothetical example of one person attending an association annual meeting: transportation ($300), accommodations for three nights ($450), food and beverage ($200), registration fee ($500), and miscellaneous ($100), for a total of $1550. Depending on the city and association, this amount could easily double. It is a complex process to create an exceptional and affordable event. If the registration fee is too high, people will not attend. If it is too low, the organization may not achieve revenue expectations. But there are more possible sources of funding available other than registration fees. These include the following:

- Corporate or association funding
- Private funding from individuals
- Registration fees
- Exhibitor fees (if trade show)
- Sponsorships
- Selling logo merchandise
- Advertising fees, such as banners or ads in the convention program
- Local, state, or national government assistance
- Selling banner ads or links on the official Web site
- Renting membership address lists for marketing purposes
- Establishing "official partnerships" with other companies to promote their products for a fee or percentage of their revenues
- Contributions in cash or in-kind (services or products)

Estimating expenses and revenues can be accomplished by first calculating a break-even analysis (see box on p. 50)—in other words, how much revenue must be collected to cover expenses.

COST CONTROL

To stay within budget and reach the financial objectives, it is important to exercise cost control measures. Cost control measures are tools for monitoring the budget. A large event for thousands of people may be managed by only a few meeting planning staff. The opportunities for costly mistakes are rampant. The most important factor is to make sure the facility understands which person from the sponsoring organization has the authority to

Break-Even Analysis

The CIC manual (2000, 30) calculates the number of attendees (break-even units) needed to achieve the **break-even point** by subtracting variable costs from the registration fee to get the contribution margin. Then, total fixed costs are divided by the contribution margin.

$$\text{Break-even Units (Attendees)} = \frac{\text{Total Fixed Costs}}{\text{Contribution Margin (Registration fee} - \text{Variable costs)}}$$

For example: The registration fee is $200. Fixed costs are $5,000 room rental, $2,000 audiovisual, and $1,000 speaker fee. Variable costs are $15 per person for refreshment breaks. To calculate the number of attendees needed to break even:

$$\text{Break-even units} = \frac{\$8000}{(\$200 - \$15)} = 44 \text{ attendees to break even}$$

Another formula can be used to determine registration fees needed to break even. Using the same figures from above, combine the total fixed costs and total variable costs (variable cost per person $\times$ number of attendees), and divide that sum by the number of attendees to determine the registration fee required to break even. *Note:* If you need to make a certain amount of profit, factor that into the fixed cost and do the calculations:

$$\text{Registration fee} = \frac{\$8000 + (\$15 \times 44)}{44} = \$196.82 \text{ fee to break even}$$

If a $1,000 profit is required, then the calculation would be

$$\frac{\$9000 + (\$15 \times 44)}{44} = \$219.55 \text{ fee to make } \$1000 \text{ profit}$$

make additions or changes to what has been ordered. Typically, the CEO and the meeting planning staff are the only ones who have this "signing authority." For example, a board member may have an expensive dinner in the hotel restaurant and say "put it on the association's bill." The restaurant cannot do so without the approval of a person who has **signing authority**. This helps keep unexpected expenses to a minimum.

Another cost control measure is to accurately estimate the number of meals that will be served. The **guarantee** is the amount of food that the planner has instructed the facility to prepare and will be paid for. If the planner estimates 500 people will attend a dinner and only 300 show up, the planner is responsible for the 200 uneaten dinners—an expensive waste of money. This is covered in depth in chapter 7, "Food and Beverage."

Outsourcing part or the entire meeting planning process can also keep costs down. Many companies prefer to hire independent meeting planners to organize and implement their events rather than keep a meeting planner on staff. The company does not have to provide salaries and benefits and can hire planners as needed. In addition, there are many ancillary activities that go into the planning and managing of a meeting that can be outsourced to other professionals, such as housing, registration, transportation, exhibits, marketing, educational programming, child care, and technology. By hiring companies that specialize in particular activities, the planner is better able to remain focused on managing the entire process.

ORGANIZING AND DIRECTING

REGISTRATION

To attend most conventions or trade shows, some type of registration is typically required. Registration is the process of gathering all pertinent information and fees necessary for an individual to attend the meeting. It is much more than merely collecting money. Registration data is a valuable asset to any association or organization that is sponsoring an event. Registration begins several weeks prior to the event and usually lasts right up to the final day. Discounts are often provided to attendees who register in advance. They are offered an **early bird special** incentive to send their money in, for example, six weeks early. The association can then use that money to pay deposits or bills coming due. By registering early, the planner can determine if registration numbers are at anticipated levels. If not, they can increase marketing or negotiate with the hotel or meeting facilities about lowering expectations and financial commitments that may have been promised.

Data collected on the registration form may include name, title, occupation, address, e-mail, phone, fax, membership category, desired workshop sessions, social functions, optional events, method of payment, and a liability waiver. A recent addition has been to ask attendees where they are staying

REGISTRATION FORM

NAME OF ASSOCIATION

DATES OF MEETING   CITY, STATE

Name: _____ _____

Address: _____

City: _____ State: _____ Zip: _____

Name as it should appear on badge: _____

Title: _____ Company: _____

Spouse or companion name: _____

Please check the appropriate box (see brochure for rates)

      Accommodations

          Single   _____nights @ $_____ per night

          Double   _____nights @ $_____ per night

          Triple   _____nights @ $_____ per night

          Suite   _____nights @ $_____ per night

                                                            Subtotal $_____

Registration (see brochure for fees)

     _____ Members   @ $_____

     _____ Nonmembers   @ $_____

     _____ Students   @ $_____

                                                              Subtotal $_____

Special Events (see brochure for fees)

          _____ Tickets for opening reception   @ $_____

          _____ Tickets for dine around   @ $_____

          _____ Tickets for closing banquet   @ $_____

          _____ Tickets for golf tournament   @ $_____

          _____ Tickets for preconference tour   @ $_____

          _____ Tickets for postconference tour   @ $_____

          _____ Tickets for children's program   @ $_____

                                                              Subtotal $_____

                                                            TOTAL $_____

Please indicate any special needs:

      Accommodations _____

      Food and Beverage _____

and length of stay so that the impact of the meeting can be determined. Some organizations inquire about the size of the company, number of employees, or financial responsibility of the attendee (does he or she make or recommend purchase decisions). This registration data can be used before, during, and after the meeting.

Prior to the meeting, the data can be given or sold to exhibitors or advertisers so they can promote their company, products, and services before the actual meeting. It may also be used to market to potential attendees who have not committed to attend. Advertising "we have 7,500 qualified buyers attending this year's convention" may entice more companies to register or exhibit. Preregistration data can also help the planner monitor interest in special events or particular workshops that may be popular. If a particular workshop is getting a lot of interest, then the planner can move it to a larger room or increase seating.

During the meeting, registration data can be used as a promotional tool with the press to gain media attention for the organization, sponsors, and exhibitors. It can also help the local CVB in justifying the costs of marketing and soliciting groups to come to their city. Hard facts, such as using 3,000 rooms and 200,000 square feet of meeting space, are music to the ears of hospitality companies. For the attendees, technology now allows us to automatically access, via computer, who is at a particular meeting and beam the entire attendee list onto a PDA for future reference.

After the meeting, registration data can be used to update association membership records, solicit new members, or sell to interested parties. Most important, it can be used to help the planner with logistics and to promote the next meeting. By examining registration data over time, it gives the organization a better view of who is attending its meeting and if there are any trends apparent, such as changes in gender, age, education, or title of attendees.

Registration Fees

There may be several different pricing structures for a single meeting. For association meetings, members typically receive a discount on the cost of registration. This helps encourage people to become members of the association. But not all members will pay the same price. For example, in 2003 PCMA charged professional members (meeting planners) $575, suppliers (hotel sales people, CVBs) $675, university faculty ($375), and student members ($175). These are the early bird preregistration prices available until about six weeks prior to the convention. After the **cutoff date**, all prices increase by $100. All attendees, regardless of how much they pay, receive the same opportunities for education and networking, and are invited to the scheduled meals, breaks, and receptions. However, additional activities, such as golf, tours, or special entertainment functions, may incur a separate cost.

For some events like the Exhibitor Show, an annual trade show for people in the exhibition industry, registration fees are priced based on what the attendee wants to attend. Entrance to the trade show is free, but education sessions may cost up to $150 per workshop. Additional events, such as dinners and receptions, may be purchased separately. All-inclusive registrations are also an option with full registration and attendance to all education programs costing well over $1,000.

Associations usually offer substantial registration discounts to their members. The "nonmember" rate to attend may well exceed the difference between the cost of membership and the member rate, making it desirable to join the association. This is a clever way for associations to increase their membership base and provides an opportunity to promote other products and services to the new members. Registration fees are often waived for VIPs, members of the press, speakers, and local dignitaries. Complimentary registrations must be monitored closely because there may be costs involved if the meeting has food and beverage or if other events are available.

Preregistration

Preregistration is the process of registering attendees weeks or months in advance of an event. This benefits the planner in several ways. It provides information about who will be attending a meeting or event. It can help the meeting planner determine room capacities for educational sessions and can help the session speaker to estimate the number of people who may attend a session. Typically, advanced payment is also required to pre-register. By receiving payment weeks or months ahead of the event, the planner can use that money to pay bills or make necessary deposits for services. The early bird discount is a major incentive to preregister. Logistically, as people are arriving for the event, preregistration can reduce congestion in the registration area as well as reduce long lines and waiting time. A quick check-in to collect a name badge and other meeting materials and to confirm the person's arrival is all that is necessary.

Whether it is paper-based or electronic, the prospective attendee must complete a registration form. The more simple and easy to complete the better. A one-sided registration form is easier to fax than a form with printing on both sides. Common information to include on a preregistration form is as follows:

- Name, date, and location of meeting
- Name and title of person
- Company name and address
- Phone, fax, e-mail address
- Fee category (member, nonmember, student) and cost
- Additional guest registration
- Early bird deadline
- Policies regarding payment method (check, money order, credit card, electronic payment) and currency accepted
- Cancellation and refund policies
- Housing information
- Official airline information
- Request for ADA accommodations
- Request for dietary restrictions accommodations
- Reservations for particular sessions
- Participation in ancillary activities requiring additional fees

On-Site Registration

Like the front desk of a hotel, the registration area is the first experience an attendee has with a meeting, convention, or trade show. A slow or inefficient registration process can set the tone for the entire meeting. The registration area should be heavily staffed the first day and should remain open throughout the event. If international guests are expected, registration materials may need to be translated, and interpreters may be necessary to facilitate a smooth check-in. For particularly large groups, the check-in process can be expedited by mailing each attendee a name badge (without the plastic holder), identification card, and other material with a confirmation letter prior to the event. The attendee has only to go to a registration counter, show identification and registration confirmation, then the registration attendant will give the attendee a badge holder, conference program, and any other materials. If a trade show is involved, having a separate area for exhibitor registration is a good idea.

Registration is one of the areas often outsourced by the meeting planner, especially for large events. It is a complex process that requires much training on the part of the registration attendants. Some hotels or convention

Registration desk at the G2E convention.
Photo by George G. Fenich, Ph.D., Professor, School of HRTA, University of New Orleans

centers have arrangements with temporary agencies that provide staff who do registration on a regular basis. Some registration management companies handle housing as well.

HOUSING

Not all meetings require housing arrangements. But if housing is needed, there are basically four methods of handling housing for attendees:

1. Attendees arrange for their own room. Lists of hotels may be provided, but the meeting sponsor makes no prior arrangements regarding price negotiations or availability.
2. A group rate is negotiated by the planner at one or more properties, and attendees respond directly to the reservations department of their choice.

3. The meeting sponsor handles all housing, and attendees book rooms through them. Then the sponsor provides the hotel with a rooming list of confirmed guests.

4. A third-party **housing bureau** (outsourced company) handles all arrangements either for a fee or paid by the CVB.

Having attendees make their own hotel reservations is the easiest method. It totally removes that responsibility from the planner. But remember, the facility is going to base its pricing to host the event on the total revenues it anticipates from the group. Sleeping rooms represent the largest amount of potential revenue for the hotel. If you do not block rooms, you will most assuredly pay a premium for renting meeting space and other services. The room block is a key negotiation tool for the planner.

The last three options require that the meeting planner establish a rate for the attendees. The room rate will reflect prior negotiations with the sales department in which the total value of the meeting to the facility is considered. A certain number of rooms will be reserved, called a "block," and rooms are subtracted from this inventory as attendees request them. This can be a gamble for the meeting planner. As with food and beverage events, the planner must estimate how many people will be attending. If the planner blocks 100 rooms and only 75 attendees show up, he or she may be held responsible for part, or all, of the cost of those rooms. The difference between rooms blocked and rooms "picked up" (actually used) is called **attrition**. This is discussed in more detail in chapter 12, on legal issues. A serious challenge to planners these days is attendees booking rooms outside the block. That is, they bypass the hotels for which the planner negotiated special pricing and find other accommodations. If the host hotel charges $199 per day and a smaller, less luxurious hotel down the street is charging $99, a certain percentage of the attendees will opt for the lower price. Sometimes, by calling the hotel directly or by using a discount hotel broker on the Internet, attendees can get better prices in the same hotel for less than what the planner negotiated. If large numbers of attendees do this, then the meeting planner is going to get stuck paying for a lot of unused rooms. One method of reducing this potentially expensive problem is to establish review dates in the hotel contract, whereby the planner can reduce (or increase) the **room block** by a certain percentage at a certain time. The closer to the actual meeting dates, the less likely the hotel will allow a reduction in room block. The hotel must have time to try and sell any unused rooms and recoup any losses.

A hotel room is a perishable commodity if it is not sold each day; the potential revenue is lost forever.

Having attendees call or reserve rooms online directly with the hotel is a good option. The attendees should benefit by the negotiated room rate, and the hotel handles the reservation processing directly. The meeting planner will need minimal involvement. For larger meetings where multiple properties are used, it is advisable to provide a range of hotel prices to accommodate the budgets of all the attendees.

Handling attendee reservations in-house is possible but is easiest with small groups. If the event is a small, high-profile event, the planner can have attendees reserve rooms with the organization, and a **rooming list** will be created to give to the hotel. The rooming list should include type of room, ADA requests, smoking or nonsmoking, arrival and departure dates, names of additional guests in the room, and special requests. Handling reservations in-house can be quite time-consuming and may require additional staffing. Alternatively, a housing bureau can be of great assistance.

Outsourcing the housing process to a third-party vendor or CVB is most prevalent with medium and large meetings. Some groups, such as the aforementioned National Association of Broadcasters or Consumer Electronics show, are so large they require most of the hotel rooms in the host city. Housing for a so-called **citywide** meeting is best left to professionals who have the most current technology and are well equipped to handle thousands of housing requests. Making reservations through a housing service can be done by mail, phone, fax, and Internet. The housing bureau may charge a fee per transaction. This cost may be paid by the sponsoring organization, or in some cases the local CVB will absorb some or all of the cost. Indeed, many CVBs and even hotels operate their own housing bureaus as a service to meeting planners.

Hotel Room Types

Hotels generally have several types of rooms to choose from, including

- *Single:* one person, one bed
- *Double:* two people, one bed
- *Double-double:* two people, two beds
- *Triple:* three people, two beds
- *Quad:* four people, two beds
- *Parlor suite:* sleeping space separate from living space

Registration and Housing Companies

Several companies have developed over the last few years that specialize in handling both conference registration and housing. Visit their Web sites at the following addresses:

http://Allmeetings.com	http://b-there.com
http://EventSource.com	http://MPBID.com
http://Passkey.com	http://PlanSoft.com
http://RegWEB.com	http://StarCite.com

MEETING & EVENT SPECIFICATION GUIDE

One of the challenges in the meeting and events profession is that there are few standardized policies, procedures, and terminology. To begin a codification of definitions and standardized practices, an industrywide task force called the **APEX Initiative** was created. As mentioned in chapter 1, *APEX* stands for Accepted Practices Exchange, and one of the first accomplishments was the development of accepted practices regarding terminology. Another APEX initiative was the standardization of resumes and work orders, which are the primary record of communication and logistics between the meeting planner and the facility. The APEX Resumes & Work Orders Panel was established in January 2002 to review common practices and to develop standards. The committee found that many terms were used interchangeably to describe the document used by a planner to communicate specific requirements for a function. Some of these terms included *catering event order, meeting resume, event specifications guide, staging guide operations manual, production schedule, room specs, schedule of services, working agenda, specifications sheet,* and *group resume* (Green and Withiam 2002). After a considerable amount of effort and input from all types of meeting planners, hotel convention service managers, destination management companies, exhibit managers, and CVBs, the panel created a format that, if adopted, will greatly facilitate the communication between planners and the entities that service their meetings.

The panel proposed that the term ***Meeting & Event Specification Guide***, or MESG, be adopted industrywide to describe this document. The MESG is a three-part document that includes the following:

1. *The Narrative:* general overview of the meeting or event
2. *Schedule of Events:* timetable outlining all functions that compose the overall meeting or event

3. *Meeting Event Orders (MEO):* specifications for each function that is part of the overall meeting or event (each "subevent" will have its own MEO)

Examples of an MESG and MEO are available for download in PDF format at http.//www.conventionindustry.org.

Part One: The narrative portion of the MESG should include the following:

- Date published
- Date revised
- Meeting name
- Group name
- Dates and times
  - Start date and time
  - End date and time
- Pre-con date and time (include attendee names)
- Post-con date and time (include attendee names)
- Key event contacts
- History of group
  - Meeting objectives, mission statement, recap of recent meetings, Web site of association
- Attendance
  - Anticipated number of attendees, demographics, ADA needs, VIP special accommodations)
- Arrival and departure pattern
  - Major arrival/departure, drive-in and fly instructions
- Space
  - Room block(s): For a citywide area, name all hotels and specify the headquarters hotel
  - Reservation method
  - Meeting rooms
  - Off-site venues
  - Registration area and staff offices
  - Reader board information (kiosk with diagrams and specific rooms used by the planner)
- Exhibits (if applicable)
  - Exhibitor profile
  - Location of exhibits
  - Exhibitor registration area
  - Number of exhibits

- ◦ Gross and net square feet of exhibit space required
- ◦ Regulations
- ◦ Schedule
- ◦ Move in and move out dates and times
- Security
  - ◦ Emergency instructions
  - ◦ Keys
  - ◦ On-site communication
- Food and beverage
  - ◦ Special requirements
  - ◦ On site and off site
  - ◦ Outlet usage
  - ◦ Concessions
  - ◦ Table of F&B functions by day
- Special activities (recreation, guest programs, tours, etc.)
- Audiovisual requirements
- Transportation needs
- Shipping and receiving (dock and freight elevator usage)
- Housekeeping instructions
- Billing instructions
- Authorized signatories

The panel also recommended a standardized timetable for communication between the planner and the facility and service providers. Recognizing that these guidelines may differ depending on the size, timing, and complexity of the individual event, they do provide a useful general format.

SIZE OF EVENT	SUBMIT MESG IN ADVANCE	RECEIVE RETURN FROM FACILITY AND VENDORS
1–500	4 weeks	2 weeks
501–1000	6 weeks	4 weeks
1000+	8 weeks	6 weeks

Part Two: The **schedule of events** should include the meeting name, group name, date published, and date revised. The rest of the information is a detailed description of exactly what is going on and when. It should include in table format each function by date and time, function name, location, and function number. For example:

| Feb. 2, 2008 | Breakfast | Ballroom A | No. 124 |

Part Three: The MEO is used by the facility to inform setup crews, technicians, catering and banquet staff, and all other facility staff of what is required for each event. Each separate function will have its own MEO. Like the MESG, prior to the APEX Initiative the MEO was called a variety of names, such as function sheet, room specs, and event order.

The MEO should contain the following:

- Meeting, group name, and function number
- Date published and revised
- Function name, location, and expected attendance
- Function date, start time, end time, setup time, tear-down time
- Post to reader board
- Room setup
  - Table and chair configurations (theater, conference, U-shape classroom, etc.)
  - Lectern and riser needs
  - Other needs, such as water and glasses, pads and pens, candy dishes, and easels
- Audiovisual Needs
  - In-house or outside vendor
  - Equipment list (flip charts, projectors, video, microphones, screens, computers, etc.)
- Food and beverage
- Time, description, guarantee, anticipated attendance, service time, price, set for
- Décor
- Decorator company, instructions, requests
- Security
- Security company, instructions, requests
- ADA needs
- Entertainment or speakers
- Entertainment or speakers company, instructions, requests
- Signage
- Signage company, instructions, requests

- Transportation
- Transportation company, instructions, requests
- Shipping and receiving
- Instructions and requests
- Utilities
  - Electrical, water, compressed air, natural gas
- Additional requests
- Key event personnel
- Authorized signatories
- Billing instructions

As you can see, the MESG contains quite a lot of detailed information. Both the meeting planner and catering and convention service staff will need access to a copy. If any changes are made, they should be recorded in all copies. Fortunately, as software is created and disseminated into the industry, this document will be easier to maintain and update. Some planners and convention service managers now download this information onto their **PDA**, so a five-pound, three-ring binder is reduced to a few portable ounces. Changes to the MESG can be made easily and beamed to the appropriate people.

PRE- AND POST-CON MEETINGS

What is certain for all meetings is that changes to the MESG are unavoidable. In fact, one of the chief responsibilities of a good meeting planner is to react and manage change—often unexpected change.

PRECONVENTION MEETINGS

A day or two prior to the actual beginning of a meeting, the planner should partake in a **preconvention** (pre-con) meeting. This is a gathering of all critical people representing all departments within the facility who will impact the group. In addition to the CSM, who is the primary contact for the planner, the following representatives may be requested to attend the meeting: catering or banquet manager or food and beverage director, audio-visual representative, sales manager, accounting manager, front desk manager, bell staff or concierge, housekeeping manager, security manager, engineering manager, switchboard manager, recreation manager, and all outside service providers, such as transportation, special events, and decorators. Often the general manager of the facility will stop by, be introduced, and welcome the planner. The pre-con meeting allows the planner to meet and visually connect with all the various people servicing the event. In most cases, this will be the first time the planner meets many of these people. Each representative is introduced, and any changes or additions of duties in their respective departments are reviewed. After the individual departments have been discussed, the planner should release the person to return to his or her duties. The MESG is reviewed page by page with the CSM. All changes are made, guarantees are confirmed, and last minute instructions are conveyed. The pre-con is basically the last time the planner has the opportunity to make any major changes without disrupting the facility. Once an event is in progress, it is very difficult and potentially costly to make major changes. If the planner decides one hour before a session that the room should be set with only chairs rather than with tables and chairs as listed on the MEO, it can cause havoc. Additional staff may be needed to remove the tables, and the planner

A preconvention meeting often includes the meeting planner, CSM, and catering manager.

Source: Dorling Kindersley Media Library

may be charged for the labor. Sometimes the last-minute request of a planner cannot be fulfilled. If fifty tables, are requested just prior to an event, the hotel may not have them available or may not have scheduled staff for set up.

POSTCONVENTION REVIEW

At the conclusion of a major meeting, the meeting planner will create a written document to record all key events of the meeting. This is used for planning the next meeting. It also serves as a "report card" for the facility and the meeting manager. It will include what went right as well as what went wrong. Then, a postconvention (post-con) meeting is held. It is smaller than the pre-con and may include the planning staff, the CSM, the food and beverage director, the audiovisual manager, and a representative from the accounting department. This is the time to address any discrepancies in billing, service failures, and problems or to praise facility staff for a job well done. Most major meetings will have a post-con; smaller meetings may not. In some cases, the planner is just too mentally and physically exhausted to conduct a post-con meeting immediately following the event. A good night's rest and peace and quiet may be needed first.

CONTROL IN MEEC

Creating and implementing most meetings is a team effort. Many meeting planners will conduct an evaluation after each meeting to obtain feedback from the attendees, exhibitors, facility staff, outsourced contractors, and anyone else involved in the event. Individual sessions may be evaluated to determine if speakers did a good job and if the education was appropriate. Overall, evaluations may collect data on such things as the comfort of the hotel, ease of transportation to the location, desirability of location, quality of food and beverage, special events and networking opportunities, and number and quality of exhibitors at a trade show convention. This information may be collected by a written questionnaire after the event as well as by telephone, fax, or Web-based collection methods. One of the fastest and least expensive is to broadcast an e-mail with a link to the questionnaire. Many software packages are available that will design, distribute, collect data, and tabulate results for you. No special knowledge of statistics is required. Programs range from no cost (http://www.Freeonlinesurveys. com) to several hundred dollars (http://www.surveypro.com). The data concerning speakers and logistics will assist the meeting planner and program planning committee to improve the programming for subsequent years (see chapter 10, on program planning).

Like setting good objectives, the meeting planner must first determine what is to be evaluated. What information is needed, who will utilize it, and how will the results be communicated to those who participate in the evaluation? Evaluations can be time-consuming and expensive to design and implement. It may cost thousands of dollars to print, disseminate, collect, and analyze evaluations. Unfortunately, some of the data collected by planners is often filed away and not used appropriately—especially if the results are negative toward the event. No board of directors or CEO wants to hear that the site they selected to hold a meeting did not meet attendees' expectations. However, negative comments may ultimately turn into a favorable marketing tool. If the attendees indicate they did not like the location of the meeting (Chicago in February), then by selecting a warmer climate (Palm Springs) for the next meeting, the planner can promote how much the attendees' opinions matter and that the organization will follow the directives of the attendees.

DESIGNING THE EVALUATION

A good evaluation form is simple, is concise, and can be completed in a minimal amount of time. An evaluation for a meeting can be a single sentence: "Was this meeting a good use of your time?" Response options can be "Yes" or "No." This would be good for short departmental meetings or training sessions. For larger events with multiple sessions and activities, a more in-depth evaluation is called for. A good source for questions can be to review your event goals and objectives. If the meeting is an annual event, it is important to ask similar questions each year so that data may be collected and analyzed over time. Self-administered surveys are the most common evaluation tool. The evaluation instrument should collect both **qualitative** and **quantitative data**. Qualitative or "hard" data is represented numerically so that data can be compared by assigning ranks or scores and calculating averages and frequencies of responses. Quantitative data can be statistically manipulated using advanced mathematical formulas and designs. However, most planners like to keep things simple. Averages and frequencies of response are the most common outcomes of interest. If, on a scale from 1 to 10, the attendees rated the hotel an average of 9.5, then the planner can demonstrate that the hotel selection was appropriate. On the other hand, if the attendees rated the quality of the food at the opening reception as a 3, then the planner needs to address what went wrong and why.

Asking open-ended questions represents qualitative data or "soft" data. It is a descriptive record of what is observed and is written in the attendee's own words. An example is asking "What did you enjoy most about the conference?," and leaving adequate space for the person to write his or her response. Qualitative data can be time-consuming to analyze and report, so this type of question should be kept to a minimum. Too many open-ended questions can result in pages of unrelated responses that will quickly be scanned and probably ignored by management. Whereas quantitative data provides hard numbers that can be statistically manipulated, qualitative data provides the "why." Quantitatively, the attendees rated the hotel a 9.5 on a 10-point scale. But what exactly did they like? The qualitative question can provide the details: "What did you like most about the hotel?"

To allow for speedy completion of evaluation forms, many planners use checklists such as the one shown below.

"What activities did you attend?"
❑ Opening reception   ❑ Breakfast   ❑ Lunch   ❑ Dinner

Another simple option is to word questions so that a minimal amount of responses are offered such as:

"Did you utilize the e-mail stations provided in the registration area?"
❑ Yes   ❑ No

Alternately, the attendee can select from a list of predetermined responses to communicate his or her opinion:

"How would you rate the opening session speaker?"
❑ Excellent   ❑ Good   ❑ Fair   ❑ Poor

Using a ranking scale is also popular:

"Please rank the following items 1–5 in their importance to you in registering for this conference, with 1 being the most important and 5 being the least important.

      Registration fee   Quality of program

      Hotel expense   Recreational activities

      Cost of transportation

Designing a questionnaire from scratch can be daunting. Building on what others have developed is a good start. The CIC (278) has the following suggestions when designing and implementing a survey:

- Keep it simple and easy to complete—one page if possible.
- Ask specific questions addressing only one concept per question.
- Avoid using professional jargon, abbreviations, and acronyms.
- Start the evaluation with easy questions. Save difficult or more personal questions for the end of the survey. People are more likely to complete a survey once they have invested time in filling it out.
- Ask personal or proprietary questions in ranges: "What is your age? 18 to 25, 26 to 35, 36 to 45, over 45." "How much does your company spend on training each year? Less than $1,000, $1,000 to $5,000, $5,000 to $10,000, over $10,000."
- Keep evaluations anonymous. People are much more honest if they cannot be linked to their responses. Providing a name should be optional.
- Include contact information on the form so it can be mailed or faxed if not collected on site.
- Number all questions to make coding easier and to avoid mistakes.
- Forms should be readable and visually simple. Fonts, graphics, and colors should be kept simple.
- If evaluating a session with multiple speakers, be sure to identify the speakers by name on the evaluation form.
- If possible, have an attendant stationed in each session room or in the hall between meeting rooms to collect evaluation forms. Alternately, have clearly marked evaluation collection boxes available.

Timing is also an issue with administering evaluations. If you collect data on site immediately after an event, you may increase your response rate. You can remind attendees to complete and return evaluations before moving on to the next session. Other planners prefer to wait a few days to ask for feedback. This gives the attendee time to digest what actually occurred at the meeting and form an objective opinion when not clouded by the excitement of the event. In fact, evaluation scores tend to decrease when attendees are surveyed a few weeks after an event, especially concerning speaker evaluations. A particularly humorous speaker may entertain the attendees and receive high marks when evaluated just after a session. In retrospect, if evaluated a week later, attendees may feel that the speaker was entertaining but did not actually teach them anything of value and may rate the speaker less positively.

Session Evaluation Feedback Form

IAEM ANNUAL MEETING
SESSION EVALUATION
FEEDBACK FORM
Win Free Registration

International Association for Exposition Management

MARKING INSTRUCTIONS
Use a pen or pencil, but do NOT use red.
RIGHT MARK: ●   WRONG MARKS: ⊗ ✓ ⊗

All completed evaluations will be entered into a drawing for a *free* registration to the June 1999 Mid-Year Meeting in Chicago, IL.

Session Title: _____

Session Number: _____

MUST
ENTER 4 DIGIT BADGE No.: | | | |

SESSION EVALUATION

Overall Content
- ○ Excellent
- ○ Very Good
- ○ Good
- ○ Fair
- ○ Poor

New/Useful Information
- ○ Excellent
- ○ Very Good
- ○ Good
- ○ Fair
- ○ Poor

Accuracy of Session Description
- ○ Excellent
- ○ Very Good
- ○ Good
- ○ Fair
- ○ Poor

This session was:
- ○ Too Long
- ○ Too Short
- ○ About Right

Speaker avoided selling his/her products/services:
- ○ Yes
- ○ No

Would you recommend this session to others?
- ○ Yes
- ○ No

EVENT EVALUATION

Please rate your satisfaction with the overall event thus far.
- ○ Excellent
- ○ Very Good
- ○ Good
- ○ Fair
- ○ Poor

YOUR BUSINESS POSITION

- ○ Association Show Organizer
- ○ Consumer Show Organizer
- ○ Independent Show Organizer
- ○ Corporate Planner
- ○ Supplier
- ○ Other _____

SPEAKER EVALUATION

Please write in the speaker name(s).

	EXCELLENT	VERY GOOD	GOOD	FAIR	POOR
Speaker A					
Presentation Skills	○	○	○	○	○
Knowledge of Topic	○	○	○	○	○
Speaker B					
Presentation Skills	○	○	○	○	○
Knowledge of Topic	○	○	○	○	○
Speaker C					
Presentation Skills	○	○	○	○	○
Knowledge of Topic	○	○	○	○	○
Speaker D					
Presentation Skills	○	○	○	○	○
Knowledge of Topic	○	○	○	○	○
Speaker E					
Presentation Skills	○	○	○	○	○
Knowledge of Topic	○	○	○	○	○
Speaker F					
Presentation Skills	○	○	○	○	○
Knowledge of Topic	○	○	○	○	○
Speaker G					
Presentation Skills	○	○	○	○	○
Knowledge of Topic	○	○	○	○	○

Additional Comments about the . . .

Speaker(s): _____
_____
_____

Session: _____
_____
_____

DC:98120   EVALUATION SERVICES BY DATA CAPTURE SOLUTIONS, INC., NEWBURYPORT, MA 01950   1-800-254-2925

The process of evaluating a meeting should begin in the early stages of meeting planning and tie-in with the meeting objectives. Costs for development, printing, postage, analysis, and reporting should be included in the meeting budget. The evaluation serves as a valuable component of a meeting's history by recording what worked or did not work for a particular event. It is a cyclical process whereby the evaluation results feed directly into next year's meeting objectives. Committees plan most large meetings. Evaluation results are the means by which information is passed from one committee to the next.

◆ SUMMARY

Association and corporate meeting planners have similar job responsibilities. It takes much organization and teamwork to produce good meetings. Setting clear meeting objectives is the first step in the planning process. The planner must begin with a clear understanding of the purpose and expectations of the meeting. The objectives will impact site or city selection, type of facility used, and the services required. Once the objectives are clear, a needs analysis should be conducted to further guide the planner in selecting appropriate meeting space, speakers, and amenities that are expected from the attendees. The demographics of attendees must also be considered. Meetings and conventions represent enormous economic potential for cities. In the site selection process, the RFP is the announcement of what is required by the planner. CVBs and individual hotels must evaluate the potential of the meeting and respond accordingly. Interested properties may invite the planner for a fam trip to visit the property.

Prior to the meeting, the planner relies heavily on outsourced companies to help with meeting arrangements, such as registration and housing. The delicate balance between cost to attend the meeting and ROI received is critical to the planner. If expenses are too high, people may not attend. If registration fees are too low, the planner will not maximize revenues. Additional cost controls must be used to ensure that the planner retains complete control of the meeting expenses.

The CSM who handles the logistics at the meeting facility will guide the meeting itself. The MESG is the guidebook to ensure that the directives of the meeting planner are carried out with the utmost efficiency and accuracy. The pre- and post-con meetings provide both direction and feedback to the planner and the facility. Evaluations of individual sessions, the overall conference, exhibitors, and other key items should be conducted to provide information for subsequent events. Creating a user-friendly format will ensure a good response.

KEY WORDS AND TERMS

For definitions, refer to http://glossary.conventionindustry.org.

APEX initiative

Attrition

Break-even point

CIC

Citywide

Convention service manager

Cutoff date

CVB

Early bird discount

Fam trip

First-tier city

Fixed costs

Guarantee

History

Housing bureau

Indirect costs

International Association of Conference Centers

Meeting and Event Specification Guide

Meeting event order

Needs analysis

Outsourcing

PDA

Preconvention meeting

Postconvention meeting

Qualitative data

Quantitative data

Return on Investment

Room block

Rooming list

Schedule of events

Second-tier city

Signing authority

Site selection

SMART

Variable costs

REVIEW AND DISCUSSION QUESTIONS

1. What are the key differences in planning an association annual meeting and planning a corporate event?

2. What are some considerations that should be addressed in the site selection process?

3. Write a meeting objective for an association annual meeting and a corporate meeting.

4. What are some ethical considerations of taking "fam" trips?

5. How does a meeting planner find information about a city, hotel, meeting facility, or service provider?

6. Why might a meeting planner select a "second-tier" city in which to hold a meeting?

7. How does a meeting planner use attendee demographics in designing and implementing an event?

8. Identify and discuss four sources of revenue for a convention.

9. Calculate the number of attendees needed to break even given the following: registration fee $100, fixed costs $2500, variable costs $20.

10. Calculate the registration fee needed to break even given the following: fixed costs $2500, variable costs $20, 32 attendees.

11. How do planners control meeting costs?

12. What are the benefits and limitations of outsourcing components of a meeting, such as housing or registration?

13. How can planners use registration data before, during, and after a convention?

14. How does preregistration assist the planner in planning a meeting?

15. Describe the four different methods of housing.

16. What is the purpose of an MESG? What information should it contain?

17. Explain the benefit of having a pre-con and post-con meeting.

18. Which is better, qualitative data or quantitative data?

19. Why do planners go through the effort and expense of evaluating meetings?

REFERENCES

Connell, B., C. Chatfield-Taylor, and M. Collins, eds. 2002. *Professional meeting management*, 4th ed. Chicago: Professional Convention Management Company.

Convention Industry Council. 2000. *The convention industry council manual*, 7th ed. McLean, VA: Convention Industry Council.

Green, R., and J. Withiam. 2003. Preliminary report of the APEX Resumes & Work Orders Panel. Conference presentation, International Association for Exhibition Management Annual Convention, Orlando, FL, December 11.

Hanson, D. 2002. "Meetings Industry Almanac." *Convene* (November): 19–22.

Jones, C. "CES Deemed a Major Success," *Las Vegas Review Journal* (January 14), http://www.Ivcva.com/press/visitor_stats_data.html (accessed January 16, 2003).

Las Vegas Convention and Visitors Authority. Expenditure and funding. http://www.Ivcva.com/press/abour_funding.html (accessed January 25, 2003).

Las Vegas Convention and Visitors Authority. 2003. Las Vegas visitor statistics. http://www.Ivcva.com/press/visitor_stats_data.html (accessed January 16, 2003).

MacLaurin, D., and T. Wykes. 1997. *Meetings and conventions: A planning guide*. Toronto, Ontario: Meetings Professional International Canadian Council.

State of the industry report. 2003. *Successful meetings*. p. s7, January.

ABOUT THE CHAPTER CONTRIBUTOR

Curtis Love, Ph.D., is an assistant professor in the Tourism and Convention Administration Department at the William F. Harrah College of Hotel Administration at the University of Nevada–Las Vegas (UNLV). His teaching and research concentrations are in the area of meetings, conventions, and exhibitions. Prior to joining UNLV, he was the vice-president of education for the Professional Convention Management Association.

◆3

MEETING, EXHIBITION, EVENT, AND CONVENTION SPONSORS

Corporations organize a significant number of MEEC events, such as this Shaklee company meeting.
Source: Pearson Education/PH College

◆ Chapter Objectives

This chapter provides the reader with an understanding of the following:

- The four major types of organizations that hold gatherings
- The types of meetings held by the different categories of organizations
- Typical lead time for planning the various types of gatherings

- The difference between the marketing strategies used to build attendance
- Several associations that support the professional development of those responsible for producing gatherings

◆ Chapter Outline

PURPOSE OF THIS CHAPTER

This chapter focuses on gaining an understanding of the organizations that sponsor different types of gatherings. Each segment of these sponsors creates gatherings to satisfy the unique needs of its organization and its constituent populations. Whether the organization is a nonprofit association or a corporation, a government agency or a private company that produces exhibitions, all have goals that may require them to call an MEEC to commemorate an event or to gain recognition for their involvement with it. Our purpose here is to identify who the sponsors are, the types of gatherings they hold, how much time they have to plan the event, who their targeted attendees are, and how they build attendance. The people who play a major role in producing the gatherings are identified, as are the professional associations who provide them with support and professional development.

WHO HOLDS THE GATHERINGS

CORPORATIONS

Virtually all businesses have needs that require them to plan and execute the production of gatherings. Publicly held companies have a legal requirement to hold a meeting of shareholders annually. All companies have varying needs to hold a press conference or to cut a ribbon on a new building. They have continuing needs to train key personnel in matters of company policy and procedures, or to develop new policies and procedures and to improve their effectiveness. Client groups may be brought together to capture their opinions in a focus group or to introduce them to a new product or service. Executive retreats may be held to improve communication or to develop long-term business plans. Gatherings are held to honor departing employees (promotion or retirement), to celebrate holidays, and to build overall morale within the organization. Companies may also be involved with sponsoring a sporting event and entertaining their clients in VIP tents at a major sporting event, such as the U.S. Open or Super Bowl.

Corporations plan and execute production of gatherings that often include a keynote speaker, such as this one.

Used by permission of Paradise Sound & Light, Orlando, Florida

Definition

Although there are numerous kinds of **corporations**, for the purposes of this section of the text we are referring to legally chartered enterprises that conduct business on behalf of their owners with the purpose of making a profit and increasing the value of the corporation. Some of these are public corporations that sell stock on the open market and have a board of directors who oversee the affairs of the corporation on behalf of the shareholders (owners) who elected them. Private corporations have the same fundamental purposes as public corporations, and their stock is not sold on the open market.

Number and Value of Corporate Meetings

When a corporation decides to hold a gathering, the corporation determines what the budget will be, where it will be held, and who will attend. Since the corporation typically pays for all expenses associated with attending the meeting, the corporation is in control. Attendance by corporate personnel is usually mandatory. Many corporate meetings are booked as needed, typically less than six months before the meeting will be held.

The typical corporate meeting has about sixty attendees. While corporations hold more meetings than any other sector, their gatherings tend to be smaller than in the others.

Decision Makers

The decision to hold a corporate meeting is typically made by persons in positions of key responsibility within the corporate hierarchy. Officers and senior managers in the sales and marketing area will call for a meeting of their regional sales managers to develop sales strategies for new product lines, or senior financial managers and controllers will call a meeting of their dispersed staffs to discuss budgets for next year.

Types of Corporate Gatherings and Events and Their Purposes and Objectives

Corporations have a variety of needs that can be satisfied by scheduling a gathering. What follows should not be viewed as a comprehensive list, but rather as an indication of the types of gatherings sponsored by corporations.

- The owners of voting shares of a corporation are invited to attend the company's annual *stockholders meeting*. Attendees are presented with reports on the state of the corporation and have the opportunity to vote on issues of significance. While most stockholders do not attend this meeting, they do participate in the governance of the corporation by filing a proxy statement in which they identify how they want their shares voted. This is an annually recurring meeting that is usually held in the city where the company is headquartered, although there is an emerging trend to move it to different locations to be more accessible to the stockholders.

- The board of directors is the governing body of a corporation. It typically meets several times a year, usually in the city where the corporation is located. While a *board meeting* may be held in the corporate headquarters, lodging, dinners, and related activities are often held at local hotels.

- There are numerous reasons for a company to hold *management meetings*. Every major division of a corporation may have a need to bring its decision makers and other important personnel together to develop plans, review performance, or improve their processes. While some of these meetings may occur on a scheduled basis, others may be called spontaneously to solve problems and situations that require immediate attention.

- As companies undergo change, it may be necessary to hold *training meetings* to bring their managers and key employees up-to-date on improved methods of job performance or to gain skills needed to operate new systems and equipment. Also, companies may use the training meeting to introduce new managers to corporate procedures and culture. Some of these meetings may be held on a regularly scheduled basis, while others may be held when conditions dictate it.

- Many corporations offer **incentive trips** to reward their top performers based on certain stated criteria. Those winning these trips may be employees, distributors, and/or customers. While these trips are often to exciting and glamorous destinations, an emerging trend is to schedule a number of activities for the participants to provide an added value to the sponsoring corporation. Companies may bring together these top performers with their corporate leadership to create a more synergistic organization.

- *Sales training and product launches* are often held to upgrade the performance of the sales staff, distributors, and retailers, and to introduce new products and services to distribution networks and the general public. These events are designed to educate and motivate those who have a significant impact on the success of the corporation.

- *Professional and technical training* meetings may be held to bring managers and others up-to-date on issues relevant to their role within the company and enhance the knowledge of their service providers. A company may have a meeting of its unit and regional controllers to discuss changes in tax law and company policies.

Attendees

Most of the attendees are members of the corporate family and persons who have a close business relationship with the company.

Need for Marketing to Build Attendance

While the purposes of corporate meetings should be carefully crafted, attendance at these meetings is mandatory for the majority of the attendees. Therefore, sending invitations or notices to those who will attend and when constitutes the majority of promotional activity. That it may be a command performance does not lessen the need to make the meeting informative, productive, and enjoyable for those attending.

Corporate Meeting Planning

Mary Jo Blythe, CMP
President, Masterplan, Inc.

Corporate meetings range from small VIP board of directors meetings to large sales meetings, customer incentive meetings, and lower tiered staff training meetings. One common thread between them is that they are always paid for (hosted) by the corporation. The funds come from a department or individual budget, thus creating a VIP(s) "host(s)" at the meeting. This VIP(s) usually expects special treatment, and it is the planner's job to ensure that the VIP(s) is taken care of well.

The planner must also embrace the corporate culture and ensure that it is depicted in all aspects of the meeting, from hotel selection to airport transportation, to menu choices and social activities. Flashy companies will have flashy meetings, and conservative companies will have conservative meetings. The planner is the ultimate controller of this element.

The meeting objectives will typically include motivation, camaraderie, brainstorming, and reviewing goals. There is also quite often an emphasis on the social events at a meeting. Although perceived as recreation, the opportunity for sidebar conversations at nonmeeting functions often will impact future corporate decisions. Social events should be strategically planned to ensure that the proper people are sitting together at dinner or assigned to the same foursome at the golf outing.

Corporate meetings, although a category of their own, can be as diverse as corporations themselves. Pay special attention to your VIP, embrace the corporate culture, and know your objectives, and your corporate meeting will be off to a successful start.

Department and/or Individual Responsible for Organizing and Planning

Corporate planners are really a hybrid group. The majority of people who plan corporate meetings have responsibilities beyond or in addition to the planning of meetings. According to the *Meetings and Conventions* magazine 2002 "Meetings Market Report," only about 25% of them spend more than 80% of their time performing the details of meeting planning; about 15% spend 10% or less on meeting planning. Only about one-third of them have job titles that would indicate that they have meeting planning responsibilities.

According to Mary Jo Blythe of Masterplan, a company that provides meeting planning services for several major corporations, "most large corporations have internal meeting planning departments." However, they do "utilize outside meeting planning firms for specific projects, overflow, or on an as needed basis."

Since the meeting planner's title, for the most part, does not indicate "meetings" responsibility, it should be no surprise that the majority do not work in a meeting planning department. They tend to work in the departments that hold the meetings (sales and marketing, finance) and have assumed meeting planning responsibility at the request of their supervisors. Only about 10% of corporate meeting planners have earned professional certifications.

Professional Associations Supporting the Corporate MEEC Industry

Many corporate meeting planners join associations to support their professional development. The associations most often joined include Meeting

Professionals International (http://www.mpiweb.org), Professional Convention Management Association (http://www.pcma.org), Society of Corporate Meeting Professionals (http://www.scmp.org), and the Society of Government Meeting Professionals (http://www.sgmp.org).

ASSOCIATIONS

The name "association" implies the act of being associated for certain common purposes, whether they are for professional, industry, educational, scientific, or social reasons. Gatherings like annual **conventions**, topical conferences, world congresses, and topical workshops and seminars are held for the benefit of the association's membership. Other gatherings need to be held for the betterment of the organization. Examples of these include board of directors meetings, committee meetings, and leadership development workshops. Many **associations** have an affiliated exhibition held in conjunction with their convention at which products or services of interest to the attendees are displayed. Besides providing value to the members

The booths at the Global Gaming Expo (G2E) reflect gambling products.
Photo by George G. Fenich, Ph.D., Professor, School of HRTA, University of New Orleans

of the association and potential recognition for the association, these gatherings also generate an important revenue stream for the organization.

According to the *Convene Magazine* "Meetings Market Survey," March 2002, associations derive about 33.2% of their annual income from conventions and exhibitions.

Number and Value of Association Meetings

A major difference between association and corporate gatherings is that attendance at association meetings is voluntary, not mandatory. Another difference is that the attendees are personally responsible for their registration, transportation, hotel, and related expenses. In some instances, employers may fund the attendance of employees at industry and professional association events that are work related.

Association meetings, especially conventions, tend to be very large, ranging from several hundred to tens of thousands of attendees. This issue of size can eliminate many smaller cities and venues from the opportunity to host these events and create increased demand by larger associations for prime locations for their gatherings. It also creates increased competition among the larger destinations to capture the major association gatherings.

To adjust to these supply and demand factors, larger associations book their major gatherings five to ten, or more, years ahead of the scheduled date to ensure that they have the space needed for their event. Small associations have a broader selection of locations that can accommodate their gatherings and therefore require less lead time to secure needed accommodations and facilities.

According to the *Meetings and Conventions* "Meetings Market Report" of 2002, the following are the top meeting destinations in the United States:

> Chicago, IL
> Washington, DC
> Orlando, FL
> Atlanta, GA
> Los Angeles, CA
> New York, NY
> Phoenix/Scottsdale, AZ
> Dallas/Ft. Worth, TX

Las Vegas, NV

Denver, CO

New Orleans, LA

San Diego, CA

San Francisco/Oakland, CA

The profile of the typical association meeting is that it has about 90 attendees and generates $78,200 in expenditures. The typical convention attracts approximately 1,050 attendees and generates $1.4 million in expenditures.

Decision Makers

The decision-making process for association meetings is rather complex and goes through several distinct stages. Once it is decided that a meeting will be held (usually by the board of directors or as stated in the association's constitution or bylaws), the location needs to be focused on. Some organizations rotate their meetings through their geographic regions, thereby dispersing hosting opportunities and responsibilities throughout their total membership. The specific city to host the meeting is decided by the board, based on the report of site visitations by the association's own meeting planner or by a contract meeting management provider.

Once the choice has been narrowed to a specific city, the meeting planner, based on site visits and inspections, will locate a venue (e.g., hotel and/or convention center) that is both available on the desired dates and well suited to the needs of the meeting. Typically, the meeting planner makes the recommendation to the association's board and, if approved, negotiates the financial and meeting details with the facility, which results in a contract that is eventually signed by both the venue and the association's senior staff person (usually the meeting planner's boss).

Types of Associations

Local: Most members are located in the metropolitan area where the organization is located.

State: Most members are located within the state where the organization is located.

Regional: Most members are located within the region (e.g., New England) where the organization is located.

National: Most members are located with the same country as where the organization is located.

International: Membership is comprised of people from several different nations.

Professional: Membership is comprised of persons from the same industry.

Not-for-profits *or* **nonprofits***:* These organizations have a special tax-exempt status granted by the IRS. Although they do not have a profit motive, these associations need to be run efficiently and must have their revenues exceed expenses. Since all revenues are used to support the mission of the organization, excess funds are allowed to stay with the organization, tax free.

SMERFs*:* These are not the little blue people from Saturday morning television. Here, this term refers to small associations with members who join for **S**ocial, **M**ilitary, **E**ducational, **R**eligious, and **F**raternal reasons. Persons attending these meetings tend to pay their own expenses; accordingly, this category tends to be very price sensitive.

Types of Association Gatherings and Events and Their Purposes and Objectives

Conventions: These are assemblies of people for a common purpose. Depending on the type of association sponsoring the convention, it may attract attendees from state, regional, national, or international markets. Many conventions have an exhibition (trade show) as an added feature. The exhibition may be a major source of revenue for the association. Exhibitors participate in these events because these events offer them an opportunity to show their products and services to a well-targeted group of potential buyers.

Board meetings: The association's board of directors typically meets several times a year to provide collective advice and direction to the association. This meeting is usually the smallest association meeting held.

Committee meetings: Many association committees will hold smaller meetings to discuss the affairs related to their purpose (e.g., government relations, convention host committee, national conference program committee, and publications committee).

Regional conferences: Organizations with a regional structure often schedule one or more events each year to bring together members who are in the same geographic area.

Training meetings: Associations often offer their members opportunities to upgrade their professional skills and knowledge through meetings targeted to specific topics. Many professions require continuing education (e.g., continuing medical education for different medical specialties). Some associations offer training meetings to develop the leadership potential of the association's elected national and regional officers.

Educational seminars: Association meetings led by an expert and allowing the participants to share their views and experiences.

Attendees

Since attendance at association meetings is voluntary, the meetings must offer appealing programs to draw members to the events.

Need for Marketing to Build Attendance

The marketing of association meetings is critical to the success of the gathering. All good association marketing should begin with an understanding of who the members are and their needs: Who are they? Why are they here? This focus should be brought into the development of all meetings.

If the meeting provides genuine opportunities for the members to satisfy their needs, the promotional aspect of marketing becomes much less intense. Since the primary group of attendees are members of the association, the key elements of promotion include providing advance notification of the date and location of the upcoming meeting along with information about the planned content, speakers, and special activities. Later, detailed registration information and a preliminary program will need to be provided.

The vehicle for communicating this information to the members has traditionally been through direct mail and notices or advertisements in the association newsletter and magazine. Technology and cost considerations have moved many associations toward the use of electronic media to communicate with their members. There is rapid growth in the use of broadcast fax and e-mail emphasizing that the recipient visit the association Web site to seek out the details.

To expand the number of attendees at the gathering, many associations send promotional materials and notices to nonmembers who have been targeted as sharing an interest in the meeting's purpose. Since the non-member fee is usually higher than the member fee, this effort, if successful, could result in attracting new members to the organization.

Association Meeting Planning

Susan Reichbart, CMP
Director, Conferences and Meetings
College and University Professional Association for
Human Resources

Associations offer their members opportunities to enhance their professional development at conferences, seminars, and workshops. These events may combine structured educational sessions of several hours or days with informal networking events, such as receptions, golf tournaments, and dinners. These activities encourage collegiality and allow members to exchange information in a relaxed social setting.

Associations encourage their members to become involved so that meetings *for* members are planned with input *from* members. The meeting planner works with the member committees from the initial planning stage through the final production of the event. Committee members can suggest program topics and speakers that their colleagues will find appealing and, at best, compelling. Local committee members may suggest local venues for social events, tourist attractions and tours, entertainment options, and golf courses for a conference tournament. One particularly enterprising volunteer researched local options and put together a comprehensive notebook rivaling those found at hotel concierge desks. Working under the supervision of the meeting planner, volunteers perform a myriad of duties during the event, such as giving out badges at registration, monitoring recreational events, and hosting social events—all duties that save the association the cost of hiring temporary staff. Member assistance is a value-added and integral part of the planning that helps ensure an event's appeal and success.

Association events are a source of revenue for associations. The greater the number of paid attendees, the greater the revenue and the more lucrative the event to the association. However, since members must pay

(continued)

registration fees and spend additional funds for travel and lodging, the association must provide programs that its members will find too valuable to miss. The meeting planner develops a marketing strategy that promotes benefits to entice members and prospects. The marketing plan may feature keynote speakers, concurrent session programs, an appealing location, and exciting social and recreational events. This information may be posted on the association's Web site, highlighted in newsletters, mailed in comprehensive preliminary programs, and sent by fax and e-mail "blasts." In addition to promoting all facets of the event to all members and prospects, additional marketing emphasis may be directed at targeted groups, such as past attendees.

Association meeting planners work with their member committees to develop worthwhile programs and then design effective marketing plans to maximize participation. The combined focus results in events that are beneficial to members and the association.

Department and/or Individual Responsible for Organizing and Planning

According to the *Meetings and Conventions* 2002 "Meetings Market Report," less than half of the association planners who responded to their survey had had the words *event, convention,* or *conference* in their job titles. More than half of the respondents had job responsibilities other than planning. Some associations, usually smaller ones, had contracted out some or all of their meetings to independent planners and multimanagement companies.

Professional Associations Supporting the Association MEEC Industry

Association meeting planners join professional associations in greater numbers than their corporate counterparts. Those associations include the American Society of Association Executives (http://www.asaenet.org), Meeting Professionals International (http://www.mpiweb.org), Professional Convention Management Association (http://www.pcma.org), International Association for Exhibition Management (http://www.iaem.org), Greater Washington Society of Association Executives (http://www.gwsae.org), and the Society of Government Meeting Planners (http://www.sgmp.org). There are also many local organizations of meeting planners that provide support and professional development opportunities for them.

GOVERNMENT

Governmental entities at all levels have continuing needs to hold gatherings, since they have continuing needs to communicate and interact with many constituent bodies. These meetings may involve the attendance of world leaders, with large groups of protestors and supporters, or a small group of elected local officials holding a legislative retreat. Government meetings are subject to rules that may influence many of the details of the meeting. The **per diem rates** that follow set limits on expenditures for lodging and meals; in addition, the ADA requires that facilities where federal meetings are held accommodate persons with certain physical limitations.

2002 Domestic Per Diem Rates (Effective 10/1/2001; Includes Lodging, Meals, and Incidental Expenses, Off and Peak Season)

Birmingham, AL	$ 97	Baltimore, MD	$179	Portland, OR	$129
Flagstaff, AZ	$101	Detroit, MI	$155	Philadelphia, PA	$164
Los Angeles, CA	$145	Minneapolis, MN	$141	Pittsburgh, PA	$125
San Diego, CA	$145	Kansas City, MO	$127	Providence, RI	$131
San Francisco, CA	$205	Biloxi, Gulfport, MS	$ 99	Hilton Head, SC	$117/137
Denver, CO	$154	Charlotte, NC	$118	Nashville, TN	$124
New Haven, CT	$125	Raleigh, NC	$112	Dallas, TX	$135
Washington, DC	$196	Manchester, NH	$123	San Antonio, TX	$133
		Atlantic City, NJ	$151/191	Salt Lake City, UT	$117/211
Miami, FL	$140	Albuquerque, NM	$103		
Atlanta, GA	$101			Richmond, VA	$115
Boise, ID	$ 99	Las Vegas, NV	$117	Montpelier, VT	$ 92
Chicago, IL	$201	Albany, NY	$138	Seattle, WA	$189
Indianapolis, IN	$112	New York, NY (Manhattan)	$254	Milwaukee, WI	$137
Louisville, KY	$107			Morgantown, WV	$100
New Orleans, LA	$131/181	Columbus, OH	$113		
Boston, MA	$205	Oklahoma City, OK	$103		

Source: http://www.gsa.gov

Decision Makers

Managers at government agencies are typically those who identify the need to hold a meeting and have the responsibility to provide funding through their departmental budget process or locate other sources of funding. Meetings, like other parts of an agency's budget, are very dependent on funding provided through the legislative process. Accordingly, as political interest grows or diminishes in an agency's mission, the budget will increase or decrease, as will its ability to sponsor gatherings.

Types of Government Gatherings and Events and Their Purposes and Objectives

The purpose of many government meetings is the training of government workers. On the federal level, many of these meetings will be replicated in several areas of the country to minimize travel expenses for the employees of the agency's branch offices.

Other government meetings may involve both agency employees and those in the general public who may have an interest in the topic of the meeting. Meetings to discuss prescription drug proposals or the future of social security are likely to go on the road to gather input from the general public.

Attendees

Attendance by employees at government meetings would generally be mandatory, while attendance by the general public would be voluntary.

Government Meetings Are Unique

Sara Torrence
President, Sara Torrence & Associates
Gaithersburg, Maryland
(Prior to her recent retirement, Sara planned special meetings for the federal government)

Meetings for the government are unique. They are different from any other type of conference. Why is this so? Because these meetings are bound by government regulations and operating policies that do not apply to other types of meetings.

First, consider rates for sleeping rooms. In an effort to save the government money, the General Services Administration (GSA) Office of Government-wide Policy sets *per diem* rates for lodging, meals, and incidental expenses for individual travelers for all locations in the continental United States (CONUS). In most cities, these rates are below those charged to conference groups, which take up a larger amount of a hotel's inventory of rooms than transient travelers. To offset this problem, GSA allows government meeting organizers to negotiate a rate up to 25% above the lodging allowance. Also, GSA's Federal Premier Lodging Program offers government travelers guaranteed rooms at guaranteed rates—right where the federal traveler needs to be—and enters into contractual relationships with hotels in the top seventy U.S. travel markets. Additionally, meetings may only be held in properties that comply with the Hotel Motel Fire Safety Act of 1990. Government regulations regarding travel are located at http://www.policyworks.gov on the Web.

Federal procurement policies also distinguish the government meeting. Bids for meeting supplies and services must be obtained from *at least* three vendors for all but the smallest purchases. Additionally, government meeting planners usually are not the people who commit federal funds. All purchases must be approved and contracted for by a federal procurement official. In some cases, meeting planners have been trained by their agencies in procurement practices, so they are able to commit a limited amount of money ($2,500, $10,000, or $25,000, for example). But private sector meeting suppliers should be forewarned to determine who has the authority to commit funds and sign contracts.

Hotel contracts are not considered "official" by the government. A hotel contract may be attached to the paperwork submitted to the procurement official, but in all cases, the government contract—not that of private sector—is the prevailing authority. This applies to all procurements for meeting services. Funds *must* be approved before the service is rendered, not after. In addition, the government *must* be able to cancel a contract without liquidated damages if funding for an event is withdrawn, if there are furloughs or closures of government facilities, or if other government actions make it inadvisable to hold the meeting. The government cannot pay for services not received. And, the government

(continued)

cannot indemnify or hold harmless anyone who is not a government employee conducting official business.

Other characteristics that make government meetings unique include the following:

- The short turn-around time for planning meetings. While associations plan their conferences with many years of lead time, most government meetings are planned only months—or even weeks—before the event. This is true for large, multifaceted meetings as well as small gatherings.
- Government meetings do not fit a particular mold. They may be elaborate international conferences for high-ranking dignitaries or small scientific conclaves for eight to twelve researchers. Some meetings may be held only once and therefore have no history.

Government meetings often require a disproportionately large amount of function space relative to the number of sleeping room nights booked. This may be because only a small percentage of attendees are coming from out of town.

- Policies for meetings can vary from agency to agency. Some agencies collect registration fees to cover expenses. Others will not allow appropriated fees to pay for lunches; collections often have to be made on site from attendees. In addition, as GSA allows each agency to implement the "up to 25%" allowance as they see fit, government lodging allowances may vary from agency to agency.
- Government meetings frequently bring together representatives from the Uniformed Services and non-Department of Defense agencies. Often, they share software applications designed for their *own* purposes, such as encrypted messaging and global directory systems that list only those with a "need to know" the information. Frequently, such meetings are classified and are required to be held in a "secure" facility, whether a government building or a public facility secured by trained personnel.

Government-sponsored meetings are far more complicated than most private-sector conferences that are often planned by people who are not full-time meeting planners. They may be budget analysts, public affairs officers, scientists, secretaries, or administrative officers. And as government meetings are perceived to provide less revenue for a hotel, they may be assigned to junior members of the hotel sales staff. Some government agencies contract their meeting planning services to outside consulting firms, and a very few agencies have their own full-time meeting planning staff.

All government meeting organizers are bound by a code of ethics that prohibits them from accepting anything from a vendor that is valued at more than $20. Those who work with the government should realize this and not put the planner in a compromising position.

Thankfully, there is an organization that specializes in providing education and resources to government planners and suppliers—the Society of Government Meeting Professionals (SGMP).

Need for Marketing to Build Attendance

Government meetings have characteristics typical of both corporate and association meetings. Mandatory attendance by government employees only requires that sufficient notice be provided so that the participants can adjust their schedules. Attracting voluntary attendees may require additional promotion so that the desired market can be attracted.

Department and/or Individual Responsible for Organizing and Planning

Government meeting planners resemble their corporate counterparts inasmuch as they are located throughout their agencies. While some of them devote all their work time to meeting planning, others handle meetings as one of their extra assigned duties.

Many government agencies hire meeting management companies or independent meeting planners to handle meetings that fall beyond their internal capabilities. In the Washington, DC, area, there are several meeting planning companies that specialize in managing government meetings.

Professional Associations Supporting the Government MEEC Industry

Meeting planners who work for the government and/or independent meeting management companies are likely to join associations to support their professional development. These associations include the Society of Government Meeting Planners (http://www.sgmp.org) and its local or regional chapters, Professional Convention Management Association (http://www.pcma.org), and Meeting Professionals International (http://www.mpiweb.org). Those who have responsibility for organizing exhibitions are likely to join the International Association for Exhibition Management (http://www.iaem.org).

EXHIBITION MANAGEMENT COMPANIES

There are a number of companies that are in the business of owning and managing trade shows and **expositions**. While both of these are events at which products and services are displayed, the **trade show** is generally not open to the public, while expositions are usually open to the public. The companies who operate these exhibitions are profit-making enterprises that have found areas of economic interest that attract, according to the purpose of the exhibition, either the general public (for an auto, boat, home, or garden show) or members of a specific industry (for high-technology communications networking).

Some associations hire **exhibition management companies** to manage all or part of their exhibitions. For their efforts, the companies are paid for the services they provide.

Among the largest exhibition management companies are Reed Exhibitions (http://www.reedexpo.com), which organizes over 470 events in 29 countries; VNU Expositions (http://www.vnuexpo.com), which creates, markets, and produces 50 trade shows and educational conferences; and George Little Management (http://www.glmshows.com), which markets and produces 27 shows. These three show management companies manage 40 of the top 200 shows, according to a study done by Tradeshow Week Inc. in 2002. Their shows serve a wide variety of industries, domestically and globally, including aerospace, art and entertainment, electronics, hospitality, security, sport and health, and travel.

According to the *2002 Tradeshow Week Data Book*, leading show producers include:

Dmg World Media

Penton Media, Inc.

Advanstar Communications, Inc.

Imark Communications, Inc.

Dallas Market Center Company

TJR Industries/The Woodworking Shows

CMP Media, LLC

Number and Value of Exhibitions

In the *Exhibition Industry Census* (published in 2001 by the Center for Exhibition Industry Research [CEIR]), the following significant data was reported:

- 11,094 exhibitions were held in the United States
- 85% (9,430) were business-to-business (B-to-B)
- 15% (1,664) were business-to consumer (B-to-C)
- 38% were held in exhibition or convention centers
- 67% (7,433) were owned by nonprofit associations
- 33% (3,661) were owned by for-profit companies

Decision Makers

The owners and senior managers of company-owned shows decide where, when, and how often they will produce their shows. The decision is driven by the profit motive—offering too many shows could lead to a cannibalization of the market. Offering too few shows creates an opportunity for the competition to enter the market with its own show.

Types of Gatherings and Their Purposes and Objectives

Trade shows: Exhibits of products and services that are not open to the general public. Trade shows may be part of a convention or may stand alone.

Public shows: Exhibits of products and services that are open to the public and usually charge an admission fee.

Attendees

Depending on the nature of the exhibition, the attendees vary greatly. For trade shows, the market is well defined by the trade or profession. For **public shows**, the attendees are basically defined by geographic proximity to the show location.

Need for Marketing to Build Attendance

The exhibition management companies have a need to market to two distinctly different yet inexorably linked publics. One group that has to be targeted is exhibitors who need to reach likely buyers of their products and services. The others are members of the trade or general public who need to view, discuss, and purchase the products and services.

The trade group only needs to be informed of the dates and location of the trade show. Direct mail and e-mail may be all that is needed for an established show. Shows appealing to the general public require extensive media advertising (newspaper, radio, and television) to communicate the specifics within the geographic region. Promotional efforts like the distribution of discount coupons is common. In both cases, it is essential that the marketing effort result in a high volume of traffic at the exhibition to satisfy the needs of the exhibitors.

The exhibition management company really is a marketing company, since it is creating the environment in which need-satisfying exchanges can occur. Their focus is on selling exhibit space and building buyer attendance.

Department and/or Individual Responsible for Organizing and Planning

In this case, the entire exhibition management company is dedicated to the organizing and planning of the exhibition.

Professional Associations Supporting the Exposition Management Industry

The associations that support the exhibition management industry include the International Association for Exhibition Management (http://www.iaem.org) for the production side of the business and the Trade Show Exhibitors Association (http://www.tsea.org) for the exhibitor side of the business. Other related associations include the Exhibit Designers and Producers Association (http://www.edpa.com), the Exposition Service Contractors Association (http://www.esca.org), and the Healthcare Convention and Exhibitor Association (http://www.heca.org).

ASSOCIATION MANAGEMENT COMPANIES

As the name of this category implies, this type of company is contracted by an association to assume full or partial responsibility for the management of the association, based on its needs. A designated person in the association management company is identified as the main contact for the association and interacts with the board of directors and members to fulfill the association's mission. If the association is small and has limited financial resources, that contact person may serve in this capacity for two or more associations. Since they managed more than one association, association management companies were formerly known as multimanagement companies. Confusion as to who they targeted their services necessitated this change.

Other employees of the association management company support the main contact and provide services as contracted (membership, finance, publications, government relations, and meeting management services). With this type of arrangement, the association office is typically located within the offices of the association management company. Examples of these types of companies include Smith, Bucklin & Associates of Chicago, Illinois, and the Association Management Group of McLean, Virginia.

MEETING MANAGEMENT COMPANIES

These companies operate on a contractual basis, like the association management company, but limit their services to providing either selected or comprehensive meeting management services. They may manage all aspects of the meeting or may be focused on site research, hotel negotiations, exhibit sales, on-site management, handling registration and housing, or any combination of these. The meeting may be held at the association's own location, or the function may be located elsewhere. Examples of meeting management companies include ConferenceDirect of Los Angeles, California, and Conferon Inc. of Twinsburg, Ohio.

Independent Meeting Managers

Experienced meeting professionals often use their expertise and contacts to set up their own business of managing meetings, or parts of meetings, for an association or several associations. An independent meeting manager may be called in to run a golf tournament that is an integral part of a gathering or provide on-site management. In some instances, an independent is called in to handle crises in the meetings department. Personnel changes in the meetings department shortly before a meeting may require hiring a competent professional to pull the meeting together and bring it to a successful conclusion.

Event Management Companies

Within the context of the meetings industry, these companies are usually brought in to manage a specific aspect of a larger gathering. They may be hired to plan, script, and supervise all aspects of the awards ceremony or the closing gala. Depending on their market and location, some of these companies may provide local event management, including the grand opening of a building or business, handle the arrangement for a parade, and do wedding and other party planning.

Professional Associations Supporting Independent Planners

The type of company individuals are associated with will dictate the type of association that they would likely join to support their professional development. Many of them will join the Professional Convention Management Association (http://www.pcma.org) or Meeting Professionals International (http://www.mpiweb.org). Others will choose to join organizations like the International Special Event Society (http://www.ises.com), the National Association of Catering Executives (http://www.nace.net), the American Rental Association (http://www.ararental.org), or the Association of Bridal Consultants (http://www.bridalassn.com).

OTHER ORGANIZATIONS ARRANGING GATHERINGS

There are a number of other entities that organize or sponsor gatherings or events. They include the following:

- Political Organizations
  - Republican or Democratic national parties
  - Local political organizations
- Labor Unions
  - The Teamsters
  - Pipe Fitters Union
- Fraternal Groups
  - Kiwanis
  - Elks
  - University fraternities and sororities
- Military
  - Army
  - Navy
  - Homeland security
  - Airport baggage screeners
- Educational Groups
  - Universities
  - For-profit education groups
  - Common interest groups
  - High schools

◆ SUMMARY

The types of organizations that sponsor gatherings are as diverse as the types of gatherings held and the people who attend them. Most of the U.S. population will participate in these gatherings at least once in their lives. For many of them, attending a meeting, convention, exhibition, or other event will be a regular occurrence. The gatherings attended reflect the personal and professional interests of the attendees.

People seeking career opportunities with sponsoring organizations will have to use targeting techniques to locate them, although these positions do exist throughout the nation. The greatest number of these positions can be found in locations where the organizations are headquartered. The metropolitan Washington, DC, area is considered to be the "meetings capital" of the world, with several thousand associations located there. Many national and international organizations are located in and around Washington, as is the federal government. State capital cities are home to many state and regional associations, in addition to agencies of state government.

Major corporations tend to be located in large cities, although many may be located in smaller cities and towns. Their meetings are typically planned at corporate headquarters.

Employment opportunities with organizations and facilities that host gatherings are located in both major cities and small towns. The organization will select a location for its proximity to access by the attendees (near a major airport or the interstate highway) or for the purpose of the gathering.

With baby boomers (the largest age group in the U.S. population) approaching retirement age, it is anticipated that there will be an increasing number of employment opportunities in the coming years on both sides of the meeting, event, exhibition, and convention industry.

KEY WORDS AND TERMS

For definitions, refer to http://glossary.conventionindustry.org.

Associations

Conventions

Corporations

Exhibition management companies

Expositions and public shows

Incentive trips

Not-for-profits and nonprofits

Per diem rates

SMERFs

Trade show

REVIEW AND DISCUSSION QUESTIONS

1. Identify the type of sponsoring organization that holds the greatest number of gatherings and the type that generates the greatest economic benefit.

2. Which type or types of sponsoring organizations have the greatest marketing challenges to ensure the success of their gatherings?

3. What changes are occurring with incentive trips to provide more value for the corporation sponsoring the gathering?

4. How do not-for-profit associations differ from for-profit organizations?

5. What type of organizations comprise the category of associations knows as "SMERFs," and what similarities do they share with each other?

6. How do government procurement officers view meeting contracts from their hotel suppliers?

7. Distinguish between the trade show and the exposition.

8. What efficiencies do association management companies bring to the management and operation of small associations?

ABOUT THE CHAPTER CONTRIBUTOR

Howard E. Reichbart is an associate professor in the Hospitality Management and Meeting, Event & Exhibition Management Department at Northern Virginia Community College in Annandale, Virginia. Professor Reichbart developed his interests in the hotel and meetings industry as a youngster working in the family hotel business. These interests led him to earn a degree in hotel administration from the University of New Hampshire. He then worked in hotel management for Hotel Corporation of America/Sonesta International Hotels in Hartford, Connecticut, and Washington, DC. He served in the U.S. Army as the club officer/manager of the Ft. McPherson Officers Club in Atlanta, Georgia. Professor Reichbart has been a faculty member at Northern Virginia Community College for thirty-three years, including almost twenty years as the program head. During his time as program head, he developed one of the first degree programs in convention management in the United States. He has also taught at the University of Nevada–Las Vegas, the University of Maryland, and George Washington University.

◆4

MEETING AND CONVENTION VENUES

An Examination of the Facilities Used by Meeting Planners,
Focusing on How Their Financial Structure Dictates Their
Relationships with Planner Clients

Cruise ships are sometimes used for meetings and conventions.
Photo by George G. Fenich, Ph.D., Professor, School of HRTA, University of New Orleans

◆ Chapter Objectives

The chapter provides the reader with an understanding of the following:

- The importance of the physical attributes of the meeting venue to your ability to use it for your event
- How the venue's financial structure impacts your ability to negotiate for your meeting
- The variations in service levels and service availability in different facilities
- Potential hazards often overlooked by novice planners
- What questions need to be asked of a facility in order to ensure the success of your meeting

◆ Chapter Outline

INTRODUCTION

Meeting planners work in a variety of facilities. These facilities range in size from **hotel** suites that hold a handful of people to major convention centers and outdoor festival sites that hold tens of thousands. Anyplace where two or more people gather is a meeting site. Whether this meeting site is a multimillion-square-foot convention center or a street corner under a light pole, people will find a place to gather. The meeting planner's job is to match the meeting and the venue. Thus, the planner must determine two things about the group: Who are they? Why are they here? Most events and meetings are appropriate only for a limited range of facilities. A national political convention would not work on a street corner. Neither would a board of directors' meeting work in an outdoor **stadium**. For an

A fashion show in an airplane hangar.
Used by permission of Paradise Light & Sound, Orlando, Florida

event to succeed, the characteristics of the event must be properly matched to the facility in which it is held. Whether the venue is the conference room at the end of a suite of offices or the flight deck of an active aircraft carrier, the goal of the meeting must fit with the choice of venue for the meeting to work.

Thus, the planner must be sure to do his or her research about the group and the facilities that may fit the group's needs, must understand the needs and expectations of the group, must communicate the benefits offered by a facility that meet the needs of the group, and must verify the arrangements between the group and the venues. In order to properly exploit this tremendous range of facilities, a meeting planner must be familiar with both the physical characteristics of the facility and its financial structure. The combined impact of these two factors determines a meeting planner's relationship with the facility management and their relative negotiating positions. Many other facility features are relevant to the success or failure of any meeting, but an understanding of the significance of the facility's physical form and its financial structure is vital for a meeting planner to effectively use the facility to support the meeting.

The vast majority of meetings takes place in conference rooms or offices on the meeting participants' property. Typically, one room in a suite of offices is designated as a conference room, and a handful of colleagues gather to address some current issue. Whether scheduled or impromptu, these meetings rarely involve a meeting planner. However, as these meetings get larger and involve more people, the person who has had the position of scheduling these on-property meetings frequently can find him- or herself planning meetings that take place somewhere else.

HOTELS

Having moved off property, the next most common place for a meeting is a hotel. Hotels and their meeting spaces vary widely in size and quality. Virtually all hotels with any meeting space have at least one small **boardroom**. These boardrooms typically seat fewer than a dozen people, and the more elegant of them have permanent large tables and furniture that would be appropriate in the conference rooms of any major corporation. At the other end of the scale, hotel **ballrooms** tend to top out at around 60,000 square feet. **Break-out rooms** would vary from little larger than the boardrooms up to about half the size of the main ballroom. The whole facility, including break-out rooms, will likely not exceed 100,000 square feet of total meeting space, although a few are larger. The Gaylord Palms, Disney's Coronado Springs Resort, Marriott's Orlando World Center, and the Walt Disney World (WDW) Dolphin–Swan complex (which is not run by Disney) all have in excess of 100,000 square feet of meeting space. There are others this size in Las Vegas, but these are a relative rarity in most parts of the country.

Hotels generally provide a variety of meeting spaces. They typically include a large carpeted ballroom with some sort of themed décor. These ballrooms are generally planned as part of the initial construction of the facility. They are typically divisible by the use of movable air walls. A common floor plan provides larger divisions flanked by smaller ones accessible from the side corridors. It is not uncommon for the ceiling to be lower in the smaller divisions than in the larger ones. This is not always obvious from printed floor plans. Break-out rooms tend to be decorated and equipped like smaller versions of the ballrooms and serve identical functions for smaller numbers of people.

The Walt Disney World Dolphin Hotel is designed for meetings and conventions.
Used by permission of Paradise Light & Sound, Orlando, Florida

Some hotels have been so successful at marketing their meeting space that they have found the need to add space. Frequently, they will level out a parking lot to facilitate the regular use of tents. Some space-intensive events can be moved to the tents. This space allows the hotel to maintain higher room occupancy levels by reducing the gap in the **shoulders** between meetings. Once the tent ceases to be a viable option, either due to weather or zoning issues, many hotels build spaces specifically designed for exhibits. These spaces have a rough, unfinished look to them and tend to be designed more for utility than beauty. These utilitarian facilities are less expensive to maintain and, due to their reduced cost structure, can be more profitable than the glamorous ballrooms.

In contrast to the stark exhibit facilities, many hotels have beautiful out-door venues to support social and "networking" functions. Pools, patios, atriums, and gardens can all be used as meeting locations. When first inspect-ing a meeting space, a planner should observe all of the physical attributes of the space. The facility's "hardware" has a significant impact on the delegates' comfort and their involvement in the proceedings.

Hotels tend to be owned by major hotel companies or are franchised by a major hotel company to a local owner who manages the facility in accordance with corporate guidelines. Almost all hotels supporting meeting space are part of a larger corporate entity. This corporate entity is likely publicly traded or a subsidiary of an entity that is publicly traded. The Rosen Hotels in Orlando and the Atlantis in the Bahamas are notable exceptions. Hotels are rarely owned by individuals and almost never owned by local governments. Some are owned by closely held corporations. While a closely held corporation is not likely to have its stock traded on Wall Street, it is just as susceptible to market variations as the publicly traded corporations are. Hotels are intended to be businesses and not charities. Their mission in life is to generate profit for the parent company.

Meetings are rarely a hotel's primary business. For almost all hotels, the primary business is the sale of sleeping room nights. Conventions are often a **loss leader** whose primary purpose is to fill what would otherwise be empty sleeping rooms. This single financial fact of life overshadows all other aspects of any negotiation between a meeting planner and a hotel. There are some hotels that derive significant revenue from their extensive meeting spaces, but these revenues are ancillary income and are intended to drive their primary business, which remains sleeping room nights. While hotels derive the majority of their revenue from the rooms, many also derive significant income from the restaurants and bars. A smaller percentage derives revenue from the **concessionaires** at the pools, beach, or spa. The dynamic changes somewhat when the hotel is associated with a theme park or casino. Casinos can be money-making machines and can have a significant impact on a planner's ability to negotiate. The hotels associated with theme parks have a similar dynamic that is discussed later in this chapter.

Conventional wisdom states that meeting planners do not pay for meeting space in hotels. However, meeting space costs the hotels money. It costs them in the interest they pay on the investment capital they needed to build the hotel. It costs them in the staff and materials to clean, maintain, and operate the meeting rooms. These costs must be funded from somewhere. The way the costs of the meeting space are covered is to require that a meeting commit to using a minimum number of sleeping rooms for a minimum number of nights. The hotel's goal is to fill the rooms that would not be filled by its regular customers. The closer the hotel gets to 100% occupancy, the happier the stockholders will be.

By linking sleeping room use with meeting space availability, hoteliers found they could induce meeting planners to use their facilities because the meeting space was free, at least to them. Unfortunately, after the system of financially linking sleeping rooms to meeting space became popular, many hotels discovered that some planners were consistently off in their projections. The hotels found they were committing large amounts of meeting space to meetings that used far fewer sleeping rooms than the planner had led them to expect. As an incentive to induce planners to project more accurately and reduce the hotel's losses from inaccurate projections, the hotels introduced **attrition** penalties. These penalties, which can be substantial, become relevant when a meeting uses less than the contracted number of sleeping room nights (see chapter 12, "Legal Issues," for more discussion of attrition).

The next most significant source of revenue for most hotels is food and beverage. The hotel's restaurants and bars are generally designed to handle the hotel's "regular" traffic, which is likely a mix of business travelers or tourists. If the hotel has a nightclub, the probability is that its intended clientele is not the meeting delegates, but rather locals or vacationers. The size and staffing levels of these outlets are rarely determined by the needs of the meeting attendees. Banquet catering is intended to fill that need. The scope and quality of hotels' banquet departments vary as much as the quality of the sleeping rooms. In a reaction to the reluctance of some meeting planners to agree to elevated sleeping room rates in order to guarantee meeting space, some hotels have linked banquet revenue with meeting space. Thus, a meeting planner who meets a threshold of spending in the catering department gets a break in the meeting room cost.

Some events do not involve sleeping rooms, and many hotels are reluctant to deal with them. However, the demand for venues in which to hold the so-called **local social** event is great enough that hotels do market to them. In order for the planner of a local social event to get "free" meeting space, he or she would have to guarantee a minimum amount of catering revenue. Since local social events do not involve sleeping rooms, they are generally a hotel's last attempt to derive some revenue out of a vacant meeting room. What revenue it derives comes from food service and the commissions paid by other support vendors for the privilege of working in the hotel. These other vendors would include the disc jockey, the florist,

Décor for a fancy dinner.
Used by permission of Paradise Light & Sound, Orlando, Florida

the limo service, and the decorator. If lighting or sound beyond the disc jockey's systems were needed, the in-house audiovisual company would pay a commission back to the hotel. All of these revenue streams are calculated in the decision to accept a piece of local social business once all other higher revenue opportunities have been exhausted. Since a planner of a local social event is just as likely to fall short of his or her projections as a planner of an event involving sleeping rooms, attrition on catering revenue projections is becoming more common for all the same reasons that attrition started becoming attached to sleeping room projections.

Hotels derive revenue from a variety of other nonmeeting services as well. The golf courses, spas, equestrian centers, and beaches all provide revenue to the hotel. Hotels often contract with exclusive vendors to provide services within the hotel. Audiovisual companies, **destination management companies** (DMCs), convention decorators, musicians, disc jockeys, florists, and bus companies can all be contracted to the hotel as exclusive vendors of their specialized services. Commissions paid back to the hotel can be as high as 40%. Some hotels charge attrition on those services as well. The hotel's theory is that the hotel and the vendor have made an investment in the facility and equipment for the meeting planner's benefit. Should the planner not elect to use these services, the services should be paid for anyway because they were available. It is not always safe to assume that the hotel's exclusive vendor has that honor because it is the most qualified. The negotiated size of the projected commission may be the determining factor.

Hotels do pay some commissions, although the discussion to this point has focused on the commissions paid to them. Travel agents and destination management companies as well as site selection companies can be paid commission for the business they bring to the hotel. One of the questions a planner must ask of every travel professional who recommends a facility is what his or her financial connection is to that facility. There is an Internet-based discussion group for meeting planners sponsored by the Meetings Industry Mall Web site (MIMList) in which the issue of commissions paid by hotels is frequently a hot topic. A planner would be well advised to ask why a specific site is being recommended.

Hotels attached to theme parks are a special case. It is not uncommon for a theme park-based hotel to include an estimate of how much money the delegates or their families will spend in the attached "entertainment" facilities when they decide whether or not to take a particular piece of business. Clauses relating the number of theme park passes purchased to the availability of meeting room space can appear in some contracts at these hotels. Meetings planned with sufficient free time to allow the delegates to avail themselves of the golf course or casino may have an easier time contracting their desired meeting space.

If the hotel is attached to a casino, it is possible for the hotel to derive more revenue from the casino than it does from the sleeping rooms. The prices charged for the sleeping rooms are fixed in advance of the guests' arrival. The potential revenue derived from the casino is limited only by the availability of credit on the guests' accounts. Meetings, then, can become a means to bring guests to the casino where they can potentially spend more money gambling than they will on other activities.

Seasonality and fluctuating occupancy levels can have a significant impact on the cost of using a facility. A hotel with a severe seasonal variation can have an out-of-season price that is as little as half its in-season price. By paying attention to a facility's seasonal occupancy patterns, meeting planners can find some true bargains. Among meeting delegates is the common misconception that the incredibly cheap rate they pay to use an exclusive resort is due to their planner's negotiating prowess when it is more likely that the great rate is because of the planner's choice of a venue with extreme seasonal variations.

Planners negotiating with hotels need to consider the entire financial package their business will bring to the facility. The more closely aligned the meeting's financial structure is to the needs of the hotel, the better deal the planner can get for his or her meeting. The entire financial package includes not just the revenue from the meeting itself but also the revenue from the sleeping rooms, the restaurants, the bars, and the exclusive vendors.

When negotiating with any convention facility, planners are not only negotiating on the basis of what they will use but on the basis of what is available whether they use it or not. The availability of specific **amenities** often drives the delegates' expectations of the facility. It is important that planners match the level of their delegates' expectations with the level of service provided by the hotel at a cost the delegates feel is reasonable.

Thus, the MEEC planner must "research, understand, communicate, and verify" that the venue meets the needs of the group.

BUT YOU COULD HAVE!

There is a story that has traveled the meeting planning circuit. A man and his wife checked into a hotel late at night after a long drive, too tired to continue. A few hours later, when they went to check out in the morning, they were presented with a bill for $250.00. The man became irate. He demanded to see the manager. The manager politely explained to the angry man that the rate was so high because the hotel had a dazzling array of special services available to its guests for their use at no additional cost. When the man protested that he did not use the services, the manager's reply was that he could have, and it was not the hotel's fault that he did not avail himself of those services. The man thought for a moment. He wrote the hotel a check for $100.00 and handed it to the front desk clerk. When the clerk asked what the check was for, the man said that his wife was in the room all night and the manager could have had sex with her and that was worth $150.00. When the manager protested that he hardly would do such a thing, the man said, "But you could have!" He then turned and left.

CONVENTION CENTERS

Conventional wisdom has it that convention centers are huge. Many are. Convention centers are designed to handle larger events than could be supported in a hotel. Several convention centers feature over a million square feet of meeting space. Their very size is both their strength and their weakness. They are meeting facilities with no sleeping rooms. Some are little more than large bare buildings with exposed roof beams. Others are mammoth architectural marvels involving magnificent feats of engineering and awe-inspiring vistas.

As compared to hotels, convention centers are more likely to devote the majority of their space to **exhibit halls** and utilitarian spaces than to plush ballrooms. Hotel lobbies are designed to be comfortable and inviting. Convention center lobbies are designed to facilitate the uninterrupted flow of several thousand delegates who are late for their meetings. This difference in design philosophy is evident in every phase of a

The Las Vegas Convention Center contains over one million square feet of space.
Photo by George G. Fenich, Ph.D., Professor, School of HRTA, University of New Orleans

convention center's operation. Just as hotels have a variety of space sizes, convention centers also have a variety of spaces. In the typical hotel, the ballrooms are the largest meeting spaces followed by the exhibit spaces. In a convention center, the exhibit halls tend to be the largest spaces followed by the carpeted ballrooms. It would not be unusual for the prefunction spaces in a convention center to be larger than the break-out rooms attached to them, unlike a typical hotel where the prefunction spaces tend to be smaller.

Convention centers are more likely to have rooms with built-in stages than hotels. They are also more likely than hotels to have "congress-style" permanent classrooms, although such rooms would not be as uncommon at conference centers. Philosophically, if hotels are designed by psychologists, convention centers are designed by industrial engineers. Engineering considerations are relevant in both types of facilities, but the impact of the difference in scale drives much of the difference between how hotels and convention centers operate.

The design of the Vancouver Convention Center breaks with tradition.
Used with permission of the Vancouver Convention Center

Convention centers are often described as utilitarian and occasionally as "cold" when compared to hotels. Convention centers generally do not have spas or swimming pools, exercise rooms, or saunas. They do not have restaurants that stay open when the center is vacant, and they do not have karaoke bars. Unlike a hotel that is open around the clock, convention centers can, and do, lock the doors at night. The staff goes home when nothing is scheduled. Whereas in a hotel someone is on duty at all times, in a convention center if someone is required to be available at odd hours, that person must be scheduled in advance. This rigidity of structure and scheduling means that the planner who uses a convention center may need to plan in more detail than the planner who holds the same meeting in a hotel.

Unlike the hotel, which is most likely part of a major corporation, most convention centers are owned by government entities. Professional management is frequently contracted to a private company that specializes in managing such facilities. SMG, Volume Services, and Global Spectrum are three such companies. Many convention centers are actively supported by the local CVB. As with everything that concerns government, the managements of these facilities are ultimately responsible to the taxpayers.

This management structure creates an environment in which the convention center can take a very long view but at the same time must think very short term. Generally, the intent of the government that built the building is that the facility be an economic driver for the whole community. Therefore, the facility can take events that benefit the community as a whole with less concern for driving sleeping room nights in the surrounding hotels. This is part of the reason why convention centers, unlike hotels, will take events like local consumer shows that generate no sleeping room nights. While the convention center may be funded in part by some kind of hotel sleeping room tax, it is generally not required to maintain a specific ratio between meeting space and sleeping rooms.

One controversial issue among convention center managers is whether the public-sector or the private-sector companies can do a better job of managing these facilities. There are strongly held opinions on both sides of the issue. Even with all the discussion, one thing is still true. The quality of a planner's event is as dependent on the planner's relationship with the individuals running the facility as it is with how well the event is planned. Especially in a convention center, the more thorough the planning, the more successful the event.

How does a convention center make money? After all, the taxpayers will not support a big building forever if it makes no money. Convention centers charge for everything they provide on a pay per use basis. Every square foot of the building has a price attached to it. Room rental, by the square foot per day, is the center's biggest single revenue source. Every chair, every table, and every service provided by the convention center has a price. The center makes money on the catering and the concessions. In a hotel, much of the real cost of holding the meeting is hidden in the sleeping room price; in the convention center, every cost is specifically itemized. This "nickel and dime" attitude is the convention center's way of charging for services used and not charging for what is not needed. The joke about the irate man checking out of the hotel would be unthinkable in a convention center.

One overlooked fact that sets convention centers apart from many other types of facilities concerns the portion of their budget spent on energy. It is not unusual for a convention center to spend more money on utilities than it does on its full-time staff. This is not a reflection of the staffing levels, but rather an indication of how expensive it is to keep a large facility properly climate controlled. Hotels have significant energy bills as well, but unlike a convention center, they are not trying to climate control huge spaces with high ceilings and massive doors that stay open all day.

Like a hotel, a convention center has relationships with vendors for services it does not provide internally. Such services might include parking, buses, audiovisual, power, data–telecom, and florists.

In a convention center, catering is more likely to be contracted to an outside vendor than in a hotel. Each of these vendors pays a commission to the center. This commission may not be in cash but may be in the form of equipment owned by the vendor installed in the building. For example, in many buildings, the facility does not own the soft drink vending equipment. The soft drink company with the exclusive rights on the facility owns and services the equipment in return for a specified level of product sales. Another debate in the convention center industry has to do with whether a facility should have "exclusive" or "preferred" vendors. It is no longer safe to assume that any vendor suggested by a facility is either exclusive or preferred unless the vendor is identified as such. Traditionally, catering was the only exclusive service, but in some facilities power, rigging, audiovisual equipment, security, and telecom can be exclusive vendors to the facility. Some of these relationships are the result of

As the old actor said in "Fantasticks," "See it in lights."
Used by permission of Paradise Light & Sound, Orlando, Florida

governmental regulations, and others are an attempt to avoid liability law-suits. In contrast, in some convention centers even the catering can be outsourced to vendors other than the ones who have the relationship with the facility. The relationships between the vendors and the facility are fluid and changing. Therefore, no planner should ever assume the nature of the relationships without asking specifically.

It is also not safe to assume that an exclusive vendor is somehow more or less competent than an outside vendor. Many convention industry sales-people have tried to paint their competition into a corner with broad-brush statements that may or may not be true. Determining the competence of the facility's preferred or exclusive vendors is one of the toughest jobs a planner must face, and while there are some guidelines, there are no absolutes. Unfortunately, the success or failure of any given meeting often depends on vendors with whom a planner has no experience.

Given the political climate in which most convention centers operate, combined with the size and scope of the events they support, they tend to be bureaucratic and inflexible. Negotiations can take longer than in a hotel, but a convention center is more likely to publish all its rate information either in print or on a Web site than is any other type of meeting facility. It is possible to go through many convention centers' documentation and know before talking to a salesperson what that event is likely to cost. This is difficult if not impossible to do in many other types of facility. With all this information readily available, it becomes the planner's responsibility to access the information and not the facility's responsibility to guide a novice planner through the process.

Due to their large size, bureaucratic nature, the complexity of the decisions, and potential impact on the events planned, novice planners should not attempt to bring a large event to a convention center without first working smaller events in other venues. There are better places to start in the meeting planning business. One of the most "planner-friendly" types of venues is the conference center.

Thus, the meeting, exposition, event, or convention planner must "research, understand, communicate, and verify" that the venue meets the needs of the group.

CONFERENCE CENTERS

For the most part, conference centers are small, well-appointed facilities specifically designed to enhance classroom-style learning. The IACC has developed a specific set of guidelines as to what constitutes a "conference center" as opposed to other types of meeting facilities. Adherence to these guidelines essentially guarantees the planner that the facility is well managed and well suited for intense, small group learning situations. Several major corporations run conference centers, including Aramark, Dolce, Sodexho, Marriott, and Hilton. Several smaller companies are also involved, including Conference Center Concepts and the Creative Dining Group.

A planner contemplating using an IACC conference center would be well advised to visit the IACC Web site and review its expectations in advance of meeting with the facility's salespeople. Conference centers can be either resident or nonresident. The biggest difference between the two is that resident facilities have sleeping rooms and nonresident facilities do not. While it is easy to draw the comparison between hotels and resident conference centers, the comparison would likely be misleading. One of the major differences concerns the conference centers' focus on teaching and learning instead of on elegant parties. This tends to translate into better furniture and a greater tendency toward permanently installed work surfaces as well as permanently installed projection and audio systems.

Many conference centers, whether resident or nonresident, employ a pricing strategy called the **complete meeting package**, which essentially means that whatever the facility owns, the planner may use at no additional charge. This puts the facility's entire inventory of easels, projectors, microphones, and sound systems at the planner's immediate disposal. For the planner, this is a flexible way to work in that he or she is freed from the task of getting scheduled speakers to provide their equipment requirements in advance.

Some conference centers are in remote locations. Some of the nonresident centers are part of large corporate office complexes and are offered to the public only when the parent company is not using the facility. The IACC guidelines have a distinctly "corporate" feel to them. The guidelines strictly control the inside of the meeting rooms. The impact in variations of location would be felt less inside the classroom than it would in the supplemental activities the delegates would partake of when not in meetings. Suburban and rural conference centers routinely feature high-quality golf courses, while the more urban centers would link to cultural and sporting activities located in the city centers. Some of the more rural facilities offer horseback riding or outdoor activities like hiking or skiing in season.

When choosing a conference center, a planner should review not only the facilities offered by the center but the expectations of the delegates attending the event. A nonresident facility might be better if all the delegates are local. A rural facility might be better if the delegates have a tendency to slip away at midday when they should be in classes. A review of the event's history is important in determining if a conference center will work for the event.

Like hotels, corporations generally own conference centers, although some are closely held family businesses. They are not government entities. Therefore, they operate more like hotels than like conventions centers except that their meeting spaces are focused almost exclusively on classroom-style education. Conference centers can also have seasonal patterns much like hotels. A conference center located in the midst of several ski slopes will be much less expensive in the summer than it will be in the winter. A conference center located in an urban area may be the same price year-round. If the event dates are flexible, moving a week or a month could yield significant savings.

Conference centers using the complete meeting package tend to be entirely self-contained. If outside vendors are used, they will likely be transparent to the planner. By using the complete meeting package concept, the facility ties all its revenue into a single bundle of services. The only variable is the number of delegates who actually show up as opposed to those who register.

Attrition takes on a new meaning in a conference center. It is not unusual for a conference center to charge a planner a fixed price for up to a certain number of delegates. If some of the delegates do not come to the event, the planner is still responsible for the full amount of the contract. This fee is not based on the ability of the facility to resell the rooms. It is based on 100% of the negotiated facility fee regardless how much of the facility is used. Although the planner's tasks on site are less intense than would be the case in a convention center, the planner's ability to predict room night use is very critical.

Thus, the meeting, exposition, event, or convention planner must "research, understand, communicate, and verify" that the venue meets the needs of the group.

RETREAT FACILITIES

Retreat facilities can be viewed as a special group, much like rural conference centers. They are more likely to be owned by a family or closely held corporation than the other facilities and have focused on a smaller portion of the conference center market. Not-for-profit entities, charitable organizations, or religious groups own many of the retreat facilities. Several evangelical organizations run retreat facilities as part of their internal training programs. Other groups can use these facilities when the parent organization is not using them. In addition to the classroom learning typical of a conference center, retreat facilities specialize in some unique extracurricular learning opportunities. Some retreat facilities are at dude ranches. Some are clusters of cabins in the woods where nature is part of the lesson plan. Others are attached to religious facilities where a spiritual message is incorporated into the program. Many planners, out of fear that their delegates may not appreciate the opportunities presented by the unique environment, can unjustly overlook retreat facilities.

These unique meeting environments can be used as a stimulus to energize a moribund group of delegates. The challenge to using these facilities derives from one of their greatest strengths—their relative isolation. Transportation and logistical issues become magnified due to the distance from airports and highways. These impediments can be overcome, and the result can be well worth the effort.

Thus, the meeting, exposition, event, or convention planner must "research, understand, communicate, and verify" that the venue meets the needs of the group.

CRUISE SHIPS

In a sense, cruise ships are floating hybrids of retreat centers, conference centers, and full-service resorts. To leave it there, however, would be to do them a disservice. Cruise ships seem underrated as meeting venues, but with proper planning, they can provide a satisfying meeting experience.

Cruise ship meeting rooms are indistinguishable from those found in a hotel.
Photo by George G. Fenich, Ph.D., Professor, School of HRTA, University of New Orleans

The quality of the planning for a cruise event has a greater impact on the success of the meeting than it does with any other type of venue. A ship moves by its own schedule that could have more to do with the tides than it does the ability of a group of guests to be at the dock on time. Failure to properly accommodate the ship's schedule into the transportation plan can have disastrous results. Unlike a building concreted into the ground, once the ship leaves port, latecomers are left behind.

Cruise ships have long been considered ideal venues for incentive trips. There are few options available to a planner that can provide as romantic an ambiance as a cruise ship. However, romantically inclined couples often have children attached. Many of the cruise lines have well-developed children's programs. In fact, the children's programs on many of the ships are better developed than in many major resorts. As for the singles, the larger ships have options for them as well.

The size and availability of meeting rooms varies widely among the different ships. Meeting planners should not look only at the spaces on the ship identified as "meeting facilities" to the exclusion of other spaces. Many of the larger ships have extensive theaters and lounge facilities that, depending on the size of the group, can be reserved for the group's exclusive use. These spaces can provide the facilities needed for the business and educational parts of the meeting.

Many cruise lines offer complete meeting packages in the same way as conference centers do. These complete packages routinely include everything except the bar tab and taxes. By carefully working with the ship's technical staff, it is possible that the entire meeting's technical needs can be accommodated with the on-board equipment. In many ways, this is no different from working with a conference center.

Cruise lines market "special interest" cruises. Some of the riverboats offer "fall foliage" cruises. Whale watch cruises and special music cruises are also available. One cruise that may present an opportunity for an unusual incentive is the "migration" cruise. Cruise ships migrate like the birds, and the cruise, as the ship changes its base of operations, could be a unique experience.

The relative isolation of many conference and retreat centers is one of their greatest strengths as meeting facilities. A ship at sea can be even more isolated. A meeting held while the ship is under way will have a different attendance pattern than the same meeting held when the ship is in port. Schedule planning coordinated with the ship's schedule can have a significant impact on a meeting's attendance. One issue many meeting planners face is keeping the delegates in the meetings. Hotels adjacent to casinos and theme parks are notorious for having low delegate attendance at the sessions. On a ship at sea, out of range of cell phones and pagers, a meeting that requires perfect attendance could have a greater opportunity for success than in many competing facilities.

Many planners overlook ships as meeting facilities except for incentive trips, but that shortchanges the potential of these mobile meeting venues. The meeting, exposition, event, or convention planner must "research, understand, communicate, and verify" that the venue meets the needs of the group.

SPECIFIC USE FACILITIES

Theaters, **amphitheaters**, **arenas**, stadiums, and sports facilities tend to be underused as meeting facilities but, depending on the needs of the meeting, they can support a variety of events. Spectacular and impressive events can be planned for any facility designed for public assembly.

An unusual venue for a hospitality event.
Used by permission of Paradise Light & Sound, Orlando, Florida

Most of these facilities are focused on events for the general (ticket-buying) public, and a closed event for an invited audience can be a welcome change for their staff. Even though the front-office staff might welcome the meeting planner, the planner needs to carefully determine that sufficient house and technical staff will be available to support the event. Entertainment events generally occur on evenings and weekends. It is not unusual for the usher staff to be people for whom this is a second job, or in the case of those who are available during the day, retirees. The availability and demographics of the staff may or may not be an issue for any given event, but it should be discussed with the facility management prior to contracting the event.

Like convention centers, these facilities are almost always owned by government agencies or are public–private partnerships. Nonprofit foundations own some, but corporations own few. They are like convention centers in the amount of planning required to use them. They are unlike convention centers in that while dealing with large numbers of people is their greatest skill, meetings are not their primary business. Depending on the facility's public event schedule, long rehearsal and setup times may not be available. If a facility has a resident sports team that might go into post-season play, the management might be reluctant to confirm space availability more than a few weeks in advance.

Finances in a special use facility can be a hybrid between the practices of the convention center and the practices of the conference center. There is generally a fixed fee for the use of the facility and a specific subset of its equipment and services. "Normal" cleanup, comparable to a public event, would likely be included in the facility rental fee. The facility would probably require a minimum level of staff for which there would be an hourly charge based on a minimum number of hours. All other labor, equipment, and services would be exactly like a convention center on a bill-per-item system.

Among the specific use facilities, theaters can be ideal meeting facilities. They come equipped with comfortable chairs arranged in sweeping curved rows for maximum comfort. They have lighting positions and sound systems built in, and they have staffs that know how to use them. If the delegates are local, they probably know where the theater is and do not need directions. The stages are designed for acoustics and the seats arrayed to enhance visibility. One of the ironies of this industry relates to the amount of time and energy expended converting hotel ballrooms into theaters and how few meetings are done in theaters.

On the surface, it would seem that the better technically equipped a theater is, the more of the theater's equipment the meeting's support team would use and the less it would need to bring in. This, however, is not usually the case. In many theaters, any equipment that is moved must be restored to its "found" location. The economics of that policy works if the equipment's found location is in a storeroom somewhere out of the way. Where the policy does not work is when the equipment's found location is in an "in-use" position. The cost of putting the equipment back to its in-use location can be greater than merely removing the rental equipment and packing it in a truck for the run back to the warehouse. This is especially true of lighting and projection. It is less true of audio. If the theater has custom draperies for the stage, those will be used because finding replacement drapes of the correct sizes can be difficult.

Another issue with using the in-house equipment has to do with reliability. Many theaters, particularly educational and community theaters, are not funded to the point where their equipment can be considered properly maintained or reliable. A lighting designer, unsure of the condition of the installed equipment, would likely import his or her own rather than take a risk.

Although all the facilities are sensitive to legal issues such as the ADA, the venues that support a lot of entertainment are more likely to be concerned with copyright laws than other facilities would be. Music is of particular concern. All music must be licensed unless it is specifically written for meeting use and the rights sold for that purpose. Copyrighted graphics must be licensed. Clip art is not necessarily in the public domain for convention use. The art might only be licensed for print use or nonprofit use. The license information is included in the original documentation that came with the material. Entertainment venues are more likely to demand to see proof of music licenses than other venues because, under the copyright laws of 1978, if a venue fails to ensure that copyright laws are enforced, they can be shut down.

Catering in a specific use facility may require more planning than in some other venues. Given that the venue's primary revenue sources are based on ticketed events, they would probably have a well-developed concessions operation, but they may or may not have as well-developed catering capabilities. Menu selection could be an issue, depending on the scope of the meeting. The kitchen equipment, intended for a concessions environment, may or may not be capable of supporting the menu needs of a meeting.

Examples of Copyright Abuses

One well-known American consumer products corporation suddenly became a major sponsor of a well-known children's television show as a result of an out-of-court settlement. The producers of the show caught the corporation using its music and characters as part of their promotional materials without having first secured permission. Another not-so-well-known corporation had its several hundred thousand dollar video presentations cut in half. The presentations included scenes pirated from videotapes and "broadcasts," which included the corporation's products and logos in the same images with very well known cartoon characters and the characters' parent company's logos. While the confrontations for both of these actual examples occurred in hotels, entertainment venues are more likely to research licensing on contract rather than waiting until later.

In stadiums and arenas, the concession operation may not support the menu needs of a meeting.

Source: Pearson Education/PH College

Entertainment venues range in size from huge outdoor stadiums to hole-in-the-wall nightclubs. Planners who wish to use these venues can be successful if they are careful to remember that entertainment and not meetings are the venue's primary business and that services considered standard in a hotel or convention center may not exist in an entertainment venue.

Thus, the meeting, exposition, event, or convention planner must "research, understand, communicate, and verify" that the venue meets the needs of the group.

COLLEGES AND UNIVERSITIES

It would seem that since colleges and universities devote all their energies to education and research, they should be ideal meeting facilities. Some are, but it is important for a planner to remember that while meetings bring often badly needed cash to an educational institution, most colleges are not set up for major meetings, and their staffs may not be as adept at responding to immediate meeting needs as a full-time meeting facility might be. The planner using an academic facility needs to investigate and coordinate well down into the institution's organizational structure. It is not sufficient to discuss with the person in alumni relations who booked the use of the faculty center after hours to ensure that the lawn sprinklers have, in fact, been turned off for the evening. The planner must verify such details directly with the department responsible.

The impact of seasonality on hotels and other meeting facilities is moderate compared to the impact of seasonality on most academic facilities. During summer vacation, most college campuses turn into ghost towns. A vacant college campus could provide an effective meeting site. The planner who wishes to use a college campus for a large meeting may have to make some extra logistical arrangements. College classrooms are generally open and airy with plenty of light, but they are not known for comfortable furniture. A student chair with a writing arm may be acceptable for a twenty-something, but it may not be acceptable for a forty-something. College dorms have beds and the rooms are generally arranged along hallways like hotels, but that is where the similarities end. College dorm rooms have single beds instead of doubles or queens, and most of those are over length so standard linen does not fit. It would probably be a good idea to contract with the college's linen service to provide bed linen and towels.

While many dorm rooms are singles, the majority are doubles. The process of arranging and processing roommate assignments can be a full-time job. If the meeting is large, it might be a good idea to hire an intern for this task. Another issue sometimes overlooked is that dorms generally have bathrooms shared among several rooms. While that might be appropriate for groups of high school and college athletes, it would likely not be acceptable for a meeting of professionals like doctors or stockbrokers. Newer dorms and some recently renovated dorms have elevators, but many older dorms still do not have ADA-compatible access to upper floors. Considerable savings can be realized using college campuses, particularly if the college's athletic facilities are part of the meeting plan; however, not all meetings will work in this environment.

Many meeting planners have less-than-fond memories of college food. With the advent of professional food service management companies operating many college food service operations, the food quality in many campuses has improved considerably. Planners should be aware, however, that a college dining hall would never be elegant. Equally important is that the quality of the food served is a direct result of the budget available. The quality of the college food that the planner may wish to forget is more likely a function of a small budget than a function of inadequate kitchen capabilities. With an adequate budget, the planner can provide high-quality meals in an academic environment.

College art museums and student centers can provide interesting and exciting locations for meetings. The art museums provide especially interesting opportunities for conversations that can enhance a "networking" event. All of the delegates to the event probably will have opinions on the art that surrounds them, and this art can be the link that motivates strangers to converse. One common mistake planners make when using art centers is the tendency to redecorate them. Without spending a lot of money, it is unlikely that the planner can provide more impressive décor than what the museum's galleries already offer. If the planner feels the need to engage in a massive redecorating project, it might well be that the art museum is not the correct venue for the event.

The art centers and theaters at colleges and universities have a unique attribute that many planners and most of the general public frequently overlook. Unlike the staff in the majority of meeting and special event venues, the venue is not just a job. It is a passion. The people who run these facilities on a daily basis take great pride in and care deeply about the condition of the building and its contents. This is not to say that people in other venues do not care. They do, but not with the intensity or even obsession that the academic theater and art people demonstrate. Any planner who intends to use one of these facilities must understand the sensitivities involved. Equally important, they must convey this message to their own staffs. The traveling staff (mere "transients" in the eyes of the permanent staff) must be sensitive to the fact that in spite of the large amount of money they will be spending on this event, they are visitors and not necessarily even welcome guests. It is entirely likely that the budget for this one event is greater than the resident staff's monthly or even annual budget, and some jealousies may arise.

If a planner and, even more importantly, the technical staff are willing to treat the facility's full-time staff with deference and courtesy, the financial savings can be significant. If, however, either side becomes adversarial, the costs will skyrocket. Managing vendors is always important, but in this case the financial impact of not managing both the "visiting" team and the "home" team is critical. One of the issues that frequently smolders in the background is the belief on the part of the facility's staff (particularly the technical staff) that they could have executed this event as well as the traveling team. That may or may not be true, but until the perception is dispelled, it can cause unnecessary friction. If the local team can properly service the event, they should be given a hand in it. If not, it is worth the time to explain to them why an outside team is being brought in. This will be less of a problem in a facility accustomed to dealing with touring shows than one that only mounts its own shows from within its own department.

How does one win the support of the local crew? Feeding them helps. Talking to them about the plans for the event helps. Explaining the goal of the event helps. In short, in a university situation, treating the in-house people more like members of the team than merely vendors will reap financial rewards far beyond their cost. Properly managed, an event in an academic environment can be financially effective for the sponsoring organization and emotionally stimulating for the delegates, but the planning burden is entirely on the visiting meeting planner and their staff.

Thus, the meeting, exposition, event, or convention planner must "research, understand, communicate, and verify" that the venue meets the needs of the group.

UNUSUAL VENUES

Meeting planners continually insist on having meetings in places never designed for meetings. Flight aprons, airplane hangars, remote islands, nature preserves, city parks, open meadows, and athletic fields are all used routinely. Perhaps the most common of these unusual venues is a large tent in a parking lot. All of these venues have more in common with each other than they have differences.

None of these venues has support equipment. Virtually everything needed for the event must be brought in. The venues have little or no staff. In addition to all the normal concerns a planner needs to deal with for an event, the planner will need to provide all the support services normally considered the purview of the facility. Such services could include portable restrooms, parking, and trash removal. Weather is an issue in any outdoor venue, but that is no different than would be the case with a pool party at a hotel.

One challenge that frequently catches planners by surprise is obtaining permits. Many local governments require permits to use parks or even private property for special events. Failure to procure the proper permits can lead to an event being shut down at the last moment. Not only must the police and fire department be notified, but in many places the building

A large tent event.
Used by permission of Paradise Light & Sound, Orlando, Florida

code office must be notified as well. Tents must usually be inspected by the fire department. In some areas, generators are under the purview of the fire department; in others, there is a special office that deals with electrical issues. This office may be part of building and zoning or may be part of a designated special events office.

Airport facilities have the additional issue of heightened security. More stringent security measures have been implemented than ever before. Failure to conform to the security procedures can be detrimental to the event. For those planners who need an aeronautical theme, an airplane museum would likely be a better choice than a working airport. Political rallies are sometimes held at airports just as they used to be held at railroad stations in previous elections. The constant noise of the aircraft in the background does give the impression of excitement, but it can also obscure important parts of a candidate's speech. The quality of the sound system, too often the last item considered, is vitally important to success of the event.

Tents routinely show up as meeting venues. Tents fall into three categories: pole, frame, and clear span. An open-sided pole or **frame tent** set up on the grass is one of the simplest of all meeting venues. It requires little advance planning beyond making sure the tent rental people can get set up in time. Permits are required in many jurisdictions. Weather is a factor, but adding tent sides and air conditioning can reduce the impact of weather. The tent may require a floor so that rain drainage flows under the floor and not over the feet of the people in the tent. Lighting or decorating a tent can be a challenge. To hang lighting in a **pole tent** requires special brackets to attach the lights to the poles if the poles are sturdy enough to support them. To support the lighting from the floor on boom stands or truss towers may be a better plan in a pole tent.

Clear span tents have a strong roof structure, and it is possible to hang lighting from the beams by using special clamps. Since the purpose of the tent is to create a meeting space where none previously existed, other support services like power, water, and restrooms may also not exist. They will have to be brought in. If lighting is to be hung in a clear span tent, the lighting should be hung before the floor is put in, since many of the tent floors will not support the scissor lifts used by the lighting and décor people during setup.

All unusual venues share the lack of support and equipment. All of them have heightened challenges with security and logistics, but some venues have additional, unique challenges.

Tent décor.
Used by permission of Paradise Light & Sound, Orlando, Florida

Access to the meeting site is an issue in some remote locations. One perfectly delightful special event venue in Park City, Utah, is only accessible via horse-drawn sleigh and then only in the winter. Another venue is in a park not far from Orlando, where the only access to the island where events are held is via a wooden bridge that is not strong enough to support a vehicle and its slatted wooden deck makes it impossible to roll catering carts. When Disney's Discovery Island was still being used as a special event venue, the only way to bring material to the island was on a float barge. The water was too shallow for anything larger to dock. There are many stories about the "**amp rack** that almost got away" on the trip to the island. There are unconfirmed rumors that one amp rack did get away and still rests on the bottom of Bay Lake.

Access can be an issue even if there are roads directly to the area. Some roads flood in the rainy season. Others are impassable in the winter. Even if the road is substantial enough to support the delivery trucks, is there a dock where it can be unloaded, or will a forklift be needed? If a forklift is needed, who supplies the driver?

One would think that outdoor sports arenas with their large arrays of seats or bleachers would be easy venues in which to work, and while they are easier to deal than many outdoor venues in that they come with restrooms, they present their own challenges. The irrigation systems for the landscaping at professional or competition fields are fragile enough that driving heavy loads over them can break the piping beneath the surface. Some venues prohibit anything heavier than a golf cart. Forget building a stage on a soccer field unless it is properly padded with plywood sheeting. Pushing that cart of riser tops across the grass is not likely to pass muster with the facility's head of grounds.

While the technicians have one set of challenges dealing with outdoor sports venues, caterers have another. It is not uncommon for caterers to dump the leftover ice out on the ground. This will kill the patch of grass underneath. Ice should be dumped in a storm drain, on the pavement, or in a mulched area. Portable bars are heavy and can damage the ground underneath. They need to be placed on pavement or have a sheet of plywood underneath. That plywood should only be in place a few hours or the grass underneath it will die. There are plastic flooring pieces that will distribute the weight and still allow the grass to breathe. These are preferable to the plywood if they are available. Portable bars also leak. If the water were clean, it would not be a problem. While most of the runoff is from the bars is melted ice, some of it is excess from the soft drink dispensers. This excess contains sugar, which attracts ants. The ants then dig up the grass in search of more sugar, and soon there is an anthill behind third base. The partially melted ice from the shrimp buffet must be disposed of properly. Otherwise, the smell from the shrimp will last long after the event is over.

Public parks can be beautiful venues except that they are open to the public. If the event is a public event like an art show, a public park with its regular traffic can be an ideal location. If the event is more private, especially if it involves alcohol, a public park may not be such a good idea.

THE STORY OF AN UNUSUAL EVENT

Every once in a while, a planner's job spreads beyond the limits of what most meeting planners are called on to do. Sometimes, people who are not meeting or event planners are called on to plan large events. Such was the case with the Osceola County (Florida) Arts Festival.

Osceola County's Annual Arts Festival had been run from time immemorial by a civic organization. For reasons beyond the scope of this

Osceola Art Festival, 2001.
Used by permission of Paradise Light & Sound, Orlando, Florida

text to explain, the management of the festival was transferred from this civic organization to the Osceola Center for the Arts. The festival had traditionally been held in October at the lakefront park. The festival was moderately successful, under the guidance of the civic organization, but had started to lose popularity and was suffering from the impact of increasing competition. This competition was not only from other art shows but also from events like a public air show traditionally held on the same weekend.

The show suffered from other problems. For the thirty-odd years the festival had been running, it had been rained on over half of those years. One of the "rains" was a hurricane. In addition, the park presented logistical problems for the artists getting their materials to their booths. There was a perception from the local arts community that the quality of the art in the show had deteriorated to the point where local artists were no longer interested in exhibiting. The show was clearly in trouble.

Immediately on taking the show over, the management of the Osceola Center for the Arts made two radical decisions. The festival was moved from October to mid-November, and it was moved from the lakefront park to the main street in downtown. No one had ever asked to block the main street in the center of town before, except for a couple of

(continued)

hours to do a parade. This was something of a shock. Moving the festival to November met with instant unanimous approval, but moving the festival from the park to the street seemed like an impossible dream.

When the plan was first presented to the center's board, the board was supportive of the idea but remained unconvinced that the city would be willing to block the street for that length of time. There was some resistance from within city government and from some of the downtown merchants. The process took a few months, but the city granted permission for the festival to be held on a four-block stretch of downtown Kissimmee. The advantages of the street location included much better access for the artists to set up their booths, dry pavement underfoot, a more recognizable location, and a ground plan that provided festival-goers an easier flow pattern through the booths, guaranteeing their ability to see everything easily.

The next step was to secure sponsors for the event. It would not be unreasonable to expect a professional meeting planner working on this event to be involved with the solicitation of sponsorships. The center advertised for artists and jurors. Artists were selected and sponsorships locked in.

Careful coordination was needed between the center and several city departments. Permits were obtained as required. Power was installed in the median on the main street because some of the booths needed power. The police and traffic departments were involved with rerouting traffic around downtown for the weekend. Parks and Recreation provided the portable stage and other support. City landscaping verified that the sprinklers in the median had been turned off. Several of the center's performing groups were scheduled to perform on the portable stage. The center's tech staff brought out the theater's spare sound system.

One of the greatest challenges became negotiating with the variety of food vendors. Each of the food vendors wanted the best location and an exclusive right on everything they sold. In retrospect, most of the center's people who were privy to the entire event agreed that the most difficult part of the event, surprisingly enough, was the food.

While the event was not flawless (few events are), it went pretty much as planned. Some "bugs got through the net," but none was severe. The distance the art had to be carried from the festival to the judging location was longer than was convenient. The food vendors squabbled the whole time. The detoured traffic pattern was more complex than necessary. The most severe on-site problem turned out to be an issue that a little better coordination could have prevented. One of the major sponsors was a local Internet Service Provider (ISP). In accordance with their agreement, they were given a booth space near the center of the show. They needed power for their booth. Power had been installed in the median, but not in the section of median adjacent to the booth. The ISP was demonstrating wireless connectivity and could not move once set up. Recognizing their need for power and that power was not available, they rented a generator. The diesel generator was both loud and smelly. Artists in booths all around complained bitterly from the time the generator was started. The solution was to run two very long extension cords from where the power had been installed in the median 300 feet away to the ISP's booth.

The bottom line on the festival is that it was successful. Had it been held on the weekend when it had traditionally been held, it would have been washed out by a hurricane. As it was, the weather was bright, dry, and unseasonably warm. Could it have been improved? Certainly. Would the influence of a professional meeting planner have avoided the conflicts that did occur? Probably. A professional planner would definitely have checked to verify that the power availability matched the power needs.

The following year, the festival suffered, as did the rest of the country, from the effects of the attacks on 9/11. Attendance was down from the previous year, but it was not as bad as some of the other festivals. The event changed slightly from the previous year. A single food service company was contracted to provide all the food. The food quality improved significantly. The traffic pattern was smoothed out. Other minor issues relating to the placement of the stage and the schedule of performances were changed. As before, the weather held. Both days were partly cloudy, but there was no rain. In spite of the reduced attendance, the festival was more successful than it had been before the move.

The third year following the move, the rains came. In spite of the rain, many of the artists had decent sales because the people who braved the rain came to buy and not just look. One of the biggest challenges that year was rumor control. As the inclement weather settled in to stay, various rumors about a variety of hazardous weather conditions spread like wildfire among the arts and food vendors. After spending the morning fending off the rumors, once the judges had been able to judge all the entries, the center management elected to shut down the festival for the afternoon. The following morning it reopened. While the weather did scare away much of the expected crowd, the second day went better than many people expected.

When planning an outdoor convention function, an indoor backup plan is vital to the success of the event. For an arts festival like this one, an indoor plan is simply not feasible. However, a professional planner should always recognize the potential for weather to have an impact on the event.

COMMON ISSUES

Regardless where an event is held, there are some issues that all events have in common. Many of these issues are logistic, like transporting the delegates from the airport. The following issues are common to most if not all meeting venues and most if not all meetings.

POWER IN ALL VENUES

Most outdoor special events and many events in smaller indoor venues have power requirements that exceed the power available. A generator usually provides this power, and generators are expensive. Properly anticipating the power needs is even more important in this type of event than one in a traditional meeting venue. With a generator, the planner will pay not only the daily cost to rent the generator but a fuel charge as well. The fuel consumption is determined by two factors: how long the generator runs and how much power is actually drawn from it. The fuel cost will be a multiple of the cost per gallon of the fuel, the time the generator runs, and the power consumption. The planner has control over two of the three elements in this equation.

For any meeting or special event using video or name entertainment, more than a few trade show booths or large scenic units will have special power requirements. Power is expensive. The power to run the sound system can be more expensive than the rental of the equipment. Many convention centers offer a discount if the power is requested early. The technical vendors can calculate power requirements fairly easily. If the discount for requesting power early is 30%, which is a fairly common discount, it would make sense to order 10 to 15% more power than estimated. In this way, ample power is available for less than it would have cost to place the power order after all the detailed requirements had been calculated.

Power charges are not based on consumption, but rather on the maximum amount of power deliverable at any one time. To meter the actual power consumption and charge accordingly is illegal in many states. This

Diesel electric generators are used as power sources for many MEEC events.
Source: AGCO Corporation

would make the facility a utility company and subject to rates regulation. It would appear that generator use is charged based on power consumption, but it is actually based on fuel consumption. A generator that is idling uses fuel even if it is supplying no power. Turning a generator off when it is not needed will save money.

RIGGING IN ALL VENUES

Plaster ceilings are a production rigger's worst nightmare. Precast concrete roofs with no steel underneath run a close second. Any event involving more than a few hundred people or video image magnification (IMAG) should involve lighting suspended from the ceiling. Unless the facility is unusually well equipped for lighting from ceiling positions, lighting must be accomplished by hanging trusses, and hanging trusses involves rigging. Theaters are generally adequately equipped for lighting without hanging trusses. The Gaylord Palms Osceola Ballroom is equipped with lighting equipment but only on the stage. The WDW Coronado Springs Resort

A lighting grid in a sports arena.
Used by permission of Paradise Light & Sound, Orlando, Florida

has adequate tracks and dimmers in the ceiling for many meetings, but the larger ones still need additional support. If the video must cover more than a single podium or a stage larger than 8 feet by 12 feet, no convention hotel in Orlando, other than the Gaylord Palms and Disney's Coronado Springs, is adequately equipped for lighting support without using lighting from trusses suspended from the ceiling.

The hotel's contracted rigging company will require all floor plans not less than two weeks in advance of the event. While it would seem that two week's lead time on a floor plan should be simple for an event contracted a year in advance, it turns out to be a challenge many planners cannot accommodate. In some jurisdictions, the fire marshal, building code inspector, or safety officer can refuse to allow a show to be hung without a detailed hanging plot. Having to ground a show at the last minute due to failure to submit paperwork can be a career-ending mistake.

Most facilities contract rigging to an outside company for liability protection in addition to the normal reasons one would outsource any task that the facility management may not have enough experience to supervise properly. Given that the riggers' normal job description involves hanging "live loads" over the heads of the general public, they take their work seriously. This sometimes obstructionist attitude is intended to keep people safe and is not meant to impede the event. Adequate advance notification of schedules and requirements can help ensure that the event is hung properly and on schedule.

FLOORS IN ALL VENUES

It is not safe to assume that just because the building has a ground level loading door big enough to drive a tractor-trailer through that once through the door the floor will support it. Even though the floor is made of 4 inches of steel-reinforced concrete on the ground, the utility boxes in the floor may not be so well designed. One Orlando area facility dug up and repoured the concrete around several of the floor pockets because the constant forklift traffic drove them into the ground. It is not safe to assume that a certain size scissor lift can be brought into the ballroom. As part of the site inspection,

Load out for a large trade show.
Used by permission of Paradise Light & Sound, Orlando, Florida

for events where these issues are relevant, the planner must ask about the floor load because the information is rarely readily available.

Ballrooms are carpeted. Exhibit halls are not. Many hotels insist that plastic sheeting be placed over the ballroom carpet during the move-in and move-out process. If the facility has such a requirement, it is important that the Exposition Services Contractor (ESC) and all technical vendors know about it in advance.

Many academic theaters have polished wood floors on the stages. Nailing or screwing into them is not recommended and is generally a fast way to be refused the use of the venue in the future. These floors are not designed for heavy loads like scissors lifts or forklifts. Staffing and equipment requirements may need to be adjusted to compensate.

ACCESS IN ALL VENUES

Not only must the delegates be able to find the venue and its entrance, but the technical support and catering people need to gain access as well. The design of the loading access can have a significant impact on an event's finances. There is a facility in south Florida where the only loading access to the ballroom is to back a truck along a sea wall for a hundred yards. A 21-foot truck will not make the corner. A 17-foot truck will. The closest a tractor-trailer can park is a quarter mile away. An event whose technical support equipment is shipped on a tractor-trailer would need to be unloaded off site and the equipment trucked in to the loading dock using a smaller truck at considerable additional expense.

The presence of truck height docks is not enough to guarantee smooth loading. Some facilities, including the WDW Dolphin and the Gaylord Palms, have elevators from the docks to the ballroom. Access to the theater at the Orange County Convention Center involves two elevators and a push down the hall between them. The number and location of the docks is significant. The only Orlando-area major convention hotels with adequate dock space are the Gaylord Palms (in spite of the elevator) and Marriott's Orlando World Center. One would think that the Orange County Convention Center, with half a mile of continuous dock space, would have adequate loading capabilities, but even that fills up on some events, as incredible as it seems. On the other hand, the Morial Convention Center in New Orleans is all on one level, with loading docks lining one entire side of the building.

◆ SUMMARY

RECOMMENDATIONS FOR DEALING WITH ALL VENUES

Accurate information is essential to successful meetings. Detailed and thorough research is the first step in the process. This first step is much easier now than it has been and promises to become even easier. The Internet and World Wide Web provide planners powerful resources with which to plan their events. Many of the best meeting facilities have extensive Web sites with volumes of information available. Some venues have 360-degree visual imaging that allows a planner to view the facility remotely. This technology is becoming more and more affordable and common. Before calling a sales representative, a planner should visit the facility's Web site and print out everything that might be of interest. Once having studied the material and determining that the facility may be appropriate for the event, then, and only then, should the planner call the facility's salespeople to open the dialogue.

The most important component of dealing with any facility is the development of an open, honest, and trusting relationship with all the parties involved. Unfortunately, there are facilities that will take advantage of that relationship, just as there are planners who do not deal honestly with their suppliers. In spite of the risks involved, the attempt must be made because the success of every event depends on the interaction between the planner and all the other parties involved. This relationship begins with understanding what each of the participants brings to the relationship and what each needs.

Communication begins with a set of requirements. The more accurate the requirements can be, the better. It is important to note, however, that "accurate" and "detailed" are not the same thing. On contract, the hotel needs to know how many people are coming, but they do not need the names until relatively close to the event. Accurate and timely listings of requirements are the first step in developing a successful relationship. Verification of the documentation returned by the venue is the other half of this communication. Not only should the planner provide requirements, but also the venue should reply and acknowledge that it understands the requirements and how it will fulfill each requirement as appropriate.

The key to working with any venue is fourfold: research, understand, communicate, verify. Research, understand, communicate, verify. Repeat until done! This chapter provides information that can be used by meeting planners in the first two steps of the process. The rest is what separates the best planners from the others.

KEY WORDS AND TERMS

For definitions, refer to http://glossary.conventionindustry.org.

Amenities

Amp rack

Amphitheater

Arena

Attrition

Ballroom

Boardroom

Break-out room

Clear span tent

Complete meeting package

Concessionaire

Destination management company (DMC)

Exhibit hall

Frame tent

Hotel

Local social

Loss leader

Pole tent

Prefunction space

Seasonality

Shoulder

Stadium

Theater

REVIEW AND DISCUSSION QUESTIONS

1. What is the single most important thing a planner can provide a venue to ensure the effective and cost-efficient execution of a meeting?
2. What is attrition, and why should a planner care?
3. What is the most significant single difference between a hotel's meeting space and a convention center's meeting space?
4. What is the most important single activity facility personnel depend on the meeting planner to provide?
5. How is the financial structure of a hotel different from that of other facilities? What is a hotel's biggest source of revenue? A convention center's?
6. Why is seasonality important to a planner?
7. Why is ceiling height significant?
8. Why should a meeting planner care about copyright laws?
9. What should be a planner's greatest concern on an outdoor event? What should a planner do about it?

ABOUT THE CHAPTER CONTRIBUTOR

Bob Cherny has spent almost his entire career on the facility side of the meetings industry. As an undergraduate in theater at Brandeis, he served as a student assistant supporting facility activities. During graduate school at the University of South Carolina, he was scene shop foreman and was responsible for the proper operation of the theater. Bob spend twenty years at the Tupperware Convention Center, starting as technical director and ending as general manager. The Tupperware Convention Center was Orlando's first full-time convention center, and until competing facilities opened, it was a pioneer in the meetings industry.

After leaving Tupperware, Bob went to Disney Event Productions, where he provided technical and facility support for clients in several of Disney's Orlando-area hotels. Bob then went to Paradise Sound & Light, supporting meeting planners in their use of meeting facilities. Bob's most recent move to the Osceola Heritage Park in Kissimmee, Florida, managed by SMG, puts him back in a building where he has an impressive array of facility services available to provide for meeting planners' needs.

◆5

EXHIBITIONS

Trade shows are used throughout the world to promote products and companies. This one takes place in Chang Rai, Thailand.

Photo by George G. Fenich, Ph.D., Professor, School of HRTA, University of New Orleans

◆ Chapter Objectives

The chapter provides the reader with an understanding of the following:

- Definitions of the types of exhibitions
- The exhibition model
- Types of exhibition facilities
- Types of exhibition programs
- How exhibition management companies operate
- The role of exhibitors
- Fundamentals of exhibition planning
- Exhibit design principles
- How exhibitors can maximize exhibition return on investment
- How exhibitors work with exhibition management and service companies

◆ Chapter Outline

THE COMDEX TRADE SHOW

Every November, over 2,000 exhibiting companies and over 120,000 visitors converge on Las Vegas, Nevada, for the annual global technology trade show called COMDEX. In the two weeks prior to the show, over 3 million square feet of empty **exhibition** space is converted into a high-tech showplace, complete with high-speed Internet access for thousands of computers and multilevel exhibits that look like they are permanent fixtures.

State of the art technology exhibit.
Source: Dorling Kindersley Media Library

When COMDEX opens to great fanfare, visitors flood the aisles and engage exhibitors with a myriad of questions about their products, services, pricing, and events. The hotels, restaurants, and casinos of Las Vegas are full of visitors and their families from around the world. Late into the night, companies sponsor events and hospitality suites to keep the conversations going with their potential customers. Breakfasts and lunches are heavily attended because industry leaders give keynote addresses.

Behind the scenes, the organizing company is solving hundreds of problems as they arise. Hotels are hosting private events by organizations and companies that are lavishing perks on their best customers. Exhibit managers for companies are frantically searching for lost deliveries of packages and keeping track of hundreds of leads, not to mention ensuring the exhibit staff are in the right place at the right time. Service contractors are responding to the demands of exhibitors and the organizer. Media personnel are searching out the new products that will make resounding profits in the coming year.

Then, when the show ends, there are immediate scrambles. The carpet begins to come up, and exhibitors frantically pack up all their belongings as service contractors dismantle the exhibits. Cabs are at a premium as thousands try to get to the airport at the same time. Within a few days, COMDEX is a memory, and the exhibit space is empty once again. Hopefully, however, exhibitors will continue their follow-ups to turn leads into sales and products into publicity. The organizing company will immerse itself into what it can do better next year, and attendees are back at work with more knowledge of the industry than they had a few weeks before.

INTRODUCTION

With over 13,000 **trade shows** and exhibitions annually in North America alone, the long history of exhibitions has turned into a thriving, ever-changing industry. This chapter provides an overview of the industry and looks at it from the perspective of organizers, attendees, and exhibitors.

HISTORY

Trade fairs began in Europe in the Middle Ages, if not before. They began when craftsmen and farmers started bringing their products to the

Interior of Amsterdam RAI in Holland with Trade Fair in progress.
Source: Dorling Kindersley Media Library

center of the town or city to meet their potential customers. These were the beginnings of the "public" trade fair, and this type of interaction between producers and buyers continues today in the crafts and food industries.

Eventually, the business-to-business industries realized the value of meeting, sharing information, and providing previews of their products to potential customers. This buyer–seller format was termed an *exhibition* and typically took place in a large city at a facility built specifically for the exhibition. This part of the industry blossomed in the late 1800s, with many facilities being built strictly for world-class exhibitions. For example, the Crystal Palace in London was opened for the "Great Industrial Exhibition of All Nations." In the United States, facilities were opened in Chicago and Philadelphia to commemorate "world's fairs" that, in reality, were trade shows highlighting the industrial advances of participating countries.

In the early and mid-twentieth century, trade associations grew and saw the potential of trade shows being held in conjunction with their annual meetings as a way to stimulate communication in the industry and expand their revenues gained from the annual meeting. As the trade shows grew, it became imperative that trade associations outsourced the management of their trade show business to outside companies—thus the growth of trade show management companies and service providers.

DEFINITIONS

To set the stage for the remainder of this chapter, a review of current definitions is in order.

A trade show is typically a business-to-business event. The exhibitor is usually a manufacturer or distributor of products or services specific or complementary to those industries. Often, attendance is restricted to buyers from the industry, and business credentials are required for registration. Educational programs may or may not be a part of the trade show program, although in recent years educational programs have expanded as a method of attracting attendees. Sponsorship or management of the trade show is usually either under the auspices of a trade association or has evolved to come under the sponsorship of a management company. Some trade shows are the result of initiatives by companies and are fully intended to be profit-making ventures. Usually, trade shows are annual events, although some occur more frequently and others less frequently. Major organizations may also have regional trade shows that are smaller than their regular national or international event. Examples of U.S.-based trade shows include the following (see chapter 14, on international issues, for more information on global trade shows):

- *COMDEX:* Held annually, this is the largest computer-related trade show in the United States. It is organized and managed by a private company. It offers over 2,000 exhibitors and typically has attendance of over 100,000.
- *ABA:* Held annually, it is the annual trade show for the American Booksellers Association.
- *CES:* The Consumer Electronics Show is held annually and is sponsored by the Consumer Electronics Association.
- *PITTCON:* The Pittsburgh Conference, which is held annually in various cities, is a large trade show directed toward the chemical industry.
- *NRA:* The National Restaurant Association trade show, held each year in Chicago, features over 1,700 exhibitors and 60,000 visitors. The NRA also holds a number of regional trade shows each year.

The definition of a "trade fair" has become close enough to that of a trade show that the terms are used interchangeably. The term *trade fair* is more often used outside the United States than *trade show*. Trade fairs are discussed in more detail in chapter 14, "International Issues." Although the historical definition of "exhibition" is quite different from today, this term has also evolved to mean a trade show or trade fair. In this chapter, we refer to trade shows and exhibitions interchangeably.

Consumer or **public shows** are expositions that are open to the public. This type of show is used by a consumer-based industry to bring their goods directly to their market's end user. Show management may or may not charge an admission fee, and attendance is usually not restricted. Types of consumer shows include:

- Automobile shows
- Sporting goods shows
- Recreation shows
- Travel destination shows
- Computer-related shows
- Garden and home maintenance shows

Automobile show.

Source: PhotoEdit

Consumer shows are often regional in nature, with exhibitors traveling from city to city with their displays and products. They also provide excellent opportunities for companies to brand or test market new products.

The term **exposition** has also evolved to be similar in meaning to trade show. An association meeting may include an exposition, or expo. This is the trade show segment of the association's annual gathering.

ORGANIZATION OF THE EXHIBITION

EXHIBITION MODEL

We now discuss a general exhibition model (see figure on p. 151) that provides an overview of how all the components of a trade show or exhibition come together to accomplish the objectives of each stakeholder.

As can be seen in the figure, the exhibition management company (organizer) is the center of the exhibition model. Although it may be a trade association, or a company subcontracted to a trade association, it may also be a separate company organizing the trade show as a profit-making

The Exhibition Model

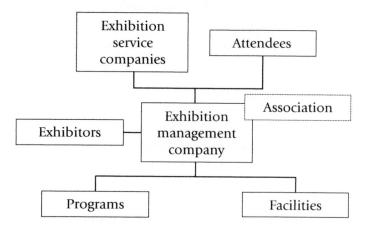

venture. The organizing company is responsible for all aspects of the trade show. Think of it as the "systems integrator" responsible for implementing the show, marketing it to buyers and sellers, and gathering together all the resources needed for success.

Buyers and sellers are also key parts of the exhibition model. Typically, sellers are the exhibitors, and buyers are the attendees. For success, the correct buyers must attend the trade show and bring sufficient business to the exhibitors (sellers) so they will continue to exhibit at subsequent trade shows.

Service contractors are the element that makes the trade show work. They supply personnel, materials, and services to the organizer, buyers, and sellers.

Obviously, facilities are needed to conduct the trade show. Facilities range from small hotels with conference centers to megaconvention centers, such as those in Las Vegas, Chicago, and Orlando. Facilities also include adjacent lodging and entertainment facilities that are used by the exhibitors and visitors.

To be profitable, the show organizer must find the right mix of buyers, sellers, service contractors, and facilities.

FACILITIES

Meeting and convention facilities have kept pace with the growth of the industry. From small, regional facilities to megaconvention centers located in major cities, regions have understood the benefits of attracting trade shows and conventions to their area. The chart that follows shows some of the largest convention centers and their plans for expansion.

The trade show organizer must take into account a number of factors in selecting the correct facility. These include:

- Facility size
- Facility amenities, including telecommunications, dining, setup, and teardown times
- Availability of service contractors
- Preferences of exhibitors
- Preferences of attendees
- Logistical considerations, such as airline service, local transportation
- Cost
- Lodging and entertainment resources in the area

Convention Center Growth

CENTER	CURRENT CAPACITY (square feet)	UNDER CONSTRUCTION (square feet)	COMPLETED CAPACITY (square feet)
Las Vegas Convention Center, Las Vegas, NV	2.0 million	918,000	2.9 million
McCormick Place, Chicago, IL	2.2 million	800,000	3.0 million
Stephens Convention Center, Rosemont, IL	700,000	140,000	840,000
Orange County Convention Center, Orlando, FL	1.1 million	1.0 million	2.1 million
Georgia World Congress Center, Atlanta, GA	950,000	500,000	1.45 million

Examples of current convention center expansion. Expansion of facilities of all sizes continues at an unprecedented rate.

Hotels are also investing in larger exhibit areas and expanding their conference centers. They must be considered as alternatives to convention centers for smaller trade shows.

PROGRAMS

The trade show management company must also consider the types of programs offered in addition to the trade show itself. Trade show programs have evolved to encompass additional programs that serve to boost attendance. Programs to consider include:

- Educational programs
- Entertainment programs
- Availability of exhibitor programs
- Special sections on the trade show floor for emerging companies, new exhibitors, or new technologies
- Celebrity or industry-leader speakers
- Meal programs
- Continuing education units (CEUs) or certifications for educational programs
- Spouse and children programs
- Internet access and e-mail centers

EXHIBITION SERVICES CONTRACTORS

As mentioned, **exhibition service contractors** (ESCs) provide products and services to the **exhibition management company** and exhibitors. Their services are often key to the success of a trade show. Typically, the trade show organizer will provide exhibitors with a list of authorized service contractors to select from and enable the two parties to deal directly with each other (see chapter 9, "Service Contractors," for more information).

Types of services that exhibition service contractors provide include:

- Freight handling
- Sound and audiovisual needs
- Marketing services
- Special lighting installations
- Arranging for exhibit furniture, carpet, and amenities
- Telecommunications needs
- Computer needs

Freight being unloaded in a convention center.
Used with permission of Paradise Sound & Light, Orlando, Florida

- Accessing electrical, gas, and water resources
- Floor plan layout
- Storing and warehousing materials
- Installation, maintenance, and dismantling of exhibits
- Providing models, entertainers, and additional exhibit staff as needed

Arranging and managing these services for a large show can be quite complex for the exhibition management company and exhibitors. Convention centers and management companies, and even exhibitors, have become accustomed to working with various arrangements and companies. Because the service contractors operate in a very competitive environment, they have learned that customer service, fair pricing, and responsiveness to customer needs are important. This enables organizers and exhibitors a level of comfort in relying on service contractors to take care of the problems that arise with organizing a successful trade show.

Service contractors, in conjunction with the exhibition management company, usually develop an exhibitor service manual that shows all details that an exhibitor needs to plan and implement an exhibit program for the trade show. It also includes the forms needed to order services from the service contractors and the rules and regulations of the exhibition management company, convention center or hotel, and local government.

Despite the controls and organization put in place by the exhibition management company and service contractors, disputes arise. When this occurs, it is important to get all concerned parties involved in achieving a successful resolution. The show manager is responsible for compliance of exhibitors, attendees, and service contractors to the show rules.

EXHIBITION PLANNING

LOCATION

Exhibition planners consider a number of variables when deciding on the location of the trade show or exhibition. Everyone will agree, however, that location has a major effect on attendance. Thus, a balance must be attained between location cost and the ideal attendance level.

Many organizations that conduct annual meetings and trade shows stay in the same city year after year. They have found that by doing so they can negotiate the best agreements with the local convention center and hotels and still retain the optimum attendance levels. Typically, these are association meetings that have strong educational programs and are held in an attractive site.

However, other organizations or exhibition management companies prefer to move their trade shows from city to city each year. This strategy also helps attract visitors. Not only is a different local attendance base able to attend inexpensively, but out-of-town visitors may be attracted by local tourist offerings as well.

Organizations and exhibition management companies often survey their membership or potential attendees to assess their preferences on location. The success of convention centers in cities like Las Vegas, Orlando, and San Francisco is indicative of organizations paying attention to the needs and desires of their members and potential audience. Expansion of the convention facilities in each of these cities indicates that the cities value the revenue generated by large trade shows.

MARKETING AND PROMOTION

Without exhibitors, the trade show or exhibition will not be successful. Without attendees, exhibitors will not return. Exhibition planners must pay serious attention to marketing and promotion programs that will fill their exhibition hall with both exhibitors and attendees. Regardless of the type of show, attendance is the key to success.

The most common form of marketing to potential exhibitors is advertising in trade publications. Until recently, well-established trade shows and exhibitions had little trouble marketing to potential exhibitors. The exhibit halls were full, and waiting lists of exhibitors were commonplace. However, the past few years have seen many companies downsizing their exhibit space or opting to exhibit at fewer trade shows. Management companies have now placed a renewed focus on marketing to potential exhibitors. Trade shows are now in competition for exhibitors, and exhibition management companies are working hard to retain existing exhibitors and attract new ones.

Exhibitors want to invest in a trade show or exhibition because their potential customers are in attendance. It is primarily the responsibility of the exhibition management company to target and market to the right

Free samples are a way for exhibitors to entice attendees to sample their products.
Photo by George G. Fenich, Ph.D., Professor, School of HRTA, University of New Orleans

audience. This is typically done through direct mail and advertising in trade publications. Management companies (for business-to-business trade shows) must provide programs beyond the exhibit hall that help attract visitors. Often, educational programs are provided as an incentive. Or, prominent industry leaders are hired to give keynote addresses that attract visitors. Contests, gifts, discount programs, and other tools to attract visitors have been commonplace.

Exhibitors are also involved in helping boost attendance at trade shows. Usually, they are given a number of free passes to the show that can be passed on to their best customers. Exhibitors are also encouraged to sponsor or conduct special events and to promote them to their customer base.

Public exhibitions also require promotion to be successful. Typically, public shows are marketed through advertisements in trade or local public media. Advertisements may offer discounts for purchasing early tickets or may promote special events or speakers that will attract the largest number of attendees. Promoting public exhibitions is a daunting task because the potential attending audience is so large that it requires a significant expense to reach them through print, radio, and television advertising. Producers must be confident that their investment in promotion will result in reaching the attendance objectives. Producers must also be attentive to other events that may be occurring during the time period that can affect attendance.

Another factor is weather. Unlike business-to-business trade shows with many people coming from outside the city, the public show usually is dependent on the local population for attendance. Locals will not venture out to a public show in the midst of a serious snowstorm. Thus, one episode of bad weather can drastically affect the bottom line of a show producer. The National Western Stock Show, held in Denver each January, is a good example of this. Years with extreme cold and snow greatly reduce attendance. During years of unseasonably mild weather, attendance skyrockets. The solution for the National Western Stock Show has been to extend the show to a sixteen-day period, ensuring there will be "good days" and "bad days." This has led to a more consistent overall attendance figure from year to year.

TECHNOLOGY

Advances in technology have made trade show and exhibition management, as well as exhibition itself, easier and more productive (for more information, see chapter 13, on technology). Let us look behind the scenes and see how technology has been introduced into the industry.

- The Internet has had a great impact on how trade shows and exhibitions are marketed to potential visitors. Most shows have sites that allow visitors to register online. Visitors can view exhibitor lists, review educational programs, and even make their travel arrangements online. They can also view interactive floor plans to efficiently plan their time.
- Lead retrieval systems are a great benefit to exhibitors. Systems are in place that enable the exhibit staff to "swipe" a visitor's card and get all of that person's contact information in a format that is usable on the company computer system, saving many hours of entering business card data.
- Technology is used in promoting a company's products as well. Many companies now give visitors inexpensive CD-ROMs instead of bulky brochures. The CD-ROMs can contain much more information and more elaborate presentations that the potential customer can view at his or her leisure.

HOUSING AND TRANSPORTATION

Housing and transportation are essential elements to success for any trade show. A large part of any organizer's time is spent negotiating room blocks in the host city and airline and car rental discounts for attendees and exhibitors. Recently, the trend has moved toward outsourcing housing and transportation arrangements to local convention and visitor bureaus or third-party housing vendors. Regardless of how housing and transportation issues are handled, the expectation is that they will be "transparent" to the attendee or exhibitor.

Hotel facilities are also a factor to be considered when determining the location of the trade show or exhibition. Are the local facilities adequate for the projected attendance? Are the negotiated room rates within the budget of the typical attendee or exhibitor? What is the proximity to the trade show site, and will local transportation need to be provided? What are the weather conditions of the host city during this period? Will weather affect attendance or even cancellation of the show? What are the safety issues that must be considered for attendees? What is the potential for labor

Bus transportation along many routes is necessary for a large convention.
Photo by George G. Fenich, Ph.D., Professor, School of HRTA, University of New Orleans

problems to arise in the host city or at host hotels? Do the convention center and local hotels comply with ADA requirements?

Additionally, the largest trade shows often require dedicated local ground transportation to assist visitors and exhibitors in getting from their hotels to the trade show site. When determining whether dedicated ground transportation is required, consider that safety is often the key decision point. Even if hotels are within walking distance from the convention center, the conditions of the city between the hotels and the center may dictate that it is in your best interests to provide transportation. For example, in New Orleans there are many hotels within walking distance of the convention center, but in the summer when temperature and humidity are both in the 90s, the meeting organizer is better off to provide transportation. When choosing ground transportation providers, be sure to take into account experience, availability, special services, insurance, condition of vehicles, labor contracts, and cost.

RISK MANAGEMENT AND CRISIS MANAGEMENT

Organizing a trade show or exhibition is a risky business. So is exhibiting at a trade show. If things are not done right, the trade show can become a colossal failure. Both trade show organizers and exhibitors need to consider having a risk management program. A risk management plan does the following:

- Provides the procedures for identifying potential risks.
- Quantifies each risk to determine the effect it would have if it occurs.
- Provides an assessment of each risk to determine which risks to ignore, which to avoid, and which to mitigate.
- Provides risk avoidance steps to prevent the risk from occurring.
- Provides risk mitigation steps to minimize potential costs if the risk occurs.

Always keep in mind that a trade show or exhibition is a business venture that should be given every chance to succeed. Knowing how to apply risk management principles will help ensure success.

Crisis management has also become critical to trade show organizers. A crisis is different from a risk in that it poses a critical situation that may cause danger to visitors or exhibitors. Examples of recent crises include the 9/11 attacks in New York City, riots during World Trade Organization meetings, and recent cruise ship illnesses. For example, trade shows that were under way on 9/11 were either canceled or curtailed midway through the schedule. Organizing companies suffered deep losses for these events.

Every trade show organizer should have a crisis management plan that addresses the prevention, control, and reporting of emergency situations. The plan should address the more likely types of emergencies, such as fire, food-borne illness, demonstrations, bomb threats, terrorism, and natural disasters. It should contain all procedures to be followed in the event of an emergency situation.

Consider having a crisis management team who is well versed in assessing the potential for a crisis, taking actions to prevent emergencies, and taking control should a situation occur. The crisis management team should be represented in the site selection process.

FROM THE EXHIBITORS' PERSPECTIVE

If exhibitors were not successful from a business perspective, trade shows and exhibitions would not exist. Exhibiting at trade shows or exhibitions is often a key part of a company's marketing strategy. Companies invest a significant portion of their marketing budget into trade show appearances and must see a positive return on their investment. This section of the chapter looks at the issues that face the exhibiting companies.

WHY EXHIBIT?

It is important for a company to know why it is exhibiting, and analysis of the potential reasons is a major part of planning for the trade show. Some of the reasons that companies participate in a trade show or exhibition include the following:

- Branding of their name in the industry
- Annual presentation of products to industry analysts
- New product rollout
- Opportunities to meet with potential and existing customers
- Opportunities to learn about customer needs
- Opportunities to meet with trade media
- Opportunities to learn about changes in industry trends and competitor products

It is important that companies exhibit at the right trade shows. Far too often a company analyzes its **ROI** and cannot understand why a particular trade show was not a success. Perhaps it exhibited at the show for years and recently their return has dropped. This is possibly due to not noticing a change in the trade show's theme and audience. It may no longer be an appropriate venue for the company.

Therefore, it is important that an exhibitor continually evaluate its trade show program and ensure that it is exhibiting at the right shows in order to meet its potential customers.

Determining trade show ROI is more critical than ever in determining whether a company is attending the right shows and is using the right strategy and planning techniques. Often, however, determining ROI is ignored because "we can't tell whether a sale was derived from a trade show lead or not" or

Trade show floor at the G2E convention.
Photo by George G. Fenich, Ph.D., Professor, School of HRTA, University of New Orleans

WHY COMPANIES EXHIBIT

It is interesting to ask companies why they exhibit. We get many different answers to this question, but too often the answer is, "Because our competitors are there." Or, "Because we have to." Obviously, these companies do not put a lot of thought or effort into their trade show programs. When attending a show in 2001, we were amazed when one company's staff did not even show up for the first day of the show. Their competitors were busy, and the show had a maximum capacity of attendees. Their exhibit was dark and empty. What message did this send to potential customers? When asked about the situation, the company gave the answers cited above. Fortunately, when the president of the company was made aware of the situation, he initiated a complete review of their trade show program, resulting in significant improvements at future shows.

"we don't have the data to be accurate." Avoid these excuses by determining actual expenses and revenue generated by the trade show exhibit leads.

When calculating ROI, establish all the expenses that are a part of the trade show. Typical expenses include:

- Space rental
- Service contractor services (electrical, computer, etc.)
- Personnel travel, including hotel and meals
- Personnel time for nonmarketing personnel
- Customer entertainment
- Preshow mailings
- Freight charges
- Photography
- Brochure printing and shipment
- Promotional items
- Training
- Postshow mailings

One method to determine revenue from the trade show is to set a time limit on business that was the result of leads from the trade show. It is easy to maintain the lead list and determine which resulted in business; after a period of time, however, the business may very well be the result of other activities and not the trade show.

EXHIBIT DESIGN PRINCIPLES

Although exhibit design may be limited by the rules established by the exhibit management company, the constraints of the facility, or the business culture of the host country, there are some general principles we can discuss. These include selecting the right layout of the exhibit to meet your purposes; selecting the right size for your company's budget and purposes; and proper use of signage, lighting, and personnel. Exhibits and the space they occupy are a significant corporate investment, and thought must be given to these factors.

Exhibit size is a major consideration if only because of cost. The more space an exhibit occupies, the more it costs in space rental, materials, labor for setup, additional staff, and maintenance. Therefore, be sure to balance the costs with the benefits of having a larger exhibit. A larger exhibit typically means being noticed by visitors, and it creates a better impression if done

CONSUMER ELECTRONICS SHOW

Over 120,000 people attend the annual Consumer Electronics Show held each January in Las Vegas. They are presented with the largest and most elaborate exhibits that companies can offer. Panasonic, Sony, Sharp, Microsoft, and other worldwide consumer electronics companies spend millions of dollars on their exhibits, events, and staff. Usually, these megaexhibits are over 100,000 square feet and filled with elaborate areas of their latest product offerings, special entertainment, and meeting rooms. They do this because the show is attended by everyone in the consumer electronics media and buyers from all over the world. It is truly an international show. Every inch of space is used for conveying the messages that the company wants to impart to buyers, media, and investors.

well. It gives the impression that the company is in a solid financial situation and is a leader in the industry. However, the space must be used well and convey the messages that the company desires to impart to potential customers.

Companies that participate in a large number of trade shows or exhibitions will have exhibits that range in size from very small (for less important or more specialized trade shows) to very large (for their most important trade shows). For example, Xerox, which exhibits at over 30 trade shows per year, has very large exhibits for information technology shows but also smaller peninsular or in-line exhibits for specialized trade shows or smaller, regional shows. Some companies even have two or three exhibits at the same trade show: a large one promoting the main theme and message they want to communicate and smaller exhibits in other halls to promote specialized products or services.

Space assignments are often given by the exhibition management company based on a number of factors, including desired space size, seniority of participation, and points garnered by participation in other marketing programs. From the organizer's perspective, this type of arrangement helps retain exhibitors and gives favor to their highest-paying exhibitors.

When selecting space, the company trade show manager should consider the following:

- Traffic patterns within the exhibit hall
- Location of entrances

- Location of food facilities and restrooms
- Location of industry leaders
- Location of competitors

It is the responsibility of the company trade show manager to notify the exhibit management company if the company is holding any special events in the exhibition, hosting any celebrities who would draw an unusually large crowd, or giving a loud presentation from a stage.

Exhibit layout is also linked to the objectives a company establishes for the trade show or exhibition. If a company's main objective is to meet as many people as possible and establish its brand in the industry, a large open exhibit is appropriate. This type of layout encourages people to enter the exhibit, and it facilitates a large amount of traffic flow. There will be a few parts of the exhibit that require visitors to stay for a period of time, such as product demonstrations.

Another type of layout may even purposely discourage people from entering, and parts of the exhibit may be by "invitation only." Why would

Standard trade show booth.
Photo by George G. Fenich, Ph.D., Professor, School of HRTA, University of New Orleans

a company do this? If their purpose at the trade show is to only meet with serious buyers or existing customers, it is important to limit visitors to only those falling in these categories. The average visitor to the trade show may be a waste of time to the staff; therefore, the exhibit is set up to minimize traffic through the exhibit.

Most trade show floor plans in the United States are based on a 10-foot by 10-foot grid, with the smallest allowable exhibit being this size. This is known as the **standard booth**.

Typically, standard booths are set up side-by-side and back-to-back with an aisle running in front of the booth. Standard booths may also be used to line the inside walls of the exhibit area. Companies may combine standard booths to create an **in-line exhibit** using multiple standard booths to give greater length to the exhibit.

Island booths are created by grouping standard booths together into blocks of four, nine, or larger configurations. Island booths have aisles on four sides and can be an excellent format for medium-sized companies.

Peninsula booths are made up of four or more standard booths back-to-back with aisles on three sides.

Multilevel exhibits are often used by large companies to expand their exhibit space without taking up more floor space. The upper floor may be used for special purposes, such as meeting areas, private demonstration areas, or hospitality stations. Exhibitors using multilevel exhibits must be aware of each convention center's unique regulations for this type of exhibit.

As mentioned, exhibitors must be aware of the location of food facilities, restrooms, entrances, and other special event areas. Each of these affect the traffic flow in the aisles and can either hinder or help an exhibit. Although many companies strive to be directly in front of an entrance, it may create more problems than expected because of the large amount of traffic. The exhibit staff may have difficulty discerning between serious visitors to the exhibit and those just trying to get in or out of the exhibit hall. Food service areas may create unexpected lines at lunchtime that spill into an exhibit area, essentially making that area useless for the time period.

Small exhibitors face a different set of problems. If they have an in-line exhibit, their options are limited in how the exhibit is organized. If they want to maximize interactions with visitors, they may "open" the exhibit by ensuring that there are no tables or other obstructions between the aisle and their staff. If, on the other hand, they want to focus interaction on serious potential customers, their approach may be to block off the inside of the exhibit as much as possible and have meeting areas within the exhibit.

Many people who pass by or through an exhibit only read the signs that the company is displaying. Signage, therefore, is important in planning the exhibit. Signs must communicate clearly and quickly the messages that the company wants to convey to visitors. Detailed itemizations of equipment specifications on signs are almost always ignored. Signs should focus on selling points and benefits to the user.

Lighting technology has come a long way in the past twenty years. Today, many companies use pinpoint lighting to focus visitors' attention on their products and signage. Color lighting is often used to accentuate certain parts of an exhibit to communicate a mood for the visitor. Lighting is also important for areas that will be used for discussions or meetings with potential customers.

Exhibit staff must also be used wisely. All areas of the exhibit must be covered, and the right people must be in the right places. For large

Lighting can enhance booth appearance and attractiveness.
Photo by George G. Fenich, Ph.D., Professor, School of HRTA, University of New Orleans

exhibits, greeters should be used to staff the outside of the exhibit. These people will direct visitors to the areas of their interest after initially greeting them. Technical staff may be stationed with the products displayed, being able to provide answers to more detailed questions a visitor may present. Corporate executives may roam the exhibit or cluster near meeting areas to enable staff to find them when needed. Often, serious customers want to be introduced to senior executives, and they need to be available.

Small exhibits have a special set of problems with staff. Usually, the main problem they face is having enough staff to cover the busy times of the trade show or having too many staff for the exhibit size. Again, it is important that the right people are used to staff the exhibit and that staff assignments are planned according to the show's busiest times.

PLANNING FOR SUCCESS

There are three phases of planning to ensure the trade show exhibit is a success. Prior to the trade show, significant planning must take place to ensure that everything arrives at the exhibition on time, including the staff, exhibit, brochures, and products. Just as important, planning prior to the show must include establishing the objectives the company wants to accomplish. The objectives set the stage for how the exhibit is presented, the messages the signage convey, and the approach that the staff takes with exhibit visitors. Establishing objectives helps the company give thought to how the exhibit will operate and the messages it needs to give to visitors.

Planning for the exhibit operation is also a key to success. Everything must work, and everyone must know his or her role. The person in charge of the exhibit must coordinate staff schedules, product demonstrations, and a myriad of other details that result in the visitor seeing a flawless exhibit. Many aspects of exhibiting must also be coordinated with the exhibition management company or service companies during the time of the trade show as well.

A post trade show plan is essential for success. Three components of the post trade show period must be planned:

- Follow-ups for all serious leads obtained during the trade show.
- Monitoring to ensure that all commitments made during the show are fulfilled. Often staff promise visitors that they will send information or have someone call the visitor.

- Evaluation of the results. This includes determining the ROI and post trade show feedback from staff to determine lessons learned for future performance improvement.

EXHIBITORS

The APEX Initiative has adopted the following definitions that relate to this area:

Exhibit Booth: Individual display area constructed to exhibit products or convey a message.

Exhibitor: (1) Person or firm that displays its products or services at the show. (2) Those who attend an event to staff an exhibit.

Exhibit Manager: (1) Person in charge of individual exhibit booth. (2) Show management staff member in charge of entire exhibit area.

A company must consider the demographics and psychographics of people attending a trade show when deciding where to exhibit and which shows to participate in. Exhibitors and booth personnel are prime examples of face-to-face marketing and are looking for a return on their investment when participating. For example, companies like Coca Cola or Pepsi exhibit at the National Restaurant Association Show in Chicago because the attendees represent businesses that purchase these products. A company that manufactures machines for folding bed sheets will not participate in this show but can be found at the American Hotel/Motel Show in New York. Large companies like Microsoft or IBM will have full-time employees who do nothing but coordinate the company exhibits and the shows in which they participate. Smaller companies will have people who work on trade shows as a part of a larger job, such as marketing manager or director of communications. A company has to be sure to determine that those attending a particular trade show are "decision makers" rather than "tire kickers." They want to interface with buyers who will undertake the transaction rather than attendees who have to get approval from a higher authority.

HOW TO WORK THE EXHIBIT

The most important part of any exhibit is the staff. A company may have a superb exhibit—attractive, open, inviting, and informative. But if the staff

Models are used to "meet and greet" potential clients at the booth.

Photo by George G. Fenich, Ph.D., Professor, School of HRTA, University of New Orleans

are untrained, communicate poorly, and do not dress professionally, the exhibit will communicate the wrong message to a visitor about the company and its products or services. Therefore, it is important that, whether a large or small exhibit, the staff are the best they can be.

Staff must be trained to "meet and greet." It is important that visitors are greeted warmly and made to feel welcome to the exhibit. Staff must also "qualify" visitors to determine if they are potential customers or not. By asking the right questions and listening to visitors, they can easily determine whether to spend more time with them, pass them to another staff member, or politely move them through the exhibit. Time is important, especially during the busy times at a trade show. Qualifying visitors is an important step in focusing your staff's time.

Many companies provide product demonstrations or even elaborate productions about their products or services. This aspect must be managed well and focus the visitors' attention on the main messages the company wants to communicate.

WORKING WITH EXHIBITION MANAGEMENT AND SERVICE CONTRACTORS

Before, during, and after the trade show, a company will be working with the exhibition management company and service contractors. As described before, these companies play a critical role in the show "coming together" and providing all the needed services to exhibiting companies.

From the exhibitor's perspective, these companies are critical for success. They provide the space, lighting, decor, carpeting, setup, teardown, lead retrieval systems, and all the other services for the trade show program. The person tasked by the company to coordinate all these activities must develop a relationship with the management company and service companies. The person must have a clear understanding of all contract requirements, deadlines, and exhibitor responsibilities.

During the trade show or exhibition, representatives from these companies are on site to assist exhibitors with problems and last-minute needs.

The exhibition management company and service companies also offer additional marketing opportunities for exhibitors to consider. Based on their objectives for the trade show, exhibitors can choose to invest in any of these types of programs:

- *General Sponsorships:* These programs usually involve the company's name being included on printed materials for the trade show or being posted in a prominent place in the exhibit hall.
- *Special Event Sponsorship:* Special events are often conducted during the trade show schedule, such as receptions, press conferences, or entertainment. Companies who sponsor these events have their names mentioned prominently in promotional materials and at the event.
- *Advertising in the Show Daily:* Large trade shows usually have a daily newspaper available to all exhibitors and attendees each morning. It reviews the previous day's events and previews what is upcoming. Exhibitors have the opportunity to advertise in the show daily.
- *Advertising in the Show Directory:* Almost all trade shows provide attendees with a show directory, packed with information about the show and exhibitors. Advertising opportunities also exist for the show directory.
- *Promotional Items Sponsorship:* Management companies may also offer sponsorship opportunities to companies for badge holders, tote bags, and other promotional items given to registered attendees.

Sign indicating where to find the office of the service contractor at a trade show.
Photo by George G. Fenich, Ph.D., Professor, School of HRTA, University of New Orleans

In Morrow (2002), Sam Lippman presents an excellent set of tips for exhibitors on how to maximize their relationship with exhibition management. He presents his tips on three levels. Level one tasks are those that are essential to exhibiting—meeting all the requirements set by the organizing company to ensure that you take advantage of the many offerings provided to exhibitors for marketing their company's exhibit.

Level two tasks require a more proactive approach. These involve tasks like organizing press conferences, advertising in the show daily, and sending special offers to attendees before the trade show.

True trade show professionals operate at level three and help ensure the show is a success. At this level, the company trade show managers work in close collaboration with the show organizers to promote the show and do not hesitate to provide special expertise to help the show succeed. Companies operating at this level provide speakers and special events that attract attendees. They also provide volunteers to help the show organizers and use their internal resources to assist show management at every level, not simply financial.

◆ SUMMARY

Whether large or small, trade shows and exhibitions are business ventures that must be planned for success. All components of the exhibition model must be blended together to create a positive experience for attendees, exhibitors, and the organizing company or association.

For an exhibiting company, a trade show is a significant investment from the marketing budget. Therefore, it is critical that planning take place that considers activities before, during, and after the trade show to maximize the ROI. Organizing companies must address the needs of attendees and, just as important, the needs of the exhibitors. Exhibitors are the lifeblood of the trade show, providing the excitement and resources that ensure a show's success.

KEY WORDS AND TERMS

For definitions, see http://glossary.conventionindustry.org.

Exhibition

Exhibition management company

Exhibition service contractor

Exposition

In-line exhibit

Island booth

Multilevel exhibit

Peninsula booth

Public show

ROI (Return on Investment)

Standard booth

Trade show

Trade fair

REVIEW AND DISCUSSION QUESTIONS

1. What is the difference between a typical trade show and a public show?
2. Give some examples of services that exhibition service contractors provide to exhibitors.
3. What attributes of an exhibit layout would a company want if its major objective is branding?
4. Describe the layout of a peninsula exhibit.
5. What kinds of additional marketing opportunities do management companies typically offer?
6. Why is risk management important to an exhibition management company? To an exhibitor?
7. What factors are considered by an exhibition management company when determining the location of a trade show or exhibition?
8. What are the three phases of planning that a company trade show manager must address?

REFERENCES AND INTERNET SITES

Trade Publications

Convene
  PCMA
  2301 S. Lakeshore Drive, Ste. 1001
  Chicago, IL 60616
Exhibit Builder
  P. O. Box 4144
  Woodland Hills, CA 91365
Exhibitor Magazine
  206 S. Broadway, Ste. 475
  Rochester, MN 55903

EXPO
>   11600 College Boulevard
>   Overland Park, KS 66210

Facility Manager
>   IAAM
>   635 Fritz Drive
>   Coppell, TX 75019

IdEAs
>   5501 Backlick Road, Ste. 105
>   Springfield, VA 22151

Meetings and Conventions
>   Reed Travel Group
>   500 Plaza Drive
>   Secaucus, NJ 07094

Tradeshow Week
>   12233 W. Olympic Blvd., Ste. 236
>   Los Angeles, CA 90064

Books

Chapman, Edward. 1995. *Exhibit marketing.* New York: McGraw-Hill.

Miller, Steve. 1996. *How to get the most out of trade shows.* Lincolnwood, IL: NTC Business Books.

Morrow, S. L. 2002. *The art of the show.* Dallas: IAEM Foundation.

Weisgal, Margit. 1997. *Show and sell.* New York: American Management Association.

Articles

Center for Exhibition Industry Research. *Exhibition Industry Census (2000).* Chicago: CEIR.

Collins, Martha. "Crisis Management." *EXPO* (February 2001), 43–45.

Professional Convention Management Association. "Crisis Response." Special section in *Convene* (December 2001), 40–71.

Internet Sites

Center for Exhibition Industry Research	http://www.ceir.org
EventWeb	http://www.eventweb.com
ExhibitorNet	http://www.exhibitornet.com
International Association of Exhibition Managers	http://www.iaem.org

Professional Convention	http://www.pcma.org
Management Association	
Trade Show Central	http://www.tscentral.com
Trade Show News Network	http://www.tsnn.com

ABOUT THE CHAPTER CONTRIBUTOR

Ben McDonald is the vice-president of BenchMark Learning, Inc. Founded in 1995, BenchMark Learning assists businesses with training and development solutions primarily in the sales and business development areas. They have since expanded their services and partnerships to include the full spectrum of sales solutions, business development, benchmarking, and competitor analysis in order to provide their clients with a total solution for increasing revenue.

6

SPECIAL EVENTS MANAGEMENT

Fireworks make an event even more special. This is a special event at a battleship in Mobile, Alabama.

Photo by Kenneth E. Manis, courtesy of Classic Fireworks by Events, Inc., Mandeville, Louisiana

◆ Chapter Objectives

This chapter provides the reader with an understanding of the following:

- A working definition of a special event
- The importance of a workable plan for staging a special event
- The planning tools used in special event management
- The city and community infrastructures when hosting a special event
- The merchandising and promoting of a special event

- Sponsorships for special events
- Target markets for procuring attendance at a special event
- The basic operations for preparing for a special event
- The components of a special event budget
- The breakdown components of a special event

◆ Chapter Outline

A WORKING DEFINITION OF A SPECIAL EVENT

The definition of *special events* is an umbrella term that encompasses all of those functions that bring together people for a unique purpose. Most events require some sort of planning on the part of the organizer. A special event, such as city festival or fair, would mean working with cities and **community infrastructures**, merchandising, promoting, and in some cases even dealing with the media. The event can be as small as the local community Kiwanis picnic or that of a global film festival. Special events are imbedded in **meetings and conventions**, and at amusement parks, parades, **festivals**, **fairs**, and exhibits.

A special event can bring organizations together for the purpose of fund-raising, establishing a city or community as a local, regional, or national destination, and even to stimulate the local economy. The event can also be an opportunity for an association or a corporation to favorably position itself within a community or with the mass consumer. Sponsoring a specific type of event could provide a marketing edge and another avenue for reaching customers.

Orchestrating the special event takes more than an idea. It takes planning, understanding your target market, having basic operational knowledge, using effective communications, working with volunteers or volunteer organizations, working within a budget, promoting the event, and even creating the logistics for breaking down an event. Simply stated, the event planner needs to understand the who, what, where, and why of the special event: Who is the group and why are they here?

One can think of a variety of special events that take place to promote and identify a destination or an occasion. One example is Punxsutawney, Pennsylvania, where millions of television viewers awake to the early morning cheers and chants for Punxsutawney Phil, the beloved groundhog who will let us know if we are in for another six weeks of winter should he see his shadow.

Another successful small city event that draws over 100,000 visitors to Central Pennsylvania is the summer Central Pennsylvania Arts Festival that attracts over 500 national and regional artists to the city of State College, Pennsylvania, home to Penn State University.

A film festival can be a dream come true for moviegoers as they seek out famous actors who might be walking right next to them, as on the streets of Park City, Utah, during the Sundance Film Festival. Each year there are over 20,000 visitors who are drawn to this quaint little town to view over 3,000 film submissions.

These special events came from an idea of historical tradition or general promotion that ultimately grew to attract thousands of visitors to some very remote areas. To continue to attract visitors, organizations require planning and the subsequent planning tools to continue the zest for the event. This is the art and science of special events management.

USING FESTIVALS IN THE OFF-SEASON: "ROCKIN' MOUNTAINS"

The typical image of the Rocky Mountains and Colorado is one of snow-covered peaks in winter. But what happens when summer rolls around and you cannot ski? What do the ski resorts do? Shut down? The answer is a resounding "No!" They put on music festivals using the same facilities occupied by skiers in the winter. The setting is idyllic, with music carrying well in the clean air at the altitude and awesome backdrop of mountain peaks.

This use of Colorado mountain ski facilities to host off-season musical events started as long ago as 1949, when concerts were held in the town of Aspen. At the time it was called the Goethe Bicentennial celebration. Some of the events included the Minneapolis Symphony Orchestra playing in a tent that could hold 2,000 people. This special event has continued and has grown into the Aspen Music Festival and School. During the summer of 2003, the event ran from June 19 through August 17 and included over 800 international musicians. During these periods, students, faculty, and visiting musicians present almost 250 classical performances ranging from symphonies to children's programs. There are three major **venues**. The biggest one is the current tent that holds over 2,000 people and is made from the same fabric as the Denver airport terminal.

Another ski resort that has turned to musical special events to attract visitors in the off-season is Telluride, Colorado. Nearly every summer weekend, the town hosts a musical event. The biggest special event is the Telluride Bluegrass Festival, which has taken place for thirty years. It runs for four days in June and attracts 10,000 people per day. Telluride also hosts a Jazz Festival, a Chamber Music Festival, and a Blues and Brews Festival.

In Winter Park just west of Denver, three weekends are occupied with music festivals. Concertgoers sit on the slopes and watch bands perform against the backdrop of the Continental Divide. A Rockfest lines up a medley of post bubble-gum artists ranging from break-out bands to performers who have boogied for decades. In July, they hold the "Hawgfest," a Harley-Davidson inspired blowout targeted to baby boomers. They also hold a Jazzfest with music that runs the gamut from smooth jazz to crossover.

The towns of Aspen, Breckenridge, and Telluride have banded together to form the Colorado Music Alliance. This year that organization will host and market events in these three locations plus a number of small, somewhat isolated communities, including Silverthorne, Crested Butte, Estes Park, Durango, Steamboat Springs, and Nederland. Festivals are a good way of drawing tourists who would not come otherwise to locales during the off-season. They bring economic activity when there would be none, and the attendees may like the location enough to come back during the high season.

PLANNING TOOLS FOR A SPECIAL EVENT

Special events management, like any other form of managing, requires planning tools. The first of these tools is a vision of your event. This vision should be a statement that clearly identifies the who, what, when, where, and why of the event. As the event begins to unfold, it is important to keep those people involved focused on the vision by continually monitoring, evaluating, and where possible measuring the progress toward the outlined goals of the event (see chapter 2, "Planning, Organizing, Directing, and Control in MEEC").

The "who" of planning an event are those people or organizations that would like to host and organize the event. In the case of the St. Patrick's Day Parade in Chicago, Illinois, it is the city *who* hosted and coordinated the march and display of floats and bands. The *what* was a parade of Irish pride and local tradition. The *where* of the St, Patrick's Day Parade was downtown Chicago, with the parade of floats and bands marching down Michigan Avenue. The big question of *why* host the St. Patrick's Parade was one of tradition, Irish pride, fun, festivities, and tourism for the city. This, in turn, promoted city notoriety and revenues to the local businesses of the area. When the city decided to serve as the host of this event, it needed to incorporate the tools of special event management.

Some of the management tools that can be used in staging events are as follows:

a. Flow charts and graphs used for scheduling certain programs that will happen at the event. Look at any program of a meeting, and you will see start times and end times of a particular seminar, when the coffee break is to occur, when and where the lunch will be held, followed by the resumption of the meeting. It could be as be as "romantic" as a wedding ceremony **agenda**. A charting of scheduling of the activities helps to guide your attendees and guests. It could be the order or sequence of floats for the parade.

b. Clearly defined work setup and breakdown **schedules** for the event. This provides the event manager with an opportunity to determine tasks that may have been overlooked in the initial planning process for the event.

Jane Byrne at the Chicago St. Patrick's Day parade.
Source: Mayor's Press Office, City of Chicago

c. Policy statements will need to be developed to help guide in the decision-making process and the fulfilling of commitments. Some of the commitments would be to human resources, sponsorships, security, ticketing, volunteers, and even to paid personnel for the event.

UNDERSTANDING CITY AND COMMUNITY INFRASTRUCTURE

Another key ingredient for planning a successful event is an understanding of the city and/or community infrastructure. "Members" of this infrastructure might include the CEO of the company, politicians, prominent business leaders of the community, civic and community groups, the media, and even social leaders within the community. Without the buy in from the city leadership, a community is less inclined to be supportive. The role of business leaders could be to provide sponsorships, donations, staff, or a possible workplace for the coordination of the event. Many times, community groups serve as volunteer workers for the event. They are also an extension of the advertising effort for a special event.

Early on, it must be recognized whether or not a community or a company is truly committed to hosting any type of special event that will call on their support not only with the financial commitment but also in the physical and mental commitment it will take to bring an event from start to finish. For a promoter or special events management company to maintain a positive reputation, there needs to be a solid infrastructure in place.

The Crewe of Barkus parade their pets during Mardi Gras in New Orleans.
Photo by George G. Fenich, Ph.D., Professor, School of HRTA, University of New Orleans

The Promotional Mix

Advertising	Direct marketing	Interactive	Sales promotion	Publicity	Personal selling
		⇩		⇩	
		Internet marketing		Public relations	

Elements of the promotional mix for successful special event management.

MERCHANDISING AND PROMOTING THE SPECIAL EVENT

Merchandising and marketing a special event is another planning tool for attracting attendance and increasing overall profitability for the event. Just because a community decides to host a craft fair or street festival does not mean that there will be the attendance necessary to meet vendors' and visitors' needs. Profit for the vendor and a memorable experience for the attendee are two main objectives for a special event. The special event requires all the promotional venues that an event management company or civic group is able to afford.

Understanding and utilizing the **promotional mix model** (see figure above) is pivotal in order to meet the goals of the event-marketing plan.

The role of promotion in special events management is the coordination of all the seller (event or promoters) efforts to set up channels of information and persuasion to sell or promote the event. Traditionally, the promotional mix has included four elements: advertising, sales promotion, publicity and/or public relations, and personal selling. However, this author views direct marketing as well as interactive media as additional major promotional mix elements. Modern-day event marketers use many means to communicate with their target markets. Each element of the promotional mix is viewed as an integrated marketing communications tool. Each element of the model (advertising, direct marketing, interactive or Internet marketing, sales promotion, publicity and public relations, and personal selling) has a distinctive role in attracting an attendee to the special event. Each takes on a variety of forms, and each has certain advantages.

DISTINCTIVE ROLES OF THE PROMOTIONAL MIX MODEL

Advertising is defined as any paid form of nonpersonal communication about the event. The nonpersonal component means advertising that involves mass media (e.g., TV, radio, magazines, and newspapers). Advertising is the best-known and most widely discussed form of promotion because it is the most persuasive, especially if the event is targeted toward mass consumers like that of a home and garden show. It can be used to create brand images or symbolic appeals for the brand and generate immediate responses to attend the event.

Direct marketing communicates directly with the target customer for an event that will generate a response. It is much more than direct mail or catalogs. It involves a variety of activities including database management, direct selling, telemarketing, and direct-response ads through direct mail, the Internet, and various broadcast and print media. Companies like Mary Kay Cosmetics or Tupperware do not use other distribution channels but instead rely on independent contractors to sell their products directly to consumers. The use of the Internet has fueled the growth of direct marketing.

Interactive or Internet marketing allows for a back-and-forth flow of information, whereby users can participate in and modify the form and content of the information they receive in real time. Unlike traditional forms of marketing communications, such as advertising, which are one-way forms of communication, this type of media allows users to perform a variety of functions. It enables users to receive and alter information and images, make inquires, respond to questions, and make purchases. In addition to the Internet, interactive media include CD-ROMs, kiosks, and interactive television. Many event attendees will go to a Web site to garner information about a special event like a concert and purchase their tickets directly online.

Sales promotion is generally defined as those marketing activities that provide extra value or incentives to the sales force, distributors, or the ultimate consumer with the intention of stimulating the sale. A popular form of sales promotion is the coupon. Many events will use a two-for-one attendance coupon to stimulate attendance on slower days.

Publicity and public relations is divided into two components. Publicity is the component that is not directly paid for or has an identified sponsor. An event planner attempts to get the media to cover or run a favorable story on the special event. It will affect the awareness, knowledge, and opinions of the attendee. Publicity is considered a credible form of promotion, but it is not always under the control of the organization or host of the event. In the case of Punxsutawney Phil, the groundhog used in the city's quest to determine if spring is but six weeks away, all of the national broadcasting television stations send a camera crew and reporter to publicize the unusual city event.

The purpose of the second component, which is public relations, is to systematically plan and distribute information to attempt to control or manage the image and/or publicity of an event. It has a broader objective than publicity because its purpose is to establish a positive image of the special event. Public relations can be the reason for hosting the special event altogether! Tobacco companies have used special events like a NASCAR race or tennis tournament to create a more positive image with consumers.

Personal selling is the final element of the promotional model, and it is a form of person-to-person communication in which a seller attempts to assist and or persuade prospective event attendees. Unlike advertising, personal selling involves direct contact between the buyer and seller of the event, usually through face-to-face sales. Typically, personal selling for an event is in the area of group tour sales, which are the best prospects to attend a special event. There are several touring companies that purchase large groups of tickets to attend special events. Some examples may include attending the Indianapolis 500 auto race, the Kentucky Derby, or the Garlic Festival in Northern California. Group tour organizers will meet face-to-face or talk via the telephone to purchase tickets for an event.

THE GREAT GARLIC COOK-OFF

Gilroy, California

The Annual Garlic Festival is held in the "Garlic Capital of the World," Gilroy, California, at Christmas Hill Park. The hours of operation are from 10:00 A.M. to 7:00 P.M. during the last full weekend of July.

This festival's origin lies in the pride of one man, Rudy Melone. Melone felt that Gilroy, California, should celebrate its superior production of the "stinking rose," otherwise known as garlic. He then began what is referred to as "the preeminent food festival in America."

In December of each year, the Gilroy Garlic Festival begins its request for original garlic recipes. Citizens of Canada and the United States are asked to participate. Recipes are then submitted by amateur chefs, and eight are chosen to participate in the festival cook-off. Winners are awarded monetary prizes for their work well done.

Another tradition practiced by the Garlic Festival is the nomination of a "Queen of Garlic." To date, only twenty-four women can claim this title. Contestants are judged on a personal interview, talent, a garlic speech, and evening gown competition. The queen represents Gilroy at various festivities before and during the festival.

Over the last twenty-four years, the Garlic Festival has raised close to $6 million for local nonprofit organizations. Volunteers are recruited to work the event and participate in activities like picking up trash, parking cars, and serving lemonade. The Gilroy Garlic Festival is not only known for its garlic pride and knowledge but for its ability to bring the community of Gilroy together.

SPONSORSHIPS FOR SPECIAL EVENTS

Sponsorships for a special event help to ensure profitable success for an event. They are an innovative way for event organizers to help underwrite and defray costs. Sponsorships should be considered more than just a charitable endeavor for a company—they can be a strong marketing tool.

Sheraton sponsors this stage at the Jazzfest in New Orleans.
Photo by George G. Fenich, Ph.D., Professor, School of HRTA, University of New Orleans

Sponsors provide funds or "in-kind" contributions to events and receive consideration in the form of logo usage and identity with the event. Recent trends of sponsorships show rapid growth. **Sporting events** have long been the leader in securing sponsorships for teams and athletes. However, their market share has dropped as companies begin to distribute sponsorship dollars toward other events, such as city festivals and the arts.

There are five compelling reasons why company sponsorships are growing:

1. Economic changes
2. Ability to target market segments
3. Ability to measure results
4. Fragmentation of the media
5. Growth of diverse population segments

This shift from sports sponsorships to that of festivals and the arts over the past decade has emerged because companies are cognizant of the effective tool that a sponsorship can be for overall company marketing plans.

When looking for sponsorships for a special event, organizers must determine if the event fits the company. Always examine the company's goal, and be sure to research the competition. Special event organizers should aid the sponsors with promotional ideas that will help them to meet their goals. Promoters of an event need to ensure that sponsors get their money's worth. Remember that sponsors have internal and external audiences to whom they are appealing.

The internal audience of a corporation is its employees, and all of these people must be sold on the sponsorship of the event. A company needs to provide opportunities for employee involvement. If the special event is a charitable running marathon, employees may be asked to actually participate in the marathon or raise funds for the charitable cause. Those employees who participate may be featured in collateral material or press releases.

Selling to the external audience (the consumer) of the corporation is done in a variety of ways. First, the company might feature the logo of the event on its product. The company can promote its affiliation with the special event by providing its logo for outdoor banners and specialty advertising items, such as T-shirts, caps, or sunglasses. The amount of specialty advertising products are limitless and excellent venues for advertising. A company may wish to appoint a spokesperson from within who may be featured on radio or television interviews.

WORKING WITH THE MEDIA FOR AN EVENT

Generating media coverage for a special event is one of the most effective methods for attracting attendance to a gathering. An event organizer ideally wants to garner free television, radio, and print coverage. In order to attract the media, a promoter must understand what makes for good TV, radio, or print coverage and what does not.

When a camera crew is sent to film an event by assignment editors at a TV station, they will look for a story that can be easily illustrated with a camera. They also look for a vignette that can entertain viewers in thirty seconds or less.

If an event organizer wants the television or radio stations to cover the event, he or she needs to call it to their attention with a press release or press conference. It should be noted that there are no guarantees that the station or the newspaper will air the footage or print the story. However, if a camera crew shoots footage or a reporter does an interview, chances are that it will air or be printed. Thus, the event has free advertising. Remember, special events provide ideal fodder for the evening news. This can take the form of an interview with a celebrity who will be attending the event or an advance look at an art exhibit.

Within the promotional mix model, the biggest way to attract attention to the event is with television, radio, and print media through publicity. This "free" type of promotion offers something that advertising cannot match, and that is credibility. These media sources are an excellent way to reach the mass consumer.

Try to present the unusual to the press. At the opening of a steak restaurant within a hotel in Tulsa, Oklahoma, a special event was staged where the management hosted a "Moo-Off." Community leaders were invited to attend a dinner featuring the signature food and beverage items. They were then asked to "Moo" according to the personality of their favorite celebrity. The audience bellowed their Mae West Moos, Jack Nicholson Moos—even an Elvis Presley Moo. Moo-ers were gonged by specially selected judges (city leaders). The winner of the event donated the cash prize to a community charity. The event caught the attention of the media and was featured on the evening news.

The event organizers used well-timed radio segments to enhance the credibility of the Moo-Off. The restaurant manager was featured on local radio stations during morning and afternoon drive times, which peaked TV interest on the day of the event.

In the case of the Moo–Off, the promoters for the event did not have to work too hard to obtain media coverage. This event sold itself!

Promoters of special events have long recognized what TV and radio coverage can do for an event. Here are some helpful hints for attracting television and radio coverage:

1. Early in the day is considered the best time to attract cameras and reporters. Remember, a crew must come out, film, get back to the studio, edit the film, and have the segment ready for the 5:00 or 6:00 P.M. newscast that night.

2. The best day of the week to attract the news crews is Friday. That is because it is usually a quiet news day. Saturday and Sunday have even fewer distractions, but most stations do not have enough news crews working the weekend who can cover an event.

3. Giving advance notice for a special event is very helpful to assignment editors. Usually about three days' notice, with an explanation of the event via a press release and telephone follow-up, is very helpful to securing media coverage. If an interview is involved, a seven-day notice is a good time allotment for coverage.

A VERY SPECIAL WEDDING

A couple from Texas wanted to be sure their wedding was special, so they decided to have it in New Orleans. They were enamored with the southern charm of the city: moss-draped oak trees, antebellum homes, and horse-drawn carriages. They decided to invite 100 people and contacted a local DMC to make the arrangements. Their specification was that the DMC arrange a rehearsal dinner for 12 people and a reception for 100. Such costs as transportation to New Orleans, hotel accommodations, and the church were not part of the bid. Their stated budget for this wedding reception and dinner was $250,000. That's right—a quarter of a million dollars or $2,500 per guest! When the planner heard this, her reaction was twofold: (1) how could she possibly put together this event and spend that much money, and (2) if that was their proposed budget, she would try to up-sell them.

The rehearsal dinner was held in a private dining room at the famous Arnaud's restaurant in the French Quarter. The real money was spent on the reception. They rented the art deco Saenger Theater for the evening, but there was a problem. Like most theaters, the floor sloped toward the stage. So, they ended up removing all the seats and built a new floor that was flat. The interior of the theater was so beautiful that it needed little decoration. The New Orleans Police Department was contracted to close the street between the church and theater to cars so that the period ambiance would not be disturbed for the couple and their guests while being transported in their horse-drawn carriages. When the couple and their guests entered for the evening, they were greeted by models in period costume and served mint juleps while a gospel group sang. A blues band followed and was topped off by not one but two performances by Gladys Knight and the Pips. The affair was catered by Emeril Legasse and only included heavy hors d'oeuvres, not even a sit-down dinner. The ultimate cost for this event was almost $300,000, and the couple was delighted.

The planner was Nanci Easterling of Food Art, Inc.

UNDERSTANDING THE TARGET MARKET FOR YOUR SPECIAL EVENT

Bringing special events to a community has not changed much over the years; however, consumers have changed. They are much more selective and sophisticated about the venues they will attend. Costs have risen, which has created discernment of how consumers will spend their entertainment dollar. This creates a demand for quality in any special event selected by the consumer to patronize.

The most valuable outcome a special event can generate for a community is positive word of mouth. In order to create this positive awareness, an organizer recognizes that the event cannot appeal to all markets. A promoter will examine whether there is a target market for the community's event.

Target marketing is best understood by clearly defining who wants to attend a certain type of event. For example, a Brittany Spears concert has been determined to appeal to a young female audience between the ages of nine and fourteen. To stage a profitable concert, promoters will direct their advertising dollars to that particular targeted audience. Subsequently, all promotional items will also be geared toward that age of attendee.

Britney Spears entertains at a concert.
Source: AP/Wide World Photos

Most communities know that a special event will have a positive economic impact on the community and the region. This has created competition to attract events. A city will commonly use inducements to lure the special event to the community. These inducements may include free entertainment space, security, parking, and even the "key to the city" to the celebrity providing the entertainment.

A successful event has two parts. One is that the community is supportive of bringing the event to the city, and second is that the event meets the consumer's need.

PREPARING FOR THE SPECIAL EVENT

Basic operations for staging an event need to be established and include the following:

1. Secure a venue.
2. Obtain **permits**.

   a. Parade permits
   b. Liquor permits
   c. Sanitation permits
   d. Sales permits or licenses
   e. Fire safety permits

3. Involve **government agencies** where necessary (i.e., if using city recreation facilities, work with the department of parks and recreation).
4. Involve the health department if there will be food and beverage at the event.
5. Meet all relevant parties in person so that any misconceptions are cleared up early.
6. Recognize the complexities of dealing with the public sector. Sometimes, public agencies have a difficult time making decisions!
7. Recognize the logistics that a community must contend with for certain types of special events, such as street closures for a marathon.
8. Set up a security plan, which may include the security supplied by the venue and professional law enforcement of the community. (Pay attention as to which security organization takes precedence.)
9. Secure liability insurance (the most vulnerable area are those liabilities attached to liquor and liquor laws).
10. Determine ticket prices if the special event involves ticketing.
11. Determine ticket sale distribution if the special event involves ticketing.

12. Other basic business support functions include:

    a. Accounting systems (general ledger, financial reporting, accounts payable, accounts receivable, and payroll)

    b. Human resource systems (recruiting, personnel records, and job classifications and descriptions)

    c. Accommodations (talent, media, officials, support staff, and spectators)

    d. Registration

    e. Ticketing (mail order, seat inventories, seat assignments, and gate sales)

    f. Scoring and results (scoreboards and displays)

The type of special event being held will determine the degree of preparedness needed.

The larger the event, the more involved the checklist. Preparedness should produce a profitable and well-managed event.

THE SPECIAL EVENT BUDGET

For any event to be considered a success, it must also be considered profitable. Profitability requires understanding the six key elements involved in the cost of an event. The basic items that make up the cost for a special event include the categories that follow.

RENTAL CHARGES

Depending on the type of event, renting a facility like a convention center or ground space to put up a tent requires payment of a daily rental charge. Convention centers usually sell the space based on a certain dollar amount per square footage used. Most facilities charge for space even on the move-in and move-out days. Multiday events can usually negotiate a discount.

SECURITY COSTS

Most convention centers, rental halls, and even hotel space provide limited security. This could mean that a guard is stationed at the front and the rear entrances of the special event. Depending on the type of event, such as a rock concert performed by a band that has raucous fans, more security may be required. Actual costs will depend on the city and the amount of security needed.

It is hard to believe that this is the inside of a tent used for a special event.
Used by permission of Paradise Sound & Light, Orlando, Florida

PRODUCTION COSTS

These are the costs associated with staging an event. The costs can vary depending on the type of special event. For example, if the special event is a large home and garden show, there are costs associated with the setup of the trade show booth. As with many home and garden shows, exhibitors bring in very elaborate garden and backyard landscapes that are very time intensive to set up and break down. Labor costs for decorators need to be calculated to estimate the production costs based on the type and size of trade show booth. There are also electrical and water fees needed for a home and garden show, and these costs must be included in the production costs. Other decorator production costs include signage or banners for each booth and pipe and drape fees to show division for the booth for the exhibitor.

LABOR COSTS

The city where the special event is being held determines the labor costs involved in the setup and breakdown of the event. Some cities are unionized, and this can add higher costs to an event because of the higher wages. Very strict union cities mean that the organizer of the event must leave more of the handling to the union crew. In some cities, the union allows the exhibitor to wheel his or her own cart with brochures and merchandise. In other cities, exhibitors cannot carry anything other than their own briefcases!

Over the years, the role of the union when selecting a facility has been an important influence on where a special event may or may not be held. Most special event organizers will pass the higher costs on to the exhibitor or will increase ticket prices.

MARKETING COSTS

The costs associated with attracting attendees can make up a large portion of the event budget (see the Statement of Revenues and Expenses below). Here, the event organizer examines the best means of reaching the targeted audience. Trying to reach a mass audience may mean running a series of television commercials, which can be very expensive. Most event

The ABC Special Event

STATEMENT OF REVENUES AND EXPENSES

REVENUES	BUDGET	ACTUAL
Admission	$ 5,000	$ 6,000
Exhibit booth sales	$ 10,000	$ 11,000
Food and beverage sales	$ 2,000	$ 4,000
TOTAL	$17,000	$21,000
EXPENDITURES		
Rental	$ 1,000	$ 1,000
Labor (security)	$ 500	$ 500
Production	$ 2,000	$ 3,000
Marketing costs	$ 3,000	$ 4,000
Talent	$ 0	$ 500
TOTAL	$ 6,500	$ 9,000
SURPLUS	$ 10,500	$ 12,000

organizers use a combination of promotions to attract the attendee. There will be elements of advertising, direct marketing, publicity and public relations, sales promotion, interactive or Internet marketing, and personal selling. All of these need to be budgeted.

The importance of planning and estimating costs and potential revenues remains essential to whether a community will host another event. Repeat events are much easier to promote the second time, especially when the organizers make a profit.

BREAKDOWN OF THE SPECIAL EVENT

Special events have one thing in common: They all come to an end! Breaking down the event usually involves a number of steps. Once the attendees have gone, there are a variety of closing tasks that an organizer must complete.

First, the parking staff should expedite the flow of traffic away from the event. In some cases, community police are able to assist in traffic control.

A debriefing of staff should take place to determine what did or did not happen at the event. There may be pending issues in regard to insurance for other liabilities that will need documentation. It is always best to have written reports to refer to for next year's event. Consider having the following sources add information to the report:

1. Interview some of the participants from the event. A customer's perception and expectation is invaluable insight.
2. Speak with the press. Ask why it was or was not a press-worthy gathering.
3. Get a variety of staff and other management involved in the event to give feedback.
4. Garner feedback from vendors of the event. They also have a very unique prospective on how the event could be improved.

Another measurement tool for evaluating the event will be the income and expense statement. Did the event break even, make profit, or experience a dollar loss?

Finalize all contracts from the event. Fortunately, most everything involved with putting together the event will have written documentation. Compare final billing with actual agreements.

Send the media a final press release on the overall success. Interviews with the press could be arranged. This could be especially newsworthy if the event generated significant revenues for the community.

Provide a written thank you for those volunteers who were involved with the event in any way. A celebration of some sort with the volunteers may be in order, especially if the event was financially and socially successful.

Fireworks can add sizzle to a special event.

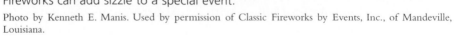
Photo by Kenneth E. Manis. Used by permission of Classic Fireworks by Events, Inc., of Mandeville, Louisiana.

Once the elements of breakdown have taken place, the organizers can examine the important lessons of staging the event. What would they do or not do next year?

ISES: International Special Events Society

About ISES

The International Special Events Society is comprised of over 3,000 professionals in over a dozen countries representing special event producers (from festivals to trade shows), caterers, decorators, florists, destination management companies, rental companies, special effects experts, tent suppliers, audio-visual technicians, party and convention coordinators, balloon artists, educators, journalists, hotel sales managers, specialty entertainers, convention center managers, and many more. . . .

ISES History

The International Special Events Society (ISES) was founded in 1987 to foster enlightened performance through education while promoting ethical conduct. ISES works to join professionals to focus on the "event as a whole" rather than its individual parts. ISES has grown to involve nearly 3,000 members active in 30 chapters throughout the world. Membership brings together professionals from a variety of special events disciplines including caterers, meeting planners, decorators, event planners, audio-visual technicians, party and convention coordinators, educators, journalists, hotel sales managers and many more professional disciplines. The solid peer network ISES provides helps special events professionals produce outstanding results for clients while establishing positive working relationships with other event colleagues.

ISES Mission

The Mission of ISES is to educate, advance and promote the special events industry and its network of professionals along with related industries. To that end, we strive to:

> Uphold the integrity of the special events profession to the general public through our "Principles of Professional Conduct and Ethics"

(continued)

Acquire and disseminate useful business information

Foster a spirit of cooperation among its members and other special events professionals, and . . .

Cultivate high standards of business practices.

What Does ISES Mean?

- Professional Development and Certification
  - Affiliation with local chapters provides education and idea exchanges.
  - ISES membership keeps you on top of industry trends through educational programs. Participate in the annual Conference for Professional Development (CPD) or other ISES-sponsored classes to challenge your knowledge. Enhance your professional credibility by working towards professional accreditation and becoming a Certified Special Events Professional (CSEP).
- Recognition
  - ISES honors industry excellence through its prestigious awards program, the ISES Esprit Awards. The Esprit Awards fuel a spirit of competition within designated categories. The categories within the Esprit De Corps Awards recognize the best and most creative within the special events industry. Esprit Awards gain global visibility and recognition for ISES members through general participation. The program honors professionals who exhibit a "spirit of excellence" in their work.
- Strategic Alliance
  - ISES and SpecialEvents magazine currently have a strategic alliance that provides benefits to ISES members. ISES recognizes SpecialEvents magazine link to www.specialevents.com as "the official and premier magazine of the special events industry in North America" and The Special Event as "the official and premier trade show for this industry in North America."
- Networking
  - Involvement means building relationships with other professionals from your region and beyond. The exchange that takes place grows your business contacts, as well as your potential

client base, and/or provides you with employment opportunities. By committing time through membership, you invest in yourself and the industry while gaining an industry edge.

The preceding information is from the ISES Web site. If you would like additional information about ISES, please contact ISES Headquarters, 401 N. Michigan Ave., Chicago, IL 60611-4267, USA; phone: 800-688-ISES (4737) or 312-321-6853; or e-mail: info@ises.com.

◆ SUMMARY

Creating a memorable event requires that an organizer meet and exceed the expectations of an attendee. Recognizing that the special event could be for a meeting or convention, a parade, a festival, a fair, or an exhibit requires understanding the objectives of the event. Having the planning tools in place is the keystone for success in managing the gathering. Special events management works with and understands the city and community infrastructures to help support the event. Looking for the merchandising opportunities and promotion of the event can be a costly venture for any special event management team when the promotional mix model of advertising, direct marketing, interactive or Internet marketing, sales promotion, publicity and public relations, and personal selling are not identified as a part of the event marketing plan. Helping to defray costs by seeking sponsorships for a special event is another way to successfully market an event. It is an important marketing tool for a corporation. Generating and working with the local and or national media is the most effective way for attracting attendance. An organizer needs to understand what makes for good media coverage, whether it be for **print** or **broadcast**. The target market, or who the consumer is, for the special event must always be considered in the objectives, the promotions, and the continuation of the event. The basic operations and/or logistics for the event follows the planning and promoting for an event. As is sometimes said, "The devil is in the details." A checklist of the items that need to be handled or looked into are a must for any planner. Create checklists that will help develop the overall special event budget that requires regular reviews of the statement of revenues and expenditures. The breakdown of the event is the final step and includes another checklist for the closure of the event. Always remember your volunteers—without them the event would not take place!

KEY WORDS AND TERMS

For definitions, see http://glossary.conventionindustry.org.

Agenda

Awards ceremonies

Community infrastructure

Corporate events

Fairs, festivals, and public events

Government agencies

Holiday and special observances

Meetings and conventions

Opening ceremonies

Permit

Print or **broadcast media**

Promotional mix model

Retail special events

Schedule

Social events

Sporting event

Theme parties

Venue

REVIEW AND DISCUSSION QUESTIONS

1. Discuss the types of events that a city might host.
2. What does the vision statement of an event provide for an organizer?
3. Discuss the types of planning tools that aid in successful event management.
4. What are the distinctive roles of the promotional mix model?
5. What are the benefits for sponsorships at a special event?
6. What are some tips for working with broadcast media?

7. What are some basic operations for staging an event?

8. Discuss costs associated with the event budget.

9. Outline the elements of breakdown for a special event.

10. Consider special event opportunities for your community. How would you offer advice as an event planner to encourage attendance?

ABOUT THE CHAPTER CONTRIBUTOR

Cynthia Vannucci holds a Ph.D. in man/environmental relations, an MBA, and a B.S. in hotel administration. She has also earned several industry certifications in marketing, sales, meeting planning, and education. She is an associate professor at Metropolitan State College in Denver, where she serves as the director of meetings and conventions.

Dr. Vannucci is a long-time hotels sales and catering executive with strong background in special event management and meeting planning. She was a national sales and marketing director for CHOICE Hotels International as well as regional sales director for Ramada and Renaissance hotels.

◆7

FOOD AND BEVERAGE

An attended buffet gives elegance to a food and beverage function.
Source: Dorling Kindersley Media Library

◆ Chapter Objectives

This chapter provides the reader with an understanding of the following:

- Types of catering operations and types of caterers
- Relationships between the catering department and other hotel departments
- Purpose of the meal function

- Types of meal functions, menu planning, menu design, and pricing
- Types of beverage functions, beverage menu planning, and pricing
- Liquor laws and third-party liability
- Space requirements and room setup

◆ Chapter Outline

INTRODUCTION

Food and beverage is an area that many meeting planners shy away from by outsourcing the planning and negotiation to third-party planners. It is a mystery to many planners as to what is negotiable and how caterers price. Where will the caterer make concessions?

The quality of the food and beverage functions can impact the overall impressions of a meeting. While many simply see food as fuel, for others it is an important component of the overall experience. From planning menus to negotiating prices, this is one area not to leave to chance. It is one of the major expenses and an area where Murphy's Law prevails.

CATERED EVENTS

Catered events generally have one host and one bill, and most attendees eat the same meal. (Exceptions would be if an attendee arranged vegetarian, low-fat, or other special meal.) A mandatory gratuity is added to the check that can range from 15 to 22% of the total bill. The distribution of this gratuity varies widely among hotel companies. In some companies, the gratuity goes exclusively to the servers and bartenders. In other hotels, a portion goes to management, such as the catering manager or the CSM. A gratuity differs from a tip, as a tip is voluntary and is given at the discretion of the client for service over and above expectations. Service charges are a murky area, but they generally do not go to the service personnel. When in doubt, ask.

Catered events can be held in just about any location. **On-premise catering** is defined as being held in a facility that has its own permanent kitchens and function rooms, such as a hotel, restaurant, or convention center. This allows the facility to keep permanent furniture, such as banquet tables and solid banquet chairs, in their inventory.

Off-premise catering transports food—either prepared, or to be prepared on site—to a location like a tented area, museum, park, or attraction. Sometimes food is prepared in a kitchen and is transported fully cooked to the event site. Other times food is partially prepared in a kitchen and is finished at the site. Or, everything can be prepared from scratch at the site. Mobile kitchens can be set up just about anywhere, using generators and/or propane and butane as fuel to heat cooking equipment. Caterers generally must rent equipment, including tables, chairs, chafing dishes, plates, flatware, and glassware.

Meeting planners are usually locked into using the catering department of the hotel at the site of the meeting. In a citywide convention, one hotel is usually named the host hotel and holds most of the food functions, although often events move attendees to a variety of venues. Many meetings have at least one off-premise event, often the opening reception or closing gala or a themed event. Attendees want to experience some of the flavor of the destination, and they often get "cabin fever" if they never leave the hotel. Events can be held at an aquarium, a museum, a winery, or an historic mansion. In Dallas, events are held at Southfork Ranch, site of the television show *Dallas*.

Logistically, in Orlando it is much easier to transport a 20-person board of directors dinner to a local restaurant banquet room than to transport

1000+ attendees to Disney World, and both may be done simultaneously. A shuttle bus system must be set up to transport attendees back and forth, which can be expensive.

Many notable and excellent restaurants have banquet rooms, and bigger restaurants have banquet sales coordinators. Arnaud's in New Orleans has a six-person sales staff, so banquets are big business. In Las Vegas, a trend in recent years has to have celebrity chefs create their own signature restaurants within the hotel, separate from the hotel's own food service operations. These restaurants, such as Spago in the Forum Shops at Caesars Palace or Delmonico's at the Venetian, also have their own banquet sales staff. The Web has made it easy to research what local restaurants have to offer. The MIM List, a free e-mail listserver for meeting planners sponsored by *Meeting News* magazine, is a great place to ask for suggestions and advice: http://www.mim.com.

For an off-premise event, the first step would be to create an RFP and send it to event managers or caterers in the area. The RFP would include basic information, such as the objective of the event, information on the company, workable dates, number of attendees, and approximate budget as well as any special requests, such as the need for a parade area. Many catering companies have online RFPs. Once the planner has had the opportunity to review the proposals submitted, an interview and, if possible, a site inspection would follow. During the site inspection, look at the ambiance of the space, the level of cleanliness and maintenance, and other amenities that may be required, such as parking and restrooms.

In many cases, off-premise events will be outsourced with a DMC. DMCs are familiar with the location and have relationships established with the unique venues in the area. For example, in Las Vegas the Liberace Mansion is available for parties. In New Orleans, Mardi Gras World, where the parade floats are made, is an outstanding setting for a party. Just about every destination has some distinctive spaces for parties: Southfork in Dallas, the Rock and Roll Hall of Fame in Cleveland, the Getty Museum in Los Angeles, and so on.

DMCs also know the best caterers, decorators, shuttle companies, entertainment, and any other product or service you may require. While DMCs charge for their services, they often can get quantity discounts because of the volume they purchase throughout the year. And if there is a problem with the product or service, the DMC can usually resolve it faster because of the amount of future business that would be jeopardized.

Two of the challenges with off-premise events are transportation and weather. Shuttle buses are an additional expense. Weather can spoil the best-laid plans, so contingency measures must be arranged. Back-up shelter should be available, whether a tent or an inside function room. A luau planned for outdoors during a recent visit to Hawaii was moved inside at the last minute due to one of the frequent tropical storms that pop up.

During the initial site inspection, obtain a copy of the facility's banquet **menus** and policies. Do they offer the type of menu items that would be appropriate for your group? Ask if they are prepared to handle custom menus if you decide not to use their printed offerings. When planning custom menus, always check the skill level in the kitchen and the availability of special products that may be required.

An important consideration is the demographics of the group. Menu choices would be different for the American Truck Drivers Association and the International Association of Retired Persons. A standing joke it that the latter prefer canned string beans rather than fresh because chefs do not cook fresh beans long enough and retired people have difficulty chewing them. The typical truck driver would probably prefer a big steak, while a retired person would likely prefer a smaller portion of chicken without heavy spices. You need to consider gender, age, ethnic background, profession, and so on.

Most meals are catered during a meeting. Serving attendees all at once prevents strain on the restaurant outlets, keeps attendees from leaving the property, and assures that everyone will be back on time for the following sessions.

Conference centers offer a complete meeting package, which includes meals. Breakfast, lunch, and dinner are generally available in a cafeteria-type setup at any time the group decides to break. This keeps the group from having to break just because it is noon if they are in the middle of a productive session. If more than one group is in the facility, they will each be assigned different areas of the dining room. Refreshments are usually available at any time as well, allowing breaks at appropriate times. Conference centers can also provide banquets and receptions on request.

Convention centers and stadiums usually have concession stands open. More and more, trade shows are holding the opening reception or providing lunch on the show floor to attract attendees into the exhibits. Most convention centers are public entities, and the food service is contracted out to companies like ARAMARK or Sodexho. These contract food service companies often have exclusive contracts, and other vendors or caterers are not allowed to work in the facility.

The above venues generally have full–service restaurants on the property as well. If the group will use the restaurant, check the capacity and hours relative to the needs of the group.

Meeting planners need to stay abreast of current food trends. They do so by reading trade journals, such as *Meeting News*, *Successful Meetings*, *Convene*, or *Meetings & Conventions*. Many of the event and food trade publications, such as *Event Solutions*, *Special Events*, *Hotel F&B Director*, and *Catering* are wonderful resources. Online versions are linked on this Web page: http://tca.unlv.edu/pub. BizBash is a great place to see creative things that others are doing: http://www.bizbash.com.

	TYPES OF FUNCTIONS
Continental breakfast	This is typically a bread or pastry, juice and coffee, although it can be upgraded with the addition of sliced fruit, yogurt, and/or cold cereals. Most are self-service, although table service is an option.
Full, served breakfast	This would be plated in the kitchen and would normally include some type of egg like Eggs Benedict, a meat like bacon or sausage, a potato item like hashed browns, fruit, and coffee.
Breakfast buffet	An assortment of foods with a variety of fruits and fruit juices, egg dishes, meats, potatoes, and breads.
Refreshment breaks	These are often beverages only but may include snacks such as cookies, bagels, or fruit.
Brunch	This is for a late-morning meal and includes both breakfast and lunch items. A brunch can be a buffet or a plated, served meal.
Buffet lunch	This can be a cold or hot buffet, with a variety of salads, vegetables, meats, etc. A deli buffet can include a make-your-own sandwich area.

(continued)

Box lunch	These are for carrying away from the hotel for a meal in a remote location. They can be eaten on a bus if there is a long ride to a destination (such as a ride from San Francisco to the Napa Valley for a day's activities) or eaten at the destination (such as a picnic area to hear the Boston Pops Orchestra). Box lunches can also be provided to attendees at a trade show.
Full, served lunch	This is a plated lunch, usually a three-course hot meal, and often includes a salad, a main course, and a dessert. A one-course cold meal is sometimes provided, such as a chicken salad served in a pineapple half.
Receptions	These are networking events where people stand up and mill around. Food is usually placed on stations around the room on tables and may be butlered. There are often bars. Light receptions may only include dry snacks and beverages and often precede a dinner. Heavy receptions would include hot and cold appetizers, perhaps a meat carving station, and are often planned instead of a dinner.
Dinner buffet	This would include a variety of salads, vegetables, meats, desserts, and beverages. Often meats are carved and served by attendants.
Full, served dinner	This could be a three- to five-course meal, including an appetizer, soup, salad, main course, and a dessert. Food can be pre-plated in the kitchen (American Service) or served from trays to guests at the table (Banquet French Service).
Off-site event	This is any event held away from the host hotel. It could be a reception at a famous landmark, such as the Queen Mary in Long Beach, or a picnic at a local beach or park.
Theme party	This is a gala event with flair. It can be a reception, buffet, or served meal. Themes can run the gamut. An example would be an international theme, where different stations are set up with food from Italy, China, Japan, Mexico, Germany, etc.

STYLE OF SERVICE

There are many ways to serve a meal, from self-service to VIP white-glove service. While there is some disagreement on a few of the following definitions, the White House protocol is being followed in this book. The White House publishes the *Green Book*, which explains how everything is to be done for presidential protocol. However, because of confusion in the area, it is important to be sure that the planner and the catering representative agree on what the service styles mean for the event. (Unfortunately, the *Green Book* is not available, as it also includes info on presidential security, etc.)

Buffet: Food is attractively arranged on tables. Guests serve themselves and then take their full plates to a table to sit and eat. Beverages are usually served at the tables. Buffets are generally more expensive than plated served meals because there is no portion control, and surpluses must be built in to assure adequate supplies of each food item. Be sure to allow adequate

White-glove service.
Source: Getty Images, Inc.

space around the table for lines to form. Consider the flow, and do not make guests backtrack to get an item. For example, place the salad dressings after the salad so that guests do not have to step back on the next guest to dress their salad. Provide one buffet line per 100 guests, with 120 being the break point.

Attended Buffet/Cafeteria: Guests are served by chefs or attendants. This is more elegant and provides better portion control.

Combination Buffet: Inexpensive items, such as salads, are presented buffet style, where guests help themselves. Expensive items, such as meats, are served by an attendant for portion control.

Plated Buffet: A selection of pre-plated foods are set on a buffet table for guests to choose from. This is helpful for portion control.

Action Stations: Sometimes referred to as *performance stations* or *exhibition cooking.* **Action stations** are similar to an attended buffet, except food is freshly prepared as guests wait and watch. Some common action stations include pastas, grilled meats or shrimp, omelets, crepes, sushi, flaming desserts, Caesar salad, Belgian waffles, and carved meats.

Reception: Light foods are served buffet style or are passed on trays by servers (**butlered**). Guests usually stand and serve themselves and do not usually sit down to eat. Receptions are often referred to as "Walk and Talks." Plates can add as much as one-third to food cost because people heap food up on the plates. Some receptions serve only finger food (food eaten with the fingers), while others offer fork food (food that requires a fork to eat).

Family Style/English Service: Guests are seated, and large serving platters and bowls of food are placed on the dining table by the servers. Guests pass the food around the table. A host often will carve the meat. This is an expensive style of service. Surpluses must be built in.

Plated/American Style Service: Guests are seated and served food that has been preportioned and plated in the kitchen. *Food is served from the left of the guest.* The meat or entree is placed directly in front of the guest at the six o'clock position. *Beverages are served from the right of the guest. When the guest has finished, both plates and glassware are removed from the right.* **American Service** is the most functional, most common, most economical, most controllable, and most efficient type of service. This type of service usually has a server/guest ratio of 1:32, depending on the level of the hotel.

Preset: Some foods are already on the table when guests arrive. The most common items to preset are water, butter, bread, and appetizer and/or salad. At luncheons, where time is of the essence, the dessert is often preset as well. These are all cold items that hold up well.

Butlered: At receptions, *butlered* refers to having hors d'oeuvres passed on trays, where the guests help themselves. At dinner, butlered is an upscale type of service, with food often passed on silver trays. Guests use serving utensils to serve themselves at the table from a platter presented by the server. (Similar to, and often confused with, **Russian Service**.)

Russian Service: Guests are seated. Foods are cooked tableside on a *rechaud* (portable cooking stove) that is on a *gueridon* (tableside cart with wheels). Servers place the food on platters (usually silver), then pass the platters at tableside. Guests help themselves from the platters. Service is *from the left.*

Banquet French: Guests are seated. Platters of food are assembled in the kitchen. Servers take the platters to the tables and serve from the left, placing the food on the guest's plate using two large silver forks or one fork and one spoon. Servers must be highly trained for this type of service. The use of the forks and spoons together in one hand is a skill that must be practiced. Many hotels are now permitting the use of silver salad tongs.

Cart French: Less commonly used for banquets, except for small VIP functions, this style is used in fine restaurants. Guests are seated, and foods are prepared tableside using a rechaud on a gueridon. Cold foods, such as salads, are prepared on the gueridon, sans rechaud. Servers plate the finished foods directly on the guest plate, which is then placed in front of the guest *from the right.* (This is the only time food is served from the right.)

Hand Service: Guests are seated. There is one server for every two guests. Servers wear white gloves. Foods are pre-plated. Each server carries two plates from the kitchen and stands behind the two guests assigned to him or her. At a signal from the room captain, all servings are set in front of all guests at the same time, synchronized. This procedure can be used for all courses, just the main course, or just the dessert. This is a very elegant and impressive style of service used mainly for VIP events because the added labor is expensive.

Waiter Parade: An elegant touch is when white-gloved waiters march into the room and parade around the perimeter carrying food on trays, often to attention-getting music and dramatic lighting. This is especially effective with a Flaming Baked Alaska Dessert Parade. The room lighting is dimmed, and the row of flaming trays carried by the waiters slowly encircles the room. When the entire room is encircled, the music stops and service starts. Guests are usually clapping at this point. (Flaming dishes should never be brought close to a guest. In this case, after the parade, the dessert would be brought to a side area, where it would be sliced and served.)

The Wave: Servers are not assigned workstations or tables. All servers start at one end of the room and work straight across to the other end—for both service and plate removal. All of the servers are on one team, and the whole room is the station. This is a quick and dirty form of service—not classy, but functional when you want fast service or the servers are inexperienced. Guests do not receive individualized attention. This is only appropriate with pre-plated foods.

Mixing Service Styles: You can change service styles within the meal. The whole meal does not have to conform to one type of service. For example, you can have your appetizer preset, have the salads "Frenched" (dressing added after salads are placed on table), the main course served American, with a dessert buffet.

MENUS

In times past, menus rarely changed. Today, change is necessary to keep pace with the changing tastes of the public. Most food trades journals run features of What's Hot and What's Not. Here are some items that are generally always "in."

Seasonal food	Locally grown produce, in season, was popularized some years ago by Chef Alice Waters. This is when food is at it peak flavor.
Ethnic foods	With the influx of peoples from other cultures into the United States has come the unique cuisine of a variety of areas of the world. The American palate has grown beyond the ethnic foods of the past—Italian, Chinese, and Mexican—to include the foods of many Asian countries, the Middle East, and South America.

High-quality ingredients	People may pinch pennies at the grocery store, but when they eat out at a banquet, they want the best. No longer satisfied with frozen, sweetened strawberries, they want fresh Driscoll strawberries on their shortcake. They want the giant Idaho baked potatoes and Angus beef.
Fresh ingredients	Frozen, canned, and dried foods, once seen as the newest, greatest technology, have worn out their novelty. The loss of flavor during preservation has made fresh food highly prized.
New and unusual ingredients	With the increased means of transportation in recent years, new foodstuffs have appeared in the marketplaces that were previously unknown to most Americans. These include Kiwi fruit, lemon grass, ugli fruit, star fruit, Yukon Gold potatoes, purple potatoes, and blood oranges.
Safe foods	Organic foods and foods free from pollution and pesticides.
Highly creative presentations	Plate presentations are increasingly important. We eat with our eyes before anything hits our taste buds.
Excellent service	Food served promptly (while still hot) and friendly, courteous service are important considerations in the enjoyment of a meal.

FOOD CONSUMPTION PATTERNS

The most important information in deciding how much food to order is the history of the group: Who are they? Why are they here? A pretty good determination can be made based on previous years. If this is a new group, or the history is not available, then consider the demographics of the attendees.

SOME GENERAL GUIDELINES

Guests will eat an average of seven hors d'oeuvres during the first hour. They will generally eat more during the first hour of a reception. This depends on whether they are blue-collar, white-collar, or pink-collar (demographics).

White-collar workers are business types who are categorized by wearing suits and white shirts. Blue-collar workers are characterized as those

TYPE OF RECEPTION	TYPE OF EATERS	NO. HORS D'OEUVRES PER PERSON
2 hours or less (dinner following)	Light	3–4 pieces
	Moderate	5–7 pieces
	Heavy	8+ pieces
2 hours or less (no dinner)	Light	6–8 pieces
	Moderate	10–12 pieces
	Heavy	12+ pieces
2–3 hours (no dinner)	Light	8–10 pieces
	Moderate	10–12 pieces
	Heavy	16+ pieces

who wear uniforms or work attire other than suits. Pink-collar workers are females in the workforce. It is safe to assume that a group of typical truck drivers would eat more (and differently) than a group of typical secretaries.

The amount of food consumed may also depend on how many square feet are available for guests to move around in (smaller equals less consumption).

MENU RESTRICTIONS

Banquet servers should know the ingredients and preparation method of every item on the menu. Many people have allergies or are restricted from eating certain items like sugar or salt due to health concerns. Others do not eat certain foods due to religious restrictions. Vegetarians do not eat meat.

Types of vegetarians:

- Type one: will not eat red meat, but will eat chicken and fish.
- Type two: "lacto-ovo" will not eat anything that has to be killed but will eat by-products (cheese, eggs, milk, etc.).
- Type three: "vegans" will not eat anything from any animal source, including honey, butter, dairy, and meat.

When in doubt, assume they are vegans. To serve a vegan a plate of vegetables with butter and/or cheese would not be appropriate.

It is a good idea to have attendees fill out a form indicating if they have any menu restrictions. This information can then be communicated to the catering manager, who will ensure the proper number and type of alternative menu items are available. At meetings of the National Association of Catering Executives, attendees are provided with complete menus of every event, along with a form where they can indicate which meals they need to have changed.

FOOD AND BEVERAGE ATTRITION

Most planners do not like **attrition** clauses, although they benefit both planner and hotel because they set down legal obligations for both sides and establish liability limits. When a contract is signed, both parties want the food and beverage guarantee to be met. But caterers want to be certain and up-front, while planners want to wait until the last minute to give the final guarantee. If the guarantee is too high, the planner might have to pay for it in the form of attrition.

Attrition hits the planner in the pocketbook if the **guarantee** is not met. The planner agrees in the contract to buy a specific number of meals or to spend a specific amount of money on group food and beverage; the caterer's obligation is to provide the service and the food. If the guarantee is not met, the planner must pay the difference between the guarantee and the actual amount or an agreed-on percentage of the actual amount (see chapter 12, "Legal Issues," for more information on attrition).

The planner may also lose concessions that he or she has negotiated. Function space often is provided free of charge because of the revenue the group brings into the hotel through sleeping rooms and catered events. If the revenue does not come in, the hotel can charge for services that normally would have been complimentary, such as labor. The hotel could also reassign or reduce space being held for the planner if minimums are not met.

Catering sales managers must strive to maximize revenue per available room. They need a way to guarantee that money when booking a group. Meeting planners should know how much revenue their meeting produces before negotiating an attrition clause. Caterers should pin down how much money the group will be spending with catering instead of getting a head count since food prices fluctuate.

When using a dollar amount guarantee, provide some flexibility as to how the money may be spent. The contract can indicate that food and beverage fees could be reduced if the catered event is replaced with other business.

AMENITIES OR GIFTS

Many hotel CSMs, the DMC, and so on, like to say "thank you for your business" with a token of appreciation that may be an in-room amenity. The meeting planner may also be offered the opportunity to send in-room amenities to meeting VIPs. When sending an in-room gift during the meeting, do not just send the customary fruit and wine basket. Give some thought to the person and what he or she might like. Sending a bottle of wine to the room of a recovering alcoholic or a big box of chocolate truffles to a diabetic would be a bad move. However, something that shows the planner gave some thought to the gift will impress VIPs. For example, if a VIP likes a particular wine, be sure that same wine is placed in the room.

Cut fruit and cheese do not last, so only send whole fruit and small packaged cheeses. In areas of high humidity, open crackers stale quickly, so only include small packages. Bottled water is always appreciated. If the sender knows nothing about the client's tastes, a gift certificate for room service would give choices and a luxury not normally indulged in. Or give the client a certificate for a massage or to the gift shop for something he or she can take back home. Flowers are pretty, but attendees do not enjoy them because they spend little time in their rooms, and flowers do not fare well on an airplane.

BEVERAGE EVENTS

REASONS FOR A BEVERAGE EVENT

Beverage events are popular and include refreshment breaks and receptions. Refreshment breaks not only provide liquid repasts and possibly a snack but also allow the attendee to get up, stretch, visit the restroom, call the office, and possibly move into another room for the next break-out session.

Receptions are slightly different because most include alcohol and probably more variety and quantity of food options. Reasons for receptions include:

Socializing: To loosen guests up—it is easier to sell to a relaxed potential client.

Networking: To look for a job or business leads.

CATEGORIES OF LIQUOR

The three categories of liquor are beer, wine, and spirits. Beer and wine are considered soft liquor, and spirits are considered hard liquor. There are three categories of spirits: **Well**, **Call**, and Premium brands.

Well Brands: These are sometimes called "house liquor." It is less expensive liquor, such as Kentucky Gentleman Bourbon. Well brands are served when someone does not "call" a specific brand.

Call Brands: These are priced in the midrange and are generally asked for by name, such as Jim Beam Bourbon or Beefeater's Gin.

Premium Brands: These are high-quality, expensive liquors, such as Crown Royal, Chivas Regal, or Tanqueray Gin.

HOW BEVERAGES ARE SOLD
By the Bottle

Common for open bars and poured wine at meal functions.

The planner pays for all of the liquor bottles that are opened. A physical inventory is taken at the beginning and end of the function to determine liquor usage. Most hotels charge for each opened bottle, even if only one drink was poured from it. This method saves money but is inconvenient to monitor and calculate. The planner will not know the final cost until the event is over. Usually, the group history will give some indication of how much consumption to expect. Open bottles may not be removed from the property. Unopened bottles may not be removed unless the hotel has an off-sale liquor license. You can, however, have them delivered to a hospitality suite or to the room of a VIP to use during the meeting.

By the Drink

Typical for a cash bar.

This method uses tickets or a cash register for control. Normally, the price per drink is high enough to cover all relevant expenses (limes, stirrers, napkins, etc.). Individual drink prices are set to yield a standard beverage cost percentage set by the hotel. This is the amount of profit the hotel expects to make from the sale of the liquor. Cost percentages range from 12 to 18% for spirits and usually around 25% for wine. The planner will not know the final cost until the event is over.

Per Person

Usually includes food. This is common for open bars.

This method is more expensive for the planner but less work and hassle. The planner chooses a plan, such as premium liquors for one hour, and then tells the caterer how many people are coming ($25 per person $\times$ 500 guests = $12,500). Costs are known ahead of time—no surprises. Tickets are collected from attendees at the door, and the guarantee is monitored.

Charge per Hour

This is similar to per person.

This method often includes a sliding scale, with higher cost for the first hour. This is because guests usually eat and drink more during the first hour, then level off. You must provide a firm guarantee before negotiating a per-hour charge. Or you can combine *per person, per hour:* $25 per person for the first hour, and $20 per person for the second hour, so hosting 100 guests for a two-hour reception would cost $4500 [$25 $\times$ 100 = $2500 (+) $20 $\times$ 100 = $2000 (=) $4500]. No consideration is given for those who arrive late or leave early; the fee is $45 per person, regardless.

Flat-Rate Charge

Similar to price per bottle.

The host pays a flat rate for the function based on the assumption that each guest will drink about 2 drinks per hour for the first hour and one drink per hour thereafter. (Check history and demographics of your group.) Costs will vary based on the number of attendees; whether well, call, or premium brands are poured; and the type of food served.

Open Bar

Also called "Host Bar."

Guests do not pay for their drinks; a host or sponsor pays for them. Guests usually drink as much as they want of what they want. Liquor consumption is higher because someone else is paying. A sponsor can be the meeting itself, an exhibitor, a similar organization, and so on. For example, at the Super Show, which features sporting goods, Nike may sponsor a bar.

Calculate Total Cost to Determine the Best Option

If the hotel charges $80 for a bottle of bourbon that yields twenty-seven $1\frac{1}{4}$ ounce drinks, each drink costs the client $2.96. If guests are expected to drink two drinks per hour, for a one-hour reception for 1,000 people, purchasing by the bottle would cost $6,000.

If purchased by the drink, at $4.00 per drink, the same group would cost $8,000.

If purchased at $10 per person (no food), it would cost $10,000.

So, you can see, the hotel makes more money selling per person.

Cash Bar

Also called "No-Host Bar."

Guests buy their own drinks, usually purchasing tickets from a cashier to exchange with a bartender for a drink. At small functions, the bartender may collect and serve, eliminating the cost of a cashier. Cashiers are usually charged as extra labor. Cashiers provide better control and speed up service. Bartenders do not have to handle dirty money and then handle glassware.

Combination Bar

A host purchases tickets and gives each attendee a certain number (usually two). If the guest wants a third drink, he or she must purchase it him- or herself. Or, the host can pay for the first hour, and the bar reverts to a cash bar for the second hour. This method provides free drinks to guests but retains control over costs and potential liability for providing unlimited drinks.

Limited Consumption Bar

Pricing by the drink. Cash register used. The host establishes a dollar amount. When the cash register reaches that amount, the bar is closed. The host may decide to reopen as a cash bar.

LABOR CHARGES

Extra charges are usually levied for bartenders and/or barbacks, cocktail servers, cashiers, security, and corkage. These items are negotiable, depending on the value of the business. For example, if a bar sells over $500 in liquor, the bartender charge may be waived.

A "barback" is the bartender's helper—restocking liquor, keeping fresh ice, clean glasses, and so on—at the bar so the bartender will not have to do it himself during service.

"Corkage" is the fee added to liquor brought into the hotel but not purchased from the hotel. The hotel charges this fee to cover the cost of labor, use of the glasses (which must be delivered to the room, washed, and placed back in storage), mixers, olives, lemon peels, and so forth.

One bar or bartender per every 100 guests is standard. If all guests are arriving at once, or if there is concern about guests standing in long lines, one bar or bartender for every 50 or 75 guests can be used. Unless yours is a very lucrative group, the hotel passes on the labor charges to you.

Number of Drinks per Bottle

		1 OUNCE	$1\frac{1}{4}$ OUNCE	$1\frac{1}{2}$ OUNCE
Liter	33.8 ounces	33	27	22
5th—750 ml	23.3 ounces	25	20	16

SPIRITS

All premium brands are available in 750 ml and 1 liter bottles. One 750 ml bottle equals 20 ($1\frac{1}{4}$ ounce) servings. A one-liter bottle equals 27 ($1\frac{1}{4}$ ounce) servings. Consumption will average 3 drinks per person during a normal reception period.

WINE

All premium brands are available in 750 ml bottles and/or 1.5 liters (magnums):

One 750 ml bottle = five 5-ounce servings
One 1.5 liter bottle = ten 5-ounce servings

Consumption will average 3 glasses per person during a normal reception period, assuming that 50% of the people will order wine; you should order thirty 750 ml bottles for every 100 guests.

Champagne should be served in a flute glass instead of the classic "coupe" because there is less surface exposed to the air, so the bubbles do not escape as fast, causing the champagne to go flat (see figure on p. 223).

Flute and Coupe

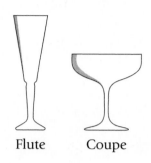

Flute   Coupe

HOSPITALITY SUITES

Hospitality suites are places for attendees to gather outside of the meeting events. They are normally open late in the evening, after 10:00 P.M., but occasionally around the clock:

Morning: Continental breakfast

Afternoon: Snacks and sodas

Evening: Liquor and snacks

Some offer a full bar, some beer and wine only. Some have lots of food, some have only dry snacks. Some offer desserts and specialty coffees. Consider ordering more food if the attendees have had an open evening.

Hospitality suites are usually held in a client's suite on a sleeping room floor, usually handled by room service, and usually sold by catering. Sometimes, they are held in a public function room and are both sold and serviced by catering.

Hospitality suites can be hosted by the sponsoring organization, a chapter of the organization, an exhibitor, a nonexhibiting corporation, an allied association, or a person running for an office in the organization.

Watch for "underground hospitality suites" where unofficial parties pop up. You gain liability and lose revenue. The resulting court case regarding the Tailhook Scandal, in which a female was groped in the hallway at a military meeting at the Las Vegas Hilton, set a precedent that a hotel can no longer claim that it does not know what is going on within the property.

Liquor laws vary from state to state and county to county. Always check the laws in your specific location.

Champagne flutes set the stage for an outdoor event.
Photo by George G. Fenich, Ph.D., Professor, School of HRTA, University of New Orleans

Examples

In Las Vegas and New Orleans, liquor can be sold 24/7.
In California, liquor cannot be sold between 2 A.M. and 6 A.M.
In South Carolina, liquor is sold in airline-size bottles.
In Atlanta, liquor may not be served until noon on Sundays.
In some states, liquor may not be sold at all on Sundays.

There are generally four types of illegal sales, wherever you are located:

Sales to minors
Sales to intoxicated persons
Sales outside legal hours
Improper liquor license

There are on-sale licenses, off-sale licenses, and beer and wine licenses. Licenses stay with the property. For example, if your hotel has a liquor license, it is not valid in the public park across the street. The caterer would need to obtain a special temporary permit.

Planners who wish to bring their own liquor into an establishment must check local laws and be prepared to pay the establishment a per-bottle corkage fee.

ROOMS

ROOM SETUPS

The way the room is set up is a critically important area to be familiar with. How the room is set up can affect the flow of service, the amount of food and beverage consumed, and even the mood of the guests. The ambiance can make or break a meal function—be it a continental breakfast or a formal dinner. (See figure below.)

Room setup includes tables, chairs, decor, and other equipment, such as portable bars, stages, and audiovisual. It is essential that you communicate *exactly* how you want the room to be set to the banquet setup manager. This is accomplished on the Banquet Event Order (BEO) and by using room layout software. These types of programs allow you to place tables, chairs, and other equipment into a meeting room. Free room layout software demos can be downloaded from the following sites:

- *Meeting Matrix:* http://www.meetingmatrix.com
- *Optimum Settings:* http://www.ceosoft.com
- *Room Viewer:* http://www.timesaversoftware.com

Room Layout

Grand Hall

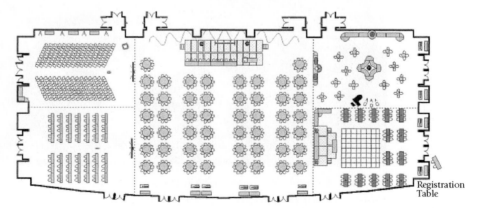

Registration Table

ROOM RENTAL CHARGES

Can they be waived? It varies depending on the venue. If the event is part of a meeting with room nights, it is easier to negotiate away the room charge from the hotel. When undertaking catering events at hotels that are handled by the catering department rather than the sales department because there are no room nights involved, a planner rarely encounters a rental fee for the space. Rather, there will be a minimum sales amount on the room. The group may have to spend $50,000 to secure a ballroom for an event, which frequently means that guests eat *very* well. However, in event venues, otherwise known as off-premise venues, it depends on how the venue has set up its charge/profit schedule. Most off-site venues charge a rental fee. Some charge a rental fee, some an admission fee per guest, a few charge both and then add on the catering, rentals, and service costs. It almost always depends on how big or profitable the event is. Everything is negotiable. At several venues, it may be possible to negotiate the rental

Banquet room set with tables for a function.
Used by permission of Paradise Sound & Light, Orlando, Florida

charge away when bringing a large or highly profitable event to the property. It varies depending on the venue. If the event is part of a meeting with room nights, there sometimes is no charge from the hotel.

Aisle Space

Aisles allow people to move easily around the room without squeezing through chairs and disturbing seated guests. They also provide a buffer between the seating areas and the food and beverage areas. Aisles between tables and around food and beverage stations should be a bare minimum of 36-inches wide (3 feet). It would be preferable to have 48 inches. Leave an aisle around perimeter of room—3 feet minimum. Cross aisles should be 6-feet wide. Check with the local fire marshal for local rules and regulations. Because of the major hotel fires in Las Vegas in the early 1980s, the local fire marshal must check and approve any layout for 200 or more people.

Tables

Allow 10 square feet per person at rectangle banquet tables. Allow $12\frac{1}{2}$ square feet per person at rounds. This assumes the facility is using standard 20- by 20-inch chairs.

Space Requirements for Tables

Rounds	60-inch round =	5-foot diameter =	Round of 8
	72-inch round =	6-foot diameter =	Round of 10
	66-inch round =	Compromise size	Seats 8–10
Rectangle	6-foot long	30-inches wide	Banquet 6
	8-foot long	30-inches wide	Banquet 8
Schoolroom or classroom	6- or 8-foot long	18- or 24-inches wide	
Half-moon table	Half of a round table		
Serpentine	$\frac{1}{4}$ hollowed-out round table		

Space Requirements for Receptions

Minimum (tight)	$5\frac{1}{2}$ to 6 square feet per person
Comfortably crowded	$7\frac{1}{2}$ square feet per person
Ample room	10+ square feet per person

Remember to deduct space taken up for furniture before calculating the number of people. Include large sofas found in many hospitality suites, buffet tables, portable bars, plants, decor and props, check-in tables, and so forth.

Allow 3 square feet per person for dance floors.

Always check local fire codes.

SERVICE

Requirements

One bartender per every 100 guests is standard. If guests will arrive all at once, or you do not want long lines, you could have one bartender for every 50 or 75 guests. There may be an additional labor charge.

Service is critical. Many excellent meals are ruined by poor service. Meal service levels can run from 1 server per 8 guests to 1 server per 40 guests. Most hotel staffing guides allow for 1/32, but most meeting planners want 1/20 or 1/16 with poured wine or French Service.

Savvy meeting planners negotiate for the following:

General

Rounds of 10 : 1 server for every 2 tables

Rounds of 8 : 1 server for every 5 tables

1 buser for every 3 servers

With poured wine or French Service

Round of 10 : 2 servers for every 3 tables

Round of 8 : 1 server for every 2 tables

Buffets 1/40

1 buser for every 4 servers

1 runner per 100 to 125 guests

French or Russian

Rounds of 8 or 10

1 server per table

1 buser per 3 tables

Supervision. One room captain. One section captain for every 250 guests (25 rounds of 10).

Set Over Guarantee. This is negotiable. It is the percentage of guests that the hotel will prepare for beyond the guarantee, in case additional, unexpected people show up.

Average overset is 5%, but you must look at the numbers, not just the percentages.

100 guests = 10% overset

100–1000 guests = 5% overset

Over 1000 guests = 3% overset

Cocktail Servers

Cocktail servers can only carry from 12 to 16 drinks per trip. Counting the time to take the order, the time to wait for the drinks at the service bar, and the time it takes to find the guest and deliver the drink, it takes at least 15 minutes per trip to the bar. This only makes it possible to serve from 48 to 64 drinks per hour. Cocktail servers are usually only used at small or VIP functions.

Service Timing

Fifteen minutes before you want to start serving, dim the lights, ring chimes, start music, open doors, and so on to get the guests to start moving to their tables.

The salad course should take from 20 to 30 minutes, depending on dressing or style of service. The main course should take from 30 to 50 minutes from serving to plate removal. Dessert should take from 20 to 30 minutes.

A typical luncheon: One hour and 15 minutes

A typical dinner: Two hours

TABLESCAPES

The tabletop is the stage—it sets expectations and should reflect the theme of the event. Once seated, the focus is mainly on the table, so it is imperative that it not be overlooked.

A garland of flowers set off this coffee station.
Source: Dorling Kindersley Media Library

The centerpiece should not block sight lines for people sitting across the table from each other. Centerpieces should be low or high with a Lucite or slender pole in the middle portion.

The *cover* is the place setting and includes placement of flatware, and china, and glassware.

Napery is the term to include all table linens, including tablecloths, overlays, napkins, and table skirting.

Other décor may include ribbons, greenery, or other items relating to the theme of the meal.

Examples

Trailing flower garlands or ribbons between place settings
Different colored napkins at each cover
Different napkin folds at each cover
Creative centerpieces
Edible centerpieces, such as a basket of bread

There are major props that can be rented from prop houses, service contractors, party stores, or owned by the hotel or club.

Other props are small, decorative pieces that can be found in many places, such as:

Junk, Goodwill, or antique shops

Auto supply stores

Toy or crafts stores

Garage sales or flea markets

Garden centers

Ethnic food stores or import shops

Travel agencies (destination posters)

Sports clubs or stores

Medical supply stores

Military surplus stores (MASH Party)

◆ SUMMARY

Food and beverage is an integral part of most meetings. Astute planning can save a tremendous amount of money. Knowing what is negotiable and how to negotiate is critical. Food and beverage events create memories and provide a necessary service beyond being a refueling stop. While most attendees do not specify food and beverage events as a reason for attending a meeting, when asked later about the meeting they will often rave (or complain) about these events. Catered events can set the tone of the meeting and create great memories that can result in future business, not only from the planner but also from every guest in attendance.

KEY WORDS AND TERMS

For definitions, see http://glossary.conventionindustry.org.

Action stations

American Service

Attrition

Buffet

Butlered

Call brands

Catered events

English Service

French Service

Guarantee

Menu

On-premise catering

Off-premise catering

Preset

Room setup

Russian Service

Spirits

Types of Functions

Well brands

REVIEW AND DISCUSSION QUESTIONS

Questions to ask when planning for food and beverage:

1. Who will I work with planning the event?
2. Who will be on site during the event?
3. When can I expect your written proposal?
4. What is your policy regarding deposits and cancellations?
5. When is the final payment due?
6. Are there other charges for setup, delivery, overtime, etc.?
7. Do you take credit cards? Do you take personal checks?
8. When must I give you my final guarantee?
9. What percentage is overset above the guarantee?
10. What is the sales tax, and what are your gratuity and/or service charge policies?
11. What are the chef's best menu items?
12. What are your portion sizes?
13. Will wine be poured by the staff or placed on the tables?

14. How many staff will be working the event?

15. What are your substitution policies for vegetarian plates and special meals?

16. Could you pass wine or champagne as guests arrive?

17. How many bartenders will be used during the cocktail hour?

18. Do you provide table numbers?

19. What size tables do you have?

20. What are the options for linen, chair covers, china, stemware, flatware, and charger plates?

21. What decorations do you provide for tables, buffets, and food stations?

22. Are you ADA compliant?

23. Can you provide a podium, mike, and overhead projector?

ABOUT THE CHAPTER CONTRIBUTOR

Patti J. Shock is a professor and chair of the Tourism and Convention Administration Department in the Harrah College of Hotel Administration at the University of Nevada–Las Vegas. She has written three textbooks on catering and teaches catering online as well as on campus. She was named one of the 25 Most Influential People in the Meetings Industry by *Meeting News Magazine* in 2002 and one of the 10 Most Powerful Women in the Convention Industry by *Successful Meetings* in 2002. For more information, visit her Web site at http://tca.unlv.edu/shock.

◆8

DESTINATION MANAGEMENT COMPANIES

DMCs arrange ground transportation. In Thailand, that includes elephant transport.
Photo by George G. Fenich, Ph.D., Professor, School of HRTA, University of New Orleans

◆ Chapter Objectives

This chapter provides the reader with an understanding of the following:

- The destination management industry
- How destination management companies (DMCs) interact with meeting planners, local hotels, event participants, and various suppliers within a destination

- How DMC business is conducted
- The competitive factors at work in the business process
- What projects DMCs pursue
- How DMCs deliver their contracted services

◆ Chapter Outline

Introduction
Services Offered by DMCs
DMC Clients and Customers
Structure of a DMC
DMC Resources
The Destination Management
  Business Process

Summary
Key Words and Terms
Review and Discussion Questions
About the Chapter Contributor

INTRODUCTION

One of the many career disciplines that exist in the MEEC industry is destination management. Careers like meeting management, hotels, convention centers, convention bureaus, airlines, catering, and restaurant management are the more commonly known outside of the meetings and events industry. However, within the industry, destination management plays a key role in the successful planning and delivery of meetings, conventions, and events.

According to the Association of Destination Management Executives (ADME),

A DMC is a professional management company specializing in the design and delivery of events, activities, tours, staffing and transportation utilizing extensive local knowledge, expertise and resources.

By contrast, APEX defines a DMC as *[a] [c]ompany or professional individual engaged in organizing tours, meetings of all types and their related activities. Same as: professional congress organizer (PCO). See also: ground operator.*

Destination management companies (**DMCs**) offer a critical layer of management and are hired by meeting planners to provide local knowledge, experience, and resources to important corporate and association gatherings. DMCs work cooperatively with airlines, hotels and resorts, convention centers, and other service suppliers in the delivery and implementation of MEEC. Successful MEEC events require comprehensive local knowledge of destination infrastructure, local laws and statutes, and regulations, plus qualified information about supplier availability, capabilities, and capacities. Each destination is unique, and only an extensive and ongoing experience in that particular destination, gained through actual project work, can ensure a successful event. While incentive travel is not a specific part of the MEEC industry, DMCs are a key element in that industry as well.

In discussing DMCs and their services, the client project—be it a meeting, exhibition, event, or convention—is typically referred to within the DMC industry as a **program**. A program includes all activities and services provided by a DMC to a customer group while visiting a destination over a finite time frame.

SERVICES OFFERED BY DMCs

DMCs are engaged by meeting and event planners to suggest what combination of destination resources might best fit and satisfy the goals for a particular gathering. After these services are determined, the DMC plans, sets up, and delivers those services. The following is a list of typical services offered by DMCs:

- Hotel selection
- Event venue selection
- Creative itineraries
- Special event concepts
- Creative theme design
- Event production
- Sightseeing options
- Team-building activities

- Meeting support services
- Transportation planning and delivery
- Dining programs
- Entertainers
- Speakers
- **VIP services**
- Staffing services
- Budgeting and resource management

DMC services often include parties and special events designed for companies and organizations to facilitate networking among attendees, to celebrate accomplishments, or to introduce new ideas and/or products. Planners rely on DMCs to provide unique and creative event concepts that will accomplish specific goals within the client's budget and other organizational limitations. In addition to typical meeting management support services like transportation and group leisure activities, all aspects of event production, such as staging, sound, and lights, are offered by DMCs. DMCs are a reliable resource for entertainment options, from a small trio for background music at an intimate cocktail party, to headline entertainment for large **special events**. Familiarity with local musicians and access to the best entertainers is vital for a good DMC. Additionally, DMCs are often expected to suggest and supply décor elements to enhance event spaces and venues. These elements include but are not limited to props, floral designs, lighting effects, table linens and decorations, and sometimes outdoor tenting.

Transportation logistics are a key element of DMCs. Airport "meet and greet" services, along with hotel transfers and baggage management, are offered by all DMCs. Multihotel convention shuttle service is often designed and managed by DMCs. Moving groups of participants—large or small—is an important component of most events that requires precise timing and execution, local expertise, and management responsibility best provided by a professional DMC.

DMCs also provide sightseeing tours, often customized to optimize the attendees' travel experience. DMCs offer recreational activities like golf and tennis tournaments, hiking, fishing, horseback riding, and team-building activities.

Because of the creative element associated with meetings and events, and the variety of each group's needs and expectations, the list of DMC services is almost limitless. One customer may require many services from

Every element of an event must come together if success is to be achieved.
Used by permission of Paradise Sound & Light, Orlando, Florida

a DMC, while another may choose to contract a DMC to provide only one or two components of the overall event.

DMCs prepare detailed proposals for services, which are based on the planner's specifications and budget. A professional meeting planner will provide the DMC with as much information about the participants as possible so that the DMCs' proposed itinerary of activities and services can be designed to best suit the group's purpose, demographics, and expectations.

Initial proposals often include more than one suggested itinerary, thus providing the client with several options, with costs and full details about each included service.

DMC CLIENTS AND CUSTOMERS

DMC clients and customers are those who plan meetings, exhibitions, events, conventions, and incentive travel programs. In this chapter, the terms *customer, client,* and *planner* are used to describe the person, organization, or company for which the DMC is providing services. The client is the representative of the customer company or organization who makes the decision to purchase DMC services. The planner, representing the customer company or organization, is the person (or persons) that the DMC works directly with on programs and events. The customer, client, and planner could be three separate entities or one in the same.

It is important to note that those who participate in the services and activities provided by a DMC are almost always associated with the same company or group, such as a corporate sales force or people who all belong to the same professional organization. Rarely do DMCs service the leisure traveler or tour groups that include "random" participants who have no common connection with others in the group. However, the value of DMC services are recognized by large tour operators and are increasingly employed to assist with transportation and/or tours for these large groups. A good example would be cruise ships that employ DMCs to manage land tours, transportation, and excursions.

A DMC may contract directly with the company or organization whose employees or members will be participating in the program, or it may contract with a professional meeting planner who is offering his or her meeting services to the participating company or organization (see flow chart on p. 240).

Most planners consider the DMC as a local extension of their own office in the destination. They expect the DMC to be their "eyes and ears" in the destination, always acting on their behalf to offer unbiased, experience-based suggestions on matters concerning logistics, venues, event concepts, and social program content. Planners depend on DMCs to help them design event programs that meet their specific needs, which can vary in size, budget, length, and purpose. Sample event programs are as follows:

Sample Flow Chart

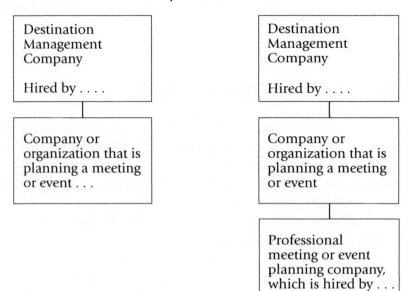

Corporate Meetings

- National sales meetings
- Training meetings
- Product introductions
- Dealer and/or customer meetings

Conventions and Conferences

- Industry trade shows (food, construction, aircraft, etc.)
- Professional trade shows and conferences (architects, doctors, teachers, etc.)
- Fraternal organizations (VFW, Lions, etc.)
- Educational conferences (medical symposia, other professional groups)
- Political conventions

Incentive Programs

- Sales incentives
- Dealer incentives
- Service manager incentives

Special Events

- Super Bowl
- Final Four basketball
- PGA Golf tournaments
- Olympics
- Important corporate occasions

DMCs offer their services to the planners, organizers, and decision makers who are responsible for these events. A DMC is both a consultant and a contractor. Customers contract with a DMC to add a layer of local, professional management at the destination level. By hiring an expert in the destination, the planner adds a critically important element to the team: local knowledge. While the meeting planner may be quite experienced at the planning and implementation of meeting programs and events, the planner is not likely highly experienced in the particular destination. The DMC becomes the voice of experience on the team when it comes to questions of logistics, choosing local suppliers, and the viability of program components.

STRUCTURE OF A DMC

Unlike hotels, resorts, convention centers, and restaurants, a DMC does not require an extensive capital investment to start up and operate its business. The DMC office is usually located in office space somewhere near the area where most meetings and events take place in its destination. Proximity to major airports is also an advantage, since so many program services involve group arrivals and departures.

Primary responsibilities and job titles for a DMC can vary from company to company. Many DMCs are small, stand-alone, single-office companies that are locally owned and operated. The owner usually runs the company and plays a major role in sales, operations, and administration. Other, larger companies may have offices in multiple destinations with local staff fulfilling management responsibilities on all levels. (See table and organizational chart on p. 242.)

Categories of DMC Job Responsibilities, with Sample Job Titles

Management and Administration

- General Manager
- Office Manager
- Accounting Manager
- Executive Assistant
- Administrative Assistant
- Receptionist
- Research Assistant

Sales and Marketing

- Director of Sales
- Director of Marketing
- Director of Special Events
- Sales Manager
- Sales Coordinator
- Proposal Writer
- Research Analyst

Operations and Production

- Director of Operations
- Director of Special Events
- Operations Manager
- Production Manager
- Transportation Manager
- Staffing Manager

Field Staff

- Meet and Greet Staff
- Tour Guide
- Transportation Manager
- Event Supervisor
- Field Supervisor
- Equipment Manager

Sample DMC Organizational Chart

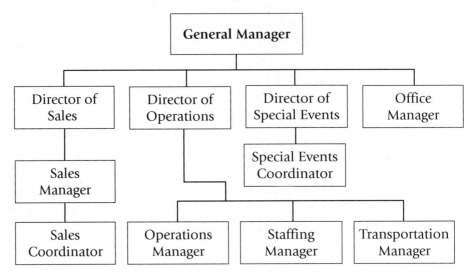

DMCs must find business opportunities, propose appropriate services, contract the business, set up and prepare for the group's arrival, deliver the contracted services to the customers, and follow up with billing and program reconciliation. Supplier companies must be contracted, **field staff** must be hired, and program staff must be assigned. Field staff, which include tour guides, hospitality desk staff, and airport "meet and greet" staff, are usually temporary, casual employees who are hired by a DMC only for the term of the program. It is common for field staff in a destination to work for more than one DMC as the needs arise for their services.

The job titles listed are examples and can vary from company to company. The fact remains that there are sales and promotion responsibilities, operations and production responsibilities, and management and administrative responsibilities. As in most companies, the levels of authority and reporting lines can and do vary, usually based on the size of the company and the qualifications of its staff. The "Director of Special Events" title appears under Sales and Marketing as well as **Operations and Production**. This is because this position can be either or both, depending on the company and the individual executive's area of expertise.

DMCs do not normally own transportation equipment (vehicles), props, décor, or other supplies that the DMC packages and sells to the customers. DMCs buy from selected suppliers and manage those products and services in the context of the larger event program. As such, the DMC becomes a "conduit" for the services of a myriad of local supplier companies, which, combined with DMC staff and management, produces the overall desired program components.

A critical characteristic for a successful DMC is its complete objectivity in recommending and selecting suppliers and services for the client's program. Meeting planners depend on their DMC to select the absolute best provider for the services that fit the client's budget and program specifications. By disassociating itself financially from the products and services offered to its clients, the client can be assured that its purchasing dollar is optimized and that there is no financial conflict of interest by the DMC as it contracts with suppliers. Clients should feel comfortable that the DMC is earning its money for its management services and not from some financial "arrangement" with the supplier companies.

DMC RESOURCES

As local experts are positioned to assist planners with their projects in a destination, DMCs are expected to provide vital resources for those planners:

- ***Products:*** The products that a DMC offers are presented in a portfolio of services. Besides logistical services, which consist primarily of transportation and related support staffing, these services may also include creative elements that the DMC has custom designed, such as theme parties, customized tours, and creative team-building activities. Some items are exclusively offered, while others are stock items usually offered by other DMCs in the same destination. New ideas are necessary to revamp offerings and create new ones. The biggest single challenge facing DMCs is the need to constantly innovate and be creative. A new idea is a valuable commodity, and DMCs have experienced difficulties with this sort of intellectual property. It is considered unethical to "borrow" a DMC's creative ideas without employing the services of the DMC.

- ***Reputation:*** The key asset for any DMC is a track record of customer satisfaction. Service being the DMC's primary product, client satisfaction is the best indicator of a DMC's reputation in the destination. Since a DMC is hired as a valued consultant and is a layer of management for the planner, it makes sense that the DMC's reputation would be a major factor in winning business. It is said that a DMC is only as good as the last program or event that has been completed. Equally important as customer satisfaction is the DMC's reputation among local suppliers. It is critical for the DMC to have established good relationships with key suppliers in the destination, and for the DMC to have earned a reputation as a quality, professional company with which to do business.

- ***Experience:*** Possibly the most valuable advantage a planner finds in a DMC is experience in the industry. Given the almost infinite number of challenges a DMC can face in the course of doing business, experience is the best teacher. Having a company that has been through the trial and error process is most important. Considering the relative ease of entry into the DMC business (primarily due to low start-up costs), experience is the critical element that distinguishes newcomers from established, professional DMCs.

DMCs may make arrangements for models, this one in costume.
Photo by George G. Fenich, Ph.D., Professor, School of HRTA, University of New Orleans

- *Relationships:* Key resources that a DMC is expected to bring to the table are relationships. In addition to established relationships with quality suppliers, also important are relationships with airports, hotels, law enforcement, regulatory agencies, city hall, and other people who can "get things done" for the planner's group while visiting the destination. The term *destination savvy* is often used when describing a DMC who has the right connections and knows how to use them.

- *Suppliers and Vendors:* Other than local knowledge, virtually everything that a DMC sells to a planner must be purchased from supplier companies—packaged, managed, and delivered. The DMC is expected to have an inventory of competent, high-quality suppliers who become partners in delivering the final program content. It is easy to determine that a caterer is needed for an off-property event. However, knowing the best of the available caterers in the area that can satisfy the specific needs and demographics of a group is what a DMC is expected to do. This knowledge and experience is required in all supplier categories, including transportation equipment, props, floral, lighting, sound equipment, event venues, and entertainers. The DMC is expected to know the appropriate combinations of suppliers that can make an event a success, and equally important, who to stay away from. Reliable vendors and suppliers are critical for a successful program.

- *Credit and Buying Power:* The DMC should have ongoing relationships in its community. It should develop good credit ratings through business volume and professional business dealings with hotels, supplier companies, and the independent staff who work for the DMC year round. Unexpected things can, and do, happen during programs that require changes and additional services to be added on site. The DMC must have the "clout" and buying power to make things happen quickly and without incident.

THE DESTINATION MANAGEMENT BUSINESS PROCESS

The DMC business process has been compared to other enterprises, particularly advertising firms. Although very different industries, there are many similarities between advertising firms and DMCs that help illustrate the DMC business process. Each is expected to be creative and innovative. Immense pressures ride on the outcome and success of the contracted services in terms of a customer company's image and reputation. The DMC, like an advertising firm, is expected to protect and enhance the image and reputation of its customers.

Comparison Between Advertising Firms and DMCs

Typically, an advertising firm identifies a target account and contacts the account's decision maker, hoping to demonstrate the advertising firm's capabilities to the potential client. This is done through direct and electronic communications, and presentations that illustrate these capabilities of the advertising company in various ways, usually with examples of successful jobs performed for other customers.

Similarly, a DMC seeks out new accounts to request an opportunity to present its capabilities that will meet the customer's requirements. DMCs also present this information through direct and electronic communications and presentations. These presentations almost always exhibit the DMC's competence using examples of successful programs operated for similar customers.

Many advertising firms are apt to make presentations to the same new customer. Typically, the customer will choose two or more advertising firms to compete for the account. At that point, the customer will give the competing firms specific guidelines outlining what is required and expected. The advertising firms will then develop more elaborate, creative advertising campaigns and services that they believe will attract the customer's favor and win the business. In most cases, these sample ad campaigns are presented to the customer without cost for the customer to use in evaluating the various advertising firms.

Similarly, the potential DMC customer will usually choose two or more DMCs to bid on its program based on a set of specifications. Each DMC then provides detailed, creative **proposals** for service, which it believes will best satisfy the client's specifications. These proposals are almost always delivered free of charge, intended to win the customer's favor and be awarded the account.

Just as the advertising firms spend valuable time and resources in pursuing potential business opportunities, so do DMCs. That time and expense is justified by winning advertising firms and DMCs as they hope to add an account on which to build future revenues and profit. Losing advertising firms and DMCs have spent valuable time and resources for no immediate return and must make up the lost expense on future, successful accounts.

A major issue in the DMC industry is the practice of providing detailed proposals at no cost to customers. Because of the often considerable cost and time required to formulate a customized proposal, DMCs must choose wisely when determining what potential business to pursue. This example illustrates one typical potential scenario for obtaining business projects. Business is secured by DMCs in other ways, which is discussed later in this chapter.

A. Basic Business Requirements

Some prerequisite items are essential to the destination management business process. The following items are some basic requirements to operate a DMC:

- Staff
- Temporary "field staff"
- Office
- Technology
- Licenses and insurance
- Community contacts
- Customer contacts
- **History**
- Destination resources

A strategically located office with competent, experienced staff and employees are a basic necessity to winning and operating business in any destination. Convenient proximity to major hotels, convention facilities, tourist attractions, and event venues is a must. Every top DMC must have access to the best possible technology available. DMC clients are usually larger companies and often major corporations that use highly sophisticated technology and expect compatible electronic communications capabilities with their chosen DMC. Communications equipment; office computer capabilities, including database management; imaging software; and high-speed Internet are all expected to be standard in today's DMC. Quick processing of information and the ability to make on-the-spot changes and produce professional documents and graphics is an industry necessity.

Without a doubt, a DMC must be legally insured for business liability as well as other standard coverage, such as workers' compensation and automobile insurance. Each destination has some unique laws and local licenses required to perform DMC services. Customers and planners must be confident that their chosen business partners are adequately insured and knowledgeable about local laws and ordinances that could affect the successful operation and production of their programs and events.

As are many businesses in the service sector, destination management is a relationship-driven industry. Customers and planners literally put their reputations and jobs on the line when selecting a DMC. DMCs must have extensive community contacts among hotels, attractions, convention bureaus, airports, law enforcement, and the supplier community. It is only with the cooperation from these valuable relationships—gained through repeated work experiences—that a DMC can properly service its clients.

Relationships outside of the destination community, that is, in the customer community, are also important to the success of a DMC. The most valuable asset a DMC has is its history of success. A DMC's reputation and track record is the best proof a planner can rely on when choosing a DMC partner.

Finally, the destination community must have the necessary resources to execute a well-run program or event. It is not enough for the community to have a caterer; it must have competitive caterers with reputations for high standards, skills, and quality. This is true for all contracted supplier services, such as transportation providers, entertainers, and attractions.

B. The Sales Process for DMCs

For DMCs to be successful, new business projects must be continually found and secured for the company. Business opportunities present themselves in a variety of ways. Not all DMCs service all business sectors. Some DMCs specialize in association convention business, some in corporate meetings and events, and others in international travel groups. Some DMCs work with individual travelers, while others focus heavily on the domestic incentive market. Most DMCs operate in multiple markets, which are usually determined by the nature of their destination.

In other words, the infrastructure and appeal of the destination dictates which of the mentioned market segments DMCs will find suitable in which to do business. Infrastructure like convention centers, convention hotels, resorts, and airport facilities all play into the equation. Destination appeal like natural and man-made attractions play heavily into whether or not corporations will plan important meetings and/or incentive travel rewards in a location. Beaches, mountains, forests, weather, quality golf availability, fishing, theater, arts, culture, gambling, and theme parks all can exhibit destination appeal.

As in most businesses, DMCs have annual business plans, which include budgets for revenue and expenses. To achieve the business plan, a sales and marketing plan is developed and implemented. Portions of this plan include items such as the following:

- Industry trade show attendance
- Sales calls on new and existing customers
- Membership and participation in various industry associations
- Community sales efforts and networking at industry events
- Utilization of representation firms
- Brochures and other collateral materials
- Company newsletters
- Partnerships and memberships in DMC industry groups

1. Identifying New Business Opportunities

The first stage of the sales process is to discover new business opportunities and pursue those customers.

Almost all new business opportunities involve going where the customers are or where the customers do business. This can be attendance at industry trade shows where potential customers are known to attend. Some example trade shows are the American Society of Association Executives (ASAE), Greater Washington Society of Association Executives (GWSAE), Meeting World, Incentive Travel & Meetings Exposition (IT&ME), and Meetings West. Sales executives representing DMCs must carefully research these trade shows to maximize their sales and marketing dollar. Knowing in advance which potential customers will attend and knowing what business opportunities they represent better ensures the DMC's prospects for creating new client relationships.

Some customers, particularly corporate customers, incentive companies, and meeting management companies, will sometimes designate a "preferred" DMC in selected destinations. For DMCs, this is known as a "house account." Whenever planners from a house account require services, the chosen DMC is in position to help without going through the often-rigorous competitive bid process with other DMCs.

These accounts are very important and require careful maintenance. There is great competition for such accounts, and competitor DMCs are always eager in their attempts to take over these accounts. Periodic visits to these customers and open lines of communication are vital in maintaining these relationships. In addition to continued good service, part of the successful "maintenance" of these relationships may include membership in the same industry organizations as the planners. Attending these organizations' conferences and meetings allows DMC representatives to visit and network among planners.

Memberships in industry organizations like PCMA, MPI, Health Care Exhibitors Association (HCEA), and the Society of Incentive & Travel Executives (SITE) are typically part of a DMC's business plan. Using these memberships to learn about managing meetings, conventions, events, and conferences, while working alongside potential and current customers, has obvious advantages.

Sales efforts on the local, destination level are considered by most companies to be an important part of any sales plan. Creating relationships with industry representatives in the community who do business with the same customers and planners as the DMC is an efficient way to identify new business opportunities. Networking at local hospitality industry functions, such as local HSMAI (Hospitality Sales and Management Association International) monthly meetings or convention bureau "mixers," is a common practice among successful DMCs. Staying abreast of industry news, people who work in the industry, and knowing changes in services and staffing within the local industry make for a well-informed DMC.

Because a local, "one-destination DMC" does not enjoy an economy of scale as that of a national DMC, such as USA Hosts, consortiums have been formed. An example of this would be "The Network Companies." This group was formed in order to pool resources from individual one-city DMCs for sales and marketing purposes. Other such "DMC groups" exist primarily for the sharing of mutual sales and marketing efforts and expenses.

In some cases, particularly with DMC groups, it makes sense to employ professional representation firms to call on particular market segments in which they specialize. Usually, this representation is contracted for a particular geographic location. New York, Chicago, and London are good examples of places where a representation firm

USA Hosts is one of the largest DMCs in the United States.
Provided courtesy of Terry Epton, Executive Vice President, USA Hosts

might be contracted. These companies typically call on existing as well as new, potential customers in the geographic area on behalf of a DMC. They will seek to familiarize planners about the DMC while trying to uncover leads for future business. When appropriate, these representation firms will sometimes also serve as a local liaison between the customer and the DMC.

Collateral materials are essential to a comprehensive sales and marketing plan. Collateral materials include brochures, letterheads, business cards, proposal shells, and fact sheets for the various activities and services offered by the DMC. In addition to these materials, a DMC will often produce a company newsletter to enhance the company's image and recognition in the industry. Brand names are difficult to establish in the DMC industry, as most DMCs are one-city companies that tend to be smaller than DMCs that operate in multiple destinations. Multicity DMCs, such as USA Hosts, have an easier time establishing brand identity due to more national exposure among clientele.

2. The Proposal Stage in the Sales Process

Once a DMC has secured the sales lead, contacted the customer, and convinced that client to consider the DMC as a possible supplier and partner in an upcoming program, the DMC will be asked to provide a proposal of services. The following items must be considered and addressed in this proposal stage:

- Project specifications
- Research and development
- Creativity and innovation
- Budgets
- Response time
- Competition

As a DMC begins to determine exactly what to offer a customer in a proposal of services, the client's project specifications become a valuable tool. A great deal of detailed information is usually included in these specifications, such as:

- Group size
- Choice of hotel, resort type
- Meeting space allotments
- Dates of service
- Types of services required
- Demographic information about the attendees
- Management's goals for the meeting or event
- Approximate budget available to produce the meeting or event
- History regarding the group's past successes and challenges
- Various other "include" and/or "do not include" items
- Deadlines for completion and proposal submission

Armed with these specifications and other information gained through ongoing customer contact, previous experience with the customer, and other research, the DMC will determine what items to offer in the proposal of services. The first step is usually a series of creative meetings among DMC staff to discuss what might best satisfy the client specifications to win the business. After these meetings, research and development of proposal components should begin. Availability of suppliers, venues, transportation, and entertainers, plus bids for services like catering, transportation equipment, and venue costs, are all reviewed and incorporated into the proposal. Costs for all items must be identified for budgeting and pricing decisions.

A winning proposal not only satisfies the client specifications but also best satisfies the client's desire to exceed the expectations of the participants of the particular program. Creativity and innovation are usually prized as high-value items in proposals. Selected programs become a reflection on the customer company; therefore, creative and innovative components, along with a thorough, well-designed program, tends to win the business. Response time is a critical factor when producing proposals. Creativity takes time, and if rushed, less creative, more "standard" items might be offered. A proposal that does not meet its deadline will seldom win the business.

A final and critical step in the proposal process is pricing. Several factors must be considered when pricing the items included in the proposal, such as the following:

- Total estimated costs for delivering the proposed services
- Staff time and involvement necessary to carry out the proposed services—before, during, and after the program
- Amount of DMC resources necessary to operate the program
- Unknown costs, which are factored into the planning stages
- Factors surrounding supplier choice and availability
- Time of the year and local business activity during a particular season
- Costs of taking staff and company capacity off the market for this customer
- Factors regarding competitive bids on the project

Depending on the competitive factors at hand, decisions must be made about how to approach a given business opportunity. DMC resources are finite and must be allocated in as efficient a fashion as possible. If a planner is entertaining bids on a project, the DMC may well be pitted against two, three, or even more competitors. Deciding how much time and company effort is appropriate to dedicate to a particular bid involves an educated management decision. The following questions are the type that a DMC should answer prior to making a final decision on how much effort to dedicate to a given opportunity. The DMC in some cases may choose not to bid at all.

- What is the revenue potential of the business opportunity?
- What is the value of a future relationship with the customer?
- How much proposal work will be involved in the bid?
- What is the bid deadline?
- How many companies are bidding?

- Which competitors are bidding?
- What success rate does your company have on similar projects?
- What success rate do your competitors have?
- What time of year will the program be operating?
- What are the approximate odds of winning the program?
- How profitable will the program be?

DMCs do not give estimates but rather design a program with suggested components and offer it at prices that are assured should their proposal be accepted. Each proposal will be different in various ways. If a selection of tours and activities are requested in the bid specifications, each DMC will offer a selection that it feels will best fit the demographics of the group, budget, and factors like time constraints and season. If a theme party is specified, the competitors will hope to prevail with a creative mix of décor, entertainment, and food and beverage. These proposals often vary greatly in style, concept, and price.

Given the variety among proposal elements offered by the competing DMCs, a customer is not in a position to choose a winning bidder based solely on price. Some other important factors must be considered, such as the following:

- Is the proposal feasible?
- What is the perceived value of services offered?
- Will the participants appreciate the suggested program?
- Will the quality be sufficient to make the program or event a success?
- Is the DMC capable of producing the program or event in an acceptable manner?

Planners tend to be measured on the outcome of the meetings and events they plan. Choosing a DMC can be a decision not entirely based on price. Some things are too important to simply award to the lowest bidder. A planner's choice must be balanced and well thought out. Planners can literally find themselves placing their job temporarily in the hands of the chosen DMC if the program is an important one. One can see the value of developing a good relationship before, during, and after the bidding process. A DMC that delivers a successful, well-run program for a planner may well become that planner's preferred supplier for years to come.

3. Site Inspections

While not always required, an often expensive component of the sales process in terms of DMC time and resources is the **site inspection**. A site inspection is a physical review of proposed venues, services, tours, and/or activities prior to the actual program. A site inspection may be required at any point in the sales process. The site inspection visit by the planner could occur prior to the proposal as a part of the information gathering, after the proposal and prior to the customer decision, or after the DMC has been chosen, as a first step in the finalization of a program or event. Site inspections can vary in time and detail but always require special attention by busy DMC sales and/or operations executives.

These inspection trips must be carefully planned and orchestrated to show a customer the places and inclusions of the proposed program and also to demonstrate the DMC's operational skills, its organization, and community contacts and relationships. The site inspection can often be the most critical step in winning a customer's business, as this is the time when the DMC has an opportunity to develop a relationship with the customer and gain the customer's confidence. Many programs have been won or lost over a seemingly simple lunch conversation during a site inspection.

C. Contracts of Services

Contracts are necessary in all aspects of the meetings and events industry. Hotels, convention centers, cruise ships, airlines, and DMCs all produce contracts, which spell out exactly what is being purchased and the details of the purchase (see chapter 12, on legal issues, for more information). DMC contracts can vary in size depending on the amount of services required. All DMC contracts should minimally include the following items:

- Accurate identification of buyer and seller
- Date of contract
- Date(s) of service(s)
- Detailed itinerary listing each activity and service with pricing
- Detailed listing of services and items that are included in each activity and service

Meeting rooms and their layouts should be checked during site inspections.
Source: Pearson Education/PH College

- Deadlines, costs, and procedure for requesting changes
- Force Majeure clause
- Guarantees (identification of services that may require a guaranteed number of participants)
- Deposit and payment policy and amounts
- Cancellation policy
- Information regarding participation by minors
- Remittance instructions

D. Program Preparation

After a program is contracted, a transition begins to take place, moving from active selling to operations and production. At this time, all suppliers that will be employed by the DMC in the course of satisfying the contract are notified that the program is definite, and their services are confirmed. Operations staff, which are usually different from the sales staff in larger DMCs, meet with the sales representatives to review the customer's needs, program goals, and any details, which will be a factor in the successful delivery of the program.

During this phase of the business process, participant numbers can fluctuate, requiring the DMC to reevaluate costs and other operational details. With active involvement by the client, other activities and services may be added or removed from the program during this planning time. It is most important that the DMC be available and responsive to these changes. As a contracted member of the customer's team, the DMC is responsible for the destination management portion of the larger, overall customer event—the DMC must be fully cooperative and flexible.

The program's project manager, either an operations or events manager, assumes primary responsibility for the entire program or event. During the setup period, each activity and service for the program is reviewed and confirmed in detail. Full-time and part-time professional program managers, supervisors, tour guides, and escorts are scheduled well in advance. Part-time staff is generally categorized as "field staff" and usually plays a subordinate role to the DMC's full-time program and event management personnel. Other managers may be assigned to various portions of the program, such as transportation, food and beverage, tours and activities, entertainment, and/or hospitality desk management.

E. Program Operations and Production

DMCs exist to produce programs and events, coordinating numerous staff and suppliers into one cohesive program of products and services. The DMC utilizes its vast experience and collective talent to provide a layer of consulting and hands-on management of a variety of assets, resources, suppliers, and staff to produce an outwardly seamless program of events. Some of the categories that are important in the on-site management of programs and events are as follows:

- Transportation management
- Event production
- Tour and activity management
- Support staff supervision
- Supplier and vendor management
- Meeting support
- Customer relations
- On-site changes, challenges, and contingencies
- Troubleshooting
- Community liaison
- Information source

After finding the opportunity, creating proposals, conquering the competition, earning the planner's confidence, contracting the program, and careful preparations, it is up to the operations and production staff to successfully deliver the program. At this culmination, everything is "on the line"—the sponsoring organization's image, the planner's reputation, the DMC's future prospects with the planner, the DMC's reputation in the destination, and depending on the program, large sums of money are all at risk.

If the program is for a major association's convention, the association's members' perception of the organization is at stake. The American Medical Association, the American Bar Association, the National Automobile Dealers Association, the National Association of Television Program Executives, and the National Association of Secondary School Principals are all examples of associations that would employ a DMC to propose and deliver selected components for their conventions. Meeting and event planners for these prestigious associations and countless others are orchestrating major events with thousands of participants. The participant's perception of the convention can easily be affected by the quality of the

DMCs may arrange outdoor performances.
Used by permission of Paradise Sound & Light, Orlando, Florida

shuttle transportation to and from the convention hall, the quality of the networking events, cocktail parties, meal service, and activities like the annual
golf tournament and optional sightseeing tours. All of these items are
potentially the DMC's responsibility. The shuttle has to operate efficiently.
The events must live up to the participants' expectations. The activities and
tours must be entertaining and well run, and provide value for price. The
participants are the association planner's customers. Membership renewals
and future convention attendance are affected by the quality of the program delivery.

Similar dynamics are in effect with corporate programs. The annual
new model dealer shows for automobile manufacturers have millions of
dollars riding on the outcome of these events. Insurance companies reward
top sales producers with **incentive programs** that effectively show the
best of their workforce how the company values their top executives.
Computer companies and software companies produce new product
introduction events either as stand-alone events or in conjunction with
industry conventions. The success of these ventures has the future of the
sponsoring companies at stake.

Through these examples, one can clearly see the tremendous pressure on running a logistically sound and high-quality program of events. This is riding on the shoulders of the meeting and event planners and the DMCs chosen to support them. The DMC's operations and production staff have one chance to deliver the program. An event cannot be rescheduled for the next day if the venue is not ready. If the bus and limousine suppliers do not provide equipment as ordered, the departure time cannot be changed. When the curtain goes up, the show must go on. Reliability and responsibility are the most important issues. Price runs a distant second to reliability on sight. The value of the DMC is indisputable now. However, all DMCs are not equal, and choosing the best fit for a particular program is essential. A close working relationship that fosters confidence, easy communication, and a mutual understanding of goals and priorities requires that the planner's DMC contact be instantly available. Similarly, the planner must be immediately available to the DMC's operation manager throughout the course of the program.

Transportation management is a major part of a DMC's business. It encompasses routing, equipment (vehicle) use, staff requirements, special venue considerations, equipment staging areas, driver briefings, staff scheduling and briefings, maps, signage, preparations for driver breaks, and the reconfirmation of all services. Transportation scenarios and requirements are usually scattered throughout the program itinerary.

Corporate programs usually begin with airport transfers. Airport transportation services customarily include "meet and greet" service and luggage management. Meet and greet service consists of DMC staff holding welcome signs and greeting arriving guests from the sponsoring company. Management of the arrival manifest by the airport transportation manager is a key component of the service. The manifest is a detailed list of each guest's arrival flight, time, and participant name. The manager schedules both staff and equipment with the arrival manifest as a guide. People change flights, miss flights, and fail to accurately supply flight information. Flights can be delayed or canceled. Because of the inaccuracies common to arrival manifest, the transportation manager must not only expect surprises but plan for them. Constant communication is necessary between the DMC and the airlines, the DMC and the transportation equipment suppliers, and the airport meet and greet staff. Equally important is the need to keep open communication with the hotel(s) to which the participants are being transferred and the meeting planner, who is probably receiving information about individual participants' changes in travel plans.

Meet and greet services are not limited to the United States. Ugandan dancers and others welcome the Malaysian prime minister.

Source: AP/Wide World Photos

When airport transfers are run properly, the participants receive a friendly welcome by someone who knows their name, after which they are directed to the proper baggage belt to identify their luggage. From there they are brought, along with their luggage, to the waiting vehicle ready to transport them to their hotel. Motorcoaches, minibuses, vans, sedans, and limousines could all be used at the direction of the planner and depending on the service purchased. A DMC must proactively manage the changes and challenges of airport transportation. The first impression made on a participant is the arrival transfers, and the last impression is the departure transfers.

Transportation requirements often include shuttle services between the shuttle focus, perhaps an event venue, and the participating hotel(s). Shuttle supervisors, dispatchers, and directional staff, sometimes referred to as "human arrows," manage this personalized service. Point-to-point transfers are often required to move groups of participants during a program.

Whatever the transportation requirement, the DMC is expected to plan, prepare, and deliver the service in a timely and efficient manner.

Event production is also a major part of destination management. Events can be large or small, on a hotel property, or in a remote location. Events can be extensive, lavish, and expensive. Events can be fun, casual, and unpretentious. Some examples are as follows:

- Cocktail receptions and networking events
- Breakfasts, luncheons, and dinners
- Dining events at unique venues
- Gala dinner events
- Extravagant theme parties
- Outdoor and indoor team–building events

These events each have a purpose and a budget. DMC production staff must deliver the contracted event in a fashion that satisfies the purpose of the event. Some examples of events are as follows:

- Events that promote corporate staff and top executives to meet and mingle with their company's middle management
- Events that provide an opportunity for the company's sales people to interact with their largest customers and dealers of the company's products
- Culminating events at the final night of an incentive program with the intent to "knock the socks off" of the attendees and fire them up about the next sales campaign
- Events to simply provide a casual atmosphere for company employees to network and renew acquaintances since their last meeting

A very large "extravaganza" event must be produced as contracted. The production staff must manage the event venue, security, suppliers of sound and light equipment, staging, entertainers, decor, floral designs, table linens, food and beverage, environmental concerns, staff, and countless other details. Experience is essential. Strong working relationships are necessary with all key suppliers; choosing appropriate staff and producing a production schedule are essential to a successful event. Preliminary meetings that bring together the key suppliers to discuss and provide input on the production schedule is a fundamental step in the planning process. Realistic setup/move–in schedules and cooperative suppliers ensure a smooth-running event.

Operations staff must be familiar with all the necessary municipal regulations regarding insurance, fire safety codes, crowd control, and police requirements. Considering all these issues, there is no substitute for experience and working with a DMC that has a known track record of success.

Whether planning and operating sightseeing tours, a scavenger hunt, a golf tournament, or running a hospitality desk, sound preparation, strong organizational skills, and a sense of commitment and responsibility are essential traits for a professional DMC operations manager. Everything is riding on his or her performance. Planners tend to bond with the managers and become dependent on them to be their on-site consultants in the community. Questions and requests for VIP arrangements are not unusual, usually on site, with little advance notice, such as the following:

> *"Where can I send my VP of marketing and her husband for a romantic dinner? She just realized that today's their wedding anniversary!"*
> *"My company president is arriving early in the corporate jet. Can we get a limo to the executive airport in forty-five minutes?"*
> *"The boss just decided he wants a rose for all of the ladies at tonight's party."*
> *"Can we get Aretha Franklin to sing 'Happy Birthday' to one of our dealers during her set at the party tonight?"*

A wise person said, "It is often the little things, the details that separate great events from ordinary ones." Knowing someone's favorite wine, song, or dessert can turn an ordinary event into one that will be remembered forever. Things that are not in the contract but become available to add special touches to an event are great opportunities for a production person with a passion for success. A production manager who has solid relationships with his or her suppliers can often see those suppliers swept up in the process and wanting to suggest additions or program improvements. Suppliers do this because they want the event that they are associated with to be the best it can be as well as to establish an ongoing relationship with the DMC for possible future events. Planners are typically pleased to be presented with options. Being offered confetti cannons for the dance floor area, additional accent lighting, or separate martini bars are good examples of on-site event upgrades.

An event producer who is on schedule and comfortable with the progress of an event's setup is likely to be the person offering the finishing touches that turn a good event into a great and unforgettable one.

DMC operations and production managers must be knowledgeable about every facet of the programs and events that they manage. They must be knowledgeable about the customer, the destination, the group's participants, the event venues, the suppliers, the staff, and numerous other factors. Onsite challenges and changes are a fact of doing business. As a result, these operations and production managers must constantly be troubleshooters, looking for what might be an issue later in the program and keeping the planner aware of every important detail that changes or may need to be changed.

Much of an operations or production manager's day is spent confirming and reconfirming services. Constant communication with vendors and suppliers who are participating in a program is critical to ensure that final participant counts and timing are accurate as well as reconfirming all service details. Another form of reconfirmation is "advancing" a venue, which is when DMC staff arrives well ahead of a group to make sure that the service staff and event location are prepared and properly set up prior to the participants' arrival. Details like number of seats, room temperature, serving instructions, menu inclusions, and beverage service are all examples of items that should be verified while advancing a dinner event.

Operations and production managers are a trusted source of information for the planners, serving as community liaisons for the DMC's customers. DMC representatives are typically asked to recommend restaurants, golf courses, beauty salons, doctors, dance clubs, antique shops, and countless other service providers. DMC representatives are expected to be experts in all facets of their community.

Throughout each program and event, operations and production managers must carefully monitor the original contracted services and all changes that occur after the original itinerary and contract are signed and approved. Each and every addition to the program, such as changes in participant counts, times of service, and additional services, must be documented. Accurate, up-to-the-minute data on the actual services delivered must be kept for billing purposes. To avoid billing disputes, it is also important to identify who authorized each change or addition. Ideally, these authorizations are in writing and approved in advance by the client.

F. Billing and Follow-Up

The final invoice for a program or event should mirror the contract of services agreed on prior to the operation of the program. Actual services delivered should be outlined along with the number of participants that each line item is based on. In most cases, items are billed on "lot" costs or per person. Lot costs are fixed and independent of the number of participants, such as bus hours, the price of an entertainer, or a décor package for a ballroom. Per-person pricing is based on the actual number of participants, such as food and beverage at a luncheon that is usually billed at a fixed price per person, plus tax and gratuities.

The contract should spell out exactly what services are authorized and at what prices. Prices, especially those that are "per person," are often based on a minimum number of participants. The per-person price of a meal may be based on 100 participants. If that is the case and only 87 people were actually served, the client would be billed for 100 people, the minimum. However, if 107 people were served, the bill would reflect the per-person price for 107 people.

All additions or deletions to the originally contracted services should appear on the invoice. The "grand total" for the program should be reflected along with all deposits and payments received prior to the final billing. Whenever possible, final billing details should be reviewed and approved by the planner or representative on site at the completion of the program, while details about the program's operation, additions, and changes are still fresh in everyone's mind. The more time that elapses between the time the program is completed and receipt of the final invoice creates opportunities for disputes about program details like participant counts, times, and items that were approved to be added to the program.

While not a standard with all DMCs, the practice of sending follow-up program evaluations is extremely valuable in obtaining customer feedback about the quality of a DMC's services. Using this critical feedback to improve services is a key to staying in the best possible form for future programs and events. The responses and comments received by the DMC can also be a valuable tool in training and evaluation of employees and management, since senior management cannot always be on site to evaluate their operations managers at work.

DESTINATION MANAGEMENT FICTIONAL CASE STUDY

It was Thursday afternoon, and American Hosts' sales manager Andrew Christensen received the call just before five o'clock as he was adding final touches to handouts and his *PowerPoint* presentation for a Monday morning meeting at the local convention and visitor bureau.

With the Genesis Automotive planners in town for a site inspection through the weekend, Andrew was not expecting any new assignments. In an hour, he was meeting the two Genesis planners at their hotel and later briefing them at dinner about the venues he had scheduled for visits on Saturday. Andrew had a town car reserved with a local livery company's best driver.

A special location was necessary for the introduction of the new Genesis SUV. Andrew had both the Sports Arena and the Water Front Amphitheater on tentative "hold." Their representatives were briefed on the client's needs and the special circumstances surrounding the event. Four other venues were also on hold, but Andrew was confident that one of his top two recommendations would meet the client's expectations.

Since the phone was already ringing, Andrew took a deep breath, cleared his head of other issues, and as he greeted the unknown caller he heard, "Andrew, I'm glad I caught you! This is Kathy Hashimoto at Randford Research. I have a project and may need your help." Andrew did not know it, but he was about to embark on his biggest sale in three years—because he was on the job, because he was prepared, and because he was open to the possibilities that this unexpected caller provided.

Andrew recognized Kathy Hashimoto's name, and everybody knew Randford Research, one of the largest defense contractors in the world, but he needed some instant background on this client. As Kathy began to introduce herself and the reason for her call, Andrew clicked into the customer profiles on his computer and reviewed the notes he had entered ten months ago after the MPI conference. Without hesitation he said, "Hello Kathy. This is a nice surprise! Of course I remember. We met in the Florentine's lobby after the final night reception at MPI. I helped carry your cartons to the taxi during that awful downpour."

"Mister, you're quick! I remember I hardly had time to hand you my card as I dashed for the taxi. But I know your company and I believed you were someone I could trust. I liked the fact that you volunteered to lend a hand when I needed one, and you didn't know if I was a customer or not. I got your note and just took a peek at your Web site."

Kathy paused a long second and began, "Hey, Andrew, I just got handed an event at the National Aircraft convention and it's only six months out. It's a crucial event for Randford and it's in your city. My regular planner is on a maternity leave and it looks like you and I are going to have to pick up the pieces."

(continued)

Andrew winced as he looked at the time, but he said, "I'll be glad to help. Do you want to give me your specifications now, or would you prefer to e-mail me your requirements?"

Kathy immediately said, "Here's the basics now, and I'll send the details in an e-mail tomorrow. First, on the night of September 20 we need a special venue for 750 people, all VIPs. Senator Germain is our keynote speaker. It has to be unique and elegant, with separate space for cocktails and passed hors d'oeuvres before a sit-down dinner. It's black tie, private sedans, and visible security on site. Andrew made notes and began to ask for more details, but Kathy continued, "That's it for now. Do some homework while I locate and send the specs. Then call me in the morning."

As Kathy ended the conversation, Andrew quickly entered the relevant program information into his computer profile. He then sent multiple voice mail messages, advising key coworkers in both sales and operations that they needed to brainstorm with him first thing tomorrow. Finally, he sent an e-mail to Kathy Hashimoto, briefly summarizing the assignment and thanking her for the opportunity and trust she was placing in him and American Hosts. He confirmed that he would call her at 9 A.M. the next morning after a short planning session with other staff in his office. With only ten minutes before his scheduled meeting with the Genesis clients, Andrew turned off his computer, picked up the printed site inspection schedules, and headed out the door.

The next morning, after meeting briefly with key sales and operations staff in his office, Andrew made the 9 A.M. call, which served to gather additional program information and demonstrate to Kathy that he could be depended on to follow through on his commitments. From the call and the subsequent e-mail, he received the following specifications:

- September 20th
- Reception 6 P.M.
- Dinner 7 P.M.
- 750 people
- Black tie
- Visible security in dress regalia
- Elegant, quiet, sophisticated
- Red carpet, white-gloved service
- No press, very strict guest list
- No cameras, no recording equipment
- Security clearances probable

- Seating in sixes and eights, tables of six preferred
- Head table of approximately ten people
- Avoid pork, veal, and game entrees
- Entertainment: Understated and refined through dinner, followed by dance orchestra, swing band or similar (no heavy rock and roll)
- Transportation: Limousines and sedans (dark colors)
- Budget: Commensurate with venue and final event scenario

Armed with these details, Andrew and his planning team would first create general recommendations and tentatively reserve several event venues to be presented to Kathy Hashimoto, along with very specific follow-up questions to identify and secure the final, "best choice." Just six months away from the actual event, time was precious and the venue had to be confirmed. To move the client toward a good, prompt decision, Andrew needed to narrow down a list of sites that fit the general criteria and were definitely available on September 20. From experience, Andrew knew that suggesting a great venue that was not available for the event could be a career-limiting mistake.

To create their initial wish list, the planning group exchanged information in a brainstorming session, concentrating entirely on the best possible venues. Other components like theme, caterer, table decoration, floral, sound and light, room décor, transportation, and security would be strongly influenced by the site selected. As they discussed potential sites—not restricting their creativity but being realistic about space requirements—they considered indoor as well as tented outdoor options. They carefully evaluated and ranked the resulting venues according to "best choices" and reasons. As the team broke to check messages, sales coordinator Melissa Unger called each of the "first choice" venues to determine availability and buyout price.

When they resumed, Melissa verified that three venues were available, but deposits would be required to hold beyond ten days—and if another client requested the space within ten days, then American Hosts would have to deposit immediately.

The group then discussed ground transportation. Sedans were specified, and for VIPS a certain number of luxury cars and limousines might also be required. At the same time, the National Aircraft convention had already created tremendous demand for the best transportation equipment.

(continued)

Melissa would call their two most dependable transportation companies and noted that quality vehicles may need to be imported from nearby cities—at an extra cost—if they were not available locally.

Before discussing remaining issues, the planning group created a list of questions to be presented to Kathy Hashimoto on Monday. Her answers would be pivotal to creating theme, décor, menu, entertainment, and other items that would distinguish this event.

1. Has this group gathered previously at a similar event?
2. If so, when and where?
3. What place did they like best? Why?
4. What place did they like least? Why?
5. What theme did Kathy think was the most successful? What entertainment? What speaker? Why?
6. What is Kathy's vision for this year's event?
7. Are there any restrictions or additional special requests for food, beverage, seating, and so on?
8. What about wine preferences, bar service?
9. What are the demographics of the group in terms of age and gender?
10. What hotel(s) will house your participants?

Andrew and Melissa reviewed their files for similar programs that had been created over the past few years. Kathy might want to know more about their experience with these kinds of VIP events. She would certainly want to know specific advantages and disadvantages of each site.

During the Monday call, Kathy was relieved to learn that good venues still were available, and she was pleasantly surprised to be presented with specific questions instead of an "off-the-shelf" program. "I get suspicious," Kathy had said, "when my DMC gives me its idea of a fabulous program this early in our planning process. It makes me think it wasn't custom designed to fit my needs." During the conversation, Kathy said two other things that made Andrew take special note. She pointed out that the senator's arrival path would not be known until four hours before the event; and two years ago, Kathy's boss objected to using stretch limousines, "because they were too 'glitzy' for this conservative crowd." Andrew knew that two or three alternate plans would be needed for the senator, allowing maximum flexibility to meet the tight restrictions of government security staff. He also knew that sedans were essential, preferably dark ones, and that creative use of nonlimousine vehicles might be considered.

Within days of their earliest conversation, Andrew had created a detailed event proposal, beginning with a summary of the basic assignment to assure that he and Kathy were communicating effectively and fully understanding one another. In addition to the basic program information in chronological order, Andrew provided a detailed description of every aspect of the event, from participant pickups at the hotels, transportation to the event itself, and return transfers to the hotels. This description helped Kathy and her staff members visualize the event as it would unfold and supplied all details so that only minor adjustments would have to be made if necessary.

A separate security plan was also included. It was created with the help of the local police department, along with supervisors from the hotel security department, the transportation supplier, and the chosen event venue—the historic Opera House. A military color guard was secured from a nearby naval air station, which provided visible security and a military presence during an opening flag ceremony. Nonuniformed personnel from the local police department who were fully knowledgeable about their city, the transportation routes, and the Opera House provided close and professional security.

Two weeks after receiving the proposal, Kathy Hashimoto visited the city on a site inspection to walk through the entire event. Andrew and his team accompanied her to the Opera House, which offered a breathtaking welcome for the all-important first impression. The venue offered spacious public areas filled with original artwork and meticulously restored design elements. However, the kitchen and pantry area offered tremendous challenges. "Our caterer is a wonder," assured Andrew. "Through the use of specially fitted trucks, portable cleanup facilities and hidden parking lot tenting, they have successfully served some of our city's most famous events."

Following the site visit, adjustments were made based on the additional details that Kathy provided. A revised document provided new specifications. All prices were included and minimum number of participants stipulated in order to calculate accurate pricing. If numbers were to vary significantly, a new price quotation would be required. Following a few minor adjustments that Kathy requested, a final document was sent to her for signature in the form of an official contract.

The American Hosts operations and production staff were offered many challenges with the Opera House. Among other "firsts" on this

(continued)

event, American Hosts had a local construction company create a temporary floor above the ground level seating area of the concert hall. This was accomplished by an elaborate use of scaffolding, plywood, and carpeting. This new floor above the seats put the dinner portion of the event in the main concert hall, which made a perfect location for classical dinner music and vignettes from the local opera company. The existing lighting and décor in the main concert hall of the Opera House provided an awe-inspiring setting for such an important occasion. Most important, the theme was set and décor embellishments were kept to a minimum, leaving the bulk of the budget for quality food and entertainment.

Six months passed, and it was the night of the big Randford event. Everything was in place. During this period, Andrew and the entire American Hosts staff had been actively involved with the Randford program. The operations and production managers for American Hosts, Dale Young and Kellie Doolan, worked long hours in efforts to make the vision a reality. This event was a first of its kind, and many details presented issues that were not previously considered by Andrew or Kathy. For example, the acoustics in the Opera House were fabulous, if not legendary. However, dinner service noise is not part of the normal Opera House equation. Felt liners in the serving trays, table padding, and some creative use of hanging acoustical baffles above the dinner area minimized the noise. Thankfully, Kellie, the production manager, was present for the sound check in the afternoon.

Important troubleshooting is an ongoing part of the preparations for any special event. There is no substitute for experience, and in this case, a minor slip could have changed the evening's outcome.

Dale Young, the operations manager, had planned three possible transportation scenarios that delivered the senator and the guests to the venue in comfort, safety, and elegance. Dale, too, had to scramble when word of an antiglobalization demonstration came to light a little over twenty-four hours prior to the event. Because Dale and Kellie had fine-tuned their production schedule and hand picked the staff assigned to the various component parts of the event, they had the time to find and fix these two potential problems.

From the time Andrew entered the initial information into the computer database, the Randford event's computer files and program templates were created for each member of the team to follow. This formed the single, centralized database for creation of the event proposal, adjustments, additions, changes, further adjustments, and a template for final billing.

The cocktail reception prior to dinner took place in the grand foyer of the Opera House, which concluded with the U.S. Marine Color Guard, obtained from a nearby military base, marching the guests into a thrilling "reveal" of the elegant dinner layout.

After dinner, Senator Germain began his presentation by stating, "I'm speechless! Mere words cannot describe how honored I am to stand here and address this group in such impressive surroundings. Never have I been so overwhelmed by an event."

The following letter accompanied the closing payment after Marsha received the final invoice.

Dear Andrew,

What a night! You, Dale, Kellie . . . your entire team created an awesome event. Our president is still raving about it. The food was spectacular; the setting magnificent, and the little special touches—menu design, flowers, and individual gifts—were perfect! You guys are great to work with, truly our partners throughout the process. Can you help me in Dallas next October?

Sincerely,

Kathy Hashimoto

This case, though fictional, shares a "slice of life" for DMC executives. Business opportunities do not always present themselves when it is convenient. As Louis Pasteur once said, "Chance favors the prepared mind." Clearly, our DMC sales executive Andrew was prepared and not overly stressed by demands on his time and attention. Successful DMC executives bring a wealth of knowledge and hands-on experience to a client's project, which includes remaining "calm, cool, and collected" throughout the process. These DMC executives have and know how to use the technology available to them. These executives draw not only on their own experience but also on the experiences of the professional staff people around them. Finally, in this relationship-oriented industry, it is vital that DMC executives earn and keep the confidence of their customers. A customer often entrusts the DMC with his or her reputation.

(continued)

This scenario was admittedly a glamorous one. Much of a DMC's work is less exciting. Research and development of program components is a part of the job, but so is creative writing and job costing, negotiating, purchasing, and management within the supplier community, the hospitality community, and the even among the staff of the DMC.

◆ SUMMARY

The DMC niche in the meetings and events industry is a secure and growing one. It is secure because the customer companies and organizations that sponsor meetings will always need local expertise. The depth of local destination knowledge, the local contacts and connections, the community standing, buying power, and hands-on experience with the implementation of programs and events are not readily available to organizations outside of the destination. DMCs have evolved in some interesting ways. The very first ones grew from the ranks of wholesale Tour Operators and Ground Operators. These companies specialized in providing tours and transportation for visiting travel groups. In the late 1950s, the specialization in association and higher-end corporate programs demanded a wider range of services, including dining programs, expanded activities, and special events. While that may seem like a long time to some of our readers, the hotel and meetings industries are ancient in comparison. Today, multi-destination, national DMC companies exist, there are DMCs on at least six continents, consortiums of local one-destination DMCs exist, and as in other industries, consolidation appears to be under way. However, just as individual one-of-a-kind hotels still prosper along with the giant hotel chains, so to do some unique and skilled one-destination DMCs.

Destination management is still establishing itself as a key component in the meetings and events industry. Founded in 1995, ADME is committed to the initiative that professional destination management is a critical and necessary component to every successful meeting or event. As a primary goal, ADME continuously seeks to identify and promote the value of destination management as a necessary resource for planners of meetings, events, and incentive travel programs. ADME's goals also include becoming the definitive source of information, education, and issues-based discussion regarding destination management for the meetings, events, incentive, and hospitality industry at large.

The professional designation "DMCP" (Destination Management Certified Professional) was introduced by ADME in January 2000. This professional certification is only available to individuals who have qualified for an extensive exam administered by ADME. Applicants are screened through a detailed questionnaire, which chronicles the applicant's experience and industry education. For more information about ADME, visit their Web site at http://www.adme.org.

As the industry goes, so goes the DMC business. The economy in general and the meetings industry in particular are good barometers for the health and vitality of the DMC industry. History has taught those participating in the meetings industry that there are some vulnerabilities to growth and maintenance of revenues. The recession of the 1980s, followed by the Iraqi invasion of Kuwait and the subsequent war in the Middle East, have taught us that travel can be interrupted and curtailed due to factors beyond the control of the corporations who are active in the industry. Airlines, hotel companies, and DMCs have learned these lessons. In 2003, after the 9/11 attacks and subsequent terrorist activities, the travel and meetings industry is in a suppressed period with little growth. Executives are consolidating resources and focusing on vital, core businesses.

The long-term outlook for the industry is bright. DMCs that are strong and financially sound stand to gain market share and greater brand recognition when temporary threats and business slowdowns are overcome.

In addition to ADME, Web sites of the following organizations are recommended for those interested in the meetings and events industry. Each of these organizations has strong DMC membership:

   SITE   (Society of Incentive & Travel Executives)
            http://www.site-intl.org

   PCMA (Professional Convention Management Association)
            http://www.pcma.org

   MPI   (Meeting Professionals International) http://www.mpiweb.org

KEY WORDS AND TERMS

For definitions, see http://glossary.conventionindustry.org.

Corporate meetings

DMC

Field staff

History

Incentive programs

Operations and Production

Program

Proposal

Site inspection

Special events

VIP services

REVIEW AND DISCUSSION QUESTIONS

1. What is a DMC?

2. Name a DMC.

3. What services are offered by DMCs?

4. Produce an organizational chart for a DMC.

5. What is the process by which a DMC gets business?

6. What resources does a DMC provide to a meeting planner or sponsor?

7. What are the basic business requirements for a DMC?

8. What are some of the professional organizations that a DMC might be a member of?

ABOUT THE CHAPTER CONTRIBUTOR

Terrence J. Epton, CITE, DMCP, is a twenty-year veteran of the DMC industry and executive vice-president of the first and largest DMC in the United States, USA Hosts, Ltd. Terry holds both the CITE (Certified Incentive Travel Executive) and the DMCP (Destination Management Certified Professional) designations. He served six years on the International Board of Directors for SITE as a director and officer, plus he has twice been president for ADME, most recently in 2002. Mr. Epton is a graduate of, and guest lecturer at, the Lester E. Kabacoff School of Hotel, Restaurant and Tourism Administration at the University of New Orleans, where he currently serves as an advisory board member.

9

SERVICE CONTRACTORS

One of the services provided by exhibition service contractors (ESCs) is booth design and construction.

Photo provided by GES

◆ Chapter Objectives

This chapter provides the reader with an understanding of the following:

- Service contractors and their role in MEEC
- General services contractors compared with specialty contractors
- Exhibitor-appointed contractors
- Associations in service contracting

◆ Chapter Outline

INTRODUCTION

An event producer or show manager (show organizer) may have all the tools at his or her fingertips to promote, sell, and execute a show or conference, but there are many pieces of equipment that he or she does not have. For example, while you might be a great cook, you do not make the frying pan or the spatula—you turn to experts for that. For exhibitions and events to be produced smoothly and efficiently, the producers and managers must rely on professional service contractors to give them, and the exhibitors, the tools necessary to create a successful show or event. These are called **service contractors**, and this chapter discusses their various roles in the process, their relationship with the organizer, and their relationship with each other.

DEFINITION OF THE SERVICE CONTRACTOR

A service contractor is anyone who provides a product or service for the exhibitor or show management during the actual show or conference. Service contractors can be the florist, the electrical company, the registration company, the models and hostesses, and just about every service you can think of. Some service contractors are hired by the show organizers to assist with their needs, and others are hired directly by the exhibitor.

MEEC service contractors and their roles have evolved over time. Historically, they were referred to as *decorators*. This is based on their earliest primary function as service contractors, which was to "decorate" the empty space of a convention center or hotel ballroom. This decorating function included pipe and drape, carpets, backdrops, booths, and furnishings.

Over the years, service contractors have expanded the scope of their activities to match the growing sophistication of MEEC. Today, service contractors can be, and likely are, involved in every aspect of the event from move in, to running the show, to teardown, and move out. As a result, the service contractor provides an important interface between the event organizer and other MEEC suppliers, such as hotel convention services, the convention center, exhibitors, local labor, and unions. Many service contractors will work with the organizer to lay out trade show floors, in part because they have spent the time to take careful measurements of every MEEC venue in the host community (Rutherford 1990).

GENERAL SERVICE CONTRACTORS

The **general service contractor** (also called the official show contractor or exposition services contractor) is hired by the show manager to handle the general duties necessary to produce the show on site.

General service contractors are responsible for assisting the show organizer with graphic treatments for the entrance and all signage, putting up the pipe and drape or hard wall exhibits, placing aisle carpet, and creating all the official booths, such as association centers, registration, lounges, and special areas. More important, the general service contractor offers the show organizer a valuable service by hiring and managing the labor for a particular show. They have standing contracts with unions and tradespeople. They know how to hire enough labor to move a show in and out based on the requirements of the show. It is their responsibility to move the

Trucks and equipment from the Freeman Companies transport and handle freight.

Photo by George G. Fenich, Ph.D., Professor, School of HRTA, University of New Orleans

freight in and out of the facility, manage the flow of the trucks coming in and out of the facility, and the storage of the crates and boxes during the show. This is called **material handling** or **drayage**.

Drayage is a somewhat confusing term and may be traced back to medieval times. According to *Webster's New Universal Unabridged Dictionary, S.V.* "drayage" (1979), *drayage* is the sum charge paid for the use of dray or drays, and a *dray* is a low, strong cart with detachable sides used for drawing heavy loads. Thus, *drayage* is the price paid for having trucks transport products. Today, the transport vehicle can be a truck or even a plane, and the fee includes many aspects of the transportation service. Service contractors may charge for services like crating an exhibit in a box, using a forklift to get the box onto a small truck that takes the crate to a local warehouse or storage facility, and then putting it onto an 18-wheeler for over-the-road transport. The reverse happens at the other end and ultimately leads to unloading at the convention center or event site. There the service contractor will also supervise the unloading of the crate and delivery of it to the proper booth. After the crate is unpacked, the service contractor will arrange for storage of the empty crate until the show is over and the whole process is reversed. The price for drayage is based on the weight, not the size, of the materials or crate. The fee is based on each one hundred pounds of weight and thus is called *hundredweight*. A "bill of lading" is completed by the shipper and delineates what the package contains, who owns it, where it is going, and any special instructions. This is the official shipping document, and authorities at checkpoints like state borders and especially national borders may insist on examining it.

Many GSCs have expanded into specialty areas. Thus, GSCs today may provide audiovisual equipment, security, cleaning, and more. This is done for a number of reasons. One is that the GSCs are building on the relationship they have established with show organizers over years of interaction and rely on the marketing concept of "relationship marketing." Provision of a wide range of services also gives the show organizer the advantage of "one-stop shopping." By using a GSC that provides general and specialty services, the show organizer does not have to deal with a multitude of companies to produce the show. As well, providing an array of services allows the GSC to increase revenues and, it is hoped, profitability.

GSCs not only serve the show organizer but are the official service contractor for exhibitors. Exhibitors can rent everything they need for their exhibit from the GSC, from a simple chair to a complete exhibit. Some GSCs will build a booth for exhibitors, store it, and ship it to other shows on behalf of the exhibitor.

The GSC adds value to his or her services by creating the **exhibitor service manual** (exhibitor services kit) along with the show organizer. This manual is a compilation of all the show information, such as dates, times, rules, and regulations for both the show manager and the city. Also included are all the forms necessary for an exhibitor to have a successful show. These forms typically include orders for carpet, furniture, utilities, setup and dismantling, and drayage. Some show organizers include promotional opportunities as well to help exhibitors do preshow and on-site promotion. The service manuals can be printed and mailed. Service manuals now exist as CD-ROMs or on the Internet, allowing exhibitors to order services and products from wherever they are.

On site, the GSC works with both the show organizer and exhibitor to ensure a smooth move in and move out. He or she is often the conduit

The primary communication link between show organizers and/or exhibitors and the ESC is the service center on the trade show floor.

Photo provided by GES

to a facility to make sure that the rules and regulations are observed. Many times, he or she solves the problems of the exhibitors by finding lost freight, repairing damaged booths or crates, and cleaning the carpets and booths in the evenings.

The services provided can include the following:

To Show Organizers

- On-site coordination of the event
- Pipe and drape
- Entry areas
- Offices
- Registration areas
- Setup and dismantling of booths
- Planning, layout, and design
- Carpet
- Furniture
- Signs
- Graphics

Signage is an important service.

Photo by George G. Fenich, Ph.D., Professor, School of HRTA, University of New Orleans

- Backdrops
- Interface with labor and unions
- Cleaning
- Transportation services
- Material handling

To Exhibitors

- Exhibit design and construction
- Booth setup and dismantling
- Carpet
- Furniture
- Signs
- Interface with labor and unions
- Rigging
- Material handling

This simple example of rigging was used to attract attention to a booth selling chairs.
Photo by George G. Fenich, Ph.D., Professor, School of HRTA, University of New Orleans

THE CASE OF EXHIBITING IN A UNIONIZED CITY

Service contractors can play a pivotal role in dealing with unionized labor. This is especially problematic since (1) the unions and rules vary throughout the United States, and (2) local labor is essential for putting together an event or trade show. The following portrays one exhibitor's interaction with unionized labor in a city in the northeastern United States. The exhibit, in its crate, was transported to the convention center in a tractor-trailer, and according to local rules, the trailer had to be driven by a member of the Teamsters Union. On arrival at the convention center, the driver opened the back of the trailer but could do no more to facilitate removal of the crate. You see, that required a forklift, and the forklift is a piece of heavy equipment, not a truck, and thus had to be operated by a member of the Heavy Equipment Operators Union. So they waited for the forklift operator, who then moved the crate to the exhibit booth and placed it on the ground. At that point, the exhibitor was anxious to get set up but could do nothing until a member of the Carpenters Union arrived to take the nails out of the crate: Wood and nails are a job for a union carpenter. The crate was opened, but the exhibitor was restricted from doing anything himself that a union member should do. Thus, he waited for a member of the Porters Union to come to take the exhibit contents out of the crate. That was followed by a string of different union members who each did a separate but distinct job and would not infringe on the responsibilities or activities of a different union. So the exhibit frame that was made from pipes had to be assembled by someone from the Plumbers Union: Only plumbers handle pipes. The products and cloth were assembled and laid out by a member of the Stage Hands Union: After all, an exhibit is part of a "show." The sign over the booth required someone from the Heavy Equipment Operators Union to drive a bucket lift, while a member of the Riggers Union occupied the bucket to "rig" the sign. The exhibitor could not even plug his VCR into the electrical outlet provided by show management—that had to be done by a member of the Electricians Union. The telephone had to be plugged into a jack provided by a member of the Communications Workers Union, and the flowers had to be "arranged" by a member of the Agricultural Union. Of course, the cleaning people, security, and other service personnel had to be members of the appropriate union. Further, part of a supervisor's pay in each these unions

(continued)

had to be paid by the exhibitor in proportion to the amount of time that union spent at his booth. Further complicating matters is that, unless special fees are paid, there can be significant time lapses between when one union member finishes one particular job and when the next arrives. And—oh yes—if any union rule is violated or the exhibitor tries to do something himself, all the unions will boycott that booth and refuse to work. Obviously, a service contractor who is knowledgeable about local union rules and has established an ongoing relationship with local labor can be worth his or her weight in gold to an exhibitor or show organizer.

Unions serve a number of laudable purposes. They represent a class of workers such as electricians when negotiating with management over pay scales and working conditions. Thus, they carry more clout than any single worker could possibly have alone. Unions also set very specific guidelines regarding termination of an employee and will provide a union member with legal council if necessary. In addition, they help to ensure that working conditions are safe and comfortable. Lastly, they work with government agencies to help establish guidelines for the construction trades.

SERVICE CONTRACTORS ARE EVOLVING

Today, service contractors are evolving and changing to meet the needs of the client and the environment. One of the major changes has been increasing the scope of their work to center on meeting the needs of exhibitors. As is the case with the organizers of events, service contractors have come to the conclusion that it is the exhibitors who are the driving force of the trade show segment of MEEC. Further, they have come to understand that exhibitors have more trade shows and vendors than ever to choose from along with increased numbers of marketing channels through which to promote and distribute their products. Thus, both service contractors and show organizers are directing their attention to the needs of the exhibitor. Exhibitors are reacting to this effort by getting much more specific about their wants and needs, and they are also becoming much more discreet and selective when choosing a service contractor. Exhibitors spend huge amounts of money to participate in a trade show and thus want the best ROI they can get. In today's economic environment, exhibiting companies have to justify the expense of a trade show and are looking to service contractors to help with the justification and show the value added by participating.

In the long run, service contractors must deliver quality service and products to the user, whether it is the organizer or the exhibitor. Otherwise, both constituents will seek other marketing avenues and strategies, with organizers left out in the cold. The status quo does not hold true any longer, and some companies have decided to forego trade shows in which they have participated for years. The well-known COMDEX Show appears to be facing exactly this type of problem, as is the National Association of Television Production Executives (NATPE). In lieu of exhibiting at an alternative trade show, some companies are developing their own private trade shows targeted to specific target markets or customers.

Still another change for service contractors is that many facilities are now offering to do in-house what used to be the exclusive domain of service contractors. For example, many convention centers are now offering to provide utilities like electricity, water, steam, and gas, and may no longer allow service contractors to do this. Venues are also offering services like cleaning, security, audiovisual, and room setups. This approach is cutting into the business and revenues of service contractors.

The advent of **exhibitor-appointed contractors** (EACs, which are discussed later in this chapter) has cannibalized the business of the service contractor. This trend began in the mid-1980s, when the courts ruled that service contractors could not have exclusive right to control and negotiate with organized labor. Thus, an EAC from out of the area had the legal right to compete with service contractors and set up a booth for an exhibitor. EACs are a subset of service contractors that, rather than work from one city or location, work for the exhibiting company and travel throughout the country setting up and dismantling their booths. Their success was based on the long-term relationship they had built with the client company and is known as "relationship marketing." Because the EAC works for the same company over many trade shows and events, the EAC is more knowledgeable about the client company's needs and can provide better service than the broader service contractor.

This competition between service contractors and EACs has encouraged the service contractors to provide more specialized, streamlined, and efficient service to exhibiting companies. For example, one service contractor now provides exhibiting companies with the same service representative before the trade show opens, during the show, and after the show for reconciliation and billing. This lets the customer deal with one source for ordering of all services and products, a one-stop service desk, and a single master bill representing every product and service used. This is analogous to an individual who gets a different credit card receipt for each transaction but a single, cumulative bill at the end of the month. A service contractor named TEG has a program called the "Gold Advantage" for its best customers that provides a special customer service representative who is available twenty-four hours a day, seven days a week, and a private service center that has a lounge, fax, phone, copy services, and so forth. The large service contractor GES is bringing the traditional service desk to the customer by equipping its sales representatives with PDAs so that they can go to a booth and provide on-the-spot service. Freeman Decorating just started a program called "ExhibiTouch," where touch screen computer kiosks are located throughout the exhibit floor. A client can go to the kiosk and transact most business requests, ascertain freight status, and print forms like order forms, invoice summaries, and shipping labels.

Service contractors are also expanding into the area of event marketing. This too is based on the desire by clients to do most of their business with someone or some company they know and trust: relationship marketing. The show organizer or association host may sponsor events, but corporations put on most events. As a result, many exhibitors are now responsible for corporate events outside the traditional trade show floor. The service contractors, having developed a long-term relationship with the exhibitor, are now developing corporate events programs, multievent exhibit programs, private trade shows, new product introductions, hospitality events for clients, multicity touring exhibitions, and more nontraditional promotional campaigns.

Technology is also changing the way service contractors do business. As with many businesses, the computer is eliminating many activities traditionally done with pen and paper. This includes updating floor plans, tracking freight, and monitoring small package deliveries. For example, as little as ten years ago, floor plans had to be drawn by hand using drafting instruments. A simple booth change, because it affects the entire show layout, could take a week or more to redraft. Now, thanks to computer technology, changes are almost instantaneous. Freeman Decorating, for example, has a program called "Design Vault" on its in-house network. Design Vault includes floor plans and artists' drawings for every major convention facility in the country. Thus, clients can take a "virtual tour" through the venue and make floor plan changes immediately.

Service contractors are also using technology to help them with drayage. Again, pen and paper is being replaced with computer technology that allows tracking of all sizes of shipments to be faster and more accurate. Everything is online so that when a truck enters or leaves a facility, it

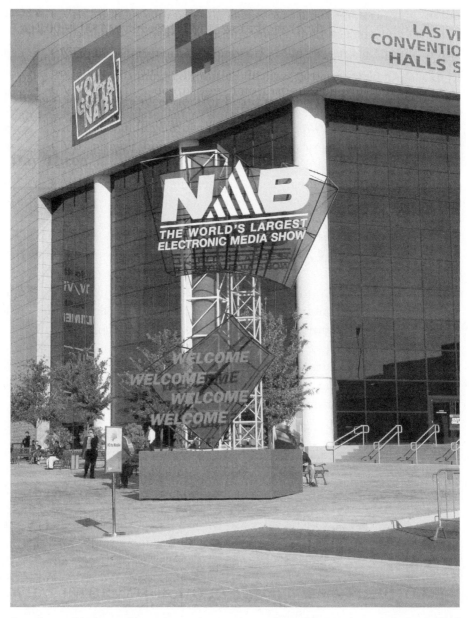

A welcome kiosk outside a convention center, such as this one, is a product supplied by a service contractor.

Photo provided by GES

is in the computer system, and freight managers can go to the central computer to check the status of not only the vehicle but its contents as well. This technological monitoring happens on the trade show floor, too. An exhibitor can contact the service contractor and know which crates are still on the truck and which have been delivered to the booth. Small packages, such as brochures, can be tracked in the same fashion.

Still another use of technology embraced by service contractors is Web site development. They produce Web sites for show organizers that include interactive floor plans, exhibitor show information, booth reservation services, and even personal itineraries for show attendees (Collins 1999).

ORGANIZATION OF A SERVICES CONTRACTING COMPANY

Service contractors are businesses, and like most businesses are organized into functional areas. This means that there are different departments grouped by a common activity or function that support the mission of the company. The department that controls and directs the company can be called "administration" and may include the general manager (GM) or CEO, marketing, assistants, receptionists, and the like. Some of the other departments or divisions are as follows:

- *Sales:* Typically divided or broken up into national sales along with local sales or special events. Some companies also have a separate "exhibitor sales" department that takes over from national sales in dealing with exhibitors. Exhibitor sales will provide each exhibitor with an inventory of the supplies available and the cost of each item. Exhibitor sales also works to encourage exhibitors to "upgrade" from standard to superior quality products at a higher price. Exhibitor sales typically will have an office and full-time presence at the trade show to facilitate interaction between production and exhibitors as well as to sell additional products and services on the trade show floor.

- *Logistics:* Handles planning, scheduling, shipping, labor relations, site selection, and preparation. This is the department that determines the flow and delivery of booth materials—with booths in the center of the hall being delivered before booths by the doors so that access is not blocked. This department may also work with the exhibit facility and lay out all the different-sized booths, aisles, food service areas, registration, and so on. Today, this is done using computer technology known as CAD/CAM.

- *Drayage and Warehousing:* Transportation of materials, booths, exhibits, etc., along with their temporary storage in the host city. Drayage may include air transport, over the road tractor-trailer, and local transportation.
- *Event Technology:* Technology, special effects, reports. This department oversees the planning and subsequent installation of the output of the production department.
- *Event Services:* Exhibitor kits, on-site coordination, registration. The exhibitor kit tells exhibitors everything they need to know about the facility, capacities, rules, regulations, labor, and move-in and move-out times, along with the array of services provided by the service contractor.
- *Production:* Woodworking, props, backdrops, signs, electrical, lighting, metal work, and so on. At Freeman Decorating in New Orleans, clients regularly request backdrops that look like the French Quarter or a swamp. They are produced on large boards like those used in theater productions. However, they are painted by two men who have worked there for years with the backdrop flat on the floor, the men standing up, using paint brushes like those used by artists doing oil painting—except that these paint brushes are five-feet long!
- *Accounting and Finance:* Accounts receivable, accounts payable, payroll, and financial analysis.

Two of the largest GSCs are Freeman Decorating (http://www.freemanco.com) and GES Exposition Services (http://www.gesexpo.com).

GES Exposition Services is headquartered in Las Vegas but has offices in all the major cities across North America. GES is a wholly owned subsidiary of Phoenix-based Viad Corp, a $1.7 billion publicly held corporation traded on the New York Stock Exchange under the symbol VVI.

The Freeman Companies include Freeman Decorating Company, Sullivan Transfer Company, AVW Audio Visual, Inc., Freeman Exhibit Company, and Freeman Decorating Ltd. Their headquarters is in Dallas, Texas, and they have offices in twenty-three cities throughout North America. Begun in 1927, they are a full-service contractor for expositions, conventions, special events, and corporate meetings. The company is privately held and owned by the Freeman family and company employees.

GES EXPOSITION SERVICES

Sallie Sargeant, Sr.
Director of Corporate Communications,
GES Exposition Services

GES Exposition Services is a premier provider of exhibition and event services in the trade show industry, staging some the most recognizable trade shows in the world. Headquartered in Las Vegas, with offices in every major convention market, GES designs and produces world-class trade shows across North America for show organizers and their exhibitors. True to its Las Vegas roots, style, and reputation, GES never fails to light up their clients' stage.

History

GES dates back to 1939, with a Kansas City company called Manncraft that specialized in signs, window trimmings, and small displays.

In 1969, the Greyhound Corporation purchased Manncraft, and growth through acquisitions began. In the early 1970s, offices were opened in Los Angeles, San Francisco, Chicago, and San Diego through acquisition as well as organic growth.

In 1973, Greyhound acquired Las Vegas Convention Services Company, and the stronghold in Las Vegas began.

In 1979, Manncraft changed its name to Greyhound Exposition Services, and GES was born.

GES expanded into the Pacific Northwest in 1991 through acquisitions in Seattle and Portland. By the end of 1992, GES was headquartered in Las Vegas with offices in most major West Coast cities. At this point, the company had 500 full-time employees.

Recognizing the projected growth of the trade show industry, GES decided to establish nationwide service. In May 1993, GES made the largest acquisition in its history by purchasing United Exposition Service Company, whose city operations included virtually every major convention market east of the Mississippi.

With the United acquisition, Greyhound Exposition Services changed its name to GES Exposition Services to reflect "The New GES." In October 1993, GES acquired Andrews, Bartlett & Associates, a major regional contractor based in Hudson, Ohio, and in November of the same year acquired Gelco Convention Services, based in Miami, enhancing the Orlando operation.

During early 1995, GES expanded into Canada through the acquisition of Panex Show Services and Stampede Display and Convention Services, gaining offices in Toronto, Calgary, and Edmonton. By June of that year, Concept Convention Service had joined the GES family, with offices in Phoenix, Tucson, and Albuquerque.

GES acquired ESR Exposition Services in May 1998, one of New York City's leading trade show and event contractors. That same year in June, GES also acquired Puliz of Utah, Inc., a noted trade show and corporate events company with locations in Reno and Salt Lake City.

In October 1998, Panex, Canada's largest trades and event-marketing company, changed its name to GES CANADA Exposition Services Limited.

Services

During the early days of conventions, the primary role of GES was to provide carpet and pipe and drape for booths. In contrast, in today's high-tech world, trade shows involve sophisticated designs and tireless technical support.

GES provides a comprehensive one-stop shop for events and trade shows that includes the following services: show planning, logistics, material handling, floor plans, exhibits and design, signs and graphics, carpet and furnishings, installation and dismantling, and extensive exhibitor services.

Exhibitor Support

Before the show, GES assists exhibitors through the GES National Servicenter, located in Las Vegas. The Servicenter is open nationwide during business hours and processes more than 25,000 exhibitor orders and answers more than 10,000 phone calls every month.

Technology

At the show, GES representatives use the GES Wireless Ambassador. These handheld computers allow GES staff members to research and place orders, check freight information, and access up-to-the minute data right from the exhibitor's booth, ensuring the highest level of customer service.

GES has also developed the Automated Freight & Package Receiving system that uses bar coding to ensure packages and deliveries are received efficiently and reliably at the show.

(continued)

Statistics

Each year, GES Exposition Services lays 56 million square feet of aisle carpet, produces more than 3,000 trade shows and events, delivers 650 million pounds of freight, prints 700,000 booth identification signs, produces approximately 7 million square feet of graphics, and rents enough extension cords to reach from coast to coast through its Trade Show Electrical division.

GES produces thousands of trade shows each year, orchestrating large volumes of people, freight, and union workers in an efficient and customer-conscientious way. There is no doubt that GES's trade show niche, specialized in the biggest of the big shows, accurately reflects its company image.

As GES has grown to provide a one-stop shop for increasingly sophisticated expositions, many of unprecedented size and complexity, it has tackled several challenges involved in the design and management of these "mega" trade shows. For example, during the world's largest gathering for the construction and construction materials industry called the CONEXPO– CON/AGG trade show held every three years, cement batch plants of colossal proportions are erected. Onlookers are often awestruck by these monoliths—large-scale machinery so immense that it must be showcased in the convention center parking lot.

High-value customer service and innovative custom design bridge yesterday's Greyhound Exposition Services, once focused on small and simple conventions, and today's behemoth, GES. GES is a modern and efficient company that capitalizes on cutting-edge technology to orchestrate large and sophisticated events. GES now produces 80% of the largest trade shows in Las Vegas, relishing in the orchestration of large volumes of people, freight, and union workers in an efficient and customer-conscientious way. There is no doubt that GES's trade show niche, specializing in the biggest of the big shows, accurately reflects its modern hometown image.

As for what lies in the future, GES sees still brighter horizons ahead. GES has begun to create the groundwork for future innovation in the industry, harnessed by its ability to design and build exhibits in ways that allow exhibitors to effortlessly market their products. In this vein, GES has led the industry with its innovative technology development that will continue to set industry standards in trade show logistics in the years to come.

Finally, GES will continue to respond to the demand of its customers, among them the companies and organizations that put on the largest and most recognizable shows in the industry. In this sense, GES demonstrates continuity with the past—the company has always specialized in offering high-value services to exhibitors and show organizers and continues this tradition of excellence.

SPECIALTY SERVICE CONTRACTORS

Specialty service contractors deal with a specific area of show production, whereas the GSC tends to be broad and generic. Specialty service contractors can either be official contractors (appointed by show management) or exhibitor-appointed contractors (see below). They handle all the services to complete the exhibit, including:

- *Audiovisual:* Services and supplies to enhance the exhibit through audiovisual methods.
- *Business Services:* Copying, printing, faxing, and other business services.
- *Catering:* Food and beverage for show organizers and for individual exhibitors.
- *Cleaning Services:* Cleaning of public areas, especially carpet along with booths, offices, and nonpublic areas.
- *Communications:* Provides PDAs, cell phones, and wired and wireless services.
- *Computers:* Rental of computers and monitors.
- *Consulting:* This can include pre-event planning, coordination, facilitation, layout and design, and booth design.
- *Drayage:* This includes over-the-road transportation of materials for the show, transfers, and delivery of materials from a local warehouse or depot to the show site, airfreight, and returns.
- *Electrical:* Brings electrical power to the exhibits.
- *Floral:* Rental of plants, flowers, and props.
- *Freight:* Shipping of exhibit materials from the company to the show and back. There are various kinds of shippers—common carrier, van lines, and airfreight.
- *Furniture:* Rental of furniture for exhibit, often fancier than in your home!
- *Internet Access and Telephones:* Rental of equipment and lines on the show floor.

- *Labor Planning and Supervision:* Expertise on local rules and regulations regarding what tradespeople to work with, union requirements, and supervision of workers on site.
- *Lighting:* Design and rental.
- *Models and Hostesses:* Temporary hiring of exhibit personnel or demonstration personnel.
- *Utilities:* Plumbing, air, gas, steam, and water for technical exhibits.
- *Photography:* For show organizers to provide publicity and to individual exhibitors.
- *Postal and Package Services:* For both organizers and exhibitors.
- *Security:* Security to watch the booth during closed hours and to control the entrances when the show is open.
- *Translators:* To work with the show organizer to do simultaneous translation of speeches and presentations. They also work with exhibitors to provide communication between sales representatives and foreign attendees.

THE TRANSLATOR WHO KNEW TOO MUCH

A small American company decided that it wanted to exhibit at a trade show in Europe. One of the thing it determined was that none of the sales managers who were going to staff their booth spoke any language except English. So it was decided that a translator fluent in Spanish, Italian, and German would be hired. The translator worked so well that she was hired to provide services at another trade show a year later. At this second show, attendees asked many of the same questions as were asked at the first trade show. Since the questions were repetitive, the translator had learned the answers and would simply answer the attendee without translating and asking the sales managers. Response at this show was low, in spite of high attendance, and reactions to the products being displayed at the booth were poor. When the company manager did a postshow assessment, he uncovered the reason. The attendees got the impression that since a mere translator knew about the products, they must be very simplistic and not cutting edge. So at all future trade shows, the translator was told to always translate, ask the sales managers, and never answer on her own!

Besides the standard needs listed earlier, each show has its own needs. A show in the food and beverage industry will have a contractor for ice and cold storage, while a show in the automotive industry might have a contractor who cleans cars.

EXHIBITOR-APPOINTED CONTRACTORS

As companies do more and more shows, their exhibits become more involved, and they often want one service supplier working with them throughout the year. Or, they have a favorite vendor who they have worked with in a city where they do many shows. This is particularly true with regard to the installation and dismantling of the exhibit. Most times, show organizers will allow this, assuming that a company meets the qualifications for insurance and licensing. This company is called an exhibitor-appointed contractor (EAC). As an EAC, they perform the same duties as a specialty contractor but only for that exhibitor, not the show manager.

Some services may be provided only by the official service contractor and are called **exclusive services**. This decision is left up to the show manager, who makes that decision based on the needs of the show and rules and regulations of the facility or to ensure the smooth move in and teardown of the show. Can you imagine what would happen if every freight company and installation company tried to move their exhibitors' freight in all at once? It would be chaos! So material handling (drayage) is a service that is often handled as an exclusive.

RELATIONSHIP BETWEEN CONTRACTORS AND SHOW ORGANIZERS

One of the first actions that show organizers take when developing an event is to hire the GSC. This partnership develops as the show develops. GSCs will often recommend cities where a show should be held, the times of the year, and the facilities that fit the event. It is important to hire this company early on.

The process for hiring service contractors is through an **RFP**. The show organizer creates a list of questions and specifications for each show. Other areas of concern include knowledge of the industry, knowledge of the

Representatives from the ESC work with show organizers and exhibitors to create a successful event.
Photo provided by GES

facility, other shows being handled in the same industry, size of the organization, and budget. A sample RFP can be found at http://www.esca.org.

As the show is developed, GSCs watch closely to suggest how marketing themes and association logos can be used in entrance treatments and signage so that when a show comes alive it looks and feels the way the show organizer wants it. Color schemes, visual treatments, and types of materials all come from the mind of the GSC.

Specialty service contractors work with show organizers to help exhibitors save time and money. Reviewing the past history of a show can tell a service contractor what types of furniture, floral, and electrical needs the exhibitors have used. This permits the specialty contractors to offer money and time-saving tips to the show organizer and pass those savings on to exhibitors. All of this creates a feeling of goodwill among exhibitors who will continue to exhibit at the show.

After a time, the service contractor knows the show as well as the show organizer. This can be added value to the show organizer because as staff changes occur, the service contractor becomes a living historian of the show and its particular nuances.

ASSOCIATIONS IN THE SERVICE CONTRACTOR INDUSTRY

There are several associations for individuals and companies in the service contractor industry, including the following:

ESCA: Exhibition Services and Contractors Association (http://www. ESCA.org). Organization serving general and specialty contractors.

EDPA: Exhibit Display Producers Association (http://www. EDPA.com). Organization serving companies engaged in the design, manufacture, transport, installation, and service of displays and exhibits primarily for the trade show industry.

EACA: Exhibitor-Appointed Contractors Association (http://www. EACA.com). Representing exhibitor-appointed contractors and other individual show-floor professionals that provide exhibit services on the trade show floor.

IAEM: International Association for Exhibition Management (http://www.IAEM.org). An association of show organizers and the people who work for service contractors.

CAEM: Canadian Association of Exposition Management (http:// www.CAEM.ca). Canadian association of show organizers and the people who work for service contractors.

NACS: National Association of Consumer Shows (http://www. PUBLICSHOWS.com). Association of public (consumer) show organizers and the suppliers who support them.

EXHIBITION CONTRACTORS ASSOCIATION

According to the Exhibition Services & Contractors Association Web site, ESCA is:

- The association for firms engaged in providing services and materials for the hospitality industry:

  Trade shows and exhibitions

  Conventions and meetings

  Sales meetings

- The voice of the exhibition service industry.
- A clearinghouse for the exchange of information between members and all other entities of the vast trade show and convention industry.
- A source for leading general service contractors, specialty contractors, independent contractors, and their suppliers.
- A source for discounts and assistance in the current business climate.

MISSION STATEMENT

ESCA is dedicated to the advancement of the exhibition, meeting, and special events industries. Through the education, information exchange, and level of professionalism shared by members and their customers, ESCA promotes cooperation among all areas of the exhibition industry.

ETHICS STATEMENT

Members of ESCA recognize the need for standards of professionalism in the relationship between contractor and customer and within the industry as a whole. They recognize that their customers come from every aspect of the exhibition, meeting, and special events industry, ranging from the organizer to the attendee. All ESCA members pledge themselves to conduct their business activities with integrity. ESCA members understand that they are responsible for the professional conduct of persons in their employ. Consequently, they undertake, through exemplary conduct at all times, to secure observance by their employees of this code of ethics.

ESCA members pledge themselves to act in accordance with the following principles of the ESCA code of ethics. Responsibilities of all members include the following:

1. *Accuracy.* ESCA members will provide factual and accurate information about their services and the services of any firm they represent. They will not use deceptive practices.
2. *Disclosure.* ESCA members will provide complete details about terms and conditions of any services, including cancellation and service fee policies, before accepting deposits.
3. *Delivery.* ESCA members will provide all services as stated in their agreement or written confirmation, or provide alternate services of equal or greater value, or appropriate compensation.
4. *Cooperation.* ESCA members will serve in a spirit of partnership with show management, other contractors, facilities management, and exhibitors.

5. *Responsiveness.* ESCA members will offer prompt, reliable, and courteous service at all times.
6. *Compliance.* ESCA members shall abide by all federal, state, and local laws and regulations.
7. *Regulations.* ESCA members will comply with all codes and standards regarding safety, performance, show rules, and regulations.
8. *Confidentiality.* ESCA members will treat every customer transaction confidentially and not disclose any information without permission of the customer, unless required by law.
9. *Conflict of Interest.* ESCA members will not allow any preferred relationships with suppliers and subcontractors to interfere with the interests of their clients.
10. *Disputes.* ESCA members will work with their customers to resolve disputes quickly and fairly, and if necessary, through mediation or then through arbitration.

Contact information for EASC is as follows:
2260 Corporate Circle, Suite 400, Henderson, NV 89074-7701;
e-mail: Info@ESCA.org;
Toll Free: 877-792-ESCA (3722); Tel: 702-319-9561;
Fax: 702-450-7732
Susan L. Schwartz, CEM, Executive Director: sschwartz@ESCA.org
Heather Geldner, Communications Director:
hgeldner@ESCA.org
Cecile Rakban, Member Relations Coordinator: crakban@ESCA.org

SO HOW DOES IT ALL WORK?

Take a look at the organizational chart on page 302, and you can see how the GSC interacts with the show organizer, the facility, the exhibitors, and the other contractors. Remember, exhibitions are like small cities, and the show organizer must provide everything a city does—from safety (security and registration) to a place to work (think of the exhibits like offices), electricity and water, and transportation (shuttle buses). But, it has to be done in a very short period of time, sometimes less than a week. Communication between everyone always must be functioning properly, and often it is the GSC who provides that conduit. The coordination of all the contractors likely is the responsibility of the general service contractor, who is acting as the right hand of the show organizer.

Relationship Between Show Organizer and Service Contractors

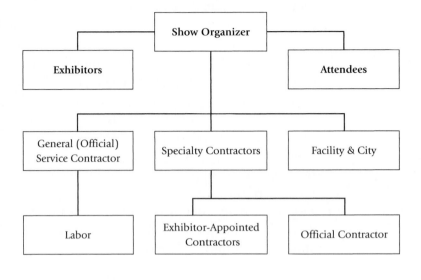

A CASE STUDY OF THE RELATIONSHIP BETWEEN SERVICE CONTRACTORS AND SHOW ORGANIZERS

On September 11, 2001, many exhibitions and events were occurring all over the world. Service contractors worked hand in hand with organizers to get shows moved out, and they held shipments for exhibitors while the airlines were not allowed to fly and trucks were being used to transport emergency equipment.

But, for the trade show industry, the most important factor was how to handle the cancellation of many of the events. Many people were afraid to fly. There were conventions and exhibitions scheduled for the Jacob Javits Convention Center in New York and the Washington area facilities that were being used by emergency crews. These shows were asked to move their dates or cancel. These decisions affected not only the show organizers but also the bottom line for the service contracting industry itself. Many had already spent money on creating show entrances and graphics, and preparing staff to work the shows.

The partnership between show organizers and service contractors allowed a compromise. Service contractors billed show organizers only for materials purchased to date and then agreed not to receive payment until the show had been rescheduled. Exhibitors were not billed for services they had not used but were asked to agree to use the same service at a later date. Everyone worked together to provide creative solutions.

Because of the partnership between service contractors and show organizers, the effect on trade shows by September 11 was somewhat minimized. Although the combination of the economic slump and the fear of travel hurt the technology shows, manufacturing shows only showed a 3 to 10% decline. Many of the shows to have been held immediately after September 11 that were canceled had successful 2002 shows, and there are indications that the future will be strong.

◆ SUMMARY

Service contractors are the backbone of the exhibition industry. Their support structure, like the backbone, allows the show organizers and exhibitors to create an atmosphere that is smooth and efficient. Understanding the responsibilities of each contractor will allow a show organizer to offer the exhibitors the best possible service as well as creating a successful environment for buyers and sellers to do business in the exhibition format.

KEY WORDS AND TERMS

For definitions, see http://glossary.conventionindustry.org.

Drayage

Exclusive service

Exhibitor-appointed contractor

Exhibitor service manual

General service contractor

Material handling

RFP

Service contractor

Specialty service contractor

REVIEW AND DISCUSSION QUESTIONS

1. What types of services do specialty contractors provide? What are some of the questions that should be asked in an RFP?

2. Describe the difference between a general (official service contractor) and an exhibitor-appointed contractor.

3. How can the GSC assist the show organizer as they prepare for the show?

REFERENCES

Collins, Martha. 1999. The evolution of the General Services Contractors. *Expo Magazine* (February): 1–5.

Rutherford, D. G. 1990. *Introduction to the Conventions, Expositions, and Meetings Industry*. New York: Van Nostrand Reinhold.

ABOUT THE CHAPTER CONTRIBUTOR

Susan L. Schwartz, CEM, is the president of ConvExx. She has been involved in every aspect of exhibition management, including registration, exhibit sales, floor management, marketing, promotion, and educational programming. She serves as the IAEM Foundation chair-elect. Schwartz currently teaches TradeShow Management courses at the University of Nevada–Las Vegas. She is the executive director of the Exhibition Services & Contractors Association.

◆10

PROGRAM PLANNING

The entire conference program is displayed on this "bigger than life size" wall graphic.

Photo by George G. Fenich, Ph.D., Professor, School of HRTA, University of New Orleans

◆ Chapter Objectives

This chapter provides the reader with an understanding of the following:

- The motivations for people to attend meetings and conventions
- How to differentiate between the duties of a corporate meeting planner and an association meeting planner
- The different types of session formats

- The importance of accurate scheduling during meetings
- Selection of appropriate food and beverage selections to maximize attendees' attention
- Determining the pros and cons of using volunteer and paid speakers
- Speaker guidelines

◆ Chapter Outline

INTRODUCTION

A meeting planner or organizer may be familiar with all of the elements of the MEEC industry. However, it takes good program planning to put these diverse elements together and "make it work." In order to accomplish effective program planning, the organizer needs to understand the group, its wants, and its needs. Then, objectives can be set that will guide the program delivery to meet these wants and needs while staying within budget constraints.

PCMA 48th ANNUAL MEETING
Program at a Glance

Saturday, January 10, 2004

8:30am–5:30pm	PCMA's College of Meeting Knowledge
	PCMA's CMP® Study Prep Course
2:00pm–6:00pm	Registration Opens

Sunday, January 11, 2004

7:30am–6:00pm	Registration
8:00am–9:00am	PCMA Board of Directors/Chapter Presidents Breakfast
8:30am–12:30pm	Hospitality Helping Hands Project
9:00am–12:00pm	Committee/Working Group Meetings
11:00am–4:00pm	Student Orientation
12:00pm–4:00pm	Chapter Leadership Day
1:00pm–5:00pm	*Executive Edge*
1:00pm–2:15pm	Hands-On Tech Labs
2:45pm–4:00pm	Hands-On Tech Labs
4:15pm–5:15pm	Annual Meeting Orientation
5:30pm–7:00pm	Opening General Session
7:15pm–9:15pm	Welcome Reception

Monday, January 12, 2004

7:00am–8:00am	CMP Breakfast
7:30am–3:30pm	Registration
8:00am–8:45am	Continental Breakfast
9:00am–10:15am	General Session
10:15am–10:45am	Morning Refreshment Break
11:00am–12:15pm	Education Sessions
11:00am–4:00pm	*Executive Edge*
12:30pm–2:00pm	AVIS® Partner Networking Luncheon at Indy Raceway
2:15pm–3:30pm	Education Sessions

(continued)

3:30pm–4:00pm	Afternoon Refreshment Break
4:00pm–5:00pm	Education Sessions
7:00pm–9:00pm	Evening Reception
9:30pm–12:30am	Party With a Purpose

Tuesday, January 13, 2004

7:30am–3:30pm	Registration
8:00am–8:45am	Continental Breakfast
9:00am–5:00pm	Faculty/Academia Track
9:00am–10:15am	Education Sessions
10:15am–10:45am	Morning Refreshment Break
11:00am–12:15pm	Education Sessions
12:30pm–1:45pm	Chapter Networking Lunch
2:00pm–3:15pm	Education Sessions
3:15pm–3:45pm	Afternoon Refreshment Break
4:00pm–5:00pm	Education Sessions
5:30pm	Indianapolis Dining Showcase Open evening for supplier functions

Wednesday, January 14, 2004

8:00am–8:45am	Continental Breakfast
9:00am–10:15am	Education Sessions
10:15am–10:45am	Morning Refreshment Break
11:00am–12:15pm	Education Sessions
12:30pm–1:45pm	2005 Hawaii Kick-off Luncheon
2:00pm–3:30pm	Closing General Session
3:30pm–5:00pm	Indianapolis Tours
6:00pm	Closing Event

SETTING OBJECTIVES

The first thing a planner needs to determine is (1) Who is the group? and (2) Why are they here? This is followed, when planning programming for a meeting, by asking, "What is the objective of this meeting?" This simple question is the basis of much of the planning process. The objective of the meeting will impact site selection, food and beverage requirements, transportation issues, and especially program content. Most people attend meetings for three reasons: education, networking, and to conduct business. Some people participate in association **annual meetings** for the networking and educational offerings. Others may attend primarily to develop business relationships and to make sales. If the planner does not design the program content and scheduling to accommodate these objectives, then the attendees may become dissatisfied. Effective program planning should take into consideration these factors and facilitate opportunities for all attendee objectives to be met. Whether planning a corporate training meeting for ten people or an association meeting for thousands, the development of SMART objectives should be the guiding force (see chapter 2).

Another key point is that program planning, especially for association meetings, begins months or years before the actual event. The average meeting attendee does not understand how much effort goes into planning even simple events, let alone something as complex as an association's annual meeting and trade show. As with much of the hospitality industry, the real work goes on behind the scenes, and unless something goes wrong, the attendees are blissfully unaware of the planning process and the coordination and cooperation necessary to produce an event. The meeting planner and the support staff should be invisible to the attendee.

ASSOCIATION VERSUS CORPORATE MEETINGS

A major difference between corporate and association meeting planning is that with association meetings, attendance is often voluntary. The meeting planner designs the entire meeting package with the intent to entice people to attend. There is a good deal of risk involved. Meeting planners have to arrange for sleeping rooms, meeting space, food and beverage, and many other costly items months or years in advance. If, for some reason, attendance is less than anticipated, the meeting planner may be held responsible for all the commodities ordered but unused (see chapter 12, on legal issues).

In corporate meetings, attendance is usually mandatory. Thus, it is usually much easier for the meeting planner to estimate attendance and plan

Corporations will often hold their meetings in exclusive resorts, such as the Boulders in Scottsdale, Arizona.

Photo by George G. Fenich, Ph.D., Professor, School of HRTA, University of New Orleans

accordingly. However, the same care and attention to detail is required of the corporate meeting planner as is the association planner. The planner may have selected the perfect location and negotiated great rates for the meeting, but if the programming is not desirable, it will impact the success of the meeting.

CORPORATE PROGRAM PLANNING

Many corporate meetings are held as needed, so the program planning timeline can be much shorter than with association meetings. The planner may have to quickly negotiate rooms, meeting space, food and beverage, and transportation needs for the attendees. Program planning for corporate meetings may be as mundane as arranging meeting space and audio-visual needs at a local hotel for a three-hour sales meeting for six people. The agenda and content of the meeting may be solely the responsibility of the manager who has called the meeting. Typically, if an organization has a history of holding many such small meetings, it is prudent to develop a relationship with one hotel or meeting facility and perhaps a specific **CSM** who will service your needs. This allows some degree of consistency and predictability for the corporate planner. On the other hand, program planning for large corporate events like large management or stockholder meetings may mirror the planning process of the typical association planner who is responsible for a major annual meeting. The planning staff may be responsible for site selection, transportation, rooms, meals, receptions, **break-out sessions**, special events, and so forth.

Corporate program planning may be designed to facilitate organizational objectives and goals like learning new computer systems, customer service and sales training, and diversity and sexual harassment **workshops** that will ultimately increase the productivity and stability of the workforce. Often, such programming will be developed in-house by the human resources department or by management. In the case of highly specialized topics, such as diversity training, an expert outside consultant may be hired. Thus, the actual content of what goes on in the meeting may not be the direct responsibility of the corporate planner. However, the overall success of the meeting will reflect on the ability of the corporate planner to anticipate the needs of the meeting sponsors and attendees. The planner is often "guilty by association" if a meeting fails to achieve the desired objectives of the group. If a training meeting suddenly develops into a brainstorming session and no flip charts are available to write down ideas, the planner may be held responsible.

Corporate programming has the added benefit of a captive audience as management may require training for all employees. Attendance is assured. However, this does not mean that the planning procedures or standards should be relaxed. Neither does it mean the meeting does not have to be effectively promoted to the attendees. Having a room full of disgruntled employees who do not know why they are meeting is just as challenging as a room full of angry association members who do not receive programming as advertised in the convention program.

ASSOCIATION PROGRAM PLANNING

According to the **ASAE** (2003), there are more than 147,000 associations in the United States. Over 127,300 are local, state, and regional associations; 20,285 are national associations; 2,409 are international associations headquartered in the United States. Membership in associations varies widely. A small association may have only a few dozen members, while the American Automobile Association currently has about 43 million members. Most associations in the United States are created as 501C corporations. This establishes the organization as a nonprofit entity, which means it receives substantial tax benefits, reduced mailing costs, and other allowances. **Nonprofit associations** are created to service the educational and professional needs of a group of individuals who share a common interest. The term *nonprofit* does not mean the association cannot generate revenues. Quite the contrary, some nonprofit organizations are quite prosperous. But monies generated by the association are supposed to be reinvested in the educational and professional growth of the membership.

Associations typically hold at least one major meeting per year. The annual meeting brings together members from around the country or globe into one place for several days of intensive networking, of education, and to provide an interactive environment to conduct business. Association annual meetings can represent millions of dollars of economic impact on the city in which it is held. Cities actively solicit associations to hold their meetings in their location. Typically, an association plans host cities three to five years out. Some associations, such as the American Library Association, select destinations over two decades out. The planner who decides in what city they will be in 2017 will be long retired by the time the meeting actually takes place.

As mentioned, associations have the additional challenge of relying on members to attend their meetings voluntarily. Forecasting three to five years in advance can be a risky proposition for the association planner. Acts of God, such as hurricanes or tornadoes, terrorism, strikes, bankruptcy, and economic downturns, can seriously impact association meetings. In our recent history, the tragic events of 9/11 had a dramatic impact on attendance at conventions and trade shows. The Center for Exhibition Industry Research (**CEIR**) estimates that attendance at trade shows decreased by approximately 30% in the months following the terrorist attacks. During the weeks following the attacks, hundreds of events all over the country were canceled. For the association community, it was an especially difficult time. Trade shows at association meetings represent the second highest revenue stream, following membership dues. If a major event is canceled, that revenue disappears.

IMPORTANCE OF EDUCATION

A key component of MEEC is to provide an environment conducive to education.

Sponsors of meetings, such as associations or corporations, are increasingly cost conscious with the planning and implementation of their events and have high expectations for the **ROI** achieved by employees or association members. Poor planning in logistics or in program content can spell disaster for the meeting planner. Gone are the days when conventions were viewed as primarily recreational events and expense accounts were plentiful. If the actual benefits of attending the meeting cannot be justified, then funding to attend or membership fees for an association

An instructor offers technical education on the inner workings of a computer.
Source: Pearson Education/PH College

may be withheld. In cases where the attendee is paying out of his or her own pocket to attend, good program content becomes a much more critical issue. People are usually much more careful with their own money than with someone else's. It is a fact that attendee expectations are seldom lowered. If you provide child care and all meals one year, then the same (or better) services will be expected the subsequent year. It is a constant challenge for the meeting planner to continuously improve the content and execution of meetings and conventions while keeping the price of attendance affordable.

Technological advances made in the last decade have provided additional challenges and opportunities for meeting planners. Web and video-conferencing technologies are becoming more sophisticated and affordable. Why spend the money to hold a physical meeting if a virtual meeting will achieve the same objective? On the other hand, using technology has the potential to bring in additional revenues by webcasting workshops, providing Internet-based distance learning, and creating virtual trade shows. In addition, CD-ROMs or DVDs of speakers and sessions can be created with video, handouts, and other resources to be offered for sale at the convention or anytime in the future. Thus, people who could not attend the meeting can still participate and benefit from the experience.

PROFESSIONAL CERTIFICATIONS

Increasingly, people within a particular industry seek to differentiate themselves by becoming "certified" or "licensed" in a specific skill or to recognize that they have achieved a certain level of competence in a career field. Most people cannot afford the luxury of quitting their job to go back to school for academic instruction. Instead, they rely on their professional associations to provide current information and continuing education in their particular field. Programs may be offered at the annual convention, at regional seminars, or through distance education over the Internet. Individuals receive continuing education units (**CEUs**) for each workshop they attend, and these CEUs will be a part of the qualifications to become certified or licensed. Physicians are a good example. To retain their medical license, doctors are required to take a certain amount of continuing medical education (**CME**) courses to keep current with innovations in health care.

In the meetings and convention industry, one of the most recognized designations is the Certified Meeting Professional (**CMP**), which is administered by the CIC. The CIC is a federation of the leading associations in the hospitality industry, including the PCMA, MPI, and International Association for Exhibition Management. To date, there are some 10,000 meeting professionals who have earned this designation, primarily those working in meeting management, convention services, and sales. One of the benefits of receiving a certification is that it demonstrates some level of competency in the profession. If the meeting planner has his or her CMP, the hotel salesperson knows that the planner has some expertise in the field. Certifications are often noted on business cards and used in correspondence to indicate what certifications have been earned. For example: John Smith, CMP, CAE, means that John Smith has earned the Certified Meeting Professional and Certified Association Executive designations. Certification programs are also a good source of revenue for associations, as application and testing fees, study materials and manuals, and periodic recertification can cost hundreds to thousands of dollars.

PROGRAM DEVELOPMENT

As mentioned previously, the first consideration when designing conference programming is to understand the objectives for the meeting. Is the programming to be designed in a way that facilitates communication between departments within a corporation? Is the programming geared toward training new employees in the use of a particular computer system? Is the programming geared to educate the members of a professional association and lead toward a certification? Are meals and networking opportunities an important consideration? Clear and concise objectives will allow the meeting planner to focus on designing the optimal learning experience for the attendees. To do so, the planner must consider several factors, including:

- Program type
- Content, including track and level
- Session scheduling
- Speaker arrangements
- Refreshment breaks and meal functions
- Ancillary events
- Evaluation procedures

PROGRAM TYPE

Each type of program or session is designed for a specific purpose, which may range from providing information to all attendees, discussion of current events in small groups, hands-on training, and panel discussions. The following are typical descriptions of the major program types and formats.

General or Plenary Session

A general or plenary session is primarily used as a venue to communicate with all conference attendees at one time in one location. Typically, the general session is what kicks off the meeting and includes welcoming remarks from management or association leadership, outlines the purpose or objectives of the meeting, introduces prominent officials, recognizes major sponsors or others who helped plan the event, ceremonial duties, and other important matters of general interest. General sessions last between 1 and 1.5 hours. Often, an important industry leader or a recognizable personality will give a **keynote address** that will help set the tone for the rest of the meeting. For a corporate meeting, this may be the CEO or the chairman of the board. An association may elect to hire a professional speaker in a particular subject area, such as business forecasting, political analysis, leadership

A general session at a convention.
Source: PhotoEdit

and change, technology, or topic that would be motivational to the audience. Many planners use highly recognizable political, sports, and entertainment personalities. These individuals are hired not because their personal knowledge of the association and the various professions it represents but as a "hook" to attract people to come to the meeting. If the National Association of Plumbing Professionals hires Jennifer Lopez to be their keynote speaker, you can bet she was not hired for her extensive knowledge of the plumbing industry. However, her presence at the meeting is sure to drive up attendance in the heavily male-dominated plumbing industry. As a note, it is not uncommon to spend $75,000 to $100,000 or more (plus travel expenses) to hire a well-known sports or entertainment figure to speak at a general session. General sessions may also be held at the end of a convention to provide closure and summarize what was accomplished during the meeting or as a venue for presenting awards and recognizing sponsors. Attendance at closing general sessions is typically smaller than with opening sessions as people make travel plans to return home early.

Concurrent Session

A concurrent session is a professional development or career enhancement session presented by a credentialed speaker who provides education on a specific topic in a conference-style format. Alternately, several speakers may form a panel to provide viewpoints on the topic at hand. Group discussions at individual tables may also be incorporated. Concurrent sessions typically serve groups of 150+ attendees, and several sessions may be offered simultaneously at a specific time. They typically last between 1 and 1.5 hours.

Workshop or Break-Out Sessions

Workshops or break-outs are more intimate sessions that offer a more interactive learning experience in smaller groups. Participants may learn about the latest trends, challenges, and technologies of a specific field. These sessions are often presented by experienced members or peers of the association and may involve lectures, role playing, simulation, problem solving, or group work. Workshop sessions usually serve groups of 150 or fewer attendees. These are the mainstay of any convention, and dozens or even hundreds of workshops may be offered throughout the course of the event, depending on the size of the meeting. A large association, such as the American Library Association, has over 1,000 workshop sessions at their annual convention! Workshops typically last between 50 minutes to an hour.

Roundtable Discussion Groups

Roundtables are small, interactive sessions designed to cover specific topics of interest. Basically, eight to twelve attendees convene around a large round table, and a facilitator guides discussion about the topic at hand. Typically, several roundtable discussions will take place in one location, such as a large meeting room or ballroom. Attendees are free to join or leave a particular discussion group as desired. Roundtables can also be useful for continued and more intimate conversation with workshop speakers. The role of the facilitator is to keep the discussion on track and not allow any one attendee to monopolize the conversation.

Poster Sessions

Poster sessions are another more intimate presentation method often used with academic or medical conferences. Rather than utilizing a variety of meeting rooms to accommodate speakers, panels or display boards are provided for presenters to display charts, photographs, a synopsis of their research, etc., for viewing. The presenter is scheduled to be at his or her display board at an appointed time so that interested attendees may visit informally and discuss the presentation. For example, a person who is conducting preliminary research may participate in a poster session to encourage other researchers to review and provide feedback about his or her project. Poster sessions help presenters gain exposure and increase the variety of educational opportunities at a convention without using a lot of meeting rooms. A poster session at one meeting may later develop into a workshop at a subsequent meeting.

PROGRAM CONTENT

The average attendee will only be able to sit through three to six sessions on any given day. It is critical that the attendee be as well informed as possible about what each session will offer and the appropriateness of the session to his or her objectives for attending the meeting. For association meetings, programming objectives are developed months in advance and used extensively in marketing the convention to potential attendees. Program content is not a "one-size-fits-all" proposition. The content must be specifically designed to match the needs of the audience. A presentation on Basic Accounting 101 might be good for a junior manager but totally inappropriate for the chief financial officer. A good way to communicate to attendees how to select which programs to attend is to create tracks and levels. **Track** refers to separating programming into specific genres, such as computer skills, professional development, marketing, personal growth, legal issues, certification courses, or financial issues. A variety of workshops can be developed that concentrate on these specific areas. **Levels** refer to the skill level the program is designed for, whether it is beginning, intermediate, or advanced. Thus, the speaker who is assigned a session can develop content specifically tailored for a particular audience. Attendees can also determine if a session meets their level of expertise.

Session Description

Workshop 14: Effective E-Mail Marketing:
Corbin Ball, CMP, Corbin Ball & Associates
3:30 P.M. to 4:45 P.M. (1530–1645)
Room 314

Over 10 billion email messages are sent daily. This is more than the combined total number of phone calls, faxes, and paper mail messages sent. This is expected to grow to 35 billion messages in 2005. How can your company develop email effectively as a primary marketing vehicle? What are the most effective options to do so?

Attend this session to:

- Discover the top ten steps in developing effective email marketing campaign.
- See recent email surveys about customer expectations.
- Understand delivery options for bulk emailing.
- Enhance your own email effectiveness.

Track: Marketing

Level: Intermediate

Adapted from the IAEM annual meeting program 2002.

SESSION SCHEDULING

Timing is critical in program development. The planner has to orchestrate every minute of every day to ensure that the meeting runs smoothly and punctually. Each day's agenda should be an exciting variety of activities that will stimulate attendees and make them want to attend the next meeting. One of the biggest mistakes planners make is double-booking events over the same time period. If a planner schedules workshops from 8:00 A.M. to 1:00 P.M. and the tee time for the celebrity golf match is at 12:30, then he or she stands to lose any of the attendees who want to attend the golfing event. Trade shows are another challenge. If workshops are scheduled at the same time that the trade show floor is open, attendees must choose between the two options. If attendees choose to attend the education sessions, the exhibitors will not get the traffic they expect. Conversely, if attendees go to the trade show rather than attend sessions, there may be empty meeting rooms and frustrated speakers.

Typical Association Meeting Schedule

While no two conventions are the same, the following time line will give you a good idea of the flow of typical meetings.

Day One

8:00 A.M. Staff office and pressroom area setup

Exhibition setup begins

Preconvention meeting with facility staff

Registration set up

Day Two

8:00 A.M. Association board meeting

Registration opens

Staff office opens

Exhibition setup continues

Set up for preconvention workshops

1:00–4:00 P.M. Preconvention workshops (with break)

    Various committee meetings

    Program planning committee finalizes duties for meeting

5:00 P.M. Private reception for board members and VIPs

7:00–9:30 P.M. Opening reception

Day Three

6:30 A.M. Staff meeting

8:00 A.M. Registration opens

    Coffee service begins

9:00 A.M. General session

10:30 A.M. Break

10: 45 A.M. Concurrent workshops

12:00–1:30 P.M. Lunch

1:30–5:00 P.M. Exhibition open

5:00 P.M. Registration closes

Day Four

6:30 A.M. Staff meeting

8:00 A.M. Registration opens

    Coffee service begins

9:00 A.M.–4:00 P.M. Exhibition open

12:00–1:30 P.M. Lunch provided on show floor

1:30–2:30 P.M. Workshops

2:45–3:45 P.M. Workshops

4:00–5:00 P.M. Workshops

    Teardown of trade show begins

5:00 P.M. Registration closes

7:00 P.M. Cocktail reception

8:00–10:00 P.M. Banquet and awards ceremony

(continued)

Day Five

7:00 A.M. Staff meeting

8:00 A.M. Registration opens

Trade show teardown continues

9:00–10:30 A.M. Closing session

Pack up staff office

Pressroom closed

10:45 A.M.–12:00 P.M. Program planning committee meets

12:00 P.M. Registration closed

3:00 P.M. Postconvention held with facility staff

Another major issue is allowing enough time for people to do what comes naturally. Do not expect to move 5,000 people from a general session into break-out sessions on the other side of the convention center in 10 minutes. Plan thoughtfully. Allow sufficient time for people to use the restroom, check their e-mail or voice mail, say "hello" to an old friend, and comfortably walk to their next workshop. If these delays are not planned for in advance, then there may be attendees disrupting workshop sessions by coming in late—or worse, by skipping sessions.

REFRESHMENT BREAKS AND MEAL FUNCTIONS

As with scheduling workshops, it is important to provide time for attendees to eat and refresh themselves throughout the day. Food and beverage functions can be quite expensive. But, depending on the objectives of the event, it may be more productive to feed attendees than have them wandering around a convention center or leaving the property to find a bite to eat. Refreshment breaks provide the opportunity to catch up with old friends, make business contacts, network, and grab a quick bite or reenergize with a cup of coffee. Breaks and meals are excellent opportunities for sponsorship. Companies gain attendee recognition by providing food and beverages. Attendees get fed, and the planner does not have to pay for it. Everybody wins!

Unfortunately, most food and beverage events are high on carbohydrates and sugar: bagels, muffins, and pastries for breakfast; cookies for breaks; rice, potatoes, and pasta for lunch. These foods are inexpensive and easy to prepare and serve but tend to make attendees drowsy. Adding some protein with nuts and cheese or adding raw vegetables and fruits to the offering is healthier and will keep attendees more focused.

Cocktail receptions and dinners provide their own set of challenges. Overindulgence in alcohol can be not only detrimental to the health of attendees but has the potential to cause liability issues for the meeting planner. If alcoholic beverages are provided, staff should be trained as to when to stop serving individuals who have consumed too much. Provide lots of healthy snacks, and limit salty foods. There are a variety of ways the planner can limit alcohol consumption. Drink tickets or a cash bar will greatly reduce consumption. Remember, hung-over attendees are not very focused!

SPEAKER ARRANGEMENTS

For large conventions, it is almost impossible for the meeting planner to independently arrange for all the different sessions and speakers. The meeting department often works together with the education department to develop the educational content of the meeting. In addition, a program committee comprised of industry leaders and those with special interests in education will volunteer to assist the meeting planner. These volunteers will work diligently to arrange what topics are appropriate for sessions and who the likely speakers might be. It is the job of the committee to be the gatekeeper of educational content. Subcommittees may be created to focus on finding a general session speaker, workshops, concurrent sessions, student member events, and so on. As you can read below in "The Life of a Session," the committee has to work quickly.

The Planning Committee Process: The Life of a Session Topic

No two organizations conduct program planning in the exact same way. In some organizations, the company makes all the decisions about topics, formats, and presenters. Other groups prefer to have programming driven by member needs. Evaluations of each session help determine good topics and speakers that may be used for subsequent meetings. A "call for topics" can alert the programming committee to perceived topics

(continued)

of interest to the membership. On average, it takes about a year to final-ize programming for a major event. However, most of the planning for next year's meeting happens in the few months directly following the current event. It is the job of the planning committee to determine topic needs, find appropriate speakers, plan logistics, and communicate the information to the graphics and Web designers to create the physical pro-gram and virtual counterpart. The following is a month-to-month overview of the planning process for the typical nonprofit association.

January 7

- Current year's annual meeting in progress
- Call for topics included in registration bags and on organization Web site
- Standing committees (finance, communications, diversity, inter-national, education, sponsorship, ethics, legal) meet and suggest topics to programming committee
- First meeting of program planning committee held on the last day of current year's meeting
- Opening comments from program planning chair, self-introductions, team-building exercise, establishment of tentative theme and objectives for next year's meeting
- Session evaluations collected and sent to evaluation vendor

January 17

- Data from evaluations returned to home office from vendor
- Written comments typed and grouped into topic areas
- Broadcast fax and e-mail call for topics to membership
- Post information about current show on Web site. Include photos and memorable events.

January 30

- Collect call for topics and evaluation results, and distribute with program planning books to committee for review

February 15

- Two-and-a-half-day program planning session at headquarters hotel for next meeting

- Divide into subcommittees and elect subcommittee chairs
  - Workshop committee
  - Concurrent committee
  - General sessions committee
  - Student program committee
  - Preconvention workshops
- Finalize theme for meeting
- Review high-scoring speakers, and consider a repeat session
- Review call for topics, and decide which are appropriate for program
- Decide session type, track, and level. Assign to subcommittee
  - Type: general session, concurrent, and workshop
  - Track: professional development, technology, and management issues
  - Level: advanced, intermediate, and beginning
- Subcommittee reviews and assigns a member to coordinate each session

March 1

- Begin artwork design for graphics for convention program and physical layout
- Design logo and color scheme

June 15

- Preliminary program copy due to staff. Includes
  - Session title
  - Session objectives
  - Speaker information
  - Session type, track, and level
  - Copy editing by staff
  - Preliminary layout with graphics department, print and Web design

July 10

- Final program committee meeting and host hotel
- Adjust speakers and/or topics
- Assign room numbers and seating requirements

(continued)

- Finalize general session speaker
- Staff approves all changes
- Graphics department finalizes program
- Web design is finalized

August

- Send speaker kits and contracts
- Planning committee members for next year's meeting are identified
- Chair and subcommittee chairs are selected

September

- Preliminary program sent to prospective attendees
- Preliminary program uploaded to Web site

October

- Early bird registration begins, and speaker contracts returned and confirmed
- Rooms and transportation arrangements made for speakers if required
- Daily monitoring of room block and registration
- Some speakers may contact early registrants and start discussing topics in Web-based chat rooms and bulletin boards
- Possible second mailing (time to react if registrations are off)

November

- Make adjustments to program
- Send final program to printer
- Copies of speaker handout due
- Prepare signage for rooms and speaker nameplates
- Arrange for a person to introduce speaker (committee member)
- Prepare session evaluation sheets

December

- Send registrant lists to speakers

January 3

- Final programs drop-shipped (delivered directly to the facility)
- Handouts printed locally and delivered to meeting site
- Programs and registration materials inserted in registration bags

January 7

- Convention begins
- Confirm speaker is present
- Appoint staff to monitor session room
- Conduct head counts at beginning and end of session
- Collect session evaluations
- The entire process repeats for the next year

Volunteer Speakers

Most associations cannot afford to pay all of the speakers at a large convention. A moderate-sized convention of 2,500 people may have 100 or more sessions offered at a three-day event. Remuneration for speakers may range from providing no assistance at all to paying a speaker fee and all expenses, such as the case with a paid general session speaker.

Benefits of Using Volunteer Speakers

- Reduces expenses (the person may already have budgeted to attend meeting, so no housing or transportation costs are required)
- Knowledgeable about what industry topics are important
- Popular industry leaders may increase attendance at sessions
- Builds relationships between speaker and event sponsor

Challenges of Using Volunteer Speakers

- May not adequately prepare for presentation
- May not be a good presenter, even if knowledgeable about topic
- May have a personal agenda; uses session to promote self or company

Paid Speakers

A more expensive but often more reliable source of speakers is to contact one of the many speaker bureaus that represent thousands of potential speakers for your event. A **speaker bureau** is a professional talent broker

Michael Jordan not only plays basketball but is a speaker as well.
Source: AP/Wide World Photos

who can help find the perfect speaker to match your event objectives as well as your budget. Typically, a speaker bureau has a stable of qualified professionals who can talk on whatever topic you desire. Fees and other amenities range from the affordable to the outrageous. If you are a small midwestern association of county clerks, you are not going to be able to afford Michael Jordan as your keynote speaker at your annual meeting. However, you might be able to afford a gold medal Olympian from the 1980s who can talk about teamwork and determination for a bargain price of $4,000.

Providing high-priced, popular, paid speakers will most likely increase attendance at your meeting. The smart way to provide such talent is to have the costs of the speaker sponsored by a key exhibitor or leader in the industry. The general session is a high-profile event, and it may be cost effective for a company to fund the keynote speaker to promote itself to a maximum number of attendees. For example, a $30,000 speaker for a group of 5,000 attendees is only $6 per attendee. That may be less expensive than designing and distributing a traditional mailing!

Another source for speakers are local dignitaries, industry leaders, and university professors. As they are local, you will not incur transportation and lodging costs. In addition, their services are often free or very affordable. The local convention and visitors bureau or university can assist you in finding people who are willing to assist you. A small gift or honorarium is customary to thank these individuals for their time and effort.

Online Speaker Bureaus

Sources for well-known or affordable speakers can be found at a variety of Web sites. Speakers are separated into several categories based on subject matter and price. Streaming video is often available for you to view actual presentations online. Otherwise, the speaker bureau should be able to supply you with a videotape of any person it represents. The best way to determine if a speaker is right for your audience is to attend an actual session and decide for yourself if he or she is worth the expense. Web sites to visit include:

- http://www.nsaspeaker.org (National Speakers Association)
- http://www.Speakers.com
- http://www.LeadingAuthorities.com
- http://www.PremiereSpeakers.com
- http://www.nsb.com

Speaker Guidelines

Speaker guidelines or speaker kits should be developed to inform the speakers (paid and nonpaid) of the logistics required to speak at an event as well as to clearly define the expectations of the organization. Speaker guidelines vary from one group to the next, but most should include the following:

- Background information about the association
- Date and location of meeting
- Special events or activities the speaker may attend
- Date, time, and location of speaker's room for presentation
- Presentation topic and duration
- Demographics and estimated number of attendees for the session
- Room set and audiovisual equipment requests and availability
- Request for short biography
- Names of other speakers, if applicable
- Remuneration policy
- Dress code
- Location of **speaker ready room**, where he or she can practice or relax prior to speaking
- Instructions for preparing abstracts or submitting final papers (typically for academic conferences)
- Instructions for having handouts prepared
- Transportation and lodging information
- Maps and diagrams of hotel or facility
- Deadlines for all materials that must be returned
- Guidelines for speaking to the group (i.e., attendees are very informal; attendees like time for questions and answers at the end of session)

It is not uncommon to include a variety of contractual agreements that must be signed by the speaker. These include the following:

Presenter Contract. This is a written agreement between the presenter and the sponsor to provide a presentation on a specific topic at a specific time. A contract should be used regardless of whether the speaker will be paid or not. The contract will verify in writing expenses that will be covered, the relationship between the two parties, promotional material needed to advertise the session, deadlines for audiovisual and handout materials, disclosure statements pertaining to any potential conflict of interest, selling or promoting products or services, penalties for failure to perform the presentation, and allowable conditions for termination of the contract.

Tape, CD-ROM, and Internet Authorization and Waiver. If the session will be recorded in any way, or if content will be made available on a CD-ROM or on a Web site via print or streaming video, the speaker must be informed and must agree. Some speakers do not want their presentation materials to be accessed on the Internet, where they may be easily copied and used by others. Selling audiocassettes or videos of programs is an additional revenue stream for associations. Since attendees are limited in the number of sessions they can attend each day, by purchasing recordings of missed sessions, they can have the information from the sessions they missed.

AUDIOVISUAL EQUIPMENT

Most hotels and meeting facilities do not allow meeting planners to provide their own audiovisual equipment, such as LCD projectors, televisions, and VCRs. The rental and servicing of this equipment is a huge revenue stream for facilities. Audiovisual equipment is extremely expensive to rent. In many instances, it costs as much to buy the equipment as it does to rent it. A 27-inch television, which may be purchased at a discount store for $250, may cost the planner that amount in rental fees *each day!* In addition, in locations that are under union jurisdiction, the planner may have to hire a union technician just to plug in an overhead projector.

Thus, controlling audiovisual costs is very important. Speakers are asked months in advance what their needs will be to ensure the availability of the equipment for the group. Realistically, most presenters do not start working on their presentation until shortly before the event. Unfortunately, there tends to be a discrepancy between what the presenter "thinks" he or she will need versus what will actually be used for a presentation. A speaker may request a TV/VCR, high-intensity LCD projector, and CD player in June, but by the time the meeting takes place in October, only a standard overhead projector is needed. This is a serious waste of resources for the planner.

Another good idea is to provide speakers with a template to use in preparing overheads and handouts. You can request that all slides and handouts be developed with a certain font, such as Arial or Times Roman, and dictate the text and background colors that should be used. Also provide a crisp logo for the organization or event. This will provide some uniformity in the "look" of your meeting.

Attendees often expect traditional paper handouts at educational sessions. In an effort to reduce expenses and conserve resources, some groups have opted to put all handouts on a CD-ROM and make it available free or for a nominal charge. Likewise, some groups will post all the handouts on their company Web site rather than distribute it at the meeting. If handouts will be used, remember to request a master copy well in advance of the meeting. You can e-mail the masters to a convenient copy shop at your destination and have everything printed and delivered to your meeting facility. Unfortunately, the fate of most handouts is to be thrown away at the hotel (too heavy to pack) or never referred to again.

MANAGING SPEAKERS ON SITE

For a large meeting with multiple speakers, keeping track of who is where and what is going on is a monumental task. Recruiting volunteers or hiring temporary staff to assist you will make a big difference. The worst thing that can happen is to have a speaker not show up for your meeting and not realize it. Likewise, most speakers expect some sort of recognition for their time and effort. They want to feel "special." The checklist that follows will help you keep control.

Keynote speaker at a political convention using high-tech equipment.
Source: Pearson Education/PH College

Speaker Checklist

- Welcome Letter: A polite letter of welcome and appreciation should be waiting for speakers at check-in. It should contain all important contact numbers, a current schedule, a map to session room, a confirmation of audiovisual requirements, and a personal thank you for attending. Any special amenities like health club or VIP lounge privileges that have been arranged should also be included.
- Ask speakers to leave you or a designated person a voice mail on their arrival.
- Assign a member of staff or volunteer to contact the speaker prior to the session for last-minute changes, emergency copying needs, and to answer any questions.
- Provide a speaker ready room, a quiet place for speakers to test equipment, have a snack, rest, and otherwise mentally prepare for the presentation.
- Assign staff or a volunteer to introduce the speaker to the audience.
- Collect evaluations of the speaker from attendees.
- Provide a complimentary copy of audio- or videotaping (if done).
- Present a small gift in appreciation. Be considerate—gift certificates, engraved pens, and other light items are appreciated. Your speaker may be heading to the airport after the presentation and does not want to be burdened with large, unwieldy items.
- Send a thank you letter and evaluation scores as soon as possible after the event.

Ask speakers to evaluate their experience at your meeting. Were the travel and lodging accommodations acceptable? Were there any problems with audiovisual or room setup?

A new trend is to develop "preconvention" session activities so that attendees come better prepared to the education session. Chat rooms may be created months in advance for people to begin discussions on a topic. The speaker may facilitate discussions and will design the actual presentation based on what has transpired online. Similarly, some speakers will do a "preassessment" of the attendees to determine the level of knowledge of the group. After the session, attendees can be reassessed, and the amount of learning that occurred may be measured. This helps demonstrate ROI.

ANCILLARY ACTIVITIES

There are a variety of activities that may be incorporated before, during, and after the actual scheduled program. In today's hectic business environment, many people try to squeeze a short vacation into their meeting schedule. More and more we are seeing husbands, wives, significant others, and children attending meetings as guests. Some meeting attendees tack on a few extra days at the beginning or end of the scheduled meeting to spend some quality time with their family and friends. Likewise, while the meeting attendee is attending workshops and trade shows, the guests want something to keep them occupied. Tours, shopping excursions, cultural events, sport events, dinners, museums, festivals, and theatrical shows are all popular diversions. Every city, no matter how small, has something of interest to explore. The key is not to let these ancillary activities interfere with your overall program objectives. **Ancillary activities** should not be more attractive than the program! Ancillary activities must be provided, and it is important that they are appropriate to the age, gender, and interests of the guests.

If possible, limit participation in planning ancillary activities for two reasons: additional effort and liability issues. As a planner, you need to concentrate on what is going on in the meeting facility. You do not want to worry about whether the bus to the mall is on time. If possible, outsource the management of ancillary activities to a local **DMC**. A DMC is a company that specializes in arranging activities and is an expert on the local area (see chapter 8, on DMCs, for more information). Likewise, if something should happen and people are injured at an event that you arranged, you do not want to worry about liability issues. A prime example is if child care is offered by the sponsoring organization. Additional insurance may be needed to protect the organization from any liability issues. Child care is definitely a service that must be outsourced to a professional child care service. Special licensing is needed to ensure the safety and security of children.

The safest route is to provide a list of local activities and the Web site address of the convention and visitors bureau. Let the attendees plan their own activities. Be warned: When holding meetings in popular resort locations like Orlando, Florida, or Las Vegas, Nevada, the "attractions" available can quickly become "distractions" for your attendees. It is not uncommon to lose a few attendees in Las Vegas when the call of the slot machines is louder than an hour-long workshop on a dry topic.

◆ SUMMARY

Setting clearly defined objectives is essential in creating effective program content and managing logistics. The first step is to understand the motivations of the attendees: Why should they attend? Is attendance voluntary or mandated by management? Planning a corporate event compared to an association event can be very different. It is a long process that often requires the input from a lot of people or committees. Education has replaced recreation as the driving force for most meetings. However, people like to be entertained as well as educated, so the planner must attend to all the needs of the attendees and provide both. The format of the education sessions as well as the setup of the meeting space should be appropriate to the objectives of the meeting. Program content should be designed with both a track and level that will target the majority of the attendees. Both paid and voluntary speakers can be utilized—each has positives and negatives. Planners should utilize speaker guidelines to assist speakers in designing program content that will be of interest. Care must be taken to ensure that speakers are adequately prepared to address the group and are contractually obligated to perform. Finally, ancillary activities like shopping trips, tours, child care, and other services that enhance an attendees' meeting experience should be planned thoughtfully so as not to interfere with the scheduled programming.

KEY WORDS AND TERMS

For definitions, see http://glossary.conventionindustry.org.

Ancillary activity

Annual meeting

ASAE

Break-out session

CEIR

CEU

CLC

CME

CMP

CSM

Concurrent session

DMC

General session

Keynote address

Level

Nonprofit association

Plenary session

Poster session

Preconvention session

Presenter contract

ROI

Roundtable session

Speaker bureau

Speaker guidelines

Speaker ready room

Track

Workshop

REVIEW AND DISCUSSION QUESTIONS

1. What are the three principle reasons people attend meetings and conventions?

2. What is the major difference between attendance at an association annual meeting and a corporate meeting?

3. Why would a planner hire a high-paid nationally known speaker for the keynote address?

4. What is the purpose of using program formats, levels, and tracks in designing effective meeting programming?

5. What is the purpose of using speaker contracts?

6. What are the benefits and challenges of using volunteer speakers compared to paid speakers?

7. Why are speaker guidelines used, and what should be included?

8. What are the benefits and challenges of providing ancillary activities?

REFERENCES

ASAE. 2003. Associations in a nutshell. http://www.asaenet.org/asae/cda/ index//,, ETI1047,00.html.

Torrence, S. 1991. *How to Run Scientific and Technical Meetings.* Van Nostrand Reinhold: New York.

ABOUT THE CHAPTER CONTRIBUTOR

Curtis Love, Ph.D., is an assistant professor in the Tourism and Convention Administration Department at the William F. Harrah College of Hotel Administration. His teaching and research concentrations are in the area of meetings, conventions, and exhibitions. Prior to joining UNLV, he was the vice-president of Education for the Professional Convention Management Association.

◆11

CONVENTION AND
VISITOR BUREAUS

DMCs attend industry trade shows to promote their city.
Photo by George G. Fenich, Ph.D., School of HRTA, University of New Orleans

◆ Chapter Objectives

This chapter provides the reader with an understanding of the following:

- The role and functions of CVBs
- The history of CVBs
- How CVBs can be organized and funded
- The activities of CVBs relative to convention marketing and sales

- An overview and definition of CVB services for meeting professionals
- The International Association of Convention and Visitor Bureaus and its services to member bureaus and meeting professionals

◆ Chapter Outline

THE ROLE AND FUNCTION OF CONVENTION AND VISITOR BUREAUS

WHAT IS A CONVENTION AND VISITOR BUREAU?

A **convention and visitor bureau (CVB)** is a not-for-profit organization supported by transient room tax, government budget allocations, private membership, or a combination of any or all three.

The bureau in each city, county, or region has three prime responsibilities. The first is to encourage groups to hold meetings, conventions, and trade shows in the city or area it represents. The second is to assist those groups with meeting preparations and while their meeting is in progress. The third is to encourage tourists to visit and enjoy the historic, cultural, and recreational opportunities the destination offers.

A CVB does not actually organize meetings and conventions. It does, however, help meeting planners and visitors learn about the destination and area attractions and make the best possible use of all the services and facilities the destination has to offer. The roots of present-day CVBs stretch back to 1895 when a group of businessmen in Detroit put a full-time salesman on the road to invite conventions to their city. Today, CVBs operate throughout the world.

Initially, convention bureaus existed to sell and service conventions. As the years passed, more and more bureaus became involved in the promotion of tourism. Many added the words "and visitor" to their names to reflect this expanded role.

THE PURPOSE OF A CVB

CVBs (known as conference and/or tourism boards in many countries) are primarily not-for-profit organizations charged with representing a specific destination and helping the long-term economic development of communities through the travel and tourism business. CVBs are usually membership organizations bringing together businesses that rely on tourism and meetings for revenue. CVBs serve as the "official" contact point for their destination for meeting professionals, tour operators, and individual visitors.

For visitors, CVBs are like a key to the city. As an unbiased resource, CVBs can serve as a broker or an official point of contact for convention and meeting planners, tour operators, and tourists. They assist planners

MEETING PROFESSIONAL AWARENESS PROGRAM

The following is a summary of a meeting professional awareness program that the Boise, Idaho, CVB developed to educate meeting professionals on the services available to them from the Boise CVB and to market themselves as an attractive and affordable meeting destination.

Bureau

Boise Convention & Visitors Bureau.

How Was This Program or Material Developed?

Jointly by bureau staff and an outside consultant or agency.

Statement of Objective

To create a campaign that would produce "top-of-mind" awareness of Boise as a sensory experience and an attractive meeting destination. The direct mail was designed to attract clients for the solicitation of meetings and conventions, enhancing the city's image as an attractive and affordable meeting location while increasing an awareness of Boise.

Implementation

The project was a hands-on, interactive three-part campaign spotlighting the sensory experiences of Boise and was targeted toward meeting planners. The initial "door opener" piece was a quad-fold mailing, featuring visual teasers of Boise that would invite the reader to "feel," "hear," "taste," and "see." The folder promised additional mailings for the recipient to anticipate. The second piece was a larger quad-fold mailer, which contained a circular, brightly colored Boise, Idaho, mouse pad with additional visual depictions of Boise's sensory highlights. The actual mailer contained testimonials from representatives of past organizations that have met in Boise. The third and final mailing continued the quad-fold

(continued)

design and contained a CD instructing the recipient to place it in a CD-ROM drive for viewing. The CD provided the viewer with a fast-paced, musical presentation of Boise's sensory experiences. At the end of the CD, the planner was invited to log onto Boise's Web site.

Evaluation

Follow-up phone calls were made to all of the clients. The mouse pad received positive remarks. The CD proved very useful for planners, as it gave a good overview of Boise as a meeting site. Because Boise is a somewhat unfamiliar destination, it was helpful for the planner to be able to log on to the Web site and view the many ways Boise makes for a great meeting city! These kinds of direct mail programs enhance marketing efforts and allow the sales staff an opportunity to further their relationships with clients. A result of direct mail may be a site visit, familiarization trip, or bid opportunities.

Entry submitted by Boise CVB at the 2002 IACVB Idea Fair.

with meeting preparation and encourage business travelers and tourists alike to visit local historic, cultural, and recreational sites.

There are a number of reasons why a CVB is valuable to a meeting planner. CVBs offer unbiased information about a destination's services and facilities. They save meeting professionals time and energy, as they are a one-stop shop for local tourism interests. CVBs can provide a full range of information about a destination, and they do not charge for most of their services.

IF CVBs DO NOT CHARGE FOR THEIR SERVICES, HOW DO THEY MAKE MONEY?

CVBs do not charge their clients—the tourist, the business traveler, and the meeting planner—for services rendered. Instead, most CVBs are funded through a combination of hotel occupancy taxes and membership dues.

WHY ARE MEETINGS AND TOURISM IMPORTANT?

Travel and tourism enhances the quality of life for a local community by providing jobs, bringing in tax dollars for improvement of services and infrastructure, and attracting facilities like restaurants, shops, festivals, and cultural and sporting venues that cater to both tourists and locals.

Travel and tourism is one of the world's largest service exports and largest employers. In the United States, for example, travel and tourism is the third biggest retail sales sector. The industry contributes more than $545 billion annually to the nation's economy and generates $94 billion in tax revenues (2001 figures). Indeed, travel and tourism is an economic engine, and CVBs are the key drivers.

HOW CVBs ARE ORGANIZED AND FUNDED

ORGANIZATIONAL STRUCTURES AND FUNDING MECHANISMS OF CVBs[1]

The following description represents the average CVB, based on a sample of 172 IACVB members.[1]

Community Profile

- Two-thirds (67%) of the destinations represented by a CVB have a convention center.
- Eighty-eight percent have a visitor center.
- The largest exhibit space available for bureaus to sell or promote averages about 198,000 gross square feet.
- The average number of hotel rooms within a bureau's primary funding city or county is approximately 10,500.
- Average tax rates are:

  - *11.6%*   *Hotel tax*
  - *8.7%*   *Car rental rate*
  - *7.1%*   *General sales tax*
  - *7.5%*   *Restaurant tax*

- For CVBs that receive funding from collected room tax, an average of 56% of room tax monies collected is dedicated toward funding the CVB.

Financial Profile

- The average CVB is funded primarily from public sources (82%), predominantly room taxes.

Jacob K. Javits Convention Center.
Source: Dorling Kindersley Media Library

- Private funding (18%) comes from such sources as membership dues, advertising, promotional participation, merchandise sales, co-op advertising, donated (noncash) services, interest, and building revenue.
- CVBs spend more than half of their budget on convention sales and marketing (27%) and tourism marketing (25%). The remainder is spent on administration expenses (20%), communications (9%), visitor services (6%), membership (4%), convention services and housing (3%), and other expenses (6%).

Organization Profile

- More than six out of ten bureaus (63%) are classified as independent 501(c)(6) organizations; only 6% are 501(c)(3).
- Twenty-four percent are some form of government agency (city, county, state, or province).
- Seven percent are a division of a chamber of commerce.
- Four out of ten bureaus are on a January–December fiscal year (42%), and a third (33%) have July–June fiscal years; 17% are on an October–September cycle.
- The average total gross revenue of a CVB is $5.1 million.
- The makeup of a typical CVB board of directors is 16 voting Board members with a 6-person executive committee.
- The average staff size of a bureau is 14 full-time employees. Factoring in regularly scheduled part-time employees brings the full-time equivalent (FTE) count to 16.4 employees. For those bureaus with part-time on-call staff (e.g., for convention registration), it is common to have 15 employees.
- A third of responding CVBs (32%) have out-of-town or satellite offices, with Washington, DC, and Chicago being the most popular locations.
- For the small number of bureaus that have employees working from home, the average is 4 employees from the main CVB office and 1.8 employees from satellite offices working from home.
- Approximately half (53%) of the respondents indicated that they are a membership organization, averaging 663 members. These members are primarily comprised of convention services and suppliers (24%), lodging establishments (20%), restaurants (15%), and retail establishments (10%).

WHAT A CVB CAN DO FOR MEETING PROFESSIONALS

WHAT MEETING PLANNERS NEED TO KNOW ABOUT CVBs

Consider a CVB to be like a meeting-planning Yellow Pages. Many people are aware of the existence of convention and visitor bureaus, but they are not aware of all the services CVBs have to offer.

Most CVBs are not-for-profit organizations representing a specific destination. Most are membership organizations bringing together businesses that rely on tourism and meetings for their livelihoods. A CVB has many responsibilities. It encourages groups to hold meetings in the city and assists groups with meeting preparations. CVBs also provide promotional materials to encourage attendance and establish room blocks, among other things.

Most importantly, CVBs serve as *the* official point of contact for convention and meeting planners. Meeting planners can access a range of services, packages, and value-added extras through a bureau.

Before going into the specifics of what a CVB can do for a meeting planner, let us examine a few common misconceptions.

Misconception 1: CVBs solely book hotel rooms and convention space.
Fact: CVBs represent the gamut of visitor-related businesses, from restaurants and retail to rental cars and racetracks. Therefore, they are responsible for introducing planners to the range of meeting-related products and services the city has to offer.

Misconception 2: CVBs only work with large groups.
Fact: More than half of the average CVBs' efforts are devoted to meetings of less than 200 people. In fact, larger bureaus often have staff members specifically dedicated to small meetings.

Misconception 3: Bureaus own and/or run the convention center.
Fact: Only 5% of CVBs run the convention center in their location. The Las Vegas Convention and Visitor Authority is one of them. Nevertheless, CVBs work closely with local convention centers and can assist planners in getting what they need from convention center staff.

Misconception 4: Planners have to pay CVBs for their services.
Fact: In truth, the services of a CVB are totally free. Michael Gehrisch, president of the IACVB, points out, "Convention bureaus are a hotel's best friend and a meeting planner's best friend. We don't charge either one. We book business for the hotel without a fee and we provide the same service,

for free, to the planner." How is it that a CVB can work for free? Most bureaus are funded through a combination of hotel occupancy taxes and membership fees.

Some may question the need to work through a CVB when planning a meeting, particularly in cases where the bulk of an event takes place at one hotel or at the convention center. However, the bureau can help a planner work with those entities and can help fill out the convention schedule (including spouse tours and pre- and post-tours) with off-site activities. Since the bureau is an objective resource, it can direct planners to the products and services that will work best to accommodate the needs and budgets of their client.

Organizational Chart for a CVB

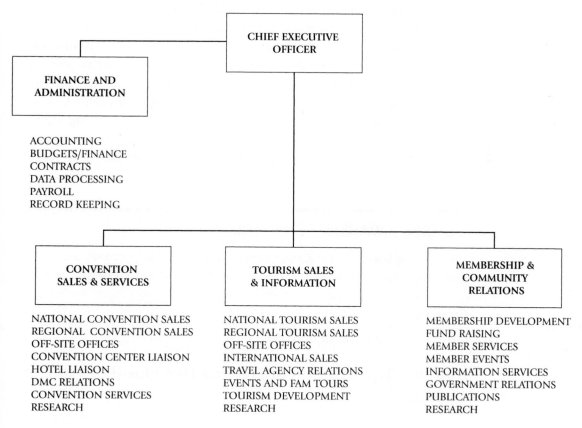

WHY USE A CVB?

CVBs make planning and implementing a meeting less time-consuming and more streamlined. They give meeting planners access to a range of services, packages, and value-added extras. Before a meeting begins, CVB sales managers can help locate meeting space, check hotel availability, and arrange for site inspections. CVBs can also link planners with the suppliers, from motor coach companies and caterers to off-site entertainment venues, that can help meet the prerequisites of any event.

No matter the size of meeting being organized, all planners are encouraged to use a bureau's services. In fact, some larger bureaus even have staff members dedicated to small meetings.

ADVANTAGES OF GOING THROUGH A CVB TO PLAN A MEETING

There are many things a CVB can do to help an organizer, sponsor, or planner to put together a meeting or event. A CVB can assist planners in all areas of meeting preparation and provide planners with detailed reference material. It can also establish room blocks at local hotels and will market the destination to attendees via promotional material, thereby encouraging attendance. A CVB can act as a liaison between the planner and community officials, thus clearing the way for special permits, street closures, etc. The bureau can offer suggestions about ways meeting attendees can maximize free time, along with helping to develop spouse programs and pre- and postconvention tours. A CVB can be an invaluable resource when putting together meetings, expositions, events, and conventions.

MEMBER AWARENESS PROGRAM

The following is a summary of a member awareness program that the Puerto Rico Convention Bureau developed for the small inns' community of Puerto Rico.

Bureau

Puerto Rico Convention Bureau.

How Was This Program or Material Developed?

By bureau staff.

Statement of Objective

To educate representatives from the small inns' community of Puerto Rico about group, meeting, and convention business, and the potential for them to generate business from this lucrative market.

To create awareness of the potential of the group market at an international level and in the United States and Puerto Rico.

To present the profile of the local group market.

To share data on the Puerto Rico Convention Bureau—what is its role?

To offer marketing suggestions for small hotels.

Implementation

Two seminars were offered, one in the West Coast and one in San Juan.

Small inns' members of the Puerto Rico Convention Bureau (PRCB) and the Puerto Rico Hotel & Tourism Association (PRHTA) were invited to participate in the seminars. Participants attended the seminar closer to their properties.

The seminars' content was designed to ensure all the objectives would be met. During the first segment, the basics of group business, its market segments, and the PRCB's role were explained. For the second segment, a DMC, a meeting planner, and a medium or large hotel were part of a panel discussion. Each of them explained how it could partner with a small inn to join forces and generate additional business.

Evaluation

Representatives from approximately forty small inns attended the seminars. They were able to meet PRCB staff and learn more about group business and the bureau.

Some of the small inns represented were not members of the PRCB (they were invited because they were members of the PRHTA), and the PRCB was able to show them firsthand the benefits of being a bureau member.

The event was featured in Puerto Rico's major newspapers, giving the PRCB great exposure among the community.

Entry submitted by Puerto Rico Convention Bureau at the 2002 IACVB Idea Fair.

Activities of CVBs Relative to Convention Marketing and Sales in Their Destinations

Professionals who work in a CVB serve as the sales representative for their destination. CVBs have hotels, restaurants, attractions, convention centers, and many other entities as their members, and they represent them to meeting professionals who need their products and services. There is an entire process that a CVB undertakes with a meeting professional to bring a meeting to its destination.

Site Review and Leads Process

Determining if a site or location can accommodate a meeting's requirements is critical. The CVB is the central information source for advice on site selection, transportation, and available local services, all with no cost or obligation to the meeting manager. CVB representatives have the knowledge and information to provide up-to-date data about the area as well as planned future developments.

Regardless of the meeting size, the CVB can serve as the first stop in the site review process. When a meeting manager contacts a CVB, a sales manager will be assigned to assist in securing the necessary information and facts to produce a successful meeting. The sales manager can gather information about preferred dates for the event and find out what facilities are available, if there are adequate sleeping rooms and meeting rooms, and whether convention facilities are available for the entire time period, including time for exhibitors to move in and out.

In order to represent all their members, most convention bureaus have a "leads" process, wherein the sales manager circulates meeting specifications to facilities and lodging entities that can accommodate the requirements. Basic information required by the bureau is indicated on the convention lead sheet. Many bureaus now distribute this information electronically.

The sales manager distributes the lead to all member-lodging properties capable of handling the meeting. However, the lead distribution may also be limited by establishing certain parameters, such as specifying a location downtown or near the airport. In cases as this, the lead would be forwarded only to properties that meet the requirements identified. If a meeting manager is familiar with the destination's properties, he or she may express interest in certain facilities by name. Then, only those facilities receive the lead.

The CVB sales manager will request that the receiving property send the information directly to the meeting manager, or the sales manager may

CONVENTION LEAD SHEET

The convention lead sheet used by CVBs will usually contain the following information:

- Name of the sales representative or account manager.
- The date that the sheet was distributed.
- The file number.
- Name of the primary contact for the group wishing to find space in the city.
  - Their title
- Name of the group or organization.
  - Address
  - City
  - State
  - Zip code
- Telephone number, fax number, and cell phone number of the primary contact.
- The total number of room nights the group anticipates using.
  - Peak room nights and date of peak.
- Dates for the event or meeting.
- Decision date.
- Total anticipated attendance.
- The occupancy pattern.
  - Day
  - Date
  - Rooms
    - In sequential order.
- Meeting space requirements
  - Exhibit space
  - Food functions
  - History
  - Competing cities
- Additional information
- Name of person who prepared the sheet and date of preparation.

Adapted from Professional Meeting Management, *4ᵗʰ Edition.*

gather the information, compile it into a package, and send it to the meeting professional. In the United States, federal antitrust laws prohibit CVBs from discussing pricing policies with hotels under consideration. All pricing discussions must take place between the meeting manager and the prospective property. A CVB salesperson may relate to a property that a meeting manager is looking for a specific price range of room rates but cannot negotiate on the meeting manager's behalf.

The CVB sales manager will communicate with the meeting manager and the facilities to ensure that all information is disseminated, received, and understood. Any additional questions will be answered, and the meeting manager will be encouraged to visit the city to personally review the properties being considered. The CVB can be of significant assistance during a personal site review by arranging site inspections. If there are several facilities to review, the CVB sales manager will develop a complete itinerary and schedule appointments with a salesperson at each property. If other facilities must be reviewed during the visit, the bureau will contact the necessary parties and include them on the itinerary. In most cases, the sales manager will accompany the meeting manager on the site reviews and respond to any questions that may arise.

The CVB can also make a meeting manager aware of any local laws and regulations that may impact the meeting. A meeting manager should ask about issues such as unions, taxes, alcohol serving laws, and any other peculiarities during the information-gathering process. For example, in Las Vegas and New Orleans, bars can stay open 24/7. A CVB representative can also discuss the condition of the local economy and local economic trends that could have an impact on the meeting. The CVB sales manager should be able to answer most of these questions or find out the answers.[2]

CVB SERVICES FOR MEETING PROFESSIONALS

The general services that CVBs provide meetings professional are as follows:

- CVBs can offer unbiased information about a wide range of destination services and facilities.
- CVBs serve as a vast information database and provide one-stop shopping, thus saving planners time, energy, and money in the development of a meeting.
- CVBs act as a liaison between the planner and the community. For example, CVBs are aware of community events with which a meeting may beneficially coincide (like festivals or sporting events). They can also work with city government to get special permits and to cut through red tape.
- CVBs can help meeting attendees maximize their free time through the creation of pre- and postconference activities, spouse tours, and special evening events.
- CVBs can provide hotel room counts and meeting space statistics as well as a central database of other meetings to help planners avoid conflicts and/or space shortages.

The specific services that CVBs can provide for meeting professionals and their meetings are as follows:

- CVBs can help with meeting facility availability—information on the availability of hotels, convention centers, and other meeting facilities.
- CVBs are a transportation network—shuttle service, ground transportation, and airline information.
- CVBs provide destination information—information on local events, activities, sights, attractions and restaurants, and assistance with tours and event planning.
- CVBs provide housing services—housing reservations for meeting delegates.
- CVBs are a liaison in destination government and/or community relations—a local resource regarding legislative, regulatory, and municipal issues that may affect a meeting or the meetings industry.
- CVBs can provide access to special venues—as most CVBs have ties to city departments, personnel have the ear of local government officials. Whether an official letter of welcome from the mayor is needed or the blocking of a road for a street party, a CVB can pave the way.
- CVBs can assist in the creation of collateral material.
- CVBs can assist with on-site logistics and registration.
- CVBs can develop pre- and postconference activities, spouse tours, and special events.
- CVBs can assist with site inspections and familiarization tours as well as site selection.
- CVBs can provide speakers and local educational opportunities.
- CVBs can help secure special venues.
- CVBs can provide help in securing auxiliary services: production companies, catering, security, and so on.

The overall job of a CVB is to sell a destination. A CVB wants clients to be happy. It is going to do everything it can to match up clients with the perfect setting and services for their meetings.

WHAT INFORMATION DO CVBs HAVE VIS-À-VIS HOTELS?

CVBs keep track of room counts as well as other meetings coming to the area. In this way, they can help planners avoid conflicts with other events. Moreover, as CVBs have firsthand familiarity with the hotels and with meeting space in the area, they can help planners match properties to specific meeting requirements and budgets.

IACVB's SERVICES TO MEMBER BUREAUS AND MEETING PROFESSIONALS

THE INTERNATIONAL ASSOCIATION OF CONVENTION AND VISITOR BUREAUS

The **International Association of Convention and Visitor Bureaus (IACVB)** represents more than 1,200 professional members from over 500 CVBs in 30 countries. Founded in 1914, the association's mission is to enhance the professionalism, effectiveness, and image of destination management organizations worldwide.

As the only association that represents CVBs exclusively, IACVB offers comprehensive year-round education programs, including two annual conferences for bureau executives to continue their professional development and network with peers. The association publishes a weekly electronic newsletter and an online membership directory, and sponsors CVB-focused research studies through its foundation.

IACVB's member bureaus represent all significant travel and tourism–related businesses at the local and regional level. The association serves as the primary contact point for its destinations for a broad universe of convention, meeting, and tour professionals.

The IACVB actively promotes bureaus worldwide, highlighting the value of using a CVB's services to the media and general public. The IACVB also offers programs and services designed to link CVBs directly with consumers and meeting planners. Direct links to individual bureau Web sites via

IACVB logo.
Source: IACVB Web site

IACVB's http://www.officialtravelguide.com offer consumers comprehensive, unbiased information on destinations around the world. Meeting planners can access their organization's postconvention history and receive reports via IACVB's Meeting Information Network database as well as submit RFPs online via the RFP/Bid Proposal Program. The IACVB also sponsors three "Destinations Showcase" trade shows every year, where bureaus exhibit their destinations to meeting professionals. The IACVB offers research, professional development, and a variety of other member services to CVBs.

OFFICIAL TRAVEL INFORMATION

OfficialTravelGuide.com is the IACVB's official Web site, linking consumers and meeting professionals directly to the CVBs and tourist boards. On this site, there is official information for 1000+ destinations, including information on hotels, conference centers, convention centers, attractions, and activities. Visit http://www.OfficialTravelGuide.com.

MINT (MEETINGS INDUSTRY NETWORK) AND ONLINE RFP

In the fall of 2002, the IACVB launched the new **Meeting Information Network (MINT)**. MINT, formerly the Convention Industry Network (CINET), is the only database in the industry that contains historical meeting data.

These enhancements have included the integration of IACVB's existing online RFP, which meeting planners submit, into the MINT database, resulting in a streamlined process for (1) accurate data collection and (2) making it easier for planners to send RFPs to multiple destinations of their choice.

This online database of 25,000-plus histories and future bookings provides critical marketing and sales direction to thousands of CVBs, hotels, and other convention industry suppliers. Meeting professionals will find that accurate information in MINT regarding their meetings will help in the negotiation process. The meeting information is entered into MINT by participating CVBs—information they received from firsthand sources, including hotels, convention centers, and meeting professionals. This is one reason why it is important for planners to participate in postconvention meetings.

Once meetings are recorded into the MINT database, meeting professionals can encourage suppliers and other interested parties to request a copy of the information in their postconvention reports (PCR). This report serves as an organization's meeting "credit report" to the industry.

Making sure of the accuracy will reduce the number of unwanted sales calls a meeting planner receives and will make available more qualified information for the next round of negotiations—whether it is with a hotel or a destination management organization. To get a copy of an organization's history report, e-mail mint@iacvb.org or visit MINT at http://www.iacvb.org.

ONLINE RFP/BID PROPOSAL PROGRAM

A meeting professional can visit **IACVB's online RFP**/Bid Proposal at http://www.iacvb.org and select the cities he or she is interested in and either fill out the RFP form provided or attach an already prepared RFP.

With the IACVB's RFP system, meeting professionals can send their meeting specifications to CVBs around the world. Visit http://www.iacvb.org to send a RFP or to seek professional assistance in planning a meeting.

DESTINATIONS SHOWCASE

Destinations Showcase is a fast-paced and productive one-day exhibition and conference sponsored by the IACVB, where qualified **meeting professionals** attend valuable **education sessions**, **network** with industry leaders and peers, and explore a full range of destinations from throughout the world. *It is where meetings business gets done.*

Destinations Showcase.
Source: IACVB Web site

Exhibitors are exclusively from CVBs and their exhibit facilities. Qualified meeting, convention, exposition, and destination planning professionals have the opportunity to meet face-to-face with professional staff representing destinations from around the world. A low planner-to-exhibitor ratio facilitates a meeting specifically for the purpose of site review and selection.

Planners are required to attend "with RFP in hand" and are encouraged to plan ahead with a pre-event exhibitor list.

Shows are held annually in Washington, DC, New York, and Chicago. Full registration is complimentary, and attendance is restricted to qualified meeting professionals only. Also look for opportunities to earn credit toward the CMP certification at Destinations Showcase! For more information, visit http://www.destinationsshowcase.com.

ExPact STUDY [A Work in Progress]

Over the course of 2002 and 2003, 500 event organizers representing a carefully selected cross section of the meeting, convention, and exhibition industry were surveyed for the Convention Expenditure & Impact Study (**ExPact**). ExPact, an ambitious research project led by the IACVB under the auspices of the IACVB Foundation, demonstrates the value of the convention and trade show industry to the overall economy.

What Is ExPact?

ExPact is short for "*exp*enditure im*pact*" and is the new abbreviated name for the Convention Expenditure and Impact Study.

ExPact updates IACVB's delegate, exhibitor, and event organizer spending information for meetings, conventions, and trade shows using an improved

ExPact Study.
Source: IACVB Web site

data collection process ("expenditure"). Additionally, ExPact also provides an estimate for the economic impact that this industry has on the United States and Canada ("impact").

An exciting new product resulting from this study is an online calculator tool that allows users to calculate the direct spending and economic impact for one or multiple meetings, conventions, or trade shows.

What Types of Events Were Surveyed?

As before, meetings, conventions, trade shows, and exhibitions held in the United States and Canada were the primary event types surveyed. A small number of consumer shows were included (but only exhibitors and event organizers were surveyed for these events). No sporting events were surveyed in ExPact. There was also a requirement that the event use a minimum of 50 rooms on a peak night.

What Kind of Information Is in the Final Report?

The final ExPact report contains industrywide expenditure data for all three surveyed audiences (delegates, exhibitors, and event organizers) and is broken down across a variety of categories, where appropriate. These include:

- Event type
- City or market size
- Geographic location (region)
- Event industry or segment category
- Event size
- Attendee scope
- Length of event
- Time of year (season)
- Event ownership: for-profit versus association/nonprofit

Where appropriate, direct spending and economic impact is shown for each category. Additionally, the data is "mined" to identify and report expenditure trends not readily apparent to the untrained eye.

The results of this study are an important promotion of the value of meetings both for the meeting professional (to prove his or her meetings' value to destinations) as well as for a CVB (to explain to local governments the power of meetings).

IACVB PROFESSIONAL DEVELOPMENT OFFERINGS

The IACVB provides professional development to CVBs and their employees. It offers the following meeting, convention, training, and certification opportunities to CVB professionals:

- Annual convention
- Professional Development Institute
- CEO Forum
- Global Executive Forum
- Sales and Marketing Executive Forum
- CFO Forum
- Sales Academy™
- Shirtsleeve Sessions

CERTIFIED DESTINATION MANAGEMENT EXECUTIVE (CDME)

The IACVB has a certification program that is the equivalent of the CMP designation in the meeting professional community.

Recognized by the CVB industry as its highest educational achievement, the CDME program is delivered under the auspices of the World Tourism Management Centre (WTMC) at the University of Calgary, and in collaboration with Purdue University and the IACVB. The CDME program is an advanced educational program for veteran and career-minded CVB executives who are looking for senior-level professional development courses. The main goal of the CDME program is to prepare senior executives and managers of destination management organizations for increasing change and competition.

The focus of the program is on vision, leadership, productivity, and implementation of business strategies. Demonstrating the value of a destination team and improving personal performance through effective organizational and industry leadership are the outcomes.

IACVB RESEARCH

Under the auspices of the IACVB Foundation, destination management professionals have access to insightful, comprehensive, and industry-specific information that they can use to enhance the effectiveness of their bureau's day-to-day operations and in their business planning. The IACVB offers a wealth of research and resources that provide statistical data and information essential for calculating economic impact, budgeting and strategic planning, marketing and promotion, and educating stakeholders.

IACVB FOUNDATION RESEARCH STUDIES
Compensation and Benefits Survey

This report, conducted in 2002, provides a baseline for more than forty job position compensation levels as well as for benefits packages offered to CVB employees.

CVB Organizational and Financial Profile

This survey, the most comprehensive of its type for CVBs, provides standards for a variety of CVB operations while also allowing CVBs to compare their operations with their peers. Conducted every two years, the 2001 report includes information on CVB funding sources, available facilities, tax rates, budgets, staff structure, expense categories, and reserves.

IACVB RESOURCE CENTER

As a new and developing industry resource, this online center houses valuable information for CVB professionals. As the center continues to grow, a wealth of resources will be provided, such as sample bureau operations documents and bureau research statistics. The Resource Center will also strive to act as a referral source of other industry-related information.

IACVB FOUNDATION

The IACVB Foundation was created in 1993 to enhance and complement the IACVB and the destination management profession through research, education, visioning, and developing resources and partnerships for those efforts.

The foundation is classified as a charitable organization under Section 501 (c)(3) of the Internal Revenue Service Code; therefore, donations to the foundation are tax deductible as charitable contributions.

A board of trustees, made up of members of the IACVB and representatives from related industry organizations, runs the foundation.

For the past ten years, the IACVB Foundation has also been honoring an individual or group in the hospitality community for contributions to the industry. This individual or group is honored with the Spirit of Hospitality Award. The award is given at the Foundation Dinner during the week of Destinations Showcase Washington, DC.

◆ SUMMARY

The world of CVBs is an integral part of the meetings and convention industry. For over 100 years, CVBs have been working diligently to bring meetings and conventions to their destinations and to service these meetings with a variety of free services. Over the years, CVBs have gone from being destination marketers to destination managers, becoming involved in every aspect of their destinations and therefore enriching the experience for meeting attendees and visitors.

The IACVB is the professional association for CVB employees, and it has been providing a wealth of member services to CVBs since 1914.

HOW TO FIND OUT MORE ABOUT CVBs

Visit http://www.iacvb.org, the official Web site of the IACVB. The site contains a listing of CVBs around the world, along with contacts and hyperlinks to more than 400 local CVB Web sites.

KEY WORDS AND TERMS

For definitions, see http://glossary.conventionindustry.org.

Convention and Visitor Bureau (CVB)

Destinations Showcase

Education session

ExPact

International Association of Convention and Visitor Bureaus (IACVB)

Meetings Industry Network (MINT)

Meeting professional

Network

Official Travel Guide

IACVB Online RFP

REVIEW AND DISCUSSION QUESTIONS

1. Define the role and function of a convention and visitor bureau.
2. Name the different ways that CVBs can be funded.

3. Name two things that a CVB does for meeting professionals.

4. Name two things that the IACVB does for meeting professionals.

5. What can the IACVB do for CVBs?

INTERNET SITES FOR REFERENCE

1. http://www.iacvb.org
2. http://www.officialtravelinformation.org
3. http://www.MINT.org
4. http://www.destinationsshowcase.org

CONTACT INFORMATION

International Association of Convention & Visitor Bureaus (IACVB)

2025 M Street, NW, Suite 500
Washington, DC 20036
Phone: +1-202-296-7888
Fax: +1-202-296-7889
E-mail: info@iacvb.org
Web address: http://www.iacvb.org

Source Notes

1. 2001 CVB Organizational and Financial Profile Report, IACVB Foundation, December 2001.
2. *Professional Meeting Management*, 4th ed., Professional Convention Management Association, May 2002.
3. IACVB Collateral Material Contributors:

   Kristen Clemens, *IACVB Communications Manager*

   Laura Powell, *Laura Powell*

   Elaine Rosquist, *CMP, Vice-President of Meeting & Professional Development*

ABOUT THE CHAPTER CONTRIBUTOR

Elaine Rosquist, CMP, is the executive vice-president for the IACVB. She is responsible for meetings and events, along with educational and professional development.

◆12

LEGAL ISSUES IN THE MEEC INDUSTRY

Knowledge of legal issues will help to keep MEEC organizers out of court.
Source: Dorling Kindersley Media Library

◆ Chapter Objectives

This chapter provides the reader with an understanding of the following:

- The fine points of negotiation between the sponsor or organizer and suppliers
- The concept of risk management and ways to deal with risk
- Taxation

- Employment laws
- The concept of intellectual property and how it relates to MEEC
- Ethics and unique applications in MEEC

◆ Chapter Outline

Introduction
Negotiation
    Information
    Flexibility
Contracts
    Negotiating Contracts
Risk
Americans with Disabilities Act
Intellectual Property
    Recording or Videotaping Speakers

Labor Issues
Ethics in MEEC
    Supplier Relations
Summary
Key Words and Terms
Review and Discussion Questions
About the Chapter Contributor

INTRODUCTION

Whether we like it or not, we live in a very litigious society. Thus, legal issues are becoming increasingly important, especially in the MEEC industry. There are legal aspects or issues in almost everything we do as meeting planners and organizers. Contracts are a part of virtually every event and have become increasingly complex: Mere humans have difficulty reading them! We enter into negotiations regardless of whether we are the buyer (events sponsors and organizers) or suppliers (hotels, DMCs, caterers, and so forth). We have to be concerned about risk like "acts of God," people getting injured, and failure to perform. We also have to be concerned with national, state, and local laws that impact how we put on an event, who we employ, and the entertainment we use. In this chapter, we delve into many of these issues and provide some insight into this important area. You are reminded that this chapter does not take the place of consulting with an attorney who is knowledgeable about MEEC and licensed to practice in your jurisdiction.

NEGOTIATION

Negotiation is the process by which a meeting planner and a hotel representative (or other supplier) reach an agreement on the terms and conditions that will govern their relationship before, during, and after a meeting, convention, exposition, or event.

While many believe that the goal of a negotiation is to create a so-called win–win situation, one in which both parties feel satisfied about the outcome, in fact the real "winner" may be the party who is better prepared entering the negotiation and has a good idea of what he or she wants. In this regard, hotel representatives generally have an advantage over planners, since the hotels usually know more about the planner's organization than the planner knows about the lodging industry or the specific hotel under consideration.

Many hoteliers, particularly those who have been in the industry for many years, sum up meeting negotiations with this simple maxim: "**Dates, Rates and Space**. You Can Only Have Two." By this maxim, for example,

Negotiating is a difficult and oftentimes frustrating experience.
Source: Dorling Kindersley Media Library

the planner can get the dates and meeting space he or she wants for a meeting but may have to give a little on the rate.

In reality, what is negotiable includes not only space, room rates, and meeting dates but also such things as complimentary room ratios, cutoff dates, rates after cutoff, attrition or cancellation clauses, meeting or exhibit space rental, comp suites, staff rates, limo service, audiovisual rates, VIP amenities, parking fees, and food and beverage provisions. In short, *everything* about a hotel contract is negotiable.

There are almost as many approaches to negotiating strategy as there are negotiators. One negotiator has offered these tips:

- ***Do Your Homework.*** Develop a "game plan" of the outcomes sought, and prioritize your needs and wants. Learn as much about the other side's position as you can.
- ***Keep Your Eyes on the Prize.*** Do not forget the outcome sought.
- ***Leave Something on the Table.*** It may provide an opportunity to come back later and renew the negotiations.
- ***Do Not Be the First One to Make an Offer.*** Letting the other person make the first move sets the outside parameters for the negotiation.
- ***Bluff, but Do Not Lie.***
- ***When There Is a Roadblock, Find a More Creative Path.*** Thinking "outside the box" often leads to a solution.
- ***Timing Is Everything.*** Remember that time always works against the person who does not have it and that 90% of negotiation usually occurs in the last 10% of the time allocated.
- ***Listen, Listen, Listen . . . and Do Not Get Emotional.*** Letting emotions rule a negotiation will cause one to lose sight of what result is important.

If a meeting planner is going to successfully negotiate with a hotel, the planner should:

- Understand the competitive marketplace in which the hotel operates, for instance, its strengths, weaknesses, and occupancy patterns.
- Understand how a hotel evaluates business.
- Position the meeting in its best perspective, using detailed information to support this approach.

To understand how a hotel approaches a meeting negotiation, the planner must first know about the hotel. Some of the necessary information is obvious:

- The hotel's location—is it near an airport, downtown, or close to a convention center?
- The hotel's type—is it a resort with a golf course, tennis court, and other amenities; a "convention" hotel with a great deal of meeting space; or a small venue with limited meeting facilities?

However, some of the information that is important to know is not so obvious and may in fact change depending on the time of the year. For example, it is important to know the mix between the hotel's transient business (that derived from individual business guests or tourists) and groups; within the group sector, it is valuable to know how much business is derived from corporate, government, and association sources. It is also important to know what the hotel regards as "high" season, when room demand is highest, and "low" season, when demand is at its annual low. This information is important because it helps the planner understand the hotel's position in the negotiation process, and it may provide some helpful hints in structuring a planner's proposal to meet the hotel's needs.

Seasonal fluctuations may be driven by outside factors, such as events in the city in which the hotel is located. For example, an informed planner will know that it is difficult to book rooms in New Orleans during Mardi Gras or during that city's annual jazz festival (in late April and early May) because hotels can sell their rooms to individual tourists at higher rates than to groups. Many hotels in Palm Springs, California, are heavily booked during spring break; therefore, favorable meeting rates may be difficult to obtain.

The arrival and departure patterns of the majority of a hotel's guests are also important for a planner to know. For example, a hotel in Las Vegas is generally difficult to book for weekend meetings, since that city attracts large numbers of individual visitors who come to spend the weekend. A hotel that caters to many individual business guests may have greater availability on Friday and Saturday nights, when business travelers are not there. A national survey indicates that, for all hotels, occupancy is lowest on Sunday evenings and highest on Wednesdays.

While hotels generate revenue from a variety of sources—and recently have become more sophisticated in analyzing these "profit centers"—the primary source of income is sleeping room revenue; one industry research report estimates that, on the whole, more than 67% of all hotel revenue is generated from sleeping rooms.

Jazzfest draws upwards of 100,000 attendees per day to New Orleans in late April.
Photo by George G. Fenich, Ph.D., Professor, School of HRTA, University of New Orleans

Sleeping room revenue is also profitable, with more than 73% of the income going to the "bottom line" as gross profit. This profit figure does not take into account expenses for marketing, engineering, general and administrative overhead, or any items related to debt service, such as mortgage payments and insurance. While food and beverage operations is the second largest source of revenue, this source is far less profitable, with only slightly more than 17% being recorded as "profit."

Hotels set their sleeping room rates—at least the published or so-called **rack rates**—in a number of ways. First, the hotel wants to achieve a total return on its investment. However, since nearly 50% of all rooms in all hotels are sold at a discount, hotels vary their actual rates depending on a number of supply and demand factors, including time of year (which is a function of demand).

Most hotels have adopted the concept of **yield management**, pioneered by the airline industry. In this approach, hotels are able to vary their rates almost daily, depending on the demand for rooms at a particular time.

The "yield management" concept may have some negative impact on meeting planners. For example, a planner who books a meeting fifteen to eighteen months in advance may find that, as the meeting nears, total hotel room utilization is lower than the hotel anticipated, so the hotel, hoping to generate additional revenue, will promote special pricing that may turn out to be less than that offered the meeting sponsor. A contractual provision prohibiting this practice—which many hotels will not agree to—or at least giving the meeting sponsor credit toward its room block for rooms booked at these lower prices—can help take the sting out of yield management practices.

When negotiating with a meeting planner, a hotel sales representative keeps in mind the hotel's booking criteria, then considers the potential business as a "package," that is, the total revenue that it can generate for the hotel and the "cost" of generating that income.

Some meetings are space intensive—in other words, a significant number of meeting or function rooms are needed. That may be acceptable to a hotel if the meeting is going to utilize all or a major share of available sleeping rooms, but it may not be acceptable if the sleeping room block is too small for the meeting rooms used. This, in effect, prohibits the hotel from using its available meeting rooms to entice other group business. This rooms-to-space ratio is one of the more important measures that a hotel uses to evaluate potential business.

While, as indicated, sleeping room utilization generates the major share of hotel revenue, food and beverage utilization is also important but only if it is the "right" kind of food and beverage function, since not all functions are equal in value. For example, a seated dinner for 100 people is worth more to a hotel—in revenue and profit—than a coffee break or continental breakfast for the same number of people.

Hotels also factor into their evaluation the type of organization sponsoring the meeting. For example, the hotel knows from experience that certain types of meeting attendees are likely to spend more on hotel restaurant meals than other types of attendees, who may venture outside the property for meals at more expensive restaurants. From experience, a hotel is also able to estimate the number of attendees who will not show up or who will check out early. This deprives the hotel of revenue that on the face of the contract they might have coming.

A meeting planner who wishes to strengthen his or her negotiating position with a hotel should keep two words in mind: *information* and *flexibility*.

INFORMATION

As indicated, a hotel may base its evaluation of a meeting, especially one it has never hosted before, on its perception of the industry or profession represented by the meeting sponsor. Thus, the sponsor can counter any negative impressions, or buttress positive ones, by providing the hotel with as much information as possible on the sponsor's meeting history.

Data pertaining to previous meeting room blocks and subsequent room utilization, total spending on sleeping rooms, or a food and beverage and ancillary service like telephones and in-room movies is especially helpful. The hotel where the meeting is conducted can supply this information; the best way to ensure it is provided at the conclusion of a meeting is to indicate in the meeting contract that the sponsor's master account will only be paid when the requested information is supplied.

When analyzing how much a meeting is worth from a financial standpoint, many planners overlook so-called "in conjunction with" activities, which technically are not part of the meeting but that would not occur if the meeting did not take place. For example, some vendors rent suites for hospitality purposes during a meeting; while these do not appear on a master

Suites like this one are sometimes rented by exhibitors and vendors to host parties for clients.

Source: PhotoLibrary.com

account, they represent a portion of the total meeting "package" just as much as a sponsor-hosted event. The planner should be sure to include in his or her contract a requirement that the hotel provide this information after a meeting so it can be utilized for future events. Thus, the planner should indicate all the activities directly and indirectly associated with the event. This can include:

- Sleeping rooms
- Meeting rooms
- Catered events
- Equipment rental
- Business services
- Recreational events
- Historical information on group eating, drinking, and entertainment consumption

Data comes in two forms: **hard** and **soft**. Examples of the former include financial information and room usage. Examples of the latter include the **profile** of attendees; a meeting of meeting planners, for which a hotel can showcase itself to others for the possibility of future business, may be worth more than a meeting of building engineers, who are not in a position to utilize the hotel for later meetings.

FLEXIBILITY

A planner can also gain some bargaining leverage with a hotel by being flexible in his or her requests. For example, if a planner understands that the meeting's space-to-rooms ratio is greater than customary, the planner can help his or her position by altering program format, eliminating 24-hour "holds" on meeting or function space that allows the hotel to sell the space in unused hours.

Changing arrival and departure dates to more closely fit the hotel's occupancy pattern can also lead to a successful negotiation. Moving the meeting forward or backward one or more weeks can also result in savings, especially if the preferred time coincides with a period of high sleeping room demand.

CONTRACTS

In far too many instances, **contracts** for meetings, conventions, and trade shows, and the ancillary services provided in connection with these events, contain self-serving statements, lack specificity, and fail to reflect the total negotiation between the parties. This is understandable since neither meeting planners nor hotel sales representatives generally receive training in the legal "rules" governing these agreements.

Before one can understand the nuances of meeting contracts, it is important to learn the basic elements of contract law. By definition in *The Meeting Planner's Legal Handbook* (Goldberg, 2003), first-year law students learn that a contract is

> [a]n agreement between two or more persons consisting of a promise or mutual promises which the law will enforce, or the performance of which the law recognizes as a duty. (p. 1-1)

A contract need not be called a contract but can be referred to as an *agreement*, a *letter of agreement*, a *memorandum of understanding*, and sometimes a *letter of intent* or *proposal*. The title of the document or understanding is not important—its contents are. For example, if a document called a "proposal" sets forth details of a meeting and contains the legal elements of a contract, it becomes a binding contract when signed by both parties.

The essential elements of a contract are:

- An offer by one party.
- Acceptance of the offer as presented.
- Consideration (i.e., the price negotiated and paid for the agreement). Although consideration is usually expressed in monetary terms, it not need be—for example, mutual promises are often construed as consideration in a valid contract.

Offers can be terminated prior to acceptance in one of several ways:

- At the expiration of a specified time (e.g., "This offer is only good for 24 hours").
- At the expiration of a reasonable time period.
- On specific revocation by the offeror. In this case, however, the revocation must be communicated to the offeree to be effective.

A rejection of the offer by the offeree or the proposal of a counteroffer terminates the original offer, but a request for additional information about the offer is not construed as a rejection of the offer. For example, if an individual responds to an offer by saying, "I accept, with the following addition," that is not really an acceptance but the proposal of a counteroffer, which the original offeror must then consider and either accept or reject.

Often, a meeting contract proposal from a hotel will contain a specified termination period for the offer. These "offers" are usually couched in the phrase "tentative first option" or in similar wording. Because the meeting sponsor pays or promises nothing for this "option," it is, in reality, nothing more than a contract offer, which must be specifically accepted by the meeting planner. There is no legal obligation on the part of the hotel to keep the option or offer open for the time period stated.

In a meeting context, the hotel or other venue is usually the offeror—that is, the written agreement is generally proposed, after some preliminary negotiation, by the hotel. The meeting sponsor becomes the offeree, but typically a counteroffer is made.

In order for an offer to be accepted, the acceptance must be unequivocal and in the same terms as the offer. Any deviation from the offer's terms is not acceptance; it is a counteroffer, which must then be accepted by the original offeror in order for a valid contract to exist.

Acceptance must be communicated to the offeror using the same means as the offeror used. In other words, if the offer is made in writing, the acceptance must be in writing. Mere silence on the part of the offeree is never construed as acceptance, and an offeror cannot impose an agreement on the other party by stating that the contract will be assumed if no response if given by a specified date.

As indicated, consideration is the price negotiated and paid for the agreement. While consideration generally involves money paid for the other party's promise to perform certain functions—for example, money paid to a hotel for the provision of sleeping rooms, meeting space, and food and beverage functions—it could also be an exchange of mutual promises, as in a barter situation.

Consideration must be what the law regards as "sufficient," not from a monetary standpoint but from the standpoint of whether the act or return promise results in a benefit to the promisor or a detriment to the promisee. The fairness of the agreed exchange is legally irrelevant; thus, the law is not concerned about whether one party "overpaid" for what he or she received. One need not make an affirmative promise or payment of money; forbearance—for instance, not doing something that someone is legally entitled to do—can also be consideration in a contract.

It is important that both promises must be legally enforceable to constitute valid *consideration*. For example, a promise to commit an illegal act is not *consideration* because the law will not require one to commit that act.

Although a contract does not have to be in writing to be enforceable, every law student learns that it is better to have a written document since there can be less chance for a misunderstanding about the terms of the agreement. Under what is called the "Statute of Frauds," however, some contracts must be in writing to be enforceable. The statute was first passed in England in 1677 and in one form or another has become a part of the law of virtually every state in the United States. The exception is Louisiana, where law is based on French Napoleonic code.

Among the agreements that must be in writing are contracts for the sale or lease of real estate and contracts that are not to be performed within one year of agreement. The latter includes contracts for meetings and other events that are to be held more than one year in the future. The former could also include a meeting contract since the agreement might be construed as a sponsor's "lease" of hotel space. The law requires these contracts to be in writing because they are viewed as more important documents than "ordinary" agreements. However, as indicated, planners are strongly encouraged to put all contracts in writing to avoid the possibility of misunderstandings.

A valid written contract must contain the identity of the parties, an identification or recitation of the subject matter and terms of agreement, and a statement of consideration. Often, where the consideration may not be obvious, a contract will state that it is entered into for "good and valuable consideration, the receipt and sufficiency of which are acknowledged by the parties."

When a contract is in writing, it is generally subject to the so-called parol evidence or "four-corners" rule of interpretation. Thus, where the writing is intended to be the complete and final expression of the rights and duties of the parties, evidence of prior oral or written negotiations or agreements or contemporaneous oral agreements cannot be considered by a court charged with interpreting the contract. Many contracts contain what is often called an "entire agreement" clause, which specifies that the written document contains the entire agreement between the parties and supersedes all previous oral or written negotiations or agreements.

Parol evidence (or evidence of oral agreement) can be used in limited instances, especially where the plain meaning of words in the written document may be in doubt. A court will generally construe a contract most strongly against the party that prepared the written document, and if there is a conflict between printed and handwritten words or phrases, the latter will prevail.

Many contracts, especially meeting contracts, contain addenda prepared at the same time or sometimes subsequent to the signing of the contract. In cases where the terms of an addendum differ from those of the contract, the addendum prevails, although it is a good idea when using an addendum to specifically provide that in the event of differences, the addendum will prevail.

Planning and executing a meeting may involve the negotiation of several contracts. Obviously, the major—and perhaps most important—agreement is the one with the hotel and/or trade show facility. However, there can also be agreements covering a myriad of ancillary services, such as temporary employees, security, audiovisual equipment, destination management (e.g., tours and local transportation), entertainment, outside food and beverage, exhibitor services or decorating, and housing bureaus. Moreover, agreements may be negotiated with "official" transportation providers like travel agencies, airlines, and rental car companies.

NEGOTIATING CONTRACTS

When negotiating meeting contracts—or any agreements for that matter—it is wise to keep some general rules in mind. While a good contract negotiation is a "win–win" situation, providing something for each party, the real "winner" in a negotiation is usually the one who is best prepared and/or the one who has the best bargaining leverage. The following general rules will help with the negotiation of a meeting contract:

- *Go into the negotiations with a plan.* A skilled negotiator knows his or her "bottom line," that is, what is really wanted and what proposals can be given up to reach a compromise result.
- *Always go into a contract negotiation with an alternative location or service provider in mind.* Bargaining leverage is better if the other party knows you can go somewhere else with your business.
- *Be thorough.* Put everything negotiated in the contract, and do not be afraid to utilize an addendum, provided it is referred to in the body of the contract. Develop your own contract if necessary.
- *Do not assume anything.* Meeting industry personnel change frequently, and oral agreements or assumptions can be easily forgotten or misunderstood.
- *Be specific.* For example, do not state "food and beverage prices will be guaranteed *12 to 18* months out." Instead, specify that "food and

beverage prices will be guaranteed (or negotiated) 12 months prior to the meeting."

- ***Beware of language that sounds acceptable but is not specific.*** For example, what does a "tentative first option" mean? Words like "reasonable," "anticipated," and "projected" should be avoided, since their meaning is different to different people.
- ***Do not accept something just because it is preprinted on the contract or the proposal is given to you by the other party.*** Everything is negotiable.
- ***Read the small print.*** For example, the "boilerplate" language about indemnification of parties in the event of negligence can make a major difference in the resolution of liability after an accident or injury.
- ***Look for mutuality in the contract's provisions.*** For example, do not sign a contract in which the "hold harmless" clause only protects one of the parties. Such provisions should be applicable to both parties. And never give one party the unilateral right to do anything, such as change the location of meeting rooms without consent of the meeting sponsor.

In addition to the general "rules" applicable to all contract negotiations, there are some special rules about hotel contracts that should also be kept in mind:

- Remember that a meeting contract provides a "package" of funds to a hotel. Think in terms of overall financial benefit to the hotel (i.e., its total income from room rates, food and beverage, and so on), and allocate this to the organization's benefit.
- Never sign a contract in which major items like room rates are left to future negotiation. Future rates can always be set as a percentage of then-current "rack" rates or as a predetermined increase (such as the Bureau of Labor Statistics' Consumer Price Index, officially called the Consumer Price Index for All Urban Consumers or CPI-U) over existing rates. And although it may be unlikely, provide for a decrease in rates if the market falls. Indicate the specific date when final rates are to be determined. For example, a contract could indicate that the room rate, if not guaranteed, is to be the increase over the CPI-U, "x" percent off the then-current rack rate, or 5% per year over the current group rate, whichever rate is less.
- Specify special room rates—such as for staff and speakers—and indicate any upgrades for these people. Indicate whether these are

included in the complimentary room formula, and specify what that formula is.

- While it is preferable to have specific meeting and function rooms designated in the contract, they should be assigned at least six to nine months prior to the meeting, depending on the time of the first promotional mailing. Do not permit a change in assigned meeting rooms without approval of the meeting sponsor.

- Provide the ability to cancel a meeting without penalty or damages if (a) hotel ownership or management is changed; (b) the meeting outgrows hotel space or substantially shrinks in size; (c) the hotel does not perform satisfactorily at an earlier meeting (e.g., in the event of a multiyear contract with the same property); or (d) an adverse change in the hotel's quality rating, as measured by the American Automobile Association or the Mobil Travel Guide.

- If a cancellation clause will trigger a monetary payment to the hotel, the payment should be specified in dollars or should be based on the hotel's lost profit rather than lost revenue. When lost room revenue is involved, make sure to measure lost sales against the normal occupancy for the particular time of the year, not against the hotel's capacity. Damages should not be payable if the hotel resells the space. While many contract drafters strive for mutuality in provisions, there is a difference of opinion with regard to specified damages in a contract for cancellation by the hotel. Some believe this is important; others point out that it only provides the hotel with a predetermined figure that it can use to "buy out" of a deal and that may not actually reflect the true damage to the meeting sponsor of hotel cancellation.

- Do not agree to any changes that are not either spelled out in the contract or a later addendum. If an addendum is used, make sure it references the underlying agreement, and if it is signed at the time of the agreement, make sure the agreement references the addendum. Be sure that all documents are signed by individuals who are authorized to bind the parties.

One of the most frequently overlooked yet most important parts of a hotel contract are the names of the contracting parties. While the meeting's sponsor is listed (an independent planner should always sign as agent for the sponsor or have an authorized representative of the sponsor sign), the name of the hotel is, in almost all cases, simply listed as the name on the hotel marquee, like "Sheraton Boston."

But the hotel's name is merely a trade name—that is, the name under which the property's owner or management company does business. In today's hotel environment, it may actually be a franchise of a national "chain" operated by a company that the planner has never heard of. For example, one of the country's largest hotel management companies is Interstate Hotels & Resorts, Inc. Included in the more than 300 hotels that it manages are properties operating under the following "chain" names: Marriott, Holiday Inn, Hilton, Sheraton, and Radisson. Thus, if a contract with one of Interstate's properties simply states that it is with the "Gaithersburg (MD) Marriott," the planner might never know that the actual contracting party is Interstate Hotels & Resorts.

Every meeting contract should contain the following provision, usually as the introductory paragraph:

> This Agreement dated _____ is between (official legal name of entity), a (name of state) (corporation)(partnership) doing business as (name of hotel) and having its principal place of business at (address of contracting party, not hotel) and (name of meeting sponsor), a (name of state) (corporation)(partnership) having its principal place of business at (address of meeting sponsor).

Attrition, cancellation, and termination provisions in a hotel are frequently confusing. If not carefully drafted, they can lead to many problems (and much expense) if a meeting sponsor does not fill its room block or wishes to change its mind for some reason.

Attrition

Attrition clauses (sometimes also referred to as *performance* or *slippage clauses*) provide for the payment of damages to the hotel when a meeting sponsor fails to fully utilize the room block specified in the contract. Most hotels regard the contracted room block as a commitment by the meeting sponsor to fill the number of room nights specified. However, in at least one case, a court determined that the room block did not represent a commitment by the meeting sponsor; that decision was predicated, in part, on contract language that indicated that room reservations would be made by individuals and not the meeting sponsor.

A well-written attrition provision should provide the sponsoring organization with the ability to reduce the room block by a specified amount (e.g., 10–20%) up to a specified time prior to the meeting (e.g., six to twelve months) without incurring damages. Thereafter, damages should only accrue if the sponsor fails to occupy a specified percentage (e.g., 85–90%) of its adjusted (not the original) room block. Occupancy should be measured on a cumulative room night basis, not on a night-by-night basis.

Because hotels sometimes offer rates to the general public as part of special promotional packages that are lower than those available to the meeting attendees, it is important that the meeting room pickup be measured by all attendance, regardless of the rate paid. This may involve some extra work on the part of the hotel and the meeting sponsor, but the result could save the organization money, especially if the meeting attendance is not as expected. For example, the meeting contract could include language similar to the following:

> Group shall receive credit for all rooms used by attendees, regardless of the rate paid or the method of booking. Hotel shall cooperate with Group in identifying these attendees and shall charge no fee for assisting Group.

Using this language, an organization would submit its meeting registration list to the hotel and ask that the hotel match the list against those guests who are in-house at the time. An alternate approach, which many hotels reject, is to have the hotel give the group its in-house guest list and have the group do the matching. This issue is so important that the IACVB has formed a task force to develop a more comprehensive approach to determining room pickup. One of their first suggestions is to have the meeting organizer ask attendees during registration to indicate where they are staying and for what nights. This information can be compared to that derived by the hotel(s) to ascertain the true impact of the meeting or convention.

Damages triggered by the failure to meet a room block commitment should be specified in dollars, not measured by a percentage of some vague figure as "anticipated room revenue." The latter may provide the hotel with an opportunity to include estimated spending on such things as telephone calls, in-room movies, and the like. The specified damages should be based on the hotel's lost profit, not its lost revenue. With sleeping rooms, for example, the average industry profit margin is 75 to 80%, so the per-room attrition fee should not exceed 80% of the group's single room rate. The industry standard for food and beverage profit is 25 to 30%. In any event, damages for failure to meet a room block commitment should never be payable if the hotel is able to resell the rooms; the contract should impose a specific requirement on the hotel to try and resell the rooms and, if possible, require the hotel to resell the rooms in the organization's room block first.

Attrition clauses often appear in the portion of a contract that discusses meeting room rental fees, with the contract providing that meeting room rental fees will be imposed, typically on a sliding scale basis, if the room block is not filled. If the clause appears in conjunction with meeting room rental, it should not also appear somewhere else, resulting in a double charge, and language should be inserted making it clear that the meeting room rental fee is the only charge to be imposed in the event that the room block is not completely utilized.

Some meeting sponsors have attempted to insert a provision that is, in essence, the reciprocal of an attrition clause. Such a provision would state that if the group exceeds its room block by a specified percentage (usually the same as the attrition percentage), the hotel would provide a monetary payment of a specified amount to the sponsor's master account, recognizing the additional revenue generated by the larger-than-anticipated attendance. Hotels, however, have been generally reluctant to agree to such a provision, even though it can be argued that it is merely the reciprocal for damages for failure to fill a room block.

Cancellation

This is the provision that provides for damages should the meeting be canceled for reasons other than those specified, either in the same clause or in the termination provision. More often than not, this provision in a hotel-provided agreement is one-sided. It provides damages to the hotel in the event the meeting sponsor cancels. A properly drafted agreement should provide for damages in the event either party (including the hotel) cancels without a valid reason. However, as indicated previously, some contract drafters believe damages should not be specified in the event of a hotel cancellation because it only provides the hotel with an amount that it can use to buy out of an agreement.

There should generally be no right for the meeting sponsor to cancel solely to book the meeting in another hotel or another city, or for the hotel to book another, more lucrative meeting in place of the one contracted for. However, a meeting sponsor should be able to cancel, without the payment of damages, if the hotel ownership or management changes, if the meeting size outgrows the hotel, if the hotel's quality rating (as measured by the American Automobile Association or Mobil Travel Guide) changes, or for reasons that make it inappropriate or impractical to hold the meeting. The latter language should be broad enough to cover so-called boycott situations, where a group decides not to hold a meeting in a particular location because of action taken by the state legislature. As an example, the sponsor of a major shooting sports trade show canceled the event after the sponsoring city sued gun manufacturers who were the show's major exhibitors.

In some cases, cancellation is provided without damages as long as it is done within a specified time (e.g., two to three years) prior to the meeting. This gives the hotel ample opportunity to resell the space.

The damages triggered by a cancellation are sometimes stated on a sliding scale basis, with greater damages being paid the closer to the meeting date the cancellation occurs. Damages should be expressed as "liquidated damages" or cancellation fee, not as a penalty, since the law generally does not recognize penalty provisions. As with damages in an attrition clause, damages should be expressed in dollar amounts, not room revenue (so that sales tax can be avoided) and should only be payable if the hotel cannot resell the space.

Termination

Sometimes called a *force majeure* or **Act of God** clause, this provision permits either party to terminate the contract without damages if fulfillment of the obligations imposed in the agreement are rendered impossible by occurrences outside of the control of either party. This usually includes such things as strikes, severe weather, and transportation difficulties.

This provision sometimes contains the "inappropriate or impractical" situation referred to above in the discussion of cancellation provisions.

Contracts provided to planners by hotels generally vary significantly from property to property, even within the same chain. Some of the variance can be attributed to the fact that some "chain" properties are managed by outside parties, making standardization difficult. Often, however, it has been the result of a lack of attention to the meeting contracting process by the chains themselves. Some hotels have resisted development of "standard" contracts, saying that all meetings are different and thus one contract cannot "fit all." More recently, though, most major hotel chains have adopted or are considering "standard" agreements, even though some of the provisions contain multiple options for use by sales representatives.

Because of the differences in contracts supplied by hotels, even ones within the same chain, and because it is often so easy for planners, even experienced ones, to overlook key elements of a contract, many meeting sponsors are developing their own "standard" contract. While many meeting sponsors may be unsure of the costs involved in having a competent attorney prepare this type of document, such costs are minimal when compared with the time (and therefore expense) involved in reviewing each and every contract proposed by a hotel, whether the review is conducted by counsel or by a meeting planner or other staff member.

A sponsor's development of its own contract will ensure that its particular needs are met and will minimize the chances of subsequent legal problems caused by a misunderstanding of the terms of the agreement.

No matter how carefully a contract is written, disputes may occur either because the parties might disagree as to their individual rights and obligations or because one of the parties may perform less than had been promised.

These controversies seldom involve precedent-setting legal issues; rather, they concern an evaluation of facts and interpretation of contract terms. When these differences arise, parties often prefer to settle them privately and informally in the kind of businesslike way that encourages continued business relationships.

Sometimes, however, such resolution is not possible. This leaves the "aggrieved" party with three options: forget the possibility of reaching a solution and walk away from the problem, go to court and sue, or resolve the dispute through other means.

Going to court can be an expensive and time-consuming proposition, with crowded court dockets delaying a decision for several months or in some cases several years. Counsel fees can mount up quickly, especially if extensive pretrial proceedings are involved. Depending on the court's location, one of the parties may have to expend additional fees for travel expenses. Since court cases are matters of public record, potentially adverse publicity may result.

For this reason, arbitration is gaining favor as a means of settling disputes. *Arbitration* is defined as "settlement of a dispute by a person or persons chosen to hear both sides and come to a decision" (*Webster's New Universal Unabridged Dictionary*, S.V. "arbitration"). Under rules administered by the American Arbitration Association, arbitration is designed for quick, practical, and inexpensive settlements. It is, at the same time, an orderly proceeding, governed by rules of procedure and standards of conduct prescribed by law. Either party can utilize lawyers, but there is a minimum of pretrial procedures. If arbitration is chosen as the dispute-mechanism procedure in the contract, the parties also generally agree that the results are binding, that is, they cannot be appealed to a court of law. The contract should also specify the location of the arbitration. Arbitration is not generally a matter of public record, so all of the proceedings can remain private.

While the filing fee required to commence an arbitration of an average daily rate (ADR) procedure is generally higher—often considerably so—than that required to begin litigation in the courts, the overall cost of arbitration is often significantly lower. This is because of the absence of extensive pretrial maneuvering and because attorneys are often discouraged, or even prohibited, from participating as representatives of the parties. The "downside" to arbitration is that some believe arbitrators may often "split the difference" in a dispute, seeking an equitable solution rather than following the letter of the law.

If the parties choose arbitration as a means of settling disputes, the choice should be made before disagreements arise, and language governing the arbitration option should be included in the meeting contract. The contract should include the location of the arbitration proceeding. If arbitration is not selected, the contract should spell out which state's law (e.g., where the meeting took place or where the meeting sponsor is located) will be utilized to resolve a court dispute.

Under the American system of justice, each party to a court suit or an arbitration proceeding is required to bear the costs of its own attorneys unless the agreement provides that the winning party is entitled to have the loser pay its attorneys' fees and costs.

Finally, a well-drafted contract should specify the damages to be awarded in the event of a breach by either party. Such an approach takes the decision out of the hands of a judge or an arbitrator and leaves the dispute resolver only to determine whether a breach of the agreement occurred. Damages are typically stated as "liquidated damages," that is, damages that the parties agree in advance will be the result of a breach. Courts will generally not honor a contract provision that imposes a "penalty" on the one breaching the agreement, so that term should be avoided.

RISK

All meetings involve an element of **risk**. The best way for a planner to manage the risk is to first understand what risks are faced. In general, all risk falls into the following categories:

- Contractual risks, such as those that the planner voluntarily and willingly undertakes by signing an agreement that calls for certain tasks to be performed.
- Operational risks, like those that occur as a result of conducting a meeting or event. These include such areas as liquor or host liability.
- Negligent occurrences, for instance, things that happen because one party did or did not take a certain action.
- Acts of God, such as damages that occur because of tornadoes and earthquakes.

After one understands what might happen, the risks can be managed in a number of ways. First, the risk can be avoided, for instance, the planner simply decides that conducting a risky endeavor is simply not worth the benefit that might accrue. Second, the risk can be transferred to another party involved in the transaction; this occurs when, for example, a planner states in a contract that the hotel is responsible for compliance with all state laws involving alcohol beverage service and will indemnify (to protect against or keep from loss, damage, and so on) the planner for any violation that results in an injury to someone. Finally, the risk can be insured, which is a form of transference, using an insurance company's money to pay any damages.

While not all risks can be insured against, there are several types of insurance policies available to minimize the sponsor's liability. Workers' compensation and comprehensive general liability are two types of insurance that are explained as follows:

- *Workers' compensation* insurance is mandatory in all states. It provides coverage for employees who are injured on the job. While most states permit employers to either self-insure or purchase coverage from private

AN UNUSUAL LIABILITY

A number of years ago, an interesting "risk" situation developed. A company sponsored a Christmas party where alcohol was served. A male and female employee each consumed enough alcohol to become inebriated and, with their moral safeguard down, decided to sleep together and have sex. The female became pregnant as a result and sued the employer company for contributing to the pregnancy by allowing her to become intoxicated. The court agreed with the woman, and the company was held liable!

companies, a few states (like Nevada) require employers to purchase this insurance only through a state fund. This could cause a problem if an organization holds a meeting in Nevada and hires temporary employees to perform services at the meeting. To avoid this problem, organizations should utilize only independent contractors for temporary staffing or hire individuals provided by a temporary agency.

• *Comprehensive general liability* (**CGL**) policies are the commercial equivalent of a homeowner's policy. They protect the organization against personal injury claims and loss (including theft) or damage to the insured's property as well as the property of others. Although these policies are designed to cover "all risks," they frequently have exclusions, and it is important to carefully review what is not covered as well as what is included within the policy's scope.

It is not clear from many of these policies whether they insure against events that occur outside of the organization's premises, such as at meetings, conventions, and trade shows. If they do not cover these types of events, they should be amended to cover them or additional insurance should be secured. Further, many general liability policies may not cover liability resulting from alcoholic beverage service without a specific amendment. Athletic events, such as "fun runs," may also be excluded from coverage without a specific endorsement. It is, in addition, important to be sure that the policy specifically refers to and covers contractual liability, like those that would be incurred under a meeting contract.

Another coverage that should be checked as part of any CGL policy is alcohol server liability. Serving alcoholic beverages at an event, especially if the guests are going to drive home afterward, can subject the sponsoring organization to the risk of litigation if an attendee becomes intoxicated at the event and then is involved in an automobile accident. Such an occurrence led to a lawsuit in the Washington, DC, area against a company holding a holiday party for its employees at an off-site location.

Planners should review the definition of who is the "insured" under the policy, since it may be important to extend coverage to the organization's employees and volunteers as well as the organization itself. Frequently, a hotel or convention center will require that it be designated as an "additional named insured"; this is easily done through the insurance broker who procured the policy.

How much insurance to carry is also a concern for planners. While multimillion dollar awards are all too common in liability cases, the typical general liability policy has coverage limits of 1 to 2 million dollars. If additional coverage is desired, it is relatively easy to obtain an "umbrella" policy that provides coverage in the 2 to 10-million dollar range.

We now discuss a third type of insurance policy:

• *Association professional liability* (**APL**) policies protect the organization and its officers, directors, staff, and volunteers against personal liability arising from their official actions. This type of policy is broader than a traditional directors and officers (D&O) liability policy in that it covers the organization as an entity as well as individuals.

Unlike many other forms of insurance, APL policies issued by different companies vary greatly, and organizations may find that certain coverages, such as antitrust or libel protection, may not be available from a particular company. Therefore, it is important to obtain several sample policies and premium quotations in order to properly evaluate options. The lowest-cost policy may not always be the best.

The APL policy generally does not protect the organization against the kind of liability that is covered by the CGL policy. APL premiums are generally considerably higher than those for general business liability, although some carriers are attempting to cut premiums by writing APL policies in conjunction with comprehensive general liability coverage.

A fourth type of insurance is the convention cancellation policy:

• *Convention cancellation* policies are a specialized form of protection, insuring against unforeseen circumstances, such as labor disputes, inclement weather, or damage to the convention or meeting facility. The nonappearance of a featured speaker or entertainer may or may not be included in the coverage. These policies often cover the organization's personal property (such as computers and other equipment) utilized at the convention or meeting and the loss or theft of on-site convention receipts. However, this coverage is generally in excess of any other existing personal property or loss of money coverage that an organization may carry. It is not intended to be used as a "first dollar" coverage against loss to personal property and/or money and receipts.

Planners should seek to include coverage for reduced attendance at an event as well as total cancellation, although most policies will not protect against lack of attendance for reasons other than unforeseen circumstances. Many policies will include so-called remedial action taken by a meeting sponsor, such as purchasing fans to deal with a failed air conditioning system. Additionally, some policies will provide automatic coverage for smaller meetings (e.g., under $50,000 budgeted gross revenue) when an organization's major meetings are covered. This coverage only applies to the period of time coverage is in force for major meetings.

These policies do not protect against liability to third parties.

We now discuss the last type of policy:
• *Exhibitors liability* policies provide protection to the organization for damage caused by exhibitors. In addition, they generally protect the organization for loss or damage that it causes as part of convention or meeting management. Many policies also provide host liquor liability coverage. One company quotes a premium on the basis of $50 per exhibitor, with a $500 minimum. This type of coverage may not be necessary if all exhibitors are major companies and the exhibitor contract includes a provision requiring indemnification of the organization for damage caused by the exhibitor's negligence.

AMERICANS WITH DISABILITIES ACT

Federal legislation over the past decade has made it illegal to discriminate against or fail to accommodate people with disabilities. The legislation resulted in passage of the Americans with Disabilities Act, Titles I and V, of 1990. The act places responsibility on the owners and operators of public facilities to make reasonable accommodations for people with many types of disabilities. This can include people in wheelchairs, those with visual impairments, hearing impairments, and food intake restrictions.

Anne Jakob, CMP, along with her husband Bob. Both require special accommodations because they use motorized wheelchairs.

Photo by George G. Fenich, Ph.D., Professor, School of HRTA, University of New Orleans

The following is the purpose of **ADA**:

1. to provide a clear and comprehensive national mandate for the elimination of discrimination against individuals with disabilities;
2. to provide clear, strong, consistent, enforceable standards addressing discrimination against individuals with disabilities;
3. to ensure that the [f]ederal [g]overnment plays a central role in enforcing the standards established in this chapter on behalf of individuals with disabilities; and
4. to invoke the sweep of congressional authority, including the power to enforce the fourteenth amendment and to regulate commerce, in order to address the major areas of discrimination faced day-to-day by people with disabilities.

Source: The Americans with Disabilities Act of 1990, Titles I and V, The U.S. Equal Employment Opportunity Commission

The act applies to meeting planners and organizers. They must (1) determine the extent to which attendees have disabilities and (2) make reasonable efforts to accommodate the special needs of those attendees at no cost to the attendee. As a result, we now see sections on registration forms asking if the attendee has any special needs. One of the most common relates to dietary needs, such as the individual who is lactose intolerant (cannot drink milk or consume milk products). The planner would have to provide milk substitutes for that attendee. Another example is the attendee who is hearing impaired. The planner would have to provide a "sign language" interpreter. Readers may have seen these interpreters in class or during important speeches. For those with a vision impairment, the planner may have to provide documents with extra large type or produced in Braille.

Failure to accommodate attendees with disabilities can result in legal action and fines. Further, the accommodations requirement is not limited to attendees. It applies to employees as well.

Guidelines for Addressing ADA

- General Areas
  - Staff training
    - Etiquette
    - Language
    - Role play
  - Provide opportunities for persons with disabilities to identify themselves and request accommodation
    - Membership applications
    - Meeting registrations
    - Certification process applications
  - Accommodations for blind and visually impaired
    - Technology orientation
      - Mobility specialists
      - Tactile maps
    - Scribes or readers
  - Accommodations for individuals who are deaf or hard of hearing
    - Technology
      - Relay service
      - TDD/TTY
      - E-mail

- ❏ Captioning
  - —Real time
  - —Open or closed
- ❏ Interpreters
  - —American Sign Language (ASL)
  - —Pidgim Sign English (PSE), and Signing Exact English (SEE)
  - —Oral interpretation
- Boards and committees
  - ○ Minutes and documents in alternative media
    - ▪ Braille
    - ▪ Text files
    - ▪ E-mail
  - ○ Voting
    - ▪ Visual signals
    - ▪ Auditory signals
  - ○ Conference calls using chat rooms or video
  - ○ At social functions

Some of the other things a meeting planner should consider:

- At least one staff member should be designated as the contact person for disability accommodations. That person should coordinate with the housing venues regarding those with disabilities who might identify themselves on one form but not the other.
- Put together a list of vendors who could provide support for people with disabilities at the conference site.
- Registration forms for the meeting or event should include places for people with disabilities to identify themselves and request accommodations.
- Registration forms for housing should also include a place for those with disabilities to identify themselves and request accommodations.
- Be sure that disability accommodations are included in your meeting budget. At least 7 to 10% of the budget should be allocated for accommodating people with disabilities.

(Source: P. Critta, and D. Hulse, 2003, "Becoming an Advocate for all attendees," *Convene,* February, pp. 48–49)

The planner must be aware of the ramification of the ADA and be sure that all facilities used meet the standards. The planner must also be sure that their activities and programs meet the guidelines set forth in the act. Be aware, however, that this act only applies to events and meetings in the United States. Canada does not have the equivalent of the ADA, and many of its facilities do not meet the standards put forth in the act. Accessibility and accommodation of those with disabilities varies significantly from county to country.

INTELLECTUAL PROPERTY

Many meetings and trade shows feature events at which music is played, either by live musicians or through the use of prerecorded tapes or CDs. Music may be provided as a background (such as at a cocktail reception) or as a primary focus of attention (such as at a dinner-dance or concert). At trade shows, individual exhibitors as well as the sponsoring organization can provide music.

Regardless of how music is provided, it is important to remember that under the federal **copyright** act, the music is being "performed," and according to many court decisions, the organization sponsoring the event is considered to be controlling the "performance," even if that "control" means only hiring an orchestra without telling them what to play. The only recognized exemption to the "performance" rule is for music played over a single receiver (radio or TV) of a type usually found in the home.

The American Society of Composers, Authors and Publishers (**ASCAP**) and Broadcast Music, Inc. (**BMI**), are membership organizations that represent individuals who hold the copyright to approximately 95% of the music written in the United States. ASCAP and BMI exist to obtain license fees from those who "perform" copyrighted music, including radio stations, retail stores, hotels, and organizations that sponsor meetings, conventions, and trade shows. A 1979 decision of the U.S. Supreme Court conferred on ASCAP and BMI a special, limited exemption from normal antitrust law principles. This decision has enabled them to develop "blanket" licensing agreements for the various industries that utilize live or recorded music.

Following negotiations with major meeting industry organizations (such as the International Association of Exhibition Managers and the American Society of Association Executives) in the late 1980s, both

ASCAP and BMI developed special licensing agreements and fee structures for meetings, conventions, trade shows, and expositions. These special agreements were designed to replace earlier agreements under which hotels paid licensing fees for meetings held by others on the property. Although the negotiated agreements technically expired at the end of 1994, ASCAP and BMI extend them on a year-to-year basis, with slight increases in licensing fees, until new agreements are negotiated with meeting industry organizations. (Copies of the current ASCAP and BMI music licensing agreements may be obtained from ASCAP at http://www.ascap.com or BMI at http://www.bmi.com.) Under court decrees, ASCAP and BMI are forbidden to grant special "deals" to individual meetings, so the agreements, which must be signed, are the same for all meetings and cannot be altered to meet the needs of a particular meeting. Failure to sign these agreements—and agreements with *both* organizations must be signed—could subject a meeting or trade show sponsor to costly and embarrassing litigation for copyright infringement.

Under copyright law, an organization cannot meet its obligation by requiring the musicians performing the music or the booking agency or hotel that provided the musicians to obtain ASCAP and BMI licenses. The organization sponsoring the event must obtain the requisite licenses.

The applicability of the music-licensing requirement to a trade show is a controversial one. Both ASCAP and BMI have pressured trade show operators to obtain the license, noting that organizations sponsoring trade shows or expositions at which exhibitors play live or recorded music need only obtain one license each from ASCAP and BMI to cover the entire show. If this is done, individual exhibitors are not required to obtain licenses. Some trade show sponsors charge slightly higher fees to exhibitors who use music to offset the license fee; others prefer to absorb the fee as a cost of running the trade show or exposition. If an organization's meeting or show features "hospitality suites" at which music might be played, the organization's license with ASCAP and BMI can be written to cover the suites as well.

If a trade show operator is going to allow exhibitors to play music, or is going to "perform" music itself, it would appear that the preferable course of action is to obtain a license covering the entire trade show, since the fees paid would be less than would be the case if individual exhibitors obtained the necessary ASCAP and BMI licenses.

RECORDING OR VIDEOTAPING SPEAKERS

An organization sponsoring a meeting will often want to make audio- or videotapes of certain speakers or programs, either for the purpose of selling copies to meeting attendees to those who could not attend, or for archival purposes.

Speakers or program participants have a common law copyright interest in their presentations, and the law prohibits the sponsoring organization from selling audio- or videotaped copies of the presentation without obtaining the written permission of the presenter. Many professional speakers who also market books or tapes of their presentations frequently refuse to provide consent to be recorded by the meeting sponsor.

Permission can be obtained by having each speaker whose session is to be recorded sign a copyright waiver, a simple document acknowledging that the speaker's session is going to be recorded and giving the sponsoring organization permission to sell the tapes made of the speaker's presentation. If the recording is to be done by a commercial audiovisual company, a sample waiver form can usually be obtained from that company, or the sample form following this summary can be used.

LABOR ISSUES

Preparation for and on-site work at meetings and trade shows often involves long hours and the use of individuals on a temporary or part-time basis to provide administrative or other support. It is therefore important for organizations to understand how federal employment law requirements impact on these situations.

The federal Fair Labor Standards Act (FLSA), adopted in 1938, is more commonly known as the law that prescribes a minimum wage for a large segment of the working population. Another major provision of the FLSA, and one frequently misunderstood, requires that all workers subject to the law's minimum wage coverage *must* receive overtime pay at the rate of $1\frac{1}{2}$ times their "regular" rate of pay *unless* they are specifically exempted by the statute.

Since the FLSA applies to all employees of organizations that gross at least $500,000 a year as well as those employees of smaller organizations that are individually engaged in interstate commerce, it is clear that the scope of the overtime pay requirements apply to virtually all employees of organizations that sponsor meetings.

There are many common misconceptions that employers have about the FLSA's overtime provisions, including the following, all of which are not true:

- Only hourly employees (and not those paid on a regular salary basis) are eligible for overtime.
- Overtime pay can be avoided by giving employees compensatory time off instead.
- Overtime need only be paid to those who receive advance approval to work more than 40 hours in a week.

As indicated, federal law essentially requires all employees to be paid overtime, unless they fall into a specified exemption.

To compute overtime, one must know the employee's "regular" rate of pay. That is computed by taking the normal workweek and dividing it into the compensation for the week. If an employee earns an annual salary, divide the salary by 52 in order to get the weekly salary; then divide that answer by the number of hours in a normal workweek.

Over the years, Department of Labor regulations and court decisions have made it clear that overtime pay cannot be avoided by a promise to provide compensatory time off in another workweek, even if the employee agrees to the procedure. According to the Department of Labor, the only way so-called comp time is legal is if it is given in the same week that the extra hours are worked or in another week of the same pay period and if the extra time off is sufficient to offset the amount of overtime worked (i.e., at the time-and-one-half rate).

The use of comp time is probably the most common violation of FLSA overtime pay requirements, and it occurs frequently, since many employees, particularly those who are paid by salary, would rather have an extra day off from work at a convenient time to deal with medical appointments, holiday shopping, or simply "attitude adjustment." Compensatory time is also frequently—but not legally—provided when a nonexempt employee works long hours in connection with a meeting or convention, then is given extra time off in some later pay period to make up for the extra work.

Overtime cannot be limited only to situations where extra work is approved in advance. The law is also clear that premium pay must be paid whenever the employee works in excess of 40 hours per week—or is on call for extra work—even when the extra effort has not specifically been approved in advance. Thus, if a nonexempt employee works a few extra hours in the days prior to a meeting to complete all assignments for that meeting, the employee must be paid overtime.

Overtime need not be paid in all cases where an employee works longer than the scheduled workweek. Take a situation where an organization's normal workday is 9 A.M. to 5 P.M. with a half-hour for lunch. That is an actual workday of $7\frac{1}{2}$ hours, and a workweek of $37\frac{1}{2}$ hours. An employee can work $2\frac{1}{2}$ "extra" hours with no extra pay required before the FLSA's overtime mandate is applicable. If the employee does work more than 40 hours, the employee must also be paid his or her "regular" rate of pay for the $2\frac{1}{2}$ extra hours worked above the normal workweek.

Overtime pay is not limited to lower salaried employees or those paid on an hourly basis. The FLSA requires *all* employees to receive overtime unless they fall under one of the law's specific exemptions. The most generally available exemptions are the so-called white-collar exemptions for professional, executive, and administrative employees.

In order to determine whether an employee falls within one of these exemptions, one should review the FLSA and applicable regulations and interpretations carefully. What is explained here is simply a summary. It is also most important to remember that the exemptions only apply to those whose actual work activity falls within the definitions; job titles are meaningless in determining whether an employee is exempt.

- The professional exemption is available only to those whose job requires that they possess a skill obtainable only through an advanced degree. This is generally limited to lawyers, physicians, architects, and some engineers. An employee whose employer prefers, or even requires, an advanced degree cannot be exempt from overtime unless the actual job being performed—such as general counsel—requires such an education.
- The executive exemption is available only to those whose primary duty is management and who regularly supervise the work of two or more full-time employees (or their part-time equivalents). Thus, someone who has the title "Director" but who only supervises an administrative assistant or secretary is not exempt from overtime under this category.

Doctors are exempted from FSLA overtime regulations.

Source: Dorling Kindersley Media Library

- The administrative exemption is probably the most difficult to understand, although it may be available to those employees who cannot qualify under either of the other two white-collar exemptions. According to Labor Department regulations, an administrative employee is one whose primary duty is the performance of nonmanual (i.e., office) work directly related to management policies and who, in the course of that work, generally exercises discretion and independent judgment. The regulations make clear that an administrative assistant is not exempt from overtime merely because he or she exercises discretion over such things as what office supplies to order or how to process meeting or convention registrations. These decisions are viewed as merely carrying out established management policy.

It is important for all employers to know which of their employees are exempt from overtime pay requirements and which are not. This is especially significant when employees are asked to work long hours at meetings or conventions, particularly those held out of town, or to "pitch in" and help complete a large mailing or project.

Overtime considerations can affect work schedules and subsequent budget determinations. Defending a complaint for overtime pay violations—the law provides for the payment of back wages, plus an equal amount in damages—or spending time at a Labor Department audit can be frustrating and embarrassing for association staff.

When in doubt about overtime, an organization should review job descriptions with a competent human resources professional or experienced counsel.

To provide on-site logistical support, such as assistance with registrations, organizations that hold meetings, particularly large ones, frequently hire individuals to work on a temporary full- or part-time basis. There is often a question as to whether these individuals are employees or independent contractors.

The distinction is an important one, for if the individuals are employees, the hiring organization must withhold federal (and perhaps state) income taxes and social security (FICA) payroll taxes; there may also be implications for the organization's benefit programs. On the other hand, the hiring organization has no such financial obligation to an independent contractor.

Unfortunately, there is no "bright line" distinction between the two types of relationships. The Internal Revenue Service itself considers twenty factors, enumerated in Revenue Ruling 87-41 (1987-1 C.B. 296), to assist it in making the determination. The essence of the IRS test is control—the more control exercised by the hiring organization (in terms of such matters as setting hours of work, determining the manner in which work is to be done, and so forth), the greater the likelihood that the relationship is one of employer–employee.

If one hired to provide temporary help at a meeting is determined to be an independent contractor, the hiring organization must file a Form 1099 for the individual at the end of the year, provided the amount paid is greater than $600. In addition, the organization should be aware that many states include the compensation paid to an independent contractor within the organization's wage base for determining unemployment compensation taxes.

Since the IRS penalties for misclassifying an individual as an independent contractor can be harsh, the safe course of action for an organization sponsoring a meeting would be to treat all individuals directly hired on a temporary basis as employees, completing all the attendant paperwork necessary for such a relationship. A simpler alternative, however, would be to procure temporary meeting assistance through a temporary help agency or through the local convention and visitor bureau. In this situation, the individuals are actually employees of the agency or bureau, and the meeting sponsor merely reimburses the agency or bureau for the individual's compensation and benefits, plus, in some cases, an administrative fee for securing the individuals.

ETHICS IN MEEC

The preceding part of this chapter deals with legal issues, and the planner can look to legislation or legal advisors for assistance in dealing with them. There are many other issues, actions, or activities in MEEC that may be legal but may raise the questions of ethics. *Webster's New Universal Unabridged Dictionary* (1972, S.V. "ethics") defines *ethics* as "(1) the study of standards of conduct and moral judgment; moral philosophy, (2) the system or code of morals of a particular philosopher, religion, group, profession, etc." Ethics guide our personal and professional lives. Further, the issue of ethics has come to center stage with the unethical practices of Enron, Imclone, Martha Stewart, and others. Ethics is addressed on the evening news and on the front page of newspapers today. The MEEC industry, by it very nature, offers a multitude of opportunities for unethical behavior or practices.

SUPPLIER RELATIONS

Many planners feel suppliers are out to make a buck and will do anything they can to get the contract for an event. Some believe suppliers and vendors will promise anything but may not deliver on their promises. While promising more than can be delivered or embellishing their abilities may be legal, it may not be ethical. On the other hand, many suppliers and vendors feel meeting planners tend toward overstatement,

GETTING COZY WITH A CATERER

The Lindy Boggs Conference Center at the University of New Orleans only allows approved caterers to supply food and beverage for events at the center. There are five approved caterers. One of the sales managers was heard saying that he tries to steer all of the clients with whom he interacts to one particular caterer, even though this caterer was the most expensive. When asked why he tries to influence his clients in this way, he said that this caterer provides the best products and service, which would be expected from the most expensive caterer. He went on to say he has become a friend of this caterer and that the caterer regularly gives him tickets to sporting events, the theater, and so on. Is this behavior ethical?

like the number of rooms they will use in a hotel and the amount their group spends on food and beverage. This too is an ethical question. The solution to these issues is to put everything in writing, preferably in the contract.

Even with a contract, the buyer (planner, organizer, sponsor) and the seller (vendor, supplier) should be as open, forthright, and honest as possible in dealing with each other. A relationship not built on trust is a fragile relationship, at best. Further, given the increasing importance of relationship marketing, honest and ethical behavior can lead to future business.

Still another ethical issue deals with the ownership and use of intellectual material. DMCs, in particular, often complain that meeting planners submit RFPs to many suppliers and the DMCs spend quite a bit of time, energy, and money to develop creative ideas and programs to secure the planners business. However, there are many cases in which a planner will take the ideas developed by one DMC and have another implement them, or the planner may then do this on his or her own. Is this legal? Yes. Is it ethical? No.

Still another issue for suppliers concerns the offering of gifts. Should a DMC employee or sales representative accept gifts and privileges from a supplier or vendor? If amenities are accepted, is there some obligation on the part of the salesperson to repay the supplier by steering business in the vendor's direction? When does one cross the line from ethical to unethical behavior? Is it proper to accept a Christmas gift but not proper to accept football tickets when offered?

Another ethical question regards fam trips. Fam trips bring potential clients on an all-expenses-paid trip to a destination with the hope that the they will bring their business to the community. But what if a planner or sponsor is invited on a fam trip to a destination but has no intention of ever holding a MEEC gathering in that location? Should the planner accept the trip? If accepted, is there some implicit expectation that the planner *will* bring business to the locale? Although it is perfectly legal to accept a trip with no intention of bringing business to the locale, is it ethical?

The planner or sponsor of a large MEEC gathering has significant clout and power based on the economic and social impact of the gathering. He or she may ask for special consideration or favors based on this power. It may be ethical to exert this influence on behalf of the group such as when negotiating room rates, catering rates, and comp services. However, is it ethical for the planner or sponsor to request personal favors that only benefit him- or herself? Is it ethical for the planner to accept personal favors from a supplier or community?

Examples of ethical issues and questions abound in the MEEC industry. An individual must adhere to a personal code of ethics, and many industry associations have developed their own code of ethics to which members must adhere. Colleges and universities have recognized the need to address ethics by implementing courses on the subject. The discussion of ethics in this chapter is meant to make readers aware that ethics is an important aspect of the study of the MEEC industry, but it is not meant as a comprehensive treatise.

◆ SUMMARY

Legal issues are an increasingly important factor in the MEEC industry. This chapter is meant to provide insights into some of these issues, such as negotiation, contracts, labor, and intellectual property. There are other issues that were not discussed, and entire books are devoted to them. Readers are reminded to seek legal counsel whenever appropriate.

KEY WORDS AND TERMS

For definitions, see http://glossary.conventionindustry.org.

ADA

APL

ASCAP, BMI

Attrition

CGL

Consideration

Contract

Copyright

Dates, Rates, Space

Force majeure, Act of God

Hard data

Negotiation

Parol evidence

Profile

Rack rates

Risk

Soft data

Yield management

REVIEW AND DISCUSSION QUESTIONS

1. Discuss the negotiation process. What are the important points for each party to be aware of?
2. Define a contract.
3. What laws are important to know with regard to contracts?
4. Discuss negotiating contracts.
5. Discuss attrition.
6. What is the difference between cancellation and termination with regard to events?
7. Discuss the different types of risks a planner may face and how to deal with them.
8. What is the ADA, and how does it impact events and gatherings?
9. What is intellectual property, and why should a planner or sponsor be aware of it?
10. What are some of the labor issues unique to MEEC?

ABOUT THE CHAPTER CONTRIBUTOR

James M. Goldberg is a principal in the Washington, DC, law firm of Goldberg & Associates, PLLC. His practice focuses on the representation of trade associations and professional societies as well as independent meeting and event planners and other providers of services to the association community.

A frequent writer and speaker on association and hospitality industry legal issues, Mr. Goldberg is the author of *The Meeting Planner's Legal Handbook*, a widely distributed publication also used as the text for his course "Meeting and Exhibition Law and Ethics," taught each fall at Northern Virginia Community College in Annandale, Virginia. The book is also used as required or recommended reading for meeting planning courses offered by George Washington University, Metropolitan State College (Denver), Prince George's (Maryland) Community College, the University of San Diego, and the University of Georgia's Gwinnett Center, where he also teaches.

Mr. Goldberg is a charter member of the Academy of Hospitality Industry Attorneys and a member of the Legal Advisory Council of the Convention Industry Council's APEX initiative. He is also an active participant in the District of Columbia Bar's Committee on Tax-Exempt Organizations.

Mr. Goldberg has an undergraduate degree in journalism from Syracuse University and received his law degree from George Washington University.

Contact information:

LAW OFFICES

GOLDBERG & ASSOCIATES, PLLC

(A LIMITED LIABILITY COMPANY INCLUDING NONLAWYERS)

Suite 1000

1101 Connecticut Avenue, NW

Washington, DC 20036

Phone: 202-628-2929

Facsimile: 202-628-4545

E-mail: jimcounsel@aol.com

Internet: http://www.assnlaw.com

DIRECTING THE FUTURE OF CONVENTION AND MEETING TECHNOLOGY

Whether it's to increase service speed and reliability, cut cost through automation, find new markets, or to add value to products, every business including exposition management, must use technology to stay current. Sam Lippman

Satellite technology is used to beam MEEC programming to remote locations.

Source: Dorling Kindersley Media Library

◆ Chapter Objectives

This chapter provides the reader with an understanding of the following:

- The Historical Perspective of Technology
- Twenty-First Century Convention Centers
- The Impact of the Internet

- Online Registration and E-Marketing
- Connectivity Options
- Convention Center Construction from the Bottom Up
- The Future of MEEC technology

◆ Chapter Outline

Introduction
The Impact of the Internet
Site Selection via the Web
    What to Look for in a Site Selection
        Tool and RFP Tool
    What to Look for in a
        Diagramming Tool
Online Registration
    What to Look for in Selecting a
        Registration Technology
E-Marketing
    What to Ask
House Bookings via the Internet
Business Intelligent Software
Evolution of Convention Center
    Technology
Twenty-First Century Convention
    Centers

Connectivity Options
Virtual Trade Shows
Videoconferencing
    Bandwidth Falls into One of
        Three Categories
    Choosing the Right Internet
        Conferencing Service Provider
A New Convention Center
    Green Technology
Summary
Glossary
Review and Discussion Questions
Source Notes
Web Sites
About the Chapter Contributors

INTRODUCTION

Technology has become a part of daily life, especially life in the MEEC business. Technology is impacting every aspect of MEEC from marketing, to information searches, to booking rooms, to running environmentally friendly facilities. Technology is also changing at a rapid pace, and what was cutting edge a year ago is old technology today. Because of this fast-paced change, the goal of this chapter is to provide some insight into how MEEC and technology are interrelated. It is not meant to be the definitive précis on meeting technology, since some aspects may change by the time you read this chapter. It is therefore suggested that you undertake your research to update what is presented.

One of the better-known experts on technology as applied to meetings and conventions is Corbin Ball. You may wish to visit his Web site at http://www.corbinball.com. The site is a veritable treasure of information on technology.

THE IMPACT OF THE INTERNET

The impact of the **Internet** has affected everyone, directly or indirectly, in this country. Every day, customers see the Internet changing the way convention centers perform a wide variety of tasks. Business has been revolutionized by Internet technology, and the MEEC industry has followed. Technology has an intimidation factor attached to it, and older generations have found it hard to adapt to its changes. Today's younger people are comfortable and driven by technology—they have been exposed to this new way of life from birth, and they are not intimidated by this medium of communication. They are prepared to use technology and will drive it aggressively into the future.

Meetings, events, convention centers, and trade shows use a myriad of Internet technology in their processes. Uses of technology include site selection, **online** registration and application practices, e-marketing, housing and bookings, logistics management, connectivity throughout buildings, virtual trade shows, videoconferencing, virtual meetings, handheld devices, and a plethora of other opportunities where Internet technology comes into play.

SITE SELECTION VIA THE WEB

Site selection is the biggest use of the Internet in the convention trade industry. The advancement of technology in the industry has been a win–win situation for both the facilities and the attendees. Along with everything else, the facility is connected via the Internet. For example, hotels, airlines, restaurants, local attractions, and so forth are available on the Internet. The savings potential is staggering from a meeting planner's perspective. For example, a planner can make arrangements for potential investor meetings, stockholders meetings, and corporate training via the **World Wide Web**. Today's Web sites allow for quick feedback on each site of interest, with very few telephone calls being made.

Web sites that invite and reward are the next wave, predicts tech seer Michael Squires. Web site design has matured from "brochure ware" to Web sites that sell, and Internet users are clicking on the new sites to buy. Forrester Research reports that 55 million households used the Internet to shop for travel last year and predicts that online bookings, worth $20.4 billion in 2002, will increase 45% over the next two years. The Neanderthal theory of Web design has changed, and now all companies shall have sites that are entertaining and informative. Internet principles of the twenty-first century are more disciplined, demanding that a site make money by helping visitors find what they want so that they can quickly conduct their transaction.

WHAT TO LOOK FOR IN A SITE SELECTION TOOL AND RFP TOOL

Web sites that host site selections provide a large array of information that may be needed in making a decision about a location. It is possible to find auction sites where exposition space can be bid on, chat rooms, **platforms** to submit your meeting specs, search utilities, and so on. Certain sites may have some or all of these features, whereas an advanced site may have options for delving into more detailed information. Some sites have three-dimensional (3D) virtual reality tours that can enhance the site selection process. All of these features aid the meeting planner in finding the appropriate space and services that fit the organization's requirements. What to look for in a site selection tool include:

- Ease of navigation.
- Robust search criteria, including location, brand, price, meeting space.
- The total number of venues or properties listed on the site. This can vary site to site and is dependent on what information is listed free of charge and what is at a premium charge to the facility.
- Amenities and services available at a site.
- An active link to a facility's Web site.
- Access to floor plans, menus, meeting space capacities, and a meeting space calculator.
- Reporting options, including the capabilities to export select data and build comparison reports.

- Access to virtual tours and multimedia presentations.
- Access or ability to download a brochure or fact sheet on selected properties.
- An RFP module with criteria that provides for meeting pattern options, preferred and alternative date options, sleeping room block information, event and function requirements (including 24-hour hold requests and pre- and postmeeting staging requirements), and the option to note response and decision dates regarding the RFP.
- Ability to store and save specific search queries, save RFPs, and modify or update an RFP.

Using site selection utilities and RFP modules can result in dramatic time and cost savings, and once you start using these robust features, you can focus your time on marketing, content development, and other core meeting or event demands.

WHAT TO LOOK FOR IN A DIAGRAMMING TOOL

- Free software! Facilities pay enormous amounts of money to have their meeting and function space measured and should provide clients with access to this free software.
- Can space be measured in metrics? This is important if you do international meetings.
- Is equipment drawn by the diagramming tool scalable and represented in a metric scale?
- Is inventory, such as chairs and tables, drawn to scale?
- Are the rules of the industry—industry defaults such as two chairs or people per six-foot table, or placement of a seat in relation to audiovisual equipment—coded within the program? Equally important, can you override these defaults to accommodate overflow or to create nontraditional seating styles?
- Are accurate line-of-sight angles available? This is important in order to assess where first and last rows should be placed in a meeting room. Have these angles been updated for plasma screen output?
- Can you label items inside and outside of a room?
- Can you place equipment outside of a meeting room or in public spaces?
- Can you print an inventory report listing all equipment required?

- Can the software plan a variety of seating layouts, such as U-shape, hollow square, theater, chevron, and banquet seating styles? Can you create your own setups?
- Can you number banquet seating and produce seating lists?
- Is there a library of symbols for stage and event props, such as bars, pianos, outlets, fire extinguishers, and exits?
- Can aisles and front-of-room delineators be set?
- Are online diagrams available at the facility's Web site, and can they be used with your software version?
- Is there an automatic seating option? Can you hit one or two buttons and automatically generate a diagram for any number of people and any size room?
- Can large-scale drawings of exhibit space, for example, be printed out to poster size or exported to a plotter? (This is a great function for staging areas.)
- Can the diagram be e-mailed or exported into a facility's version of the application?

Floor plan or room diagramming is here to stay and in wide use throughout the world. This tool should be a part of every meeting professional's arsenal and made available at all meeting facilities and special event venues.

ONLINE REGISTRATION

Online registration is a huge benefit to attendees. It is one of the most used technologies in the industry, along with **e-mail** and vendor research. For an attendee to simply go online and register is quick, efficient, and cost effective for both parties. It is also important to understand the scale of the organization and to apply appropriate and relevant technology. This is how the real savings come into play. The general rule is the more registration transactions—including travel and housing—made throughout the organization, the greater the potential savings, according to E. J. Siwek. There are four categories of technology-based options: over-the-counter (OTC), PC-based software, industry-specific applications, and highly customized applications.

1. *OTC applications* are user-friendly and inexpensive options that use well-known programs, such as word processing, spreadsheet, e-mail

management, and calendar and task management utilities. It also uses a relational database (a database in which the records are organized in individual tables). This option, however, does make it difficult to generate savings through the actual process.

2. ***Meeting management software PC solutions*** often provide a relational database structure, with core interfaces for session tracking, registration, speaker management, budgeting, and financial management. Most offer predefined reporting, custom report capability, and badge and ticketing options. A level of customization is needed to operate the housing and marketing functions. This application can be viewed by the organization or seen on a network.

3. ***Web-based e-marketing and front-end registration applications*** is a category of product that can provide strong e-marketing abilities from design to implementation and analysis. Most solutions of this type provide for event-based, Web site integration for handling online registrations, e-market tracking and analysis, and **real-time** reporting. The strongest benefit results in both cost and time savings within marketing creation, distribution, and analysis cycles. Strong in their marketing aspects, these solutions often fall short in addressing the general meeting management functionality—such as room setup requirements, audiovisual specifications, food and beverage planning, event budgeting, and speaker management—offered by PC-based systems.

4. ***Enterprisewide applications*** is a category of product often managed from a centralized department and distributed at an enterprisewide level. As a result, incorporated planning tools like site selection, registration, travel, and housing are easily available to all who need access to the application.

Highly dependent on meeting volume, these multifunctioned applications provide degrees of functionality within travel, housing, e-marketing, and meeting management areas. The more widely these applications are used within an organization, the greater the time savings, the more enhanced the data for negotiations, and the more stringent the travel and meeting policy adherence.

From a management perspective, enterprise-level deployment allows an organization to truly assess spending levels. For the largest associations, these systems can bring the greatest return on investment.

WHAT TO LOOK FOR IN SELECTING A REGISTRATION TECHNOLOGY

- Flexible pricing options for setting and tracking registration fees.
- Options for branding marketing messages and event sites.
- Ease of importing and updating your marketing list.
- Knowing which version and web browser will work with an online application.
- Annual support policy.
- How many simultaneous users can the site handle?
- Does the system trap for errant or duplicate entries, for instance, can someone register for more than one session held at the same time?
- Can you integrate the solution with your internal databases?
- How long does it take to get up and running?
- Can you create sessions and combined event packages?
- Can multiple pricing levels be set?
- Can you print name badges in the format and for the hardware you utilize?
- How does the system manage vendor information?
- Will the budgeting interface support your needs?
- How are hotel blocks managed?
- Is there subblock management?
- How are cancellations and changes processed?
- Can the system be integrated with third-party services?
- Can you check out a meeting to manage while on site, or will you need ongoing Internet connectivity when using a system on site?
- Protection of your data.
- Ability to segment and re-sort your marketing list or list of registrants.
- Ability to analyze return rates, bounce rates, and conversion rates.
- How the cost is set and calculated—by user or by transaction?
- Cost for credit card processing.
- Availability of support when you need it.
- Cost for customization.
- Wait list management.
- How registrations acquired through offline channels are to be processed.
- Ability to personalize e-mail messages.
- Ability to process multiple credit card accounts.

E-MARKETING

Marketing has changed drastically with the advent of technology. The ability to extend marketing quickly and cheaply has reshaped the craft of marketing. E-marketing has a very desirable attraction to the convention and trade world due to the richness of the World Wide Web. New e-marketing software tools have been very successful in the industry. This technology has the capability to save time and money as it increases business within the industry. The downfall of e-marketing technology is its newness. Many inexperienced managers have been thrown into the game without really understanding it.

WHAT TO ASK

- *In what delivery channel formats do my messages need to be readied?* Some of the channels might include the Internet, wireless devices, e-fax, e-mail, traditional print, and phone.
- *How will you edit information for each channel, and what information needs to be supplied to each channel?* For instance, a phone recording may only mention an opportunity and where to receive updates, and not the finer details of a promotion. Due to screen and memory limitations, PDA content should be a scaled-down version of information found on the Web.
- *Are there items requiring secured transfer of personal data?* Obviously, credit card data is one of these. However, just as important these days are e-mail addresses, government ID numbers, and member numbers.
- *Where are the bottlenecks? How many transactions are anticipated? Is there a manual step in the process that might become a bottleneck?* For instance, how do you authorize a credit card transaction or process a fax when it is received?
- *Will you personalize print response forms with unique identifiers like a name or membership number? How are they processed when received?*

The great advantage of e-marketing is that planners and managers can quickly develop user profiles. Some Internet users will prefer to register online and purchase other items online as well. For future marketing, then, convention center managers may offer conference materials online and discontinue traditional mailers. If planners and managers continue to mail to profilers as well as e-market, then the process is not being utilized.

They should always provide Internet users with the ability to opt out. All of these measurements should be tracked with each campaign, and managers should work at improving them on an ongoing basis.

HOUSE BOOKINGS VIA THE INTERNET

Another segment of the industry that has been helped tremendously by the use of the Internet is house bookings. This application is highly sophisticated; it will impact how people book rooms. Rooms are in real time, with up-to-date information on single rooms or block of rooms' availability. This allows for quick decisions on room reservations without overbooking. Data is now shared among service bureaus, individual registrants, and meeting professionals. Internet bookings thus cut cost and saves time.

The Product Types for Handling Housing Transactions Divide into Three Basic Categories

1. At the highest level of integration, systems designed for real-time processing with integration into data warehouses. These allow for up-to-date or real-time review by both the room buyer and seller.
2. Vendors that have carved out strategic relationships with industry-wide housing switches, such as Pegasus Systems. Depending on the servicing agreement, the depth of the integration and number of facilities served can and will vary with each facility relationship.
3. A database, often with front-end Web access, for holding attendee housing information. The captured data is then batch-processed at contracted facilities. In this category, real-time processing in its truest form is not available, especially after rooming cutoff dates.

BUSINESS INTELLIGENT SOFTWARE

Business intelligence (see figure on p. 413) can be defined as the manipulation and application of the collective body of knowledge about a business for the purpose of accomplishing its management and operation at optimum levels of efficiency and profitability. Business Intelligent software (BIS) is software designed to create databases and to offer processes for manipulation and presentation of data in a manner most effective for

BI Process Overview

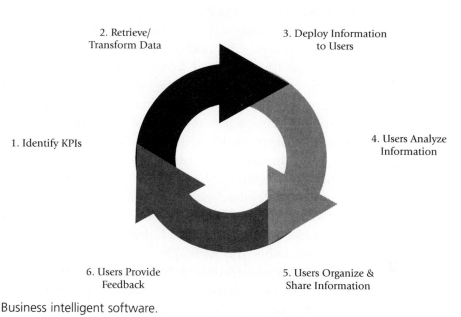

Business intelligent software.

managers and other users. In order for this software to be effective, it must have the following characteristics and/or capabilities:

1. Full capability to sort, analyze, and present data to *reveal trends* within a business.
2. Ability to integrate corporate data in order to *support decision making*.
3. Capacity to gather and store all relevant information needed to make *informed business decisions*.
4. Ability to integrate and transform raw data into organized *knowledge*.
5. Capacity of the data must be easy to interpret, allowing for *more rapid decision-making* processes.
6. Ability to *highlight trends* associated with past operating procedures and experiences in order to discover opportunities and uncover weaknesses.

Within the hospitality industry, and particularly within the sector of conventions, expos, and large-scale meetings, BIS has been developed and employed in a very innovative and effective way. An operator's ability to collect, transmit, and analyze transaction data in a way that allows for concurrent availability to the hotel or convention center property offers major opportunities to trim costs and boost revenue. For example, Cognos, a prominent vendor of BIS, calls its software product *PowerPlay*. This product is designed to investigate business data and display multidimensional reports for analysis. With *PowerPlay* software, convention hoteliers are able to customize data presentations and perform multidimensional analysis of corporate convention data for essential decision making and trend analysis. Users (managers) work with the *PowerPlay* administrator, who is usually the **chief information officer (CIO)** of the convention property. Together, they identify key performance indicators (KPIs). KPIs are measures and attributes that best indicate business performance at the departmental or enterprise level.

Once the KPIs are identified, the CIO retrieves organizational data that best describes the KPIs. The data is transformed and provided to users/managers in a form of a *PowerPlay Cube* (see the figure on p. 415) that can be easily analyzed and navigated. Convention site managers then navigate the data, tailoring the analysis to their individual needs. During analysis, data may be easily shared throughout the enterprise. Cognos' *PowerPlay* and the PowerPlay Cube ensure that data sharing conforms to the convention center's security and sensitivity guidelines. Users, after analyzing and sharing information, provide feedback to the CIO. The CIO leverages user feedback to provide more information to users or to refine current information offerings.

The PowerCube is the container of convention center data provided to users/managers by the CIO. The PowerCube presents the conventions data in a format that information users can easily interpret and analyze. Information users access the PowerCube(s) via the BI application software, *PowerPlay*. *PowerPlay* allows managers with minimal vendor-supplied training to navigate through the convention property's data, which is contained in the cube, to create custom views and reports. Cubes are usually focused on one subject or departmental area (e.g., sales). This configuration facilitates the management of KPIs. Single-subject cubes also make security and distribution easier. Cubes are designed for "top-down" analysis. Since they are optimized for portability and maneuverability, cubes typically do not contain data at the transaction level.

Unlike traditional reports, PowerCubes are not static. Cubes contain source data that is as current as the last Cube update. The convention center

- PowerPlay (and use of PowerCubes) is at center of BI process

- PowerCubes built directly from source data or Data Warehouse

PowerPlay/Power Cubes.

general manager can *navigate* the cube data—filtering, organizing, and displaying the data in any way the user desires. Furthermore, each user/manager may save various views of the cube (reports) to share with others, such as the chief financial officer or the chief operation officer, to navigate further. Cubes contain multiple attributes and measures and may be used to display revenue, cost, inventory units, staff counts, and so forth. Virtually any KPI, qualitative or quantitative, can be incorporated into a cube for navigation and analysis.

In other approaches to designing and supplying BIs, vendors have opted to centralize and store information in data warehousing scenarios and have provided processes to retrieve and present the data to its end users. Such a system is called *Market Player*, developed by Passkey in 1996. Its solution employs back-end technologies that allow for tracking and management of reservations from a range of sources, including traditional service bureau processing of mail, call-in, and fax-back reservations as well as those submitted online. The secured, centralized database design provides data warehousing that enables the tracking of user profiles. This reduces data entry time and provides individual transaction data.

To date, more than 2,000 hotels in 90 cities are Passkey enabled, and more than one million reservation transactions have been processed through the system. Traditional clients include convention and visitor bureaus, third-party services like Par Avion and Conferon, travel agencies, trade show managers, and corporate and association planners who handle their own group housing needs.

Passkey's latest product, HotelDirect™, is a hotel-facing technology for managing single-property meetings. It lets hotels share event housing data with planners. HotelDirect is the first technical site to allow hotels to create on-the-fly Web reservation pages for any event that can be branded jointly by the planner and hotel. Through the use of a shared standard, planners or housing managers who choose a Passkey-enabled housing supplier can have access to real-time reports and provide attendees with the ability to shop for hotels based on price, location, or brand. Outputs include trend analysis reports, accurate histories, and property-level room inventory reports. The system is secure and scaleable, regardless of the event size and demand on room inventory. Passkey provides several products for the convention housing business that address individual processing needs, ranging from convention and visitor bureaus to trade show managers, third-party providers, and others.

Founded in 1997, http://www.b-there.com provides a comprehensive solution set that includes housing block management as one of its integrated modules. The housing module allows online individual reservations through a customized Web site designed by the planner or housing manager. The site's design allows attendees to view basic information on available hotels contracted by the planner. On selecting their choice, attendees can instantly secure a reservation.

At this time, approximately 1,000 properties can accept electronic data transfers from planners using b-there.com's housing module. By using this system, attendees can take advantage of an integrated process that includes event registration, travel planning, reservations, and housing needs.

EVOLUTION OF CONVENTION CENTER TECHNOLOGY

In the race to keep up with rapidly changing technologies, no one is huffing and puffing any harder than convention center managers. A few years back, they could not even spell **Integrated Services Digital Network (ISDN)**; now, they are being pressed to provide the newest and fastest ways to accommodate event organizers' needs and thus remain competitive. Cities are scrambling to make big decisions on whether to completely renovate, just rewire, or tear down and rebuild outdated convention center structures. There is a momentum that is carrying the convention center industry into the future. This is a direct result of the Internet phenomenon and has forced the industry to re-examine the age-old question of why people gather. Research still suggests that most business transactions are performed in a face-to-face traditional business format. This simple ritual is what will keep convention centers growing in the future; however, prospective users will demand the latest technology.

To understand how the evolution of technology in a convention center environment came about, we must look at the evolution of convention centers. Convention center evolution can be broken into four generations. Generation 1 (G1) centers were basically a "box with a dock"; G2 centers were "pretty boxes"; G3 were "boxes with very large hotel rooms"; and G4 convention centers are designed today with the surrounding culture in mind as well as a abundance of integrated high technology.

First-generation convention centers were moved from the hotels into a structure similar to a warehouse. There was very little thought put into the appearance or design of the buildings, thus taking up very large areas of city real estate and receiving failing grades by urban designers and planners.

Second-generation centers brought city leaders and urban planners together to rethink the structures. The results of the first-generation convention centers in the business districts proved damaging to the image of the areas. The solution was to make the boxes more attractive. Designers concentrated on the exterior of the facilities to help camouflage the convention centers into the business districts. This was, in reality, little improvement over the first-generation convention centers.

Third-generation convention centers were designed to replicate "very large hotel rooms." These convention center designs were focused on a very polished look inside and out. More emphasis was put on lobbies, ballrooms, and meeting places. The convention centers were installed with all the wall and ceiling trimmings along with custom carpets and lighting fixtures. In reality, it was an extension of the G2 convention center. Although plush and grand, the end result was a box.

Fourth-generation convention centers are the future, and several are just now coming into play. They are a revolution in the industry—not just an extension of past generations in design and technology. G4 centers are being structurally reengineered to capture a city's physical ambience and culture. They have personalities reflecting that of their own city. For example, the Vancouver Convention and Exhibition Center at the waterfront has a distinctive roof with five sails that resembles the sailing vessels that line the docks adjacent to the center. Pittsburgh boasts a new high-tech facility that has a dramatically curved roofline that pays homage to the many suspension bridges in the city. Meeting planners are seeing more and more cities joining the revolution in design and technology.

This generation of convention centers needs to be aesthetically pleasing, spacious, and environmentally smart; the building design also needs to be supremely functional. In today's business environment, it is important to understand that managers are not managing a property but, more importantly, a medium of communication. Technology is playing a huge role in the future of convention centers. An example is high-speed and wireless Internet access needed and used in meeting rooms, conference centers, and convention hotels. This new medium of business communication has changed how trade shows and exhibitors are doing business today. And the Internet is changing the whole way we think about convention centers. This is important because managers will soon see how the Internet and convention centers are interfacing, communicating with large audiences across a global marketplace. The convention center does have some advantages over technology: Customers can interact with each other while physically handling the product of the advertiser or vendor.

TWENTY-FIRST CENTURY CONVENTION CENTERS

For a convention center to survive well into the twenty-first century, technology will be needed to ensure its competitive advantage in the future. It is important that managers understand and market this technology as part of their product. For example, Price Waterhouse research delineates how technology has impacted convention centers:

- Cities, CVBs, and convention centers are utilizing the Internet to market themselves to prospective clients.
- Conferencing tools allow event planners to work online with suppliers and CVBs as well as allow centers to coordinate events.
- Show managers provide online registration for exhibitors and attendees, and also secure Web sites for capturing credit card information.
- Development of the "Smart Card," a data-storage device, facilitates meeting planning and security. It also provides centers and associations

Information	EXISTING AVAILABILITY		Planned/ Recommended
	At Centers	To Event/Attendees	
Marketing			
Center Info Online	87%	54%	95%
CVB Info Online	85%	55%	94%
Online Event Planning			
Book Events	20%	12%	62%
Order Supplies	18%	16%	81%
Plan Setup	22%	16%	85%
Accommodations	16%	13%	75%
Equipment/Service			
Teleconferencing	58%	69%	90%
Videoconferencing	50%	64%	85%

Existing availability of technology.

Source: *1998 Convention & Congress Center Annual Report,* Price Waterhouse LLP

with valuable attendee information (e.g., registration, session attendance, purchases of products or publications, and evaluations of meetings and the center).

• User requirements for information technology services include fiber-optic and **broadband** data and voice and video transmissions, allowing exchange of information with outside parties.

The following information shows existing technology, improved service, and recommendations. This information is used to determine future needs in order to achieve a competitive advantage for facilities.

USE OF TECHNOLOGY

Having information online, such as teleconferencing, and videoconferencing were highly recommended by the Convention & Congress Center Annual Report. Convention Center Bureau information, bookings, procurement management, floor plans and setup, and even accommodations like hotels and restaurants nearby the convention center were mentioned. Other recommendations were copper CAT 5 wiring, fiber optics, Internet access, **digital** and **analog** setups, and a variety of data lines, such as ISDN, network setup, switch 56K, and cable modems.

Information	At Centers	EXISTING AVAILABILITY To Event/ Attendees	Planned/ Recommended
Wiring			
Fiber-Optic	72%	67%	90%
Copper CAT 5	59%	59%	83%
Copper CAT 3	51%	47%	50%
Copper CAT 1	29%	33%	48%
Internet Access	77%	61%	90%
Digital	88%	83%	91%
Analog	71%	76%	77%
Data Lines			
ISDN	73%	80%	86%
T-1	51%	52%	68%
T-2	35%	48%	65%
Sonet	14%	30%	57%
Switch 56K	34%	45%	73%
Other	44%	50%	64%
Network Setup	72%	63%	80%
Cable Modems	53%	48%	73%

Existing communication access.

Source: *1998 Convention & Congress Center Annual Report,* Price Waterhouse LLP

Type of Technology

The figure above indicates that most of the centers have a network setup and ISDN lines. Cellular and wireless technology availability is very important in marketing the convention center property. Another recommendation is the use of access cards for security. A business center offering computers, fax service, phone service, e-mail access, and Internet access is needed. Along with the technical services, a very strong information technology support system is required to handle any problems that could arise.

Accessing Technology

The figure on page 421 shows the necessities for support to the end users. This aspect of customer service is critical for attendees to communicate

Information	EXISTING AVAILABILITY		Planned/ Recommended
	At Centers	To Event/ Attendees	
Subscriber Line			
High-Speed Digital			
Asymmetrical Digital	28%	35%	59%
Other	21%	38%	67%
Cellular Technology	17%	0%	50%
Satellite Communication	65%	67%	76%
Smart Card Access	55%	61%	68%
Wireless Technology	22%	27%	68%
Simultaneous Interpretive	60%	56%	80%
Booth	53%	58%	65%
Security			
Access Cards	43%	18%	75%
Other Areas			
Business Center	62%	75%	89%
In Business Center: Laptop Hookup	62%	63%	84%
Fax Service	89%	93%	94%
Phone Service	76%	82%	89%
E-mail Access	61%	63%	82%
Voice Mail Access	43%	50%	72%
Internet Access	61%	63%	89%

Accessing technology.

Source: *1998 Convention & Congress Center Annual Report,* Price Waterhouse LLP

outside the property. Customer service and support will continue to gain emphasis in the future with the desire for faster more reliable services. There are many good facilities and a flood of new facilities being built across the country. To receive and maintain business, it will be the facilities that make sure customer service is a number one priority. The Washington State Convention and Trade Center in Seattle initiated a service plan that is essential among all employees who work in the facility. The vision is to "provide ordinary service in an extraordinary manner." This statement says details, no matter how small, are of great importance. This is an example of a corporate culture that can and will compete in the marketplace throughout the twenty-first century.

CONNECTIVITY OPTIONS

Today's convention centers and trade shows have to provide a wide range of technologies. From the show room floor to meeting rooms, today's center has to be wired with the right stuff. With safe, secure speed, the networks are becoming more flexible, making them more valuable to everyone.

Some Technology Options Available

- *High–Speed Connectivity.* This provides secure, reliable, and fast connections, which also allow corporate users access to Virtual Private Networks (VPNs)—private networks that connect remote sites through a public network, such as the Internet. Users can access VPNs to facilitate training, view online demonstrations, and conduct e-commerce—all on site at a convention. VPNs also can provide authorized users access to needed files or programs when off site.
- *Design Flexibilities.* Centers that have lodging affiliations or city-wide connectivity can provide either a wired or wireless network, with possible connectivity back to guest rooms. Clearly, the trend is toward wireless networks. Without a doubt, these wireless networks allow for much faster setups on site, reducing labor costs and providing connectivity that is twice as fast as a T1 line and twenty-three times faster than older ISDN lines.
- *Bandwidth.* Unfortunately, not all users have network cards installed on laptops, so a facility should provide flexible **bandwidth** that allows access for even low-bandwidth users. If this is only a bank of pay phones with data ports, it is still an on-site requirement.
- *Information Kiosks.* Such kiosks allow show and meeting information, sponsor messages, and industry news or world news to be broadcast to attendees throughout a facility.
- *Dedicated Recording Facilities.* As needs grow to provide live or archived program content, access to dedicated recording rooms to facilitate both audiorecording and session duplication becomes an important feature of convention centers.
- *Videoconferencing Functionality.* Such functionality, including voice- and video-over information processing (IP) and broadcast-quality lighting, is also an essential need for webconferencing or **webcasting.**

- *Availability of "Dark Fiber" Cabling.* These fiber-optic cables remain inactive until hardware is connected, and it is a state-of-the-art feature that allows companies to establish private networks outside of the convention center network.
- *Event Boards.* Plasma or LED event boards located throughout the center and connected to a **local area network (LAN)** give organizers a real-time ability to promote sponsors and communicate information to attendees.
- *Guest Room Connectivity Linking Back to the Convention Center.* Certainly, this feature is a must-have for citywide gatherings.
- *Cybercafes and Kiosks.* Multifunctional kiosks can provide information like product locators for trade show booth locations, session locations, attendee management, e-mailing, message centers, Internet phoning capability, on-site surveying to provide general event information for handling technology needs, PDA **download** stations, and handheld computing synchronization.
- *Audience Response.* Can the facility provide this capability in meeting spaces?
- *Wireless Lead Retrieval and Tracking Systems.* Due to the growing number of wireless networks, options for processing leads and communicating with show attendees have come into fashion. Bluetooth Technologies, for example, provides availability to these process-saving technologies. Also, one can research two-dimensional (2D) bar coding when reviewing lead retrieval systems.
- *Fully Equipped Business Centers with Extended Operating Hours.* Often, such centers can serve as backup to services offered on site.
- *Wireless LAN Network Access.* This may not be available in smaller meeting rooms due to soundproofing requirements. In these cases, a hard-wired network should be available. This is certainly a detail to confirm during a site visit.

VIRTUAL TRADE SHOWS

There has been an interest in virtual trade shows in the last few years. Their popularity is growing; their evolution, however, is slow. Virtual trade shows probably can be recognized as an additional marketing tool. Virtual spaces allow for 24/7 access to presentations, which is a huge benefit to attendees.

With the help of high-quality technology in sound, light, and viewing, such as plasma screens, there is a comfortable platform to launch virtual reality shows. Although virtual trade shows are efficient and cost effective, they lack any kind of real emotion or face-to-face value.

Guidelines to Virtual Reality

- First, benchmark the services provided by a physical trade show in your industry sector. Many of these features should be offered online, depending on the needs of your audience. If the expectations of your audience are not clearly met or exceeded, then your virtual experience will be less than rewarding.
- If available, also benchmark any virtual sites within your industry niche.
- Consider simple and easy design with useful and intuitive site navigation.
- Do not go overboard with graphics. Not only do they have a slow transmission time, but they quickly grow old and can be annoying. Keep the site simple and attractive.
- Do capture and qualify users, especially if a need of the site is to generate revenue.
- Offer exhibitors a range of value-added services, such as the ability to stream audio and video, the option for providing on-site demonstrations and training, and preferred locations on the virtual show floor.
- Provide attendees with value-added features, such as e-mail and chat rooms.
- Apply basic marketing concepts, and cross-promote your virtual site with members, exhibitors, traditional advertisers, and so on.
- Provide online giveaways or discounted promotions.
- Offer online credit card processing.
- Clearly state your privacy policy on handling names and personal data captured on the site.
- Make absolutely certain you secure all transactions.
- Provide a database of vendors who are exhibiting online.
- As with any implementation, be certain to outline your requirements of the virtual space, and carefully select suitable applications and/or service providers. Virtual sites require a great deal of ongoing maintenance.

VIDEOCONFERENCING

One fact that remains true: Individuals cannot be everywhere at once, but sometimes need to be. This reality is what keeps the idea of videoconferencing alive. The events of 9/11 proved this to be true, when the air space over the United States was shut down for several days. As much as technology has advanced with mobile devices used for management of business from remote locations, the loss of productivity is still prevalent. Today, there are many applications that promote virtual meeting alternatives. With high bandwidth, the technology is continuing to improve. A mix of low- and high-bandwidth technologies are close to creating perfect virtual meeting alternatives.

BANDWIDTH FALLS INTO ONE OF THREE CATEGORIES

Broadband: Greater than a Pentium III and a 128K modem. This Internet speed allows for some very sophisticated services, such as full-motion video and reliable audio **streaming**.

Medium Band: Pentium II with a 56K or better modem. Medium band conferencing services include streaming video and audio but are less reliable than broadband. The audio can get distorted, and the video may become choppy if line conditions are not stable. Medium band conferencing technologies also can deliver low bandwidth style of conferencing with audioconferencing support and the program visuals provided on the Internet.

Low Band: Pentium I with a 28K or less modem. Low-band conferencing technologies need to be supported by audioconferencing services. The Internet portion of the conference would support such components as program slides, polling screens, **hyperlinks** to Web sites, and online "Q and A" features. This type of conferencing technology is often referred to as Web-enhanced audioconferencing services.

CHOOSING THE RIGHT INTERNET CONFERENCING SERVICE PROVIDER

Upfront Planning. Understand the information you need to communicate and what media will be used to present the information.

One-Way Session. Do you need one-way communication with intensive video and no interaction or perhaps delayed interaction through a call-in line for taking questions from remote participants?

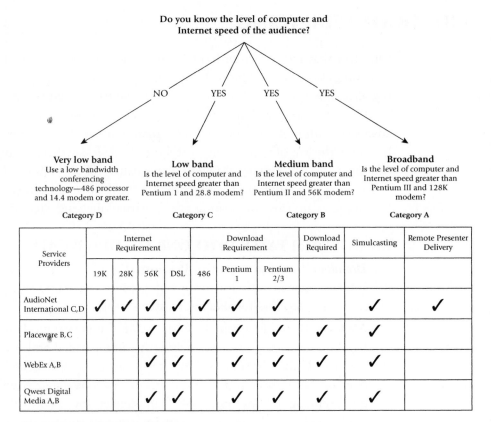

Service Providers	Internet Requirement				Download Requirement			Download Required	Simulcasting	Remote Presenter Delivery
	19K	28K	56K	DSL	486	Pentium 1	Pentium 2/3			
AudioNet International C,D	✓	✓	✓	✓	✓	✓	✓		✓	✓
Placeware B,C			✓	✓		✓	✓	✓	✓	
WebEx A,B			✓	✓		✓	✓	✓	✓	
Qwest Digital Media A,B			✓	✓		✓	✓	✓	✓	

Choosing the right provider.

The webcast presentation can be live or taped. Taping the session allows time for editing and the inclusion of value-added material. It then can be broadcast via the Internet, a satellite, or a CD. Remember, broadcast quality sound and lighting are highly recommended, as are speaker rehearsal and coaching. Consider hiring a production manager whenever mission-critical communications are required.

Two-Way Session. Do you need a high degree of interaction among members of a smaller team? Examples of this type of group collaboration utility include Microsoft's Net Meeting or Symantec's PC Anywhere. These two applications require technical know-how, since third-party services are not used. Do not forget that many people now deploy firewalls; if connectivity is a problem, firewall settings may need to be changed.

These approaches also require advance knowledge of who will be authorized to participate, and each PC will need to load the software and appropriate settings prior to the call.

Third-Party Services. Offering technical services for participants and leaders, moderating services, and scheduling services, third parties provide great control and quality assurance. All participants will be required to preload either a client application or a leader application. This is made available by the service provider and can be downloaded and set up in little time, with a third party being used to encourage all participants to test their connectivity. Service providers will offer useful utilities to validate that both hardware and connectivity are appropriate. All links and phone numbers should also be pretested by your staff or the service provider. The best features of service providers are online technical assistance if a participant is dropped and the ability to have multiple leaders. The latter is very useful: Should one designated leader have a temporary computer problem, the lead can be silently passed to a secondary leader and the presentation can continue. The best part is that no one in the audience even needs to know. Of course, leadership control and presentation coordination need to be reviewed and rehearsed in advance among the leaders for the best experience.

Two-Way, with High-End Media. Is two-way communication required along with higher-end media? Such an interactive webcast event requires serious advance production and coordination. Will you do point-to-point or point-to-multipoint? Will you broadcast to service centers where an audience can gather or to other corporate locations? Will you broadcast via satellite or push through the Internet? These sessions call for broadcast-quality lighting, sound, and production.

A NEW CONVENTION CENTER

The city of Pittsburgh constructed a new convention center that tripled the size of its exhibit space from the previous building. It is the new David L. Lawrence Convention Center. The facility became fully operational in 2003. Architect Rafael Vinoly, who was inspired by the suspension bridges that connect the city to its neighbors, was the lead project designer. He imitated this by designing an upward swooping roofline that flows with the bridges. The structural plans received input from civic leaders in the fields of hospitality, planning, architecture, and economic development as well as input from the local arts.

This $331 million center is an outstanding example of form and function. Merged within the cultural district and business district allows a perfect fit for diversity. Visitors will find points of interest that are appealing while attending functions within the convention center. The Lawrence Convention Center boasts the following:

- Prefunction area facing Allegheny River
- 330,000 square feet of exhibit space
- 250,000 square feet of column-free exhibit space
- 80,000 square feet in secondary hall
- 34,000 square-foot ballroom
- 53 meeting rooms and two 175-seat lecture halls, totaling nearly 90,000 square feet
- 12,000 square-foot main kitchen
- 37 highly accessible loading docks
- 750 parking spaces
- 3,000 committable hotel rooms in downtown business district
- New adjoining hotel in development
- State-of-the-art **teleconference** and telecommunications capabilities
- Internet access throughout
- Pedestrian walkway to river and riverfront trail

The building's technology is at the forefront of modern architectural design. It has been wired with category 6 cables. Convention goers are able to hook up to the Internet, use videoconferencing, and use wireless technology in the building. There are no dead spots for wireless users in the building.

Utilities in Each Floor Box Include the Following:

- Water Supply: $\frac{3}{4}$-inch male quick coupler
- Air Supply: $\frac{3}{4}$-inch male quick coupler
- Plumbing Drain: 4-inch iron drain with dome strainer
- (2) 20 amp GFI duplex receptacles and (3) breakers
- (1) 30 amp 120/208 3ph/4p/5w receptacle and (1) breaker
- (1) 100 amp 120/208 3ph/4p/5w power receptacle
- (4) RJ-45 jacks for telephone and Internet connections
- (1) Jack for microphone/audio visual

A shadowed image of the David Lawrence Convention Center.
Source: With permission of David Lawrence Convention Center

GREEN TECHNOLOGY

Not only does the David L. Lawrence Convention center boast state-of-the art technology, but it also can claim it is the first environmentally smart convention center in the United States. The goal of the design team was to receive a gold rating under the U.S. Green Building Rating System. The center estimated that 30 to 50% could be obtained in energy savings.

Water for the convention center is taken from an underwater aquifer that exists under the city. An aquifer is a formation of permeable material that yields a sufficient amount of water to wells and springs. This water is used to reduce the energy consumption for heating and cooling. All the plants and landscape around the center are native. There is no need for water sprinklers around the facility, thus conserving water.

Energy conservation is helped by the design of the sloped roof by pulling up cool breezes off the water, creating the first naturally ventilated exhibit hall of its size in the United States. Natural lighting is used throughout the building, and blackout shades are available to darken rooms or to control temperatures.

The convention center is using materials in the building that emit fewer toxins; 25% of the building was constructed with recycled material, and local materials were used in order to cut down transportation costs.

This was a new direction for convention centers, and Pittsburgh took the helm and ran with it—the superior technology that the center was wired with, to a new green technology that was just on the horizon, to the award-winning service that the Greater Pittsburgh Convention and Visitor Bureau team has had for years.

Buildings that bear the Green standard are at the forefront of an innovative way of constructing new buildings. The issue of the environment has helped the world to see that not only a more environmentally friendly building can be achieved but also a much more efficient and cost-effective building can be constructed.

◆ SUMMARY

Technology and the Internet are the drivers that will take MEEC into the future. Futurist Joseph Coates, of Coates & Jarratt, is involved in a company that is one of a dozen companies in the United States that does full-time future work. Coates states "information technology" will be the dominant issue. He also points out that "facilities will have to be wired for the information era." John Swinburn, executive director of the International Association of Assembly Managers, also agrees that technology will be the major issue of convention centers. He sees that greater interchangeability of technologies and information will have an effect on how the facilities of the future operate. Technology and the Internet have reshaped and revolutionized convention centers. The Internet has been the biggest part of technology, changing everything. "Whether it is to increase service speed and reliability, cut cost through automation, find new markets, or to add value to products, every business including exposition management, must use technology to stay current." Globalization has changed the competitive market in such a way that reaches out into the world much further and faster with a fewer boundaries and new audiences. Technology and the advent of the Internet have impacted the convention center so permanently that it will continue to influence the value of the convention center and trade show far into the future.

GLOSSARY

With new technology comes new jargon, and often it takes years before we can agree on the proper spelling and usage of words that seep into our vocabulary from common usage. The proliferation of words that have sprung up since the development of the Internet is a prime example of this phenomenon. Although for some words there are generally agreed-on spellings and usages, there are others that are used with less standardization and therefore vary from publication to publication. Definitions are included in this chapter because they relate to technology, not just MEEC.

Most stylebooks and dictionaries agree that the words "Internet" and "Web" (when referring to the World Wide Web) should always be capitalized because they are proper nouns. There is only one Internet and only one World Wide Web.

Analog: A signal that is received in the same form in which it is transmitted; amplitude and frequency may vary.

American Standard Code for Information Interchange (ASCII): The standard 8-bit code used in data communications, from which files may be interchanged from one software program to another and from PC to Mac formats.

Asynchronous: Communication in which interaction between parties does not take place simultaneously.

Bandwidth: Information-carrying capacity of a communication channel.

Broadband: Telecommunications that provide multiple channels of data over a single communication medium.

Browser: Software that allows you to find and see information on the Internet. Commonly used browsers are Microsoft Internet Explorer and Netscape Navigator.

Chief Information Officer (CIO): The highest-ranking information system officer in the organization, usually a vice-president, who oversees the planning, development, and implementation of IS and serves as leader to all IS professionals in the organization.

Cyberspace: The place where humans interact over computer networks.

Digital: An electrical signal that varies in discrete steps in voltage, frequency, amplitude, locations, and so forth. Digital signals can be transmitted faster and more accurately than analog signals.

Download: Using a network to transfer files from one computer to another.

Electronic Mail (e-mail): The transmission of messages from one computer user to another.

File Transfer Protocol (FTP): The format standard that allows users to move files between a distant computer and a local computer using a network like the Internet.

Fully Interactive Video (Two-Way Interactive Video): Two sites interact with audio and video as if they were colocated.

High-Definition TV (HDTV): A television that delivers resolution far exceeding the current NTSC standard, resulting in a brighter and clearer picture. It requires bandwidth five times the capacity of a conventional TV signal.

Host: A network computer that receives data from other computers.

Hyperlink: Images or text within Web documents that move a user to a different location or present a different page once selected.

Hypertext: Text that is coded so that users may select and click on elements within a document to connect to further information.

Hypertext Markup Language (HTML): The language in which Web documents are written. Browsing software interprets the elements of the language, or tags, for display on the Web.

Hypertext Transfer Protocol (HTTP): The format standard used to define how documents are formatted and transmitted on the Web, and what action servers and browsers should take in response to various commands.

Integrated Services Digital Network (ISDN): A telecommunications standard that allows communication channels to simultaneously carry voice, video, and data.

Internet: Global information network connecting millions of computers. Also called the Net.

Local Area Network (LAN): A network of computers connected within an office either in a wired or wireless environment. When connected, computers can share files and programs and other devices connected to the network.

Multimedia: Any document that uses multiple forms of communication, such as text, audio, and/or video.

Net: A shortened term for the Internet.

Online: A computer is considered online when others can see Internet and its IP address on a network.

Platform: The underlying hardware or software of a computer system. Platform-independent and cross-platform applications run on various computer systems.

Plug-in: Downloadable software that adds enhanced capabilities to a browser, enabling the user to view, hear, or interact with nonstandard display formats.

Portable Document Format (PDF): A file format developed for Adobe Acrobat Reader that captures formatting information from a variety of desktop publishing applications and preserves the intended format for display on a recipient's monitor or printer.

Protocol: An agreed-on set of standards, rules, or formats for exchanging data that assures uniformity between computers and applications.

Real Time: Communication in which interaction between parties takes place simultaneously and "live." Also referred to as "synchronous."

Search Engine: Web-based software tools that search for and return documents on the Web based on specified key words.

Server: A computer that is established as the common link on a network to all other computers on that network. The server acts as a gateway for file access and sharing.

Streaming: A continuous sequence of video images and/or audio that is sent in compressed form over the Internet and displayed by the viewer as it arrives. A special program called a "player" uncompresses, or expands, the data for display and/or reception through a browser.

Teleconferencing: Two-way electronic communication between two or more groups in separate locations via audio, video, and/or computer systems.

Uniform Resource Locator (URL): The address of a document or site on the Web.

Uplink: The communication link from the transmitting earth station to the satellite.

Video on Demand: The delivery of digital movies via cable, telephone, or wireless, in which the user has the ability to start and stop the movie at any time.

Webcasting: Uses push technologies to simultaneously broadcast live video and/or audio via the Internet to multiple computers. The quality of webcast reception can vary greatly and is highly dependent on bandwidth, hardware quality, and so on.

World Wide Web: A global, networked system that serves data images, documents, and multimedia on the Internet.

REVIEW AND DISCUSSION QUESTIONS

1. Explain the evolution of convention centers and provide examples.
2. List and explain the myriad of Internet technology and their processes.
3. What should you look for in site selection tools and RFP tools?
4. What should you look for in the selection of a online registration tool?
5. What is business intelligence? What benefit does BI not provide for the convention facility?
6. What are some of the new technological innovations being developed in convention centers constructed today?

SOURCES NOTES

Cognos, Inc. http://cognos.com.

Elliott, Suzanne. 2001. "A Showcase of-and-for- Technology." *Pittsburgh Business Times*. (December 28).

"Follow-up: Convention Center Technology." 1999. *Convene*, http://www.pcma.org.

Garvin, Michael. 2001. "Alternative Delivery—The Flow of Information." *Convene* (December): 19, http://flashpointtech.com/sandiego.

Greusel, David, and Todd Voth. 2002. "Generation 4: The Future of Convention Centers." *Auditorie Magazine* (January).

Kasavanna, Michael L., and John J. Cahill. 1997. *Managing computers in the hospitality industry.* Michigan: Educational Institute of the American Hotel & Lodging Association.

Lippman, Sam. 2000. "Constructing the New Skill Set for Show Managers." *Convene* (July): 46, http://flashpointtech.com/sandiego.

Ordonez, Brenda. 1994. "Convention Center 2000: How Will It Be Operated?" *EXPO Magazine* (February).

Rudd, Denis, and Lincoln H. Marshall. 2000. *Gaming operations.* Upper Saddle River, NJ: Prentice Hall.

Siwek, E. J. 2001. "Finally! . . . Real-time Housing Information." *Convene* (September): 29, http://flashpointtech.com/sandiego.

Siwek, E. J. 2002. "CHAPTER 1—Meeting Logistics." *San Diego Guide to Meetings Technology* (May 15), http://flashpointtech.com/sandiego.

Siwek, E. J. 2002. "CHAPTER 2—Registration, Housing, and Destination Management." *San Diego Guide to Meetings Technology* (May 15), http://flashpointtech.com/sandiego.

Siwek, E. J. 2002. "CHAPTER 5—Exhibitions." *San Diego Guide to Meetings Technology* (May 15), http://flashpointtech.com/sandiego.

Siwek, E. J. 2002. "CHAPTER 7—Audience Communications." *San Diego Guide to Meetings Technology* (May 15), http://flashpointtech.com/sandiego.

Siwek, E. J. 2002. "CHAPTER 8—Audiovisual Advances." *San Diego Guide to Meetings Technology* (May 15), http://flashpointtech.com/sandiego.

Skolinik, Rayna. 1999. "Convention Centers: Tending the Tech Crop." *Technology Meetings* (March 1).

WEB SITES

Domestic Convention Centers
Palm Beach County Convention Center
http://www.palmbeachfl.com
Pittsburgh/David L. Lawrence Convention Center
http://www.pgh-sea.com
Anaheim Convention Center
http://www.anaheimconventioncenter.com
Illinois Convention Center
http://www.rosemont.com
Minnesota Convention Center
http://www.decc.org

Austin Convention Center
   http://www.austinconventioncenter.com
El Paso Convention & Performing Arts Center
   http://www.elpasocvb.com
Washington D.C. Convention Center
   http://www.dcconvention.com
Pittsburgh Convention Center
   http://www.pittsburgh-cvb.org
   http://www.planpittsburgh.com

International Convention Centers
Australia
   http://www.mecc.com.au
Canada
   http://www.congresmtl.com
Germany
   http://www.congresscenter.de
United Kingdom
   http://www.aecc.co.uk
Puerto Rico
   http://www.prconvention.com

ABOUT THE CHAPTER CONTRIBUTORS

Denis P. Rudd, Ed.D., CHA, FMP, PTC, is a professor and director of Hospitality and Tourism Management at Robert Morris College of Pennsylvania at both the Coraopolis and Pittsburgh campuses. Dr. Rudd received his bachelor's degree in finance and commerce from Rider College, Lawrenceville, New Jersey; a master's in business administration; a master's in education counseling; a specialty in higher education administration; and a doctorate in educational counseling from the University of Nevada–Las Vegas. Dr. Rudd is currently a member of Council on Hotel, Restaurant and Institutional Education (CHRIE), the Association of Corporate Travel Executives (ACTE), the American Culinary Federation, the National Restaurant Association (NRA), the Travel and Tourism Research Association (TTRA), and the Society of Travel and Tourism Educators (STTE).

Dr. Rudd is a fifth-generation hotelier and has worked in hotels in New York as well as in Florida. He served in the United States Army as an

S-1 and club and slot machine officer for the Third Brigade Fourth Armored Division. In 1995, he moved to Robert Morris College. Dr. Rudd has recently published a text entitled *Introduction to Casino and Gaming Operation*, published by Prentice Hall.

His interests are varied, and he has done research and made presentations on gaming operations, ADA, bed and breakfast, innkeeping, marketing, ABA, the senior market, and casino operations. In addition, Dr. Rudd has received certification as a Certified Hotel Administrator (CHA) and Foodservice Management Professional (FMP) from the NRA and the Educational Institute of the American Hotel Motel Association.

Kathleen Taylor Brown holds a master's of liberal studies degree from Duquesne University and a bachelor's degree from Lock Haven University. She is currently pursuing a master's of business administration degree at Duquesne as well a doctorate in information systems and communications at Robert Morris University. Taylor Brown has taught part-time at Robert Morris University since 1997.

◆14

INTERNATIONAL ISSUES IN MEEC

MEEC organizers must be prepared to work with diverse people and cuisines.

Source: Merrill Education

◆ Chapter Objectives

This chapter provides the reader with an understanding of the following:

- How trade fairs and exhibitions vary around the world
- The status of the trade fair industry in different regions
- The terminology and protocol differences
- Aspects to consider before committing to an international trade fair

◆ Chapter Outline

INTRODUCTION

The growth of international communications and travel has caused phenomenal changes in how the world does business. Twenty years ago, only the largest companies were considered "international"; today, few large companies do not have an international presence.

Consequently, the meetings and exhibitions industries have grown much more international. In this chapter, we look at how the international scope of meetings and exhibitions has evolved and how it differs in various parts of the world.

The 69th UFI (Union of International Fairs) Congress held in October 2002 in Munich, Germany, announced some incredible statistics about the international trade fair industry. For example, Dr. Hermann Kresse, AUMA CEO, announced that the economic impact of trade fairs in Germany was 23 billion euros and employment reached 250,000 full-time jobs in the exhibition industry. Similarly, Michael Duck, vice-president of CMP Asia, stated that in 2001 Greater China and Asia organized 1,159 trade fairs that generated almost $1 billion in revenue.

Regardless of the location, the purposes of international meetings and exhibitions remain the same—communication, learning, and marketing.

REPORT FROM CeBIT 2002

The information technology (IT) industry may be going through a bad time, but not CeBIT. This international trade fair for the information technology industry is held annually in Hannover, Germany. In 2002, it hosted 8,152 exhibitors (as compared to 8,093 in 2001). To meet demand, the show was extended one day, to a total of eight. International participation was stronger than ever—3,120 exhibitors (2001: 3,059). Exhibiting companies come from 58 countries. Taiwan led the international sector with 555 exhibitors, followed by the United States at 512. In addition, many companies with worldwide operations are represented by their German subsidiaries. CeBIT is truly an international event!

The next CeBIT is in 2004.

HOW MEEC VARIES AROUND THE GLOBE

Despite similarities of purpose, cultural and business influences have created different models for meetings and exhibitions in various parts of the world. In this section, we survey the types of meetings and exhibitions held in different regions of the world, how they differ in scope and operation, and what areas of the world are embracing trade fairs as a primary method of marketing. At the end of this chapter is a compilation of international trade fair organizations with their corresponding Web addresses.

EUROPE

The trade fair industry has its roots in Europe. During the Middle Ages, the concept began with farmers and craftsmen bringing their products and wares to the town center to link with their customer base. Although the world wars of the twentieth century devastated European industry, today Europe is the focal point of international trade fairs and exhibitions.

The Grassmarket has been a focal point in the Old Town for 500 years and a trading place since the beginning of the city of Edinburgh, Scotland.
Source: Getty Images, Inc.–Hulton Archives Photos

There are two primary reasons for this. First is location—Europe has always been the crossroads of the world. International hub airports in Frankfurt, London, Amsterdam, Paris, and Rome enable visitors and cargo to easily arrive from all parts of the world. In addition, a superlative network of rail transportation within Europe enables many cities to be within a day's transportation from one another. The second reason for the growth of trade fairs is the industrial base of Europe. With postwar reconstruction help from the United States, Europe was able to recover its manufacturing and distribution base within a few decades. With the help of

LARGEST EXHIBITION VENUE

Hannover, Germany, is the model for government and private industry working together to create a successful trade fair venue with an unparalleled economic impact on a region. Managed by Hannover Messe A.G., the world's largest exhibition venue consists of over 5 million square feet of indoor exhibit space and 1 million square feet of covered outdoor space, restaurants, warehouses, and meeting facilities. More importantly, the regional government and the management company have worked together to establish excellent transportation and lodging facilities. Local companies have also contributed to making the facilities the best in the world.

their governments, European industrial centers develop trade fair facilities that are unrivaled in other parts of the world.

Germany is usually thought of as the center of industry and trade fairs in Europe. Trade fairs and exhibitions are a $10.5 billion business in Germany alone. Over 165,000 exhibitors participate in 133 international events each year. Over 40% of trade fair exhibitors in Germany are from countries not in the European Union. Four of Europe's top five trade fair facilities are located in Germany (Hannover, Frankfurt/Main, Cologne, and Dusseldorf). In addition, five of the world's top international trade fairs and exhibitions are held in Germany:

- Hannover Fair—Industrial; over 7,000 exhibitors
- CeBIT—Information Technology; over 8,000 exhibitors
- Domotex—Flooring; over 3,000 exhibitors
- Frankfurt Book Fair—Over 4,000 exhibitors
- Biotechnology—Over 3,000 exhibitors

Italy is another center of international trade fair activity. Milan is the fashion trade fair center of the world and attracts buyers from around the world for its almost constant fashion-related trade fairs. Rome opened a new exhibition center in 2001 and hopes to rival Hannover and Dusseldorf for industrial trade fairs. Many trade fairs and exhibitions in Italy are sponsored by the strong network of world trade centers in cities across the country.

FACTS ABOUT *HANNOVER FAIR 2004*

Milestones in Innovation

World's Leading Event for Technologies and Automation

GENERAL INFORMATION

Show Dates Monday, 19th April to Saturday, 24th April 2004

Hours: 9 a.m. – 6 p.m. (daily)

Venue: Hannover Fairgrounds (Messegelände), Hannover, Germany

Organizers: Deutsche Messe AG, Messegelände, D-30521 Hannover

Contact in USA: Hannover Fairs USA, Princeton, NJ, 08540 • Angela Dessables – Project Manager – adessables@hfusa.com, ☎ 609-987-1202 • 🖶 609-987-0092, adessables@hfusa.com • www.hannoverfair.com

Show Statistics
- Over 6,000 exhibitors from 70 nations
- Approximately 200,000 visitors from 120 countries
- 4,000 journalists
- 100 official government delegations

Exhibit Information
Indoors exhibit area: 18 buildings, 2.09 million square feet

Trade Fairs 2004	Exhibitors	Visitors	Space m2 net display area
Interkama	800	40,000	30,000
Factory Automation	1,200	126,000	60,000
Surface Technology plus PCE	600	35,500	20,000
MicroTechnology	300	21,000	5,000
Subcontracting	1,800	44,000	32,000
Energy	900	43,000	38,000
Research & Technology	550	35,000	9,200
Total	**6,150**	**344,500**	**194,200**

Tickets + Prices

Ticket prices

Tickets	Price in EURO
Day ticket, advance sale	18.00
Full-event ticket, advance sale	42.00
Day ticket, purchased at ticket counter	23.00
Full-event ticket, purchased at ticket counter	50.00
Discount day ticket (for students 15 and above or young people doing military or community service)	10.00

Do you have any questions about tickets you already ordered? Our service team will be happy to help!

The latest information on tickets, prices, advance sale, etc. is available at: http://www.hfusa.com/hannoverfair/

Catalogue (printed version)

The catalogue of **HANNOVER FAIR 2003** can be ordered via Internet, Fax or E-Mail at the price of EURO 25,00 (plus p&p):

LETTERSHOP BRENDLER GmbH
Magdeburger Str. 6
D-30880 Laatzen
Fax: +49-(0)5102/93 59 40
baerbel.triller@brendler-vkf.de
www.hannovermesse.de/catalogue

The **HANNOVER FAIR 2004** catalogue will be ready for advance sale about 2 weeks prior to the event.

Catalogue (online)
The online search for exhibitors and products of **HANNOVER FAIR 2003** is available all the year round: www.hannovermesse.de/search. The **HANNOVER FAIR 2004** online search will be available about six weeks prior to the event.

Travel + Accommodation
The latest information and search facilities for planning your journey to Hannover as well as information on accommodation, Hannover's cultural program, etc. is available here:

> Special Services Department
> housing@hfusa.com
> Phone (609) 987-1202
> Fax (609) 987-0092, ext. 219

Or visit:

www.hannovermesse.de/travel, www.travel2fairs.com

HANNOVER FAIR 2004 PROGRAM SUMMARY

INTERKAMA+ 2004
The leading trade fair for Process Automation
INTERKAMA+ at HANNOVER FAIR2004: Unlocking new sources of potential. A complete array of automation technology at a single venue – this is the guiding philosophy behind the new collaboration between INTERKAMA+ and the HANNOVER MESSE. INTERKAMA+ will be taking place for the first time under the umbrella of the HANNOVER MESSE. The combination of INTERKAMA+, Factory Automation and Industrial IT at a single venue will cover the entire spectrum of industrial automation technology. The product categories will complement each other perfectly and underline the leading role of INTERKAMA+ as well as the HANNOVER FAIR– to the benefit of visitors, exhibitors and the participating industry associations.

Factory Automation 2004
The leading trade fair for Production Automation
As the world's leading trade show in its sector Factory Automation serves as a meeting-place for professionals from electrical engineering and electronics, robotics, assembly and handling technology, industrial image processing as well as IT and software. This is where you can contact top decision-makers and users – trade professionals who come to this leading event for holistic solutions in factory automation.

SurfaceTechnology plus
Power Coating Europe 2004
The leading trade fair for Surface Technology SurfaceTechnology, the no. 1 international showcase for this sector, and POWDER COATING EUROPE, Europe's key event for innovative powder coating technology, have joined forces. As of 2004, POWDER COATING EUROPE will take place in conjunction with SurfaceTechnology as an integral part of the HANNOVER FAIR at the Hannover Exhibition Grounds. Whether it's state-of-the-art technology, universal innovations or application-oriented solutions, only this leading event offers a comprehensive survey of innovative surface treatment and trend-setting processes and solutions.

MicroTechnology 2004
The leading trade fair for Applied Microsystems Technology and Nanotechnology
MicroTechnology is the ideal business forum and showcase for innovative solutions, technologies and trends and offers a comprehensive survey of integrated microsystems technology for all areas of industry – all at the same time and under one roof. Here you can meet decision-makers and users from factory automation, the communication sector, the automobile industry, the energy sector and the life sciences who are looking for forward-oriented solutions.

Subcontracting 2004
The leading trade fair for Subcontracting and Industrial Materials
As the world's leading marketplace for innovative processes, materials and services, Subcontracting is an ideal meeting place for professionals from mechanical and plant engineering, electrical engineering, electronics and the automobile industry. The number of top decision-makers and users will also be swelled by the exhibitors from the other trade shows at the HANNOVER MESSE. In short, this event offers excellent opportunities to meet the right target groups.

Energy 2004
The leading trade fair for Energy Management, Energy Technology and Renewable Energy
Only the Energy covers such a broad spectrum. From traditional aspects of energy technology to the entire range of innovative renewable energy and diverse services such as energy marketing, distribution and contracting – all under one roof. Customized planning, management and services geared to specific energy projects and concepts also form a keynote theme.

Research & Technology 2004
Innovations Market Research and Technology
As the leading marketplace for innovative areas of technology such as microsystems technology, nanotechnology, photonics, bionics, the life sciences and new materials, Research & Technology serves as an annual meeting-place for top international decision-makers and users from industry. In short, it is not only an ideal business forum where market oriented solutions can be shown to a high-caliber audience, but also a place where exhibitors can meet potential business partners and cultivate contact with existing clients.

Hannover
Fairs USA, Inc.

212 Carnegie Center • Princeton, NJ 08540 • Phone 609-987-1202 • Fax 609-987-0092 •
hannoverfair@hfusa.com • www.hfusa.com

The nations of the United Kingdom hosted over 1,800 exhibitions in 2001, attracting 17.3 million visitors to over 450 venues. Top exhibitions included:

- Birmingham Spring Fair
- World Travel Market (London)
- Furniture Show (Birmingham)
- Birmingham Fall Fair
- Security Solutions (Birmingham)

The Benelux nations also have a strong trade fair program. Excellent facilities exist in Amsterdam, Rotterdam, Brussels, and at Schipol Airport. New Congress facilities in Paris are attracting new trade fairs as well. Again, world trade centers in these cities are the focal point of promotion and operation of trade fairs.

Perhaps the greatest growth of trade fairs in Europe is occurring in the countries of Eastern Europe. New facilities are opening in Zagreb, Belgrade, Warsaw, and most recently Moscow.

It is anticipated that the growth of the European Union, common currency with the euro, and removal of trade barriers and tariffs will only make the European trade fair and exhibition industry continue to grow.

ASIA

The growth of trade fairs and exhibitions in Asia has been phenomenal over the past ten years. New facilities and government promotion have taken the industry from its infancy to world class in little more than a decade. Primarily, Asian trade fairs focus on high technology, consumer electronics, and food. However, all types of manufacturing and service industries are well represented. Asian trade fairs and exhibitions are either sponsored by trade organizations, such as the world trade centers, or individual governments.

Taiwan and Singapore have been the backbone of Asian trade fairs and exhibitions. Taiwan has excellent facilities and routinely sponsors trade fairs in the semiconductor, consumer electronics, and food industries. Taiwan is also the world's leader in exhibiting at trade fairs and exhibitions in North America and Europe.

Singapore is a major "destination" city and consequently attracts many visitors to its textile, fashion, food, and electronics trade fairs. It has multiple facilities all linked to world-class shopping and entertainment complexes. Singapore is also attractive because it provides excellent transportation

The Merlion is the symbol of Singapore. It is half fish and half lion.
Photo by George G. Fenich, Ph.D., Professor, School of HRTA, University of New Orleans

facilities with a world-class airport serving every continent, and every facility or attraction is within walking distance or a short taxi ride. The government of Singapore is very active in promoting exhibitions. The Singapore Trade Development Board is the lead agency for marketing

Singapore as an international exhibition city. It provides financial and marketing support for trade fairs organized by both Singaporean and international organizers. It also chairs the Exhibition Management Services Council, a public/private partnership of government agencies, industry associations, chambers of commerce, and exhibition companies.

China, as it opens up to international trade, is expanding the number and quality of its trade fairs and exhibitions. Major new facilities have been built in Hong Kong, Shanghai, and Beijing. The Shanghai International Exhibition Corporation facility covers over 1.5 million square feet. Recent trade fairs have focused on consumer goods, food, and electronics. In Hong Kong, there are more than thirty fair organizers belonging to the Hong Kong Exhibition and Convention Organizers' and Suppliers Association. These include for-profit companies, associations, and government agencies.

Thailand is a major center for clothing and textile trade shows. Excellent transportation facilities in Bangkok make it easy for visitors to arrive from around the world.

Other countries nurturing trade fair programs with government promotion include Vietnam, Malaysia, and India. In these countries, the facilities are usually owned and operated by the government, and promotional activities are sponsored by various government agencies. Vietnam has taken a strong position in clothing and food trade fairs, while India is at the forefront of Asian information technology and software shows.

AFRICA

Both Cairo and Johannesburg are heavily promoting continental trade fairs with new facilities and incentives for international exhibitors. Because Johannesburg is relatively difficult and expensive to travel to, the government of South Africa works with major trade organizations and other countries to provide incentives for regional and country pavilions. The U.S. Department of Commerce is providing specialized assistance to companies that plan to exhibit at African trade fairs. Special rates for participating in the U.S. pavilion and assistance from trade professionals from the Department of Commerce help make it easier for U.S. companies to exhibit in Africa. In addition, the new National Exhibition Centre in Johannesburg offers almost a half-million square feet of covered exhibit space.

MIDDLE EAST

Trade fairs and exhibitions in the Middle East are concentrated in Dubai and Abu Dhabi in the United Arab Emirates. This concentration is the result of excellent government promotion, new facilities, and ease of travel access. Both Dubai and Abu Dhabi host international airports with service to every continent. This "crossroads" concept, as well as the fact that exhibition facilities are located at or near the international airports, is emphasized heavily in promotional materials. For example, both Dubai and Abu Dhabi strongly promote the duty-free zones near their airports and the extensive duty-free shopping available at their facilities. In addition, the regional market for consumer goods is very strong and puts the focus of trade fairs on items like furniture, automobiles, and consumer electronics.

LATIN AMERICA

The huge population base of Latin America makes it well suited for trade fairs and exhibitions. Until recently, most of the Latin American trade fairs and exhibitions have been regional. However, new facilities and promotional efforts have set the stage for a growth in international exhibitions. New facilities in Sao Paulo, Brazil; Santiago, Chile; and Mexico City are the hubs for this activity. The Feria International de Santiago contains over 1 million square feet of covered exhibition space and almost the same amount of open-air space. The Las Americas Exhibition Center opened in December 2001 in Mexico City and provides the latest in technology to support exhibitors and attendees. Additionally, the center is built within an entertainment complex that includes a horse race track, restaurants, hotels, and a shopping center.

OWNERSHIP, SPONSORSHIP, AND MANAGEMENT MODELS

In the United States, many trade shows are adjuncts to association meetings and are owned by the association. Others are sponsored by private, entrepreneurial companies and operated on a for-profit basis. Ownership and management are usually accomplished by two companies working toward the success of the show. Other service companies support the industry by helping both the trade show management company and exhibitors.

This model is not typically followed for international trade fairs and exhibitions. In other countries, associations do not play a major role in the organization and sponsorship of trade fairs. Often governments, in collaboration with organizing companies, plan and operate the trade fairs. For example, the government of China plays a major role in the sponsorship of most trade fairs presented in Beijing, Hong Kong, and Shanghai.

WORLD TRADE CENTERS ASSOCIATION

The **World Trade Centers Association** was created in 1970 as a not-for-profit, apolitical organization to promote the concept of world trade centers worldwide and to encourage reciprocal programs between all of its members. Today, there are more than 300 world trade centers in 91 countries servicing more than 750,000 international businesses.

The purpose of a world trade center is to bring together businesses and government agencies involved in international trade. Most world trade centers provide business services to their member companies, such as support and meeting facilities, videoconferencing, secretarial services, and translation capabilities. Many also conduct group trade missions to help businesses explore new markets.

Many world trade centers have also found the benefits of trade fairs and exhibitions appealing to their member companies. Thus, most of the world trade centers have built exhibition centers as part of their facilities. Throughout the year, the center sponsors trade fairs and events that showcase their members' products.

World trade centers also sponsor trade meetings and educational events open to businesses in their area and internationally.

INTERNATIONAL MEEC CONSIDERATIONS

LESSONS TO BE LEARNED

It is important for trade fair and exhibition managers to learn the reasons for success in different aspects of the international marketplace. For example, North American trade show managers can learn from their European colleagues in three areas:

- *Excellence of Infrastructure:* Few American facilities rival those of Germany. In addition, public transportation systems in Europe provide excellent support of trade fairs and exhibitions. We have already discussed the case of Hannover, Germany, earlier in this chapter. Other European cities are following their model, including Dusseldorf, Berlin, Cologne, and Rome. Berlin has invested heavily in infrastructure to support its facilities.
- *Logistics:* International trade fair organizers are, by necessity, experts in logistics. Because the lifeblood of many international shows is the international exhibitor, many have specialized departments devoted to

helping exhibitors overcome obstacles for exhibiting in their countries. Shipping and storage procedures are simplified and expedited by these agencies to help make exhibiting in their countries as easy as possible.

- *Support Organizations:* In America, many trade shows are sponsored and organized by associations. Although well done, trade shows are often a secondary mission of associations. In other parts of the world, trade fairs and exhibitions are sponsored and organized by trade promotion organizations, such as the world trade centers or government agencies.

By the same token, many international trade fairs can learn from how North Americans conduct trade shows. For example, although the typical trade show staff in America can use additional boothmanship training, this is a dire need in most other countries. What American exhibitors consider "sins," such as smoking in a booth or leaving a booth unattended, are commonplace in some other countries.

METHODS OF EXHIBITING

There are a number of differences between exhibiting at an American trade show and at an international trade fair or exhibition. These differences need to be a part of the basic research before initiating an international trade fair program.

Typically, companies have choices in how they will exhibit at an international trade fair or exhibition. The U.S. government sponsors U.S. pavilions at many trade fairs, and the U.S. company can work through the government to be part of the U.S. exhibit. If this is the chosen method, the U.S. Department of Commerce can provide significant help.

Another option is to exhibit under the auspices of another company that is organizing a pavilion. Similar to U.S. government sponsorship, a private company may be the main interface, and contractual arrangements are made with them. Companies should fully investigate this type of situation to ensure that the organizing company is reputable and has experience in the host country and with the desired trade fair.

Joint ventures can also be formed between companies, particularly when one has experience exhibiting at the desired trade fair. In this case, it is important that companies be sure that their products or services do not compete with each other. This type of arrangement works best when the two companies' products complement each other, and it is an excellent way for a company to enter the international trade fair marketplace and gain valuable experience.

"Going it alone" is another option for companies entering the international trade fair arena. Many large companies choose this route because they have the budget and staff to support the complexities of exhibiting internationally. Smaller companies must ensure that they have a clear understanding of all the requirements, costs, and scheduling before committing to this route. For example, smaller companies must factor in all the personnel time and costs involved in verifying that all tasks are completed. Assuming that preparation is the same as that for a domestic trade show can be a very costly mistake.

TERMINOLOGY

In many parts of the world, an exhibit is not called an exhibit—or even a booth. Rather, it is called a **stand**. And this is only the beginning of the differences in terminology. Depending on where the trade fair is being held and who is managing it, participating companies must be familiar with those differences.

For example, in Germany the following terms must be understood:

- **Ausstellung:** Consumer Show
- **Congress:** Meeting or Convention
- **Gesellschaft:** Company or Society
- **GMBH:** Limited Liability Company
- **Messe:** Trade Fair
- **Messegelande:** Fair Site
- **PLC:** Public Limited Company
- **Trade Exhibition:** Trade Show

CONTRACTUAL AND PROCEDURAL ISSUES

In addition to terminology differences, contractual and procedural differences abound. Labor rules in the United States are very different from those in Europe or Asia. In Asia, there are few unions and no jurisdictional issues. Exhibitors have much more freedom in what they can do within their exhibit. In Europe, although there are unions, they are much more flexible than many in the United States.

Companies should not assume that setup or logistical contracts read the same as those in their home country. Substantial differences exist from country to country and from trade fair to trade fair. Companies should read each contract closely and adhere to all the requirements. If something is not understood, it should be brought to the attention of show management immediately.

CUSTOMS CLEARANCE

Exhibition organizers at international shows provide access to experienced international freight forwarders, who also act as custom brokers, to ensure that everything is in order and arrives on time. The freight forwarders are knowledgeable about the custom regulations for the host country and take action to ensure exhibitors know of every requirement and deadline.

Typically, goods can be temporarily imported to an international show site without having to pay duties or taxes, using either a **carnet** or a **trade fair bond**. A carnet can be very complicated to obtain, and a hefty bond must often be established. However, most trade fair venues offer trade fair bonds, which are simple to arrange. Again, the international freight forwarders are the point of contact for trade fair bonds. Be sure to inquire about host country rules on giveaways and promotional materials. In some countries, duty is charged when the value is above a certain limit; in others, duty is not charged for materials used for this purpose.

Freight forwarders are also cognizant of the estimated time for materials to clear customs, and they factor these times into the schedules they provide exhibitors. Companies must be fully adherent to these schedules to ensure that their materials arrive on time. Countries vary widely in the amount to time to clear customs, so be very aware of the differences if you are exhibiting in more than one country. Do not assume that because it takes only one day to clear customs in Paris or Frankfurt that it will be the same in Dubai or Taipei.

FIRST INTERNATIONAL TRADE SHOW

At one point before joining academe, Dr. George G. Fenich had the job of running all the marketing and trade shows for a company. The first international show in which the company participated was held in Innsbruck, Austria. The equipment to be displayed was airfreighted well in advance of the trade show, and the written material and brochures were sent later but with ample time to clear customs. Dr. Fenich sent one of his technical representatives to man the booth. On arrival, the tech rep called Dr. Fenich and was frantic. Although the crate was delivered to the booth and appeared in good order, when the container was opened it was found that a critical high-tech component was missing, and in its place was a box of inexpensive nails. Some time during shipment, probably while waiting to clear customs, thieves had opened the box and stolen the equipment. They replaced it with the box of nails so that the weight of the container would remain the same and not draw suspicion. There was no time to get another piece of high-tech equipment to Austria before the show closed.

On another occasion, the tech rep arrived at a trade show the day before it was to open only to find that the written materials and brochures had been lost. He called back to the company and asked that a new set of brochures be sent "overnight express" to be there in time for the opening of the show. The problem was that, while the shipment could get there overnight, it would take three or four days to clear customs, and the trade show would have ended.

PROTOCOL

It is the responsibility of the company trade fair manager to research the business customs of the host country and the individual trade fair. Staff should then be thoroughly trained on these differences before departing for the trade fair. Always remember that what is acceptable in one country or at one trade fair may very well be offensive in the next country or at another trade fair. Although English is normally the "official" language of international trade fairs, it is not safe to assume that all attendees or other exhibitors speak English. The wise company will ensure that at least some of the staff is bilingual, particularly in the host country's language.

Exhibit staff members will be greeting people from many countries to their international exhibit. It is imperative that they be familiar with the appropriate greetings for different cultures and forms of address. Although most visitors will not be offended if protocol is not strictly followed, it does give visitors a positive impression if their cultural standards are observed. It is also important for visitors to be aware of negative gestures for various cultures. What is a normal gesture in one culture may be extremely offensive in another. Gift giving and invitations are other areas that require research and training before embarking on an international trade fair program. Staff should also be aware of other cultural factors concerning dining and traveling in the host country. If spouses are traveling to

USING A TRANSLATOR

Dr. George G. Fenich represented his company at a trade show in Europe. Knowing that attendees spoke many different languages, in none of which Dr. Fenich was fluent, he hired a translator who spoke many of those languages. The translator worked out so well that she was hired to do translations at the next trade show. However, the reception by attendees at the second trade show was less than stellar. In analyzing the cause, Dr. Fenich realized it was the interpreter. At the first show, she knew nothing about the product, so each time an attendee had a question, she translated it for Dr. Fenich, who answered, and then she translated back for the attendee. By the second trade show, the same question kept coming up, and rather than translate and ask Dr. Fenich, she simply responded in the appropriate language. The attendees felt that if the product was too simple that the interpreter knew the answers, it could not be a very good or complex product.

the host country they should be given briefings on the host country and its cultural expectations as well.

Examples

- In Indonesia, greetings are stately and formal. Do not rush. Hurried introductions (which commonly occur in trade fair settings) show a lack of respect.
- In the Netherlands, always avoid giving an impression of superiority. Egalitarianism is a central tenet of Dutch society. Everyone in a Dutch company, from the boss to menial laborers, is considered valuable and worthy of respect.
- When interacting with French visitors to an exhibit, never use first names until you are told to do so.
- Germans generally take a long time to establish a close business relationship and may appear cold in the beginning. This will change with time.
- Be very careful regarding what your exhibit staff wears. What is the customary business dress for the host country? What colors should not be worn? For example, avoid wearing yellow in Singapore; it is the color worn at funerals.

- At a business meeting in Saudi Arabia, coffee is often served toward the end of the meeting as an indication that the meeting is about to end.
- Also, in most Arabic countries, the left hand is considered dirty, so you should never eat or accept anything with this hand. Be sure when giving gifts or promotional materials that you do so with the right hand.
- When giving away gifts in Switzerland, avoid giving away knives—it is considered bad luck.
- If a Japanese person gives you a gift, do not throw away the wrapping or tear it up. It is considered part of the gift.
- Aside from handshakes, there is no public contact between the sexes in many countries. Do not kiss or hug a person of the opposite sex in public—even if it is your spouse. On the other hand, in some countries contact is permitted between people of the same sex. Men may hold hands with men and even walk with arms around each other; this is interpreted as nothing but friendship.
- Westerners frequently find Arabic names confusing. The best solution is to request the names of anyone you meet, speak to, or correspond with. Find out their full names (for correspondence) as well as how they are to be addressed in person.
- Understand the hierarchies of doing business with a foreign country. For example, the managing director in England equates to the CEO in an American firm.
- Keep in mind that the English do not consider themselves European. This is vital when discussing issues regarding the European Union.
- In many European countries, employees get four or five weeks of summer vacation. Many countries virtually shut down for the month of August.
- Eye contact among the French is frequent and intense—often this is intimidating to U.S. visitors.
- When negotiating in China, always give many alternatives so the Chinese negotiators have room to negate several options with dignity. Also, always keep the same negotiating team throughout the process.
- The traditional Chinese greeting is a bow. When bowing to a superior, you should bow more deeply and allow him or her to rise first.
- In many Asian countries, it is not appreciated to pat people on the shoulder or initiate any physical contact.

- When negotiating in Italy, a dramatic change in demands at the last minute is often a technique to unsettle the other side. Be patient— just when it appears impossible, the situation will clear itself.
- In Japan, the host will always treat when you are taken out. Allow your host to order for you. Be enthusiastic while eating and show great thanks afterwards.
- As well in Japan, business cards are presented after a bow or handshake. Present your card with the Japanese side facing your colleague, in such a manner that it can be read immediately. Handle cards very carefully, and do not put them in your pocket or wallet. Never write on a person's business card in his or her presence.
- Age and rank are very important in Korea, so it is usually easiest to establish a relationship with a businessperson of your own age.
- The Swedes tend to be very serious, and humor is not part of the business environment.
- Hospitality is very important in Taiwan. Expect to be invited out every night after hours. This will entail visiting local nightspots and clubs, and may go until the wee hours of the morning.

Japanese persons exchanging business cards.
Source: Stock Boston

- Avoid pouring wine at a social occasion in Argentina. There are several complex taboos associated with wine pouring that a foreigner can unknowingly violate. For example, pouring with the left hand, a common practice in the United States, is a major insult in Argentina.
- In the United States, the hand gesture where the thumb and forefinger are forming a circle with the other three fingers raised is considered the "OK" sign.
  - In Brazil, it is considered a vulgar or obscene gesture.
  - In Greece and Russia, it is considered impolite.
  - In Japan, it signifies money.
  - In southern France, it means zero or worthless.
- In the United States, waving the hand back-and-forth is a means of saying hello.
  - In Greece, it is called the *moutza* and is a serious insult: The closer the hand is to the face of the other, the more threatening it is.
  - In Peru, waving the whole hand back-and-forth can signal "no."
- In most of the world, making a fist with the thumb raised means "OK."
  - In Australia, it is a rude gesture.

These are simply a few of the cultural issues that foreign business-people must face. Before traveling to any country, it is wise to consult as many sources as possible to learn the appropriate business and social behaviors. Take the time to learn the appropriate behavior in the host country and the greeting expectations for potential visitors to the trade fair.

The following are some other differences between international trade fairs and U.S. trade shows. Keep in mind that these are generalizations and do not apply to all situations.

- Hospitality events are generally held on the exhibit floor, with many companies providing food and beverages as a matter of course in their exhibit.
- Height restrictions may be nonexistent. Many large exhibits may be two or three levels.
- Rules on smoking in the exhibit hall may not exist, and many exhibitors and attendees may smoke in the exhibits.
- Some trade fair organizing companies may not offer "lead retrieval" systems that U.S. companies are accustomed to. It is always wise for a company to bring its own method of capturing leads.

- International trade fairs are often longer in duration than U.S. trade shows and often are open on weekends as well. Although in Europe the show may run from 9 A.M. to 6 P.M., in Brazil or other Latin American countries it is common for trade fairs to open at 2 P.M. and run until 10 or 11 at night.
- Be aware that most of the world outside the United States is metric. Voltages may differ, and exhibitors may need plug-in adaptors or transformers. The video format may be different, so the VHS video-tapes you hand carry to the show may be worthless if the television only accepts PAL format.

DETERMINING WHETHER TO PARTICIPATE

Because exhibiting at an international trade fair or exhibition is a significant investment, it is important that companies seriously consider if this move makes good business sense. First, consider the following top-level questions:

- Would international trade fair exhibiting support our business objectives?
- Who is our international audience that can be reached through a trade fair program?
- What trade fairs or exhibitions are available in our industry?
- What is the audience profile for each potential trade fair or exhibition?
- Do we have a system in place to determine our return on investment?

If these questions support a company's decision to initiate an international trade fair program, the following questions help analyze the situation before making a final decision:

- What are the costs associated with exhibiting at each potential trade fair or exhibition? Companies must be sure to calculate the costs for travel, shipping, translated materials, and other items that are not a normal part of domestic exhibiting.
- What are the cultural consequences of exhibiting at each potential trade fair or exhibition? Investigate how the fair operates, what cultural rules may apply, and provide training for all staff who will participate.
- Does the company have the personnel resources to support adding international trade fairs to its marketing mix? International trade fairs are often longer than domestic trade shows and therefore may require more staff.

- What type of participation is best for the company? Explore the options that are available—U.S. Pavilion, joint venture, or going it alone.
- Have all the requirements for each trade fair been identified and analyzed? Every trade fair is different, and an exhibiting company must be clear on all requirements before committing funds and resources.
- Does senior management support an international trade fair program? An international trade fair or exhibition is a serious investment— one that should require commitment from the highest levels of company management.
- Are the logistic requirements fully understood? Although trade fair management companies generally provide detailed instructions to exhibitors, it is imperative that key people in the company understand all the requirements, especially deadlines, for shipping materials.

TRADE FAIR CERTIFICATION

The **U.S. Department of Commerce** has developed a program to promote exports of U.S. products and services abroad. The **Trade Fair Certification Program** endorses independent and association show organizers who manage

Trade Fair Certification.

Source: http://www.usatrade.gov/Website/Website.nsf/WebBySubj/TradeEvents_TradeFairCertification

and organize overseas events. The certification helps trade fairs attract more exhibitors, provides additional support and value-added services for exhibitors, and promotes the event through a variety of publications and sources. Requirements for Department of Commerce Trade Fair Certification include the following:

- Must have either a U.S. Pavilion or commitment to attract at least ten U.S. exhibiting companies.
- Must have a U.S. office or agent.
- Must have taken place before.

◆ SUMMARY

The growth of international trade fairs and exhibitions has been phenomenal over the past ten years. The historical home of trade fairs, Europe, continues to strengthen its hold on the world's largest trade fairs and those with the most significant economic impact. Asia has made great strides by building state-of-the-art facilities and promoting its efforts throughout the world. The Middle East, Africa, and Latin America all have strong efforts under way to capture a piece of the international trade fair and exhibition market.

Worldwide communications, easy travel access, and open markets have been a boon to the international trade fair and exhibition industry. Few large companies can afford not to be in the international marketplace today. What was once the playground of only the world's largest companies is now a necessity for most companies of any size. Trade fairs and exhibitions are the easiest method for these companies to enter the marketplace and meet their potential customers.

Exhibiting at international trade fairs is not easy. Cultural and business differences present a new set of problems for the exhibitor, along with more complex logistics and travel procedures. Companies must seriously analyze all factors before committing to an international trade fair program.

KEY WORDS AND TERMS

Ausstellung

Carnet

Congress

Gesellschaft

GMBH

Messe

Messegelande

PLC

Trade exhibition

Trade fair

Trade fair bond

Stand

World Trade Centers Association

U.S. Department of Commerce Trade Fair Certification Program

REVIEW AND DISCUSSION QUESTIONS

1. List some ways that international trade fairs may differ from U.S. trade shows.

2. What are two reasons for Europe's strength in the international trade fair industry?

3. What is the purpose of the World Trade Centers Association?

4. What are some of the complexities that a company must consider before exhibiting at an international trade fair or exhibition?

5. What options does a company have for participating in an international trade fair or exhibition?

INTERNET SITES

Address (URL)	Description
http://www.aeo.org.uk	Association of Exhibition Organisers (U.K.)
http://www.ufinet.org	Union des Foires Internationales
http://www.auma-fairs.com	Association of German Trade Fair Industry
http://www.caem.ca	Canadian Association of Exhibition Management
http://www.fairlink.se	Scandinavian Trade Fair Council
http://www.exhibitions.org.hk	Hong Kong Exhibition and Convention Organisers and Suppliers Association

http://www.inter-expo.com	Association
http://www.saceos.org.sg	Singapore Association of Convention Organisers and Suppliers Association
http://www.thaitradeshow.org	Thailand Tradeshow Organization
http://www.ccpit.org	China Council for Promotion of International Trade
http://dcoem.com	China events
http://emeca.com	European Major Exhibition Centres Association
http://www.fil.be	Association des Expositions, Foires et Salon Wallonie
http://www.exobel.be	Federation Belge des Activites de l'Expos
http://www.febelux.be	Federation des Foires et Salons de Belgiq du Grand-Duche de Luxembourg
http://www.ffme.org	Federation Francaise des Metiers de l'Exposition
http://www.francecongres.org	France-Congres
http://www.foiresaloncongres.com	Foires Salons et Congres de France
http://www.fama.de	Fachverband Messen und Ausstellungen
http://www.famab.de	FAMAB Design-Exhibition-Event
http://www.fme-net.de	Forum Marketing-Eventagenturen
http://www.gcb.de	German Convention Bureau
http://www.idfa.de	Interessengemeinschaft Deutscher Fachmesse Ausstellungsstadte
http://www.assoexpo.com	Associazione Promozione Mostre
http://www.aefi.it	Associazione Enti Fieristici Italiani
http://www.federlegno.it	Associazione Nazionale Aziende Allestrici Fieristici Mostre
http://www.feram.org	Feram I&CT
http://www.eaaoffice.org	European Arenas Association
http://www.esah.nl	Exhibition Services Association Holland
http://www.fbtn.nl	Branchevereniging voor Beurzen & Evenemen
http://www.nlcongress.nl	Netherlands Convention Bureau

http://www.nvbo.nl	Netherlandse Vereniging van Beursoorganisato
http://www.afe.es	Associacion de Ferias Espanolas
http://www.osec.ch	Schweizerische Zentrale Fur Hándelsforderung
http://www.myswitzerland.com	Switzerland Convention & Incentive Bureau
http://www.expo-event.ch	Swiss Expo & Event Makers
http://www.messenschweiz.ch	Vereinigung Messen Schweiz
http://www.beca.org.uk	British Exhibition Contractors Association
http://www.exhibitionvenues.com	Exhibition Venues Association
http://www.primary.uk.com/naa	National Arena Association
http://www.efct.com	European Federation of Conference Towns
http://www.esae.org	European Society of Association Executives
http://www.ettfa.org	European Tourism Trade Fair Association
http://www.evvc.org	Europaischer Verband der Veranstaltungs
http://www.xmeurope.com	Associated European Exhibition Organization
http://www.afida.com	Asociacion de Ferias Internacionales de Am
http://www.aipc.org	Association Internationale des Palais de Congres
http://www.bie-paris.org	Bureau International des Expositions
http://www.cope.org.uk	Confederation of Organisers of Packaging Expositions
http://www.iaam.org	International Association of Assembly Managers
http://www.iacvb.org	International Association of Convention and Visitor Bureaus
http://www.iapco.org	International Association of Professional Congress Organizers
http://www.icc.org	International Chamber of Commerce
http://www.icca.nl	International Congress and Convention Association

http://www.iela.org	International Exhibition Logistics Associates
http://www.iesaj.org	International Exhibit System Association
http://www.ifesnet.org	International Federation of Exhibition Services
http://www.uia.org	Union des Associations Internationales
http://www.venue.org	World Council for Venue Management
http://www.wtca.org	World Trade Centers Association

ABOUT THE CHAPTER CONTRIBUTOR

Ben McDonald is the vice-president of BenchMark Learning, Inc. Founded in 1995, BenchMark Learning assists businesses with training and development solutions primarily in the sales and business development areas. They have since expanded their services and partnerships to include the full spectrum of sales solutions, business development, benchmarking, and competitor analysis in order to provide clients with a total solution for increasing revenue.

◆15

PUTTING IT ALL TOGETHER

MEEC events are like puzzles—eventually they must be put together.
Source: Dorling Kindersley Media Library

◆ Chapter Objectives

This chapter provides the reader with an understanding of the following:

- The key tasks in creating a citywide meeting
- How to create a statement of conference objectives
- How to identify budget expenses and income sources
- When different meeting planning tasks are implemented in the timetable
- The process of conducting a site inspection
- How to assess the success of the meeting

◆ Chapter Outline

INTRODUCTION

Many books contain a concluding chapter that repeats and summarizes the elements of the earlier chapters. In this book, a fictitious case study of a citywide convention serves the same purpose. The overall goal of this case study is to bring together all the previous chapters. Throughout this text, you have read about the tasks associated with meeting planning. Through this case study, you will learn more about topics from the previous chapters and how they apply to a citywide annual conference for 3,000 attendees. The objective of this case study is to help you understand the various tasks a meeting planner must complete in order for a meeting or convention to be successful. In addition, this case study will help you to understand the complexities of the budget, timetable, and the many people with whom the planner must communicate.

This case study uses a three-year planning timetable for one citywide conference. The meeting planning cycle is continuous, and it is important to understand that two of the key skills a meeting planner must possess are the abilities to organize and multitask. Meeting planners typically work on three to five meetings simultaneously, each in different stages of development.

As you review the budget portion of the case study, it is important to understand that many variables will affect the budget, including the time of year the meeting is held, the planner's ability to negotiate, the value of the business to the facility, and trade outs. This budget is broad and was created to highlight the many details the planner must consider.

THE ASSOCIATION

As a meeting planner, it is important to understand your audience—the attendees of the meeting. For association meeting planners, this is critical as they market the conference to association members and to potential members. The meeting planner must also communicate information about his or her association members to suppliers for the convention. The better a supplier understands the audience of the meeting planner, the better the supplier can serve them. For example, if a hotel knows that the majority of the people attending a meeting are women, the hotel might add products that women use like hand cream or shower caps to the room amenities.

The American Small Animal Association (ASAA) is an example of a typical association in the United States. The ASAA is an 8,000 member nonprofit association whose members are veterinarians from thoughout the United States specializing in the care for small animals. The ASAA was founded ten years ago by a group of veterinarians who saw the need to update research and network with other veterinarians specializing in small-animal care. Over 60% of the membership operate independently owned veterinary clinics. The remainder of the association members are suppliers to the veterinary industry. The suppliers include pharmaceutical companies, prescription food companies, and product suppliers. Although women members are increasing, 70% of the members are male. Sixty percent of the members are Caucasian, 30% African American,

AMERICAN SMALL

ANIMAL ASSOCIATION

and 10% are a mix of Latino, Asian, and Native American. It is important to know the makeup of the organization so that the event can meet its wants and needs. The planner or organizer must ask (1) Who is the group? and (2) Why are they here?

An executive committee and a board of directors operate the ASAA. The executive director and seven committee members oversee the day-to-day operation of the association. Members of the board of directors are elected from seven established regions and serve two-year terms. All board elections take place during the annual meeting and are announced during the final night.

Sue Rodriguez is the director of meetings for the ASAA and is a full-time employee. Sue is one of the five full-time employees and is responsible for coordinating the seven regional meetings and the annual conference. She reports directly to the executive director. Planning for the annual conference begins three years in advance of the meeting date. For the past five years, attendance at the annual conference has increased 5% per year. Last year, 37% of the membership attended the meeting. This increase is attributed to the success of the trade show portion of the conference that was added five years ago.

ASSOCIATION GOALS

To begin preparation for the annual conference, Sue reviews past annual conference evaluations from attendees and members of the board of directors. The board of directors wanted to save money by cutting down on the cost related to networking activities, but the members indicated how important it is to have time to meet other professionals from around the country. The board also would like to see the money collected from this conference increased by 10%. Other than membership dues, the annual conference is the largest revenue source for the association. Last year, the ASAA created the Small Animal Preventive Disease Certificate (SAPDC). During the annual convention, veterinarians earn 5 CEUs and learn about the preventive medicines that can be used to save the lives of small animals.

To help focus her thoughts, Sue reads the ASAA mission statement. The mission of ASAA is to provide an educational forum for members to exchange ideas and develop ways to ensure the health of small animals. This mission is accomplished by providing quality education for its members, offering assistance to new veterinarian clinics, and providing a forum for members to meet and to assist each other with emerging technologies.

To help Sue measure **return on investment** (ROI), she creates an operational and educational objective. The operational objective for this conference is to increase meeting profits by 5% over last year's conference. Sue works with the program committee to create the educational objective. The educational objective for this meeting is to increase the number of attendees enrolled in SAPDC classes by 10% and to provide additional networking opportunities. Sue hopes to meet these objectives by offering a four-day conference focused on education and networking that will result in an increase of conference profits by 5%.

BUDGET

To create the budget (see figures of budgets on pp. 472–473), Sue reviews the past meeting budgets. For her expenses, she includes the cost of the convention center, host hotel, decorator, audiovisual, speakers, and entertainment. In addition, Sue must consider operational objectives for the meeting. To locate income sources, Sue looks at past meeting **sponsors** and exhibitors.

The hotel budget will include meeting room rental, food and beverage, staff sleeping rooms, and services charges and gratuities. In creating the budget, Sue knows that she will have some negotiation opportunities based on the ASAA sleeping and meeting room usage ratios. The better ASAA's use of meeting rooms to sleeping rooms match the hotel ideal sleeping room to meeting room ratio, the better the rate can be negotiated. To assist in managing the hotel blocks, Sue uses a housing bureau and includes that cost in the hotel expense item.

BUDGET			
INCOME			
REGISTRATION			3,000 attendees
Members			1,680 attendees
early	(at 60% = 1008 people)	$600 p/p	$604,800
late	(at 40% = 672 people)	$800 p/p	$537,600
Nonmembers			
early	(at 50% = 300 people)	$700 p/p	$210,000
late	(at 50% = 300 people)	$900 p/p	$270,000
Student	(at 5% = 120 people)	$100 p/p	$12,000
Speakers	(100 people)	$300 p/p	$30,000
Exhibitors		Included in exhibit fee	
Registration Total			**$1,664,400**
SAPDC	(500 people)	$100 p/p	$50,000
Exhibitors	(500 exhibitors)	$3000 p/exhibit	$1,500,000
Sponsors			$120,000
Extended Learning			$10,000
Other			$5,000
Total Income			**$3,349,400**
Expenses			$1,881,438
Net Income			**$1,467,962**

The convention center expenses will include the cost of space for meeting rooms, exhibit hall, electricity, Internet connection, garbage pickup, and staffing for coffee and food stations. To maximize dollars, Sue plans the majority of her educational events at the convention center. This not only enables her to use the daily rate for the rooms at the convention center but also is a selling point for the exhibitors who want attendees near the trade show.

BUDGET

EXPENSES

Convention Center	$350,000
Host Hotel	$212,643
Decorations	$102,245
Signage	$80,000
Audiovisual	$125,000
Webcasting	$60,000
Pressroom	$50,000
Transportation	$18,250
Off-site Venue	$50,000
Golf Event	$150,000
Marketing Committee	$185,000
Program Committee	$10,000
Speakers	$52,000
Entertainment	$17,000
Security	$180,000
Insurance	$100,000
Special Services	$5,000
News Delivery	$30,000
Temporary Staff	$67,200
Tote Bags	$30,000
Site Visits	$2,100
Other	$5,000
Total Expenses	**$1,881,438**

Sue will need to identify an **exposition services contractor** (ESC) to provide decorations and to set up the trade show. She will also need to assess audiovisual (AV) needs for both the hotel and convention center. The ESC will provide staging for the reception, general session, trade show, and awards night, and the **AV company** will provide sound and light. In order to provide an accurate quote, the ESC must be given information on carpeting request, number of trade show booths, estimated freight use, and types of staging needed for the opening session, general session, and awards dinner. The AV company will need to know sound and lighting needs for each venue and the type of production for the general session, opening reception, and awards dinner. The general session will be webcasted to members unable to attend. Sue lists this as a separate expense (see budget on p. 473).

To budget transportation, Sue looks back at past budgets to determine how many attendees used the shuttle service for airport transfers. Sue knows this expense will vary greatly depending on the existing transportation options in a given city. At this point, she includes full shuttle service for each day of the conference, VIP transportation, and transportation to the off-site events and golf tournament. In addition to ground transportation, Sue's transportation budget includes air transportation for staff and VIPs and freight shipping. Of the transportation items budgeted, freight shipping is the least expensive. Due to the large shipping volume of exhibitors, the ASAA is charged a minimum for association shipping needs.

The budget for the off-site golf tournament will vary greatly depending on the conference location. To include these items, Sue uses the amount from the last meeting and increases the cost by 5%.

Reviewing the budget history is also a good starting place when Sue allocates funds for marketing. With a minimum of five marketing pieces being created, this can become very expensive; however, with the increased use in the Internet, more money is being spent on Web development rather than large marketing brochures.

Seventy-five percent of the speakers for the ASAA are members presenting research papers. To encourage members to make presentations, ASAA offers presenters a 50% discount on the early registration fee. The majority of the money allocated for speakers actually is used for a keynote speaker and entertainment. To locate the keynote speaker and entertainment, Sue uses a speaker bureau. The speaker bureau fee is included in this expense item.

In order to have a smooth meeting, Sue will need to hire temporary staff. This budget item includes the cost for registration personnel, on-site assembly of attendee packets, room monitors, distribution of evaluations, and other duties as needed. Sue will need to bring temporary staff in one day prior to the meeting for training and will pay staff for their time.

Security is an ongoing expense that ASAA must include in the budget. The ASAA is increasing its involvement in new research for small animals. This new research is both confidential and controversial.

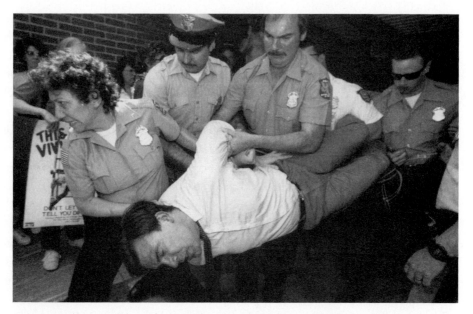

Sammy Busby, a member of People for the Ethical Treatment of Animals, was arrested during protests at the National Institutes of Health in Bethesda, Maryland. Several people were arrested while demonstrating against the use of animals for experimentation as part of World Laboratory Animal Liberation Day.

Source: AP/Wide World Photos

Insurance is another increasing expense. Sue includes insurance to cover attrition, loss of revenue due to acts of God, terrorism, and liability. The $100,000 budgeted represents 5% of the cost to host this meeting.

To cover expenses for attendees with special needs, Sue includes a special services item in the budget. This will be used for members who identify themselves as needing translators, written material to be published in Braille, sign language interpreters, special accommodations for seeing eye dogs, and so on. For example, Sue knows that one of her key sponsors is legally blind and has a seeing eye dog. To accommodate him, Sue makes sure that water and dog food is available. About five of the ASAA members are hearing impaired. For these members, Sue arranges for sign language interpreters to be on site to escort them throughout the conference.

When Sue creates the budgets, she contacts city officials where the meeting will be held. As a nonprofit, the ASAA is exempt from most city and state taxes, but she must file the documents to ensure the exemption. Further, Sue will need to bring forms proving that ASAA is a not-for-profit organization. The forms will also be filed with suppliers.

Sue includes some expenses in the budget even though she knows that these expenses will be picked up by sponsors. Each year, Sue has no problem finding a company to sponsor tote bags given to all attendees, the on-site newspaper, transportation, the meal for the opening reception, and the entertainment for the VIP dinner. It is important that Sue includes this in the budget to document these expenses.

To allow for unexpected expenses, Sue creates the "other" expense category. This is used to cover additional expenses that do not occur every year or are not planned for. For example, if the cost of stamps increases, this contingency would be covered.

INCOME

The income (see budget on p. 472) will offset the expenses for the meeting. Estimated expenses for this meeting are $1,886,437.50. To reach the financial objective and make a profit, Sue must not only pay all expenses, but she must build in a profit.

In determining the income, Sue starts with income generated from the registration fees. She first takes the expected attendance of 3,000 and subtracts 500 exhibitors whose registration fee is included in the exhibitor fee, then subtracts the 100 speakers who will pay a reduced registration. The ASAA has three registration fee categories: member, nonmember, and student. Convention history shows that 70% are members, 25% nonmembers, and 5% students. In order to reduce attrition fees, Sue creates an early registration fee and a late fee for members and nonmembers. Typically, 60% of the members and 50% of the nonmembers will register early. Sue estimates that if registration alone will cover expenses, she must charge $629 per person. With this in mind, Sue's registration fee structure is $600 for an early member, $700 for an early nonmember; $800 for a late member, and $900 for a late nonmember. Students only pay $100, thus encouraging them to join when they are employed in the field. Sue estimates her registration income to be $1,664,400.00.

Following the income generated from registration fees, the exhibitors are the largest single source of income for the ASAA. It will cost the ASAA approximately $10 per square foot for the convention space, ESC, and AV. The ASAA will sell this trade show space for $30 per square foot. History shows a steady 10% increase in exhibitors per year. At the last conference, about 450 companies ordered booths. Sue estimates exhibitor income for this year to be $1,500,000 (500 exhibitors spending $3,000 each for a ten-foot by ten-foot booth).

Other sources of income that Sue will include in the budget are rebates generated from hotel rooms, the transportation company, and the ESC. Rather than accept commission for these items, the ASAA negotiates a rebate per room night that becomes an income stream. There is a small amount of money raised by the sale of extended learning products, including videotapes, CDs, books, and audiotapes.

Income from the CSEP is $100 per person, in addition to the registration. Last year, the ASAA charged $200 per person. The cost is low to encourage attendees to take classes toward certification.

REQUEST FOR PROPOSAL

Once the meeting objectives are laid out and a budget determined, Sue creates a **Request for Proposal** (RFP). In creating the RFP, Sue wants to include accurate information to help hotels and cities submit good proposals. She includes meeting specifications on ASAA and explains that the RFP is sent three years prior to the annual conference date. Sue collects proposals and reviews them with Dave Rogers, executive director, and Elizabeth Rice, a board member serving as the convention chair. Sue, Dave, and Elizabeth will choose two cities to visit in order to conduct an initial site inspection. After the initial site inspection to all selected cities is complete, a decision will be made, and Sue and Dave will conduct a second site inspection to the chosen city to begin contract negotiations. In order to avoid any bias, the ASAA will pick up the cost of the site inspection with the understanding that when a city is selected, the host city will rebate the cost of the site inspections.

The RFP will include a list of cities under consideration and the preferred dates. Although the dates may vary between the months of March and April, the days of the week must be Thursday to Sunday. The annual conference is held around the country, primarily in large cities near places where members of the board of directors reside.

Sue's RFP includes a detailed grid of her meeting room needs. She includes special requests; for example, her classroom sets require two chairs per six-foot table and a water station set in the back of the room. She also includes a food and beverage summary that notes special dietary needs of attendees. Her meeting room grid includes the event, number of attendees, and room set.

The ASAA prefers to use no more than five hotels in a given city. A grid is created requesting the number of suites, singles, and double rooms that ASAA anticipates using at each hotel. In considering a city, Sue looks for downtown hotel properties that offer a large range of room prices. Hotels need to be in close proximity to each other. The host hotel must be willing to block a minimum of 900 rooms. In addition to the sleeping room block, the host hotel will be the site of the opening night reception and break-out rooms for special interest groups.

A detailed history, in the form of a grid of the last three years, is included in the RFP. The history grid shows the peak room nights, meeting room block, sleeping room block, pickup for the host hotel and the room block, and pickup at each of the nonhost hotels. She also includes a food and beverage section showing reported use. The ASAA reports a 10% increase in meeting attendees per year over the last two years and has an attrition rate of only 2%.

The final portion of the RFP is a two-page questionnaire for the hotel to complete and submit with the proposal. Questions include comp room policy, deposit policy, definition of "sold out," attrition policy, master accounts, split folios, shuttle service availability, tax rate, nonprofit tax policy, gratuity distribution, Internet connection, phone charges, and fitness facilities. She also includes questions about how the hotel handles "In Conjunction Withs" (ICWs) and exhibitor room blocks, and if they will work to create priority housing for members over nonmembers. Sue found that this form provides a quick way for her to compare hotels.

The RFP is sent to the **Convention and Visitor Bureau** for distribution to appropriate hotels. Included in the RFP is a questionnaire for the CVB to complete. The questionnaire includes questions regarding state, local, and hotel room taxes as well as holidays, union contracts, special venues, CVB services, and citywide events or holidays that take place during the ASAA meeting dates.

FIRST SITE INSPECTION

Sue, Dave, and Elizabeth have reviewed the proposals and identified two cities with available dates to host the ASAA citywide: Chicago and Dallas. She calls the CVBs in those cities to arrange to spend three days in each city. Sue explains to them that the team plans to conduct a detailed site inspection to look for hotels, off-site venues, and golf courses. She sends the site inspection form that the team will use to evaluate the city and properties. Sue explains that the team will stay at the hotels under consideration as host properties and will conduct short tours of nonhost hotels under consideration. For the nonhost properties, the team only needs to meet with the hotel sales contact, see a standard room, and tour the outlets.

DAY ONE

Mark Tester, vice-president of sales, Chicago CVB, meets Sue, Dave, and Elizabeth at Chicago's O'Hare airport. On arrival, Mark gives a driving tour of downtown, passing by all the hotels under consideration. They have lunch at the Chicago Museum of Art, where they are joined by Kesha Evans, owner of Windy City, and a **destination management company**. Kesha explains the various services she can provide, including transportation and arranging off-site events, spouse tours, and private dining. Tom Delaney, catering manager at the Chicago Museum of Art, introduces himself and takes the group on a tour of the private function areas of the museum and recommends the best area for an off site. He gives Sue a sales packet with sample menus and pricing.

After lunch, Mark takes the inspection team to the Hyatt Regency McCormick Place to meet with sales manager Bob Taylor and general manager Larry Rose. They tour the property, looking at sleeping rooms, suites, singles, and doubles; the meeting and ballrooms for possible location of the opening reception and special interest group meetings and available outlets. After the tour, they meet in one of the conference rooms to discuss available dates and rates.

Then, Sue, Dave, and Elizabeth meet at 6 P.M. in the hotel restaurant for dinner. During dinner, they make observations, noting how the guests are treated, quality of the food, time food is served, and the attentiveness of the wait staff. They order different entrées to sample the many types food their attendees might order if they stay at this hotel. After dinner, Sue walks the meeting space, looking into the meeting rooms to see how the rooms are set.

DAY TWO

At 8:30 A.M., Mark meets the team, who have already eaten breakfast and checked out of the hotel. Mark has arranged for a 9:00 A.M. meeting with Randy Moses, senior sales manager of McCormick Place Convention

Center. Randy gives a tour of the facility, taking time to show them what he sees as the best location for their functions, loading docks, shuttle drop-off and pickup, and areas where sponsored items like banners are allowed. Sue asks about available dates, food and beverage concession hours, taxes, union rules, and contract renewal dates. Randy provides this information and discusses the security and their medical and emergency procedure guidelines. Both Mark and Randy explain to Sue, Dave, and Elizabeth how the CVB and convention center work as a team to help market the Chicago meeting to attendees. They discuss marketing options, including premailers and on-site promotions the year prior to coming to the host city.

For lunch, Mark takes the group to the Golden Princess, a luxury yacht owned by ABC Charters, a company that provides dinner tours of Lake Michigan. Rich Cunningham, general manager of ABC Charters, meets with them. Today, they are having a special lunch for meeting planners to sample the menu and enjoy a minicharter experience. The president of Chicago DMC Services, Deborah Adams, explains her services and has photos showing other off-site locations Sue may want to consider.

The afternoon is spent making contacts and touring the hotels under consideration. Mark arranges thirty-minute tours of each nonhost hotel and explains to the hotel sales contact that they only want to see sleeping rooms and restaurants areas.

By 4 P.M., Sue, Dave, and Elizabeth are ready to check in to the Hyatt Regency Chicago, the second hotel under consideration as the headquarters hotel. Rachel Monroe introduces herself as the association sales manager and begins the tour. She is excited about a new ballroom that was recently added and explains how the ballroom could be used for the opening reception. After the tour, Richard Moore, the general manager, joins the group to look at available dates and rates.

Sue, Dave, and Elizabeth take an hour break and meet in the restaurant for dinner. During dinner, they review all notes from the past two days. After dinner, Sue takes her tour of the meeting rooms.

DAY THREE

The team checks out early and waits in the hotel lobby. They notice a line forming as people check out of the hotel. They take mental notes, observing the speed of the checkout and how courteous the employees are at the front desk and bell stand. Mark arrives at the hotel and takes the group to the first stop, Harborside International Golf Center, a four-star course only twelve miles from downtown Chicago. The group meets with the special event manager of the Harborside to discuss the optional golf outing that is part of the ASAA event. The tournament is held Thursday afternoon, prior to the opening reception. Mark takes the group to one more golf course and on two more hotel site inspections before they depart for the airport.

Sue, Dave, and Elizabeth thank Mark for his time and inform him that they will be touring Dallas next month and plan to make a decision in two months. After the Dallas site inspection, the ASAA will make their decision and will contact the bureau regarding that decision.

One month later, Sue, Dave, and Elizabeth go to Dallas for another three-day site inspection. Patty Towell, the sales manager of Dallas CVB, arranges for the group to meet with hotels, the convention center, and off-site locations.

After both site inspections conclude, the inspection team reviews their notes. Due to the conflict of dates with other industry meetings, they decide to meet on St. Patrick's Day. In evaluating Chicago, they are concerned about room availability, the renewal dates for some union contracts, and finally the fact that the cost to hold the meeting in Chicago is 25% more than in Dallas. This increase in cost might be offset by the number of attendees who prefer to meet in Chicago over Dallas, but this meeting will attract more attendees seeking the SAPDC—thus location will not be a much of an issue. Dallas is selected for the annual conference. Sue calls Mark from the Chicago CVB, expresses their concerns, and explains why Dallas was selected. Sue reminds Mark that they have not held a meeting in Chicago in five years and would like to look again to them in the future.

SECOND SITE INSPECTION

DAY ONE

Sue sends Patty Towell, at the Dallas CVB, a letter of intent to hold the conference in Dallas and contacts her to help arrange a second site inspection. This second site inspection will only include Sue and Dave and will be for two days. The goal is to finalize nonhost properties, select off-site venues and golf course, select the DMC and transportation company, and begin contract negotiations. When Sue and Dave arrive in Dallas, they rent a car and take a self-guided tour of the city. They check in at the Hyatt Regency Downtown, the location of the headquarter hotel for the meeting.

At the Hyatt Hotel Downtown Dallas, Sue and Dave meet with Nancy Simonieg, the senior sales manager, and Rizwan Naqvi, CMP, LES, the **convention service manager** (CSM). Once the contract is signed, Sue will work with the CSM for the remainder of the meeting. During this meeting, Sue and Nancy will begin negotiations for sleeping rooms, meeting rooms, shuttle service, and so on.

After the meeting with the hotel, Sue meets Sonja Miller, sales manager of the Dallas Convention Center; Erika Bondy, CMP, senior event coordinator; and Bill Baker, director of catering. Once the contract is signed, Sue will work with Erika on all her meeting details and with Larry on meeting F&B requirements. Today, Sue beings negotiating rates with the Dallas Convention Center. It will be a meeting where she will review her needs and see what is the best "win–win" for her attendees and the convention center.

Sue and Dave have lunch at the Dallas Museum of Art and meet with the catering sales manager, Cindy Hartman, to review rates for having the VIP dinner in the restaurant. Carolyn Petty, president of EMC, a DMC, joins Sue and Dave for lunch to discuss what the DMC can provide for the ASAA meeting, including gift baskets and general transportation needs.

In the afternoon, Patty has arranged with Sue to meet with two of the nonhost hotels under consideration in the city for sleeping room space. At each hotel, she meets the sales manager to negotiate the rates and amenities. For dinner, Patty takes Sue and Dave to a small Mexican restaurant that is a favorite of the locals. At dinner, Patty discusses the services the bureau can assist with, including registration personnel, marketing, slides, leads for suppliers, transportation, Internet services, and on-site brochures. She will staff a promotional booth at the meeting prior to the one in Dallas.

DAY TWO

The morning is spent touring and reestablishing contact with the remainder of hotels that will provide sleeping rooms. Sue has lunch at the Dallas World Aquarium. She is looking for a "fun" site for the VIP meeting and meets with Jose Lopez, sales manager, for a tour and to discuss possible dinning options. Although this is an option, it might be too casual for the group. Jose brings a portfolio with pictures of events held and the aquarium, and Sue's concerns end.

In the afternoon, Sue tours two golf courses. For each course, she makes contacts, has the event sales manager take her on a nine-hole tour, and begins discussing rates. Sue pays attention to where the group might meet before and after the tournament. Is there an area where the group might meet as they finish playing golf?

Her evening is free to review her notes. Sue will catch up on e-mails missed during her day of meetings and will carefully look at all the brochures she is given. She really likes the idea of having the VIP dinner in an unusual location.

DAY THREE

Sue begins the day with meeting the ESC contact, Jack Boyd, account executive for the Freeman Companies, and Darren Temple, vice-president of sales, AVW TELAV Audio Visual Solutions, part of the Freeman Companies. Jack, Darren, and Sue meet first at the Dallas Convention Center, then at the Hyatt Hotel to discuss ESC and AV needs. They tour each venue, discussing specific staging, setup, and AV needs for each event. Sue realizes the impact the ESC and AV have in making a meeting successful. Sue takes the time to review all meeting details. For example, since this is a medical meeting and attendees will receive CEUs for poster session presentations, the poster session must be set up at least 4 feet from any exhibitor. Once all the details of each venue are known, the ESC and AV company can provide an accurate estimate of expenses.

MARKETING COMMITTEE

ASAA has both an in-house marketing department and an outside advertising agency. They both work together to create the marketing pieces for the annual conference. After Sue returns from the second site inspection, she meets with George Day, the ASAA director of marketing, and Julie Love, the account manager for Idea Maker, Inc., an advertising company. She discusses the convention location and the meeting objectives. She also explains how important promoting the new SAPDC is for this conference.

After two weeks, Sue meets with George and Julie again. Julie brings theme ideas and visuals for the marketing pieces. After reviewing several themes, "Power of Prevention" is selected. The visual will be the skyline of Dallas with the Hyatt Regency Hotel ball of lights brightly shining on the downtown area. The ball of lights represents the power, and the light shining on the city shows its power.

After reviewing the success of past marketing pieces, it is decided that four marketing tools will be used. A four-color postcard-size mailer will be developed as a teaser and mailed to all past conference attendees and targeted to potential members. This teaser will also be used as an advertisement that will be placed in industry newsletters and magazines. The second piece will be a magazine-style brochure to be sent to all association members. This brochure will include a convention agenda listing dates, times and speakers, a program at a glance grid, current sponsors, and convention and housing registration forms. Idea Maker, Inc., designs Web pages and maintains ASAA's e-mail newsletter. The third marketing approach will be a Web page that will serve as an electronic brochure, allowing people to register for the meeting and make hotel reservations online. The final approach will be through the e-newsletter that features convention information and will include testimonials from people who have earned their SAPDC.

In creating the meeting program to be given to attendees on check-in, Sue meets with George and Dan to discuss content of the program. Dan is concerned that attendees will take the wrong class because they will not understand the level of instruction. George assures Dan that each session will be color coded to provide easy identification of the education level. This color-coded scheme will be repeated in the program. Among topics discussed are the size of sponsors' ads and how much copy will be given for educational event descriptions. All agree that to support the objective, the SPDC should receive a full-page description in the front of the program.

During each conference, a new board of directors is introduced, awards are given, and important announcements must be made. Sue, George, and Dave meet to discuss the types of presentations that will be made and the scripts that George and his team will write. Sue is responsible for arranging rehearsal time for each presentation.

The marketing committee is responsible for creating press releases that will be sent to professional publications. For each conference, a new piece of research is featured, and the marketing committee works to promote this research to the public.

CREATING THE PROGRAM

When Sue returns from the Dallas site inspection, she meets with the program committee to begin creating the educational content of the meeting. Serving on the program committee is Doug Walker, board member and chair of the Small Animal Preventive Disease Certificate, SAPDC; Dan Dearing, board of director chair of the Program Committee for the Power of Prevention annual convention; and his appointed committee members Liz Stewart and Mark Collins along with Donna Smith, ASAA administrative assistant. These five people and Sue will work together to create the content of the meeting.

Sue begins the meeting by giving each committee member a notebook with responsibilities of the committee members, past convention notes, and the meeting theme, the "Power of Prevention." Sue wants to make sure the committee members understand the objective of the meeting is "[t]o increase the number of members attendees taking the SAPDC by 10% by offering a four-day conference that is focused on education that will increase meeting profits by 5%."

The committee agrees to follow the same meeting agenda as in the past: opening reception, general session, awards dinner, and a poster session to run at the same time as the trade show. The conference will include an ASAA VIP dinner, a golf tournament, and a total of 120 ninety-minute education sessions in two days. The one change in the schedule is to add 2 four-hour segments for the SAPDC class. The committee will locate speakers for SAPDC and all break-out sessions. ASAA members will present 100 of the 120 educational sessions. To help the program committee, a separate committee—called the paper review committee— is created. This committee will issue the call for papers, grade and evaluate papers, and will inform the program committee of their final selection for presentations and poster session. Sue will use a speaker bureau for the opening reception, general session, awards dinner, ASAA VIP dinner, and all entertainment.

Sue reviews the timeline with the committee. The paper review committee will begin the call for papers one-year prior to the meeting. Six months prior, the paper review committee will provide the program committee with the final selection, and the program committee will make initial contact with presenters and speakers. The committee will recommend speakers for all sessions. Once speakers and back-up speakers have been identified, Sue will send out invitation letters. In her letter, she will ask the speaker to sign a commitment sheet and require the speaker to provide an abstract of the presentation and his or her biography.

The committee will be responsible for contacting all the speakers and following up with those not responding. There will also be a point person for all speaker questions. Once speakers have been selected, Sue's role is to collect information, assign time slots, and correspond, including letters of acceptance and a reminder letter.

One key feature in the conference is the exhibitors. Jill Kochan, ASAA staff, is the ASAA trade show manager for the conference. Jill is responsible for all communication with the exhibitors and ESC at they set up the trade show. Jill will work closely with Sue to communicate exhibitor needs. Jill will meet with the ESC to create specifications for the exhibitor prospectus.

PARTNERSHIP

As Sue prepares for this meeting, she knows the importance of her meeting partners. Throughout the conference, Sue depends on many companies to provide excellent service and create a memorable experience for the ASAA members. She reviews her contact list, looking at the many companies she will partner with for the upcoming conference.

Although most housing bureaus can provide a complete housing package, including hotel selection, negotiation, and contract, Sue prefers to work with the housing bureau after she has selected the hotels. Once the selections have been made, the housing bureau will manage the hotel room block. The housing bureau will create a Web link for attendees to book rooms online and a paper form for attendees to complete and fax. Once an attendee selects a hotel, the housing bureau will send a confirmation letter. One of the best aspects about Sue's partnership with the housing bureau is room block management. Rather than call all the hotels used, Sue calls the housing bureau for monthly, weekly, and daily rooming reports as needed. Sue also depends on the housing bureau to manage the exhibitor room block.

Sue likes to partner with a local DMC for the annual conference. For this conference, Sue uses the DMC for arranging the airport transfers,

VIP transportation, and shuttle service from hotels to convention centers. The DMC made all logistical arrangements for the VIP dinner. This allowed Sue to concentrate on VIP invitations and content of the event. Sue also appreciates the fact that a DMC normally has access to many motorcoach suppliers. Transportation is always an area of concern for Sue. While in Washington, DC, a few years back, Sue contracted with a motorcoach company, and one of the motorcoaches broke down with all her attendees in it. The company had no back-up motorcoaches, and her attendees waited almost an hour to be rescued and taken to the event.

For key speakers and entertainment, Sue uses a speaker bureau. Sue does not have the time to research the many speakers and entertainers who could speak to ASAA members. The speaker bureau will make recommendations on the best speakers and entertainers, and once Sue makes her selection, the speaker bureau will handle all arrangements. They will ensure that the speakers are at the meeting on time, and if something happens, the speaker bureau can quickly arrange for a back-up speaker.

Sue selects an online registration company to help with the many attendees that prefer this registration method. The designated registration company will accept registrations electronically, automatically send attendees a confirmation letter, and will store the registration for easy retrieval to create name badges to have available at the meeting site.

Sponsors are important partners for the ASAA conference. Sue will work with each sponsor to ensure that they receive exposure to members in exchange for their financial and/or in-kind support. Sue realizes that without annual conference sponsors, ASAA would not reach its convention financial objectives.

The ASAA has always included meeting security for attendees' safety and exhibitor products. For this conference, Sue will increase security. An animal rights association contacted ASAA and plans to protest a new test being conducted on laboratory rats. Sue realized that she must allow this group to protest, but she wants to ensure that they protest peacefully and do not disturb meeting attendees.

A key partner in making the conference a success is the ESC providing decorations and AV company. Sue considers the ESC as the "partner" that brings the theme to life. The decorations must wow attendees visually. In addition to the conference, Sue recognizes the important role the ESC plays in keeping the exhibitors happy. This is important to the ASAA, as the exhibitors generate 44% of the revenue for the conference.

Sue loves to work with the AV company. This partner is crucial for every meeting event. Without proper projection and sound, the attendees would not be able to learn. Sue works closely with AV during the meeting. One burned-out light bulb or malfunctioning microphone can ruin a break-out session.

In selecting an ESC and AV company, Sue chooses to use the Freeman Companies. Unlike other ESCs and AV companies, the Freeman Companies offers both ESC and AV supplier services under one company. This makes communication more smooth. Additionally, the organizational structure of the Freeman Companies allows Sue to have one contact from sales to service of the meeting.

In order to keep things running efficiently at the conference, she hires temporary staff. She builds a partnership early with these people. They will be part of the team and represent ASAA during the conference.

"The Total Show" is a promotional concept used by the Freeman Companies.
Photo by George G. Fenich, Ph.D., Professor, School of HRTA, University of New Orleans

CONTRACTS

Sue has a contract for each convention partner and every service provider. Each contract specifies the exact services that are expected and penalties if the expectations are not met. Early in Sue's career, she worked with an association that signed a contract that did not include a realistic attrition clause. The association did not meet their room block and paid the hotel over $10,000 for unused rooms. At least one year out, Sue reviews each contract carefully. Before the meeting begins, Sue will have contracts finalized with the host hotel, housing bureau, airlines, off-site venue, golf course, speaker bureau, security, audio visual, DMC, ESC, and many others.

ONE-YEAR TO SIX-MONTH COUNTDOWN

Sue looks at her **meeting time line** and realizes that she is eighteen months away from the Power of Prevention annual conference. She takes out her meeting resume and reviews all contracts. She meets with George and Julie from the marketing committee to look at the blue line of the marketing pieces and the first draft of the program. The blue line, or proof as it is also called, is the final copy that will be reviewed before the marketing piece is printed. If Sue and her team miss an educational session or a grammatical error is made, then that is the way it will be printed. If the mistake is important enough, the marketing piece will be reprinted and the expenses billed to the cost of the conference.

She arranges a meeting with Doug and Dan from the program committee to select the speakers for the convention. On selection, Sue mails out the acceptance letter to the speakers. In her letter, Sue requests that the speaker confirm his or his commitment by sending the speaker biography, presentation abstract, and audiovisual needs form. Sue makes a point to contact the speaker bureau to check the status of the motivational speaker and entertainment. She requests that all AV needs are identified one year prior to the meeting. By doing this, Sue is able to have a more accurate budget item for AV and can catch any potential fire hazards with AV usage.

Sue secures ten sponsors for the meeting, including Small Vets Pluss, a company that supplies the vaccines for small animals, for the tote bags; Houver Pharmaceutical, a small-animal antibiotic producer, for transportation; LabSmlab, provider of medical instruments used in surgery, for the opening night reception; Mix-a-vet, developer of special food for small animals, to sponsor the newspaper; Smalco, a pet store featuring small-animal products; and Smallvets will cosponsor the VIP entertainment and the awards dinner. Sue will contact each sponsor to confirm commitment and sign contracts. In her conversation, Sue reminds sponsors that she needs them to return a form that has the exact spelling of their company name and what the sponsor signage should be.

The trade show floor plan for the Dallas conference was created and approved fourteen months prior to the Dallas meeting. Exhibit space for the Power of Prevention conference was sold on site at the ASAA conference prior to Dallas. The ASAA has an 87% exhibitor retention. Nine months out, the ESC updates the floor plan and mails exhibitor packets to potential exhibitors.

In addition to the trade show, Sue works with the ESC in finalizing the setup for the opening reception, general session, and awards dinner. She determines where the media center will be located and the registration area. Sue depends on the ESC to recommend the best location to place sponsor banners and signage. Most convention centers have strict rules regarding banner and signage placement. ESCs that work with convention centers frequently know the rules and have great ideas on how sponsors can be recognized.

SIX MONTHS TO DAY OF THE MEETING

Fast forward to the six-month countdown for the Power of Prevention annual conference. The marketing committee writes and sends press releases. If timed correctly, the press releases will be published within a month of when the convention ads are scheduled to run.

Early registration forms begin to arrive within weeks after being sent. In reviewing the registration forms, Sue notices that three of the attendees indicated that they have mobile disabilities and will need special accommodations. In compliance with ADA laws, Sue will work with all meeting partners to ensure that these attendees are able to fully participate in the conference. She will need to arrange for handicapped rooms and note that the meeting rooms will need to be set with aisles to accommodate theses attendees.

Sue receives the menus from the hotel catering manager and selects the meals. She makes a special note informing catering that she will require five special meals for attendees with dietary needs.

She contacts the host hotel and convention center to get the names of the meeting rooms that will be used for the Power of Prevention conference. It is important for Sue to get the name of the location of the meeting rooms so that this information can be added to the convention program. Hotels and convention centers rarely want to give this information out early, as they do not want to commit to a particular meeting room that might be sold to another planner. Good communication and flexibility is important.

Sue works with the DMC to review the menu and the ESC for the VIP dinner at the Dallas World Aquarium. The DMC located a florist that will create floral arrangements that look like coral reefs on the sea bottom. The entire event is designed to make attendees feel like they are under water.

Sue contacts Larry Grant, the event organizer at Tennison Golf Course, to finalize tournament rules. It looks like this will be a great year for this event—ten people already registered for this event. Sue gives Larry the names and handicaps.

During this time, Sue will contact the DMC to finalize shuttle routes to all events, enabling her to begin ordering signage for transportation. Sue learns each year how even highly educated people get lost at meetings. It baffles her that vets cannot read material in their program. Sue must clearly list all events, their locations, and the shuttle service times. Signage is very important in the total conference experience.

MONTH FIVE

Five months prior to the meeting, Sue sends out reminders to all speakers. She works with the marketing committee to finalize and send the marketing brochure and the e-mail announcement. She arranges quiet time to proofread the meeting program and to create a detailed work schedule for staff, temporary employees, and volunteers. Sue orders meeting name badges and meeting supplies, and calls the security company to review needs.

MONTH FOUR AND MONTH THREE

During the fourth and third month prior to the meeting, Sue monitors registration on a weekly basis. At the third month, Sue reviews registration and makes adjustments to her room block. Sue negotiates this option in her hotel contracts as a way to control attrition.

Hotel	Hyatt Regency Downtown Dallas	Fairmont	Lowes Anatole	Le Meridian	Holiday Inn
Initial Room Block	1000	500	500	500	500
90-Day Room Block Review	700	500	300	300	100
Room Block Adjustment	Over will add +50 rooms	No change	On schedule	On schedule	Under will remove −200 rooms
New Room Block	1,050	500	500	500	300

Sue looks at her initial room block and compares it with current hotel registration. Convention history shows that 60% of the people register early, indicating that in a perfect world, the host property would have 600 rooms reserved and the remaining properties 300 each. In looking at the actual hotel registration, Sue notices that all rooms have been filled at the Fairmont. She is unable to get additional rooms and will need to close reservations for the Fairmont. The Lowes and Le Meridian are right on schedule and will require no changes. The Holiday Inn is 200 rooms less than what it should be. Sue reduces the block by 40% and is now obligated for 300 rooms rather than 500. She has the opposite problem with the Hyatt Regency, the host hotel. The host property is 100 rooms over what she expects, so she conservatively increases the block by 5% and is obligated for 1,050 rooms.

In addition to the room block adjustments, she has received calls for changes from the convention center to move the location of meeting rooms and calls from speakers needing to cancel. These changes affect the information in the program, and it must be revised. She sees this as a time of many changes. These changes are all part of Sue's job. The work she did a year ago is paying off. A speaker cancels, so she contacts the program committee to see who they have planned as a back up.

MONTH TWO

At two months out, Sue arranges another trip to Dallas. Anna Murphey, CSM Dallas CVB, arranges for Sue to meet with all the key contacts to make the Power of Prevention conference a success.

Rizwan, CSM, Hyatt Hotel Downtown, meets with Sue to conduct a property walk-through, and he will introduce Sue to the catering manager to review the menu, the accounts receivable contact to explain the bill review process, the front desk manager to confirm pre-key guests and check-in and check-out process, and the director of security and medical staff to review emergency procedures. The CSM explains that he is the hotel contact and will assist Sue in providing information needed from the hotel from room pickup to bill review. Rizwan and Sue will work closely together.

As with the hotel, Sue will meet with Erika Bondy, senior event coordinator at the Dallas Convention Center, to conduct a walk-through. She invites the ESC and AV contacts to join her. By doing this, Sue has many eyes looking for potential problems that might occur. She will also spend time with the catering manager to review the menu for lunch and awards dinner.

Sue meets with the DMC to walk-through hotel transportation routes and finalize menus, decorations, and entertainment for the VIP dinner at the Dallas World Aquarium. Sue will meet with the event coordinator at the Tennison Golf Course to update the player list and review pairings.

When Sue returns from Dallas, she makes final changes to the program and sends it to the printer. She ships material to the convention site and works with the marketing committee on the final scripts. Sue also reviews her staging guide that has all her contacts, the time line, contracts, menus, and notes for her to review.

MONTH ONE

One month prior to the meeting, Sue continues weekly monitoring of the registration. She sends reminder letters to all the speakers. She works with the advertising firm to approve press releases to announce research findings that will be presented at the Power of Prevention conference. She works with the staff to finalize work schedules, marketing, scripts, and rehearsal times. Sue will create a checklist and pack her convention material. Sue thinks of the month before the meeting as a tennis match. Emergencies, like five to ten tennis balls thrown at the same time, can hit the planner, and Sue must be ready with her racket in hand to successfully hit the balls over the net and be ready for the next forty or so balls. She is a good planner and has thought about back-up plans for her activities. So, if the golf tournament is rained out, the group will spend the morning on a sports tour of Dallas.

PREMEETING ACTIVITIES

Three days prior to the meeting, Sue and her staff arrive in Dallas to set up the meeting headquarters. She is happy to see that all her convention material arrived safely. She meets all contacts to finalize meeting plans. She arranges a walk-through of the host hotel and the convention center with her staff, temporary employees, and volunteers. The host hotel arranges a pre-con meeting where everyone working on the meeting will get together and review the meeting resume for any changes or concerns.

Sue monitors the setup of all meeting events and conducts on-site troubleshooting. Something always needs to be changed; it might be a sponsor sign with an error that needs to be redone by calling the ESC or more a complicated situation like the space for the registration being too small. This is a time of constant problem solving.

Sue joins George and the marketing staffs as they rehearse for the general session, set up the pressroom, and conduct a press conference. George takes time to review the press list with Sue. Sue needs to know the names of press attendees to ensure that when they arrive, someone from the ASAA staff can quickly assist them. Good publicity can ensure success of future conferences.

MEETING DAY ACTIVITIES

The meeting begins, and Sue is busy working with the staff to ensure all meeting rooms are set properly and that all speaker materials and evaluations are ready. Her role is to work behind the scenes to make the attendees' experience perfect. She is the first one to arrive on site and will be the last person to leave. The day is filled with questions that she must clarify or problems that need to be solved. This is the time that excites Sue, and this is when she sees all her hard work become a reality. She uses the contacts she made to quickly solve problems. The AV equipment in one of the rooms is not working, so Sue calls the AV company, and the problem is quickly solved. At the beginning of each day, Sue meets with the hotel CSM and the accounts receivable department to conduct a bill review. She checks with the housing bureau to follow up on a comparison of the ASAA registration with the in-house guest list to ensure that ASAA attendees are properly coded to the ASAA block. This helps with future history.

A special ASAA exhibitors headquarters office opens at the convention center. Ruth, the ASAA's trade show manager, will remain in this office to handle any problems that might occur during the trade show and to accept exhibitor bookings for next year's ASAA conference.

POSTMEETING ACTIVITIES

A tired Sue sips coffee and takes a moment to review the success and areas of opportunity of the Power of Prevention Annual Conference. Before leaving Dallas, Sue will facilitate a post-con meeting to evaluate this year's conference. People who attended the pre-con meeting will be present to discuss the conference. What were the problems? What could be done to improve this situation for future conventions? She will work with the hotel and vendors to reconcile registration numbers, review all pickups, and estimate ancillary business.

Planning a convention is a team event. Sue takes time to thank all speakers, sponsors, committee members, and facilitators for helping with the conference. Sue also rewards her staff by having a free day in Dallas for the team to relax.

TWO-MONTH POSTMEETING

The statistics and evaluations have been reviewed. Sue begins her report to the executive director and to the board of directors regarding conference ROI. It is important after each conference that an evaluation is conducted. In creating this conference, Sue and her team said that the convention objective was to "increase the number of attendees taking the SAPDC by 10% by offering a four-day conference that is focused on education and networking that will increase conference profits by 5%." What is the point of having a convention if the success is not measured? Part of the meeting planner's job is to demonstrate how a convention or meeting helps achieve organizational goals. By establishing objectives and reviewing ROI, a planner can show his or her role in supporting company objectives and the bottom line.

Sue is excited about the Power of Prevention convention. The industry press gave excellent premeeting coverage, with over $50,000 tracked as nonpaid advertising. Sue believes this third-party endorsement definitely increased attendance. The meeting objectives were met, 500 people took the classes for SAPDC—a 10% increase from the 454 that took SAPDC classes last year, and meeting profits grew from $1,393,297.60 to $1,462,962.50—a 5% increase.

Sue finishes her report and takes a call from the Orlando Convention Center, the location for the next year's annual conference. She is ten months away from the conference and is receiving the names of the meeting rooms that will be used . . . and the meeting cycle continues.

◆ SUMMARY

In this chapter, you have learned about the process of creating a citywide meeting. This is a large task for one person and requires many partners to make the conference successful. Through this example, you have been able to see a day in the life of a meeting planner on a site inspection and have looked at the many tasks leading up to the conference. The chapter began with creating a conference objective and budget, and ended with evaluating ROI to determine the success of the meeting.

KEY WORDS AND TERMS

For definitions, see http://glossary.conventionindustry.org.

AV company

Convention service manager

Convention and Visitor Bureau

Destination management company

Exposition services contractor

Meeting time line

Requests for Proposal

Return on Investment

Sponsor

REVIEW AND DISCUSSION QUESTIONS

1. Who is the group? Why are they here?
2. Where else has the group met?

3. What are the steps Sue goes through to plan this meeting?

4. Who does Sue work with on her staff?

5. Who does Sue work with in the city where the meeting is being held? Which suppliers or vendors?

6. What does Sue do after the meeting is over?

ABOUT THE CHAPTER CONTRIBUTOR

M. T. Hickman, CTP, CMP, is the program coordinator for the Travel, Exposition and Meeting Management program at Richland College in Dallas, Texas. She began her career at the Irving, Texas, CVB, where she worked in many departments, including tourism sales, convention sales, and special events. Over the years, she worked as director of marketing for the National Business Association and as a proposal writer for World Travel Partners. In 1995 to 1996, she served on the board of directors for the Dallas–Fort Worth Chapter of MPI. In 1997, she became head of the Richland College Travel, Exposition and Meeting Management program. Hickman is active in the meeting and exposition planning associations, including MPI, PCMA, and IAEM. She holds a B.S. in journalism/public relations from the University of Southern Mississippi and an M.S. degree in communication from the University of North Texas.

Other Chapter Contributors

Dana Nickerson-Rhoden, CMP, CMM, *Manager Scientific & Corporate Meetings, American Heart Association*

David Gisler, *Director of Sales and Training, Total Show University, The Freeman Company*

Nancy Simonieg, *Senior Sales Manager, Hyatt Hotel Downtown Dallas*

Erika Bondy, *CMP Senior Event Coordinator, Dallas Convention Center*

Patty Towell, *Sales Manager, Dallas Convention & Visitor Bureau*

This appendix includes a detailed example of a Site Selection Sample Request for Proposal (RFP). It is used with permission of the originator, Joan L. Eisenstodt.

Forms for Use in Requesting a Proposal and On-Site Selection

The sections that follow provide a number of forms, or frameworks, that are used by meeting professionals. Studying and reviewing these documents will help provide the reader with a better understanding of the myriad of details that a meeting professional must deal with.

<u>*Site Selection*</u>—*Sample <u>R</u>equest <u>f</u>or <u>P</u>roposal (RFP)(v. 18b)*

Group or Meeting Sponsor: *Full name of organization (acronym in parentheses)*

Contact Information: *Name(s) including alternate contacts, title(s), address(es), communication numbers (phones, fax, email, tdd/tty), and contact times and time zones*

Organization: *Provide brief organizational description—structure, mission, purpose.*

The Meeting: *Provide brief description—purpose, goals and objectives, general format, and audience profile.*

History: *Provide up to 2 years of meeting history—dates, attendance, hotel(s) used, rooms blocked and picked up, and range of rates.*

Schedule for Future Meetings; Future Years for <u>This</u> Meeting

Considerations for This Meeting:

Destination(s) and site(s)

*Dates (acceptable <u>**and**</u> unacceptable)*

Rates

Special requirements/information (transportation, attractions/restaurants, quirks)

References: *Request for meetings of similar size, focus/scope, held in last 6 to 12 months*

Proposals Due/Decision Process: *Provide date by which proposal must be received and what collateral materials should be included. Describe decision process and date by which decision is expected.*

Meeting Specifications:

Sleeping Room Block: *Describe day-by-day, including early arrivals/late departures; bed and room types; suites.*

Meeting Space: *Provide day-by-day description of the program, including meeting/ conference office space, speaker ready room, lounges, and times needed.*

Exhibit/Display Space: *For literature tables, other displays or exhibits and the times the space is needed. Include move in and move out times.*

Site Selection
Request for Proposal
Organization Name
Attachment A

If you plan to submit a proposal, please keyboard all information and upload these forms to (*e-mail address*).

Property name _____ *City/State* _____

Property contact name/title/e-mail and phone _____

Year property built   _____   ☐ Last building inspection and results:

Number of floors _____   Total number of rooms _____ suites _____

Single/one-bedded rooms _____   Double-double/two-bedded rooms _____

Number of nonsmoking rooms _____   Number of disability-accessible rooms _____

Year of last guest room renovation _____   Year of last public space renovation _____

Scope of Planned Renovation and Schedule:

Type of property

      ☐ *meeting/convention*   ☐ *resort*   ☐ *full service*   ☐ *limited service*
Market tier: ☐ *luxury*   ☐ *upscale*   ☐ *moderate*
Property location: ☐ *suburban*   ☐ *downtown/city center*

Property ownership & management

Chain owned? (Y/N) _____ If no, name of owners. _____

Management Company _____

Franchise? (Y/N) _____

Owner's company is at least 51% owned, controlled and operated by an American citizen minority? (Y/N) _____

Owner's company is at least 51% owned, controlled and operated by an American citizen nonminority woman? (Y/N) _____

Site Selection
Request for Proposal
Organization Name
Attachment A

If you plan to submit a proposal, please keyboard all information and upload these forms to (*e-mail address*).

Property name _____ *City/State*_____

Property contact name/title/e-mail and phone _____

Rating
AAA Diamonds   *1*   *2*   *3*   *4*   *5*   not rated
Mobil Stars   *1*   *2*   *3*   *4*   *5*   not rated

Other rating(s) (specify) _____

Outlets
Name _____ Location _____ Hours _____
Full or Ltd. Service _____ Nonsmoking?_____

Transportation and Parking
Airport One
Name   _____ 3-Letter code _____
Distance from property _____ miles
       Minutes/rush hour _____ Minutes/nonrush hour_____
Complimentary shuttle (Y/N) _____
Estimated taxi charge (each way) _____
Alternate mode of transportation _____ Cost each way _____
Driving directions (attach)

Airport Two
Name   _____ 3-Letter code _____
Distance from property _____ miles
       Minutes/rush hour _____ Minutes/nonrush hour _____
Complimentary shuttle (Y/N) _____
Estimated taxi charge (each way) _____
Alternate mode of transportation _____ Cost each way _____
Driving Directions (attach)

Number of parking spaces at property _____ Charge for self-park _____
Charge for valet park _____
Identify facility's parking capacity for large trucks, semitrailers, etc.: _____

Taxes, service, and/or gratuity charges
The current rooms tax is ____% plus $____ occupancy tax.
    → There is ___ is not ___ a ballot initiative in the next election to raise those taxes.
There is a ____ gratuity or a ____ service charge of _____% on group food and beverage.
    → This is taxed at _____%.

Site Selection
Request for Proposal
Organization Name
Attachment A

If you plan to submit a proposal, please keyboard all information and upload these forms to (*e-mail address*).

Property name _____ *City/State* _____

Property contact name/title/e-mail and phone _____

Facilities/Services on Property (check all that apply)

☐ Cocktail lounge
☐ 24-hour room service OR
　　☐ Room service Start time _____ End time _____
☐ Safety deposit boxes/lobby area
☐ Express check in and out　　　☐ Video review/check out
☐ Full business center　　Hours _____ A.M. to _____ P.M.　　Days of the week _____
☐ Gift/newsstand　　　　 Hours _____ A.M. to _____ P.M.　　Days of the week: _____
☐ Full-service health club　Hours ___ A.M. to ___ P.M.　　Days of the week: _____
☐ Laundry/valet service (circle applicable responses)

Circle one: On property or *Sent out*

　　Circle service: 5 days/week　　*6 days/week*　　*7 days/week*　　*overnight service*
☐ Shoe shine service
☐ Indoor pool　☐ outdoor pool
☐ Airline desk(s)　　　　　　　(specify) _____, _____
☐ ATM (Current use fee is $ ___.___.)
☐ Car rental desk(s)　　　　　 (specify) _____, _____
☐ Evening turndown service　　☐ All guests　　　　☐ VIPs only
☐ Golf course
☐ Tennis court(s)
☐ Racquetball courts
☐ Other (specify) _____

Guest Rooms

☐ In-room safe　　　　☐ No charge　　　　☐ Charge to use ($_____/day)
☐ Working desks with outlets above floor
☐ Voice mail　　　　　☐ Personalized voice mail
☐ 2 line phones/all rooms　☐ 2-line phones/concierge/specialized rooms only
☐ Data ports on all phones　☐ Digital or analog phone lines
☐ Phone in bathroom　　☐ bathroom phone/concierge or specialty rooms only
☐ Access charge for local phone calls _____ Access charge for toll-free calls _____
☐ AM/FM radio　　　　☐ with cassette player　　☐ with CD player
☐ Color TV
☐ Remote control TV　　☐ Cable TV　　　　☐ Satellite TV
☐ All news cable channel　☐ Weather channel
☐ Other special channels (specify) _____
☐ In-room movies on demand
☐ Closed-circuit television (CCTV)

Site Selection
Request for Proposal
Organization Name
Attachment A

If you plan to submit a proposal, please keyboard all information and upload these forms to (*e-mail address*).

Property name _____ *City/State* _____

Property contact name/title/e-mail and phone _____

Guest Rooms (cont.)

☐ In-room video players
☐ Iron/ironing board
☐ Mini-bar   ☐ Refrigerator on request
☐ Coffee/Tea maker   ☐ Daily complimentary coffee/tea
☐ Working desk/desk lamp
☐ Free **daily** paper delivered to room   ☐ Paper/**weekdays only**

Reservations and Check-in/out

☐ Reservations may be made through a toll-free number.
   ☐ That number is _____   ☐ Number is accessible throughout United States.
   ☐ A number that can be used for those residing in the state in which the reservations department is located:
   ☐ A reservation number for those outside the United States is ( ) _____.
   ☐ The TTY/TDD number is ( ) _____.
   ☐ The fax number for reservations is ( ) _____.
   ☐ Reservations may be made on line at http://www._____,
   ☐ or by email to _____.
☐ All rooms in a group's block are released to the toll-free number.
☐ The property has an in-house reservations department.
☐ The reservations department is located off-site.

Check-in time is _____. Check-out time is _____.

☐ The facility will audit the room reservations using a group's registration list.

<u>Site Selection</u>
<u>Request for Proposal</u>
Organization Name
Attachment A

If you plan to submit a proposal, please keyboard all information and upload these forms to (*e-mail address*).

Property name _____ *City/State* _____

Property contact name/title/e-mail and phone _____

<u>*Safety and Security (check all that apply)*</u>

☐ Smoke detectors in all guest rooms   Hardwired?   *Y/N* _____
☐ Smoke detectors in hallways   Hardwired?   *Y/N* _____
☐ Smoke detectors in public areas   Hardwired?   *Y/N* _____
☐ Audible smoke detectors   ☐ Visual alarms for people with hearing impairments
☐ Sprinklers in all guest rooms   Sprinklers in hallways
☐ Sprinklers in public areas
☐ Fire extinguishers in hallways
☐ Automatic fire doors
☐ Auto link to fire station
☐ Auto recall elevators
☐ Ventilated stairwells
☐ Emergency maps in guest rooms/hallways
☐ Emergency information in all guest rooms
☐ Emergency lighting
☐ Safety chain on door   ☐ Doors with viewports ("peep holes")
☐ Deadbolts on all guest room doors
☐ Restricted access to guest floors
☐ Property has AEDs (automatic external defibrillators)
    ☐ Staff has been trained to use defibrillators   *Per shift* ____
☐ Staff trained in CPR   CPR-trained staff *per shift* _____
☐ Staff trained in first aid   *Per shift* ____
☐ Secondary locks on guest room glass doors
☐ Room balconies accessible by adjoining rooms/balconies
☐ Primary guest room entrance accessible by interior corridor/atrium
☐ Guest room accessible by exterior entrance only
☐ Guest room windows open
☐ Uniformed security
☐ 24-hour security throughout facility   Number of staff ___
☐ Public address system
☐ Video surveillance in public areas/elevators
☐ Video surveillance at entrances
☐ Video surveillance in hallways
☐ Staff trained in issuance of duplicate keys/cards
☐ Emergency power source: _____
    ☐ SOPs for power outages _____

Food Safety:
Detail the frequency of inspection by county or city health inspectors and the results of the last three (3) inspections.

Site Selection
Request for Proposal
Organization Name
Attachment A

If you plan to submit a proposal, please keyboard all information and upload these forms to (*e-mail address*).

Property name _____ *City/State* _____

Property contact name/title/e-mail and phone _____

Emergency call response time (for fire, police, EMTs) in minutes to your property _____
Does property have an emergency evacuation plan? (Y/N) _____
   How often does property conduct emergency evacuation drills? _____
Nearest police station (blocks/miles) _____ Nearest hospital (blocks/miles) _____
Does facility comply with all country/state/local fire laws? (Y/N) _____

Please describe

—The actions your facility took beginning 9/11/01 for the safety and comfort of your guests:

—Any change of policies governing safety/security instituted or reinstituted since 9/11/01.

—The communication tree among your property and local/state/federal emergency management officials.

—Any policies in effect that govern "containment" of guests in the property for issues of bioterrorism? Inability to travel because of airport closures?

"Oversold/Underdeparted" ("Walk") Policies or Guidelines
☐ Property will arrange accommodations at comparable or superior property within 10 minutes of this property.
☐ Property will pay directly for one room night and tax at comparable property.
☐ Traveler will be provided with transportation.
☐ Traveler will be reimbursed for (number) _____ of phone calls to home and/or office.
☐ Other (specify) _____

<u>Site Selection</u>
<u>Request for Proposal</u>
Organization Name
Attachment A

If you plan to submit a proposal, please keyboard all information and upload these forms to (*e-mail address*).

Property name _____ *City/State* _____

Property contact name/title/e-mail and phone _____

Staff and Staffing
☐ Average length of employment at this property:
   Management staff _____ years   line staff _____ years
☐ Staff organized for the purpose of collective bargaining (List unions and staff positions, contract renewal dates on separate sheet.)

Policies and Miscellaneous Charges
☐ Credit cards are charged when reservation is made.
   ☐ If charged, is it for _____ first night _____ last night _____ all nights
☐ Guest may cancel guaranteed reservations without penalty/charge
        _____ to 4 P.M./day of arrival   _____ to 6 P.M./day of arrival   _____ 24 hours
        _____ 48 hours   _____ 72 hours   _____ other
☐ Guest substitutions are allowed, at any time, without penalty or charge to group and/or individual.
☐ Guest substitutions are not allowed without a charge to group and/or individual.
☐ Extended stays (based on availability) are allowed at no charge.
☐ Early checkouts incur a charge of $_____ if the front desk is not notified at check-in.
☐ The property charges $____/page for receipt of faxes.
☐ The property charges $___/page to send faxes.
☐ There is a charge of $_____ for receipt of packages.
☐ There is a charge of $_____ for property to send packages.
☐ There is a charge of $_____ to deliver packages to individual or group.

<u>Site Selection</u>
<u>Request for Proposal</u>
Organization Name
Attachment A

If you plan to submit a proposal, please keyboard all information and upload these forms to (*e-mail address*).

Property name _____ *City/State* _____

Property contact name/title/e-mail and phone _____

Policies and Miscellaneous Charges (cont.)

☐ Is a resort or hotel or other fee added to the room rate? Y/N _____
  ☐ If so, the current amount per room (or per guest) per night is $_____ which is/is not taxed.
    ☐ This covers:
  ○ Contractual issues that must be included in our contract are attached to this document.

Energy Issues

☐ The property does charge an energy surcharge of $_____ per room per night. This charge is or is not taxed. (Is _____ Is not _____) If taxed, it is at _____%.
☐ The power supply for the property is from _____.
☐ Describe the property's backup power source(s):
☐ Describe the property's emergency procedures for brownouts and blackouts:
☐ Describe the property's backup systems for water and phones:
☐ Define any charges for use of electrical outlets for meetings and/or in public space and/or in guestrooms:

Environmental Issues

○ Our property recycles the following materials:
  _____ paper _____ plastic _____metal/tin/aluminum
○ The method by which guests may recycle is:
○ We ask guests to advise us by use of a card if they want their towels and/or bed linens changed every day.
○ Other areas we protect the environment are:

<u>**Site Selection**</u>
<u>**Request for Proposal**</u>
Organization Name
Attachment A

If you plan to submit a proposal, please keyboard all information and upload these forms to (*e-mail address*).

Property name _____ *City/State* _____

Property contact name/title/e-mail and phone _____

Other Groups

During the group's preferred dates, the other events confirmed in the city, including conventions, festivals, other public and private events that are known to the bureau or the facility, are:

During the group's preferred dates, the other events confirmed in the facility are:

City/County Labor Issues

Note any groups organized for the purpose of collective bargaining in the city or county whose contract deadlines are 2 months on both side of preferred dates, and their history of labor actions:

<u>Audio Visual Equipment</u>

The in-house or recommended company is _____.

The facility has the ability to negotiate prices on behalf of the AV company. (Y/N) ____

A discount of _____% off list prices can be offered for AV equipment for the meeting.

The service charge is _____%. It is taxed at _____%. It is not taxed. ____

If an outside AV company is brought in by our organization, there is ____ is not ____ a fee.

   If there is a fee, it is _____.

<u>Electricity Supply/Vendor</u>

Electricity (for exhibits and meeting space) is provided to the facility by _____ in-house or _____ external vendor. (If external, specify _____.)

The facility has the ability to negotiate prices for meeting and exhibit electrical service.
   (Y/N) ____

Electricity is available to the outdoor portions of the facility (for outside exhibits).
   (Y/N) _____

A discount of ____% off list prices can be offered for meeting room and exhibit electricity for the meeting.

Site Selection
Request for Proposal
Organization Name
Attachment A

If you plan to submit a proposal, please keyboard all information and upload these forms to (*e-mail address*).

Property name _____ *City/State* _____

Property contact name/title/e-mail and phone _____

Operations and Technology

☐ *Our sales/convention services staff use* _____ *word processing software, version* _____.

☐ *Sales and convention services personnel use e-mail.* _____ *yes* _____ *no*
   E-mail addresses are:
      ☐ *Sales* _____
      ☐ *Convention/Catering services* _____
      ☐ *Reservations* _____

☐ *Sales and convention services have Web access.* ___ *yes* ___ *no*
☐ *Reservations is fully automated and can respond by e-mail.* ___ *yes* ___ *no*
☐ *Our Web site address is* _____.
☐ *Group/Meeting reservations can be made on line.*
      ☐ *If reservations may be made on line, please specify information that must be included in any published URLs and any restrictions and/or policies.*

NATIONAL SALES RESPONSE FORM
(year/meeting) Site Selection
Request for Proposal: (name of organization)

Please complete and return this form <u>after</u> reading the RFP. To allow us to track proposals, please advise to which properties in which cities you will send the RFP. **Please upload this to (e-mail address), or fax this form to** *(name, fax number)* **to be received by** *(day, date, time/time zone).*

Please print or type in black:

Company _____

Contact name/title _____

Direct phone no. _____

Direct fax no. _____

E-mail address _____

The RFP is being sent to the following properties:

_____/City _____

_____/City _____

_____/City _____

_____/City _____

_____/City _____

_____/City _____

Comments:

CVB RESPONSE FORM
(Year/Meeting) Site Selection
Request for Proposal: (Organization/Meeting Name)

Please complete and return this form <u>after</u> reading the RFP. To allow us to track proposals, please advise to which properties you will send the RFP, keeping in mind that it should only be sent to properties not represented by the companies noted in the cover note and only to those that meet the criteria. If responses are received by properties that do not meet the criteria, or by vendors for whom we do not need services, we will reject the proposals.

Please upload this to (*e-mail address*), **or fax this form to** *(name, fax number)* **by** *(day/date/time/time zone)*.

Please print or type in black:

CVB _____

Contact name/Title _____

Direct phone no. _____

Direct fax no. _____

E-mail address _____

The RFP is being sent to the following properties:

                                 _____

                                 _____

                                 _____

                                 _____

                                 _____

                                 _____

Comments:

Property RESPONSE FORM
(Year/Meeting) Site Selection
Request for Proposal: (Organization/Meeting)

Please complete and return this form <u>after</u> reading the RFP but before sending a proposal. There is no need to send a follow-up letter or e-mail, or to call once this form has been sent. **Please upload this to** (*e-mail address*), **or fax to** (*organization/fax number*) **to be received by** (*day/date/time/time zone*).

Full proposals and collateral are due by (day/date/time/time zone).

Please complete and return this information <u>whether or not</u> a proposal is being submitted. If completing by hand, please use black ink.

Property name/City _____

Contact name/Title _____

Direct phone no. (_____)_____

Direct fax no. (_____)_____

E-mail address _____

URL *http://www.* _____

Check/complete all applicable responses:

_____ We will send proposal and collateral to be received by (*due date*).
_____ Dates noted on first option basis are being held for this group.
_____ Dates will *not* be held until a contract is signed.

Dates available/First option   **Dates available/Second option**

_____   _____
_____   _____
_____   _____
_____   _____

_____ We regret we are *unable to send a proposal* for the following reason(s):
_____ None of preferred dates available.
_____ Meeting space and/or sleeping rooms not appropriate for meeting.
_____ Unable to meet rate parameters.
_____ Other (specify):
            _____
            _____

Comments:

◆ INDEX

A

P